Modern Classics

Modern

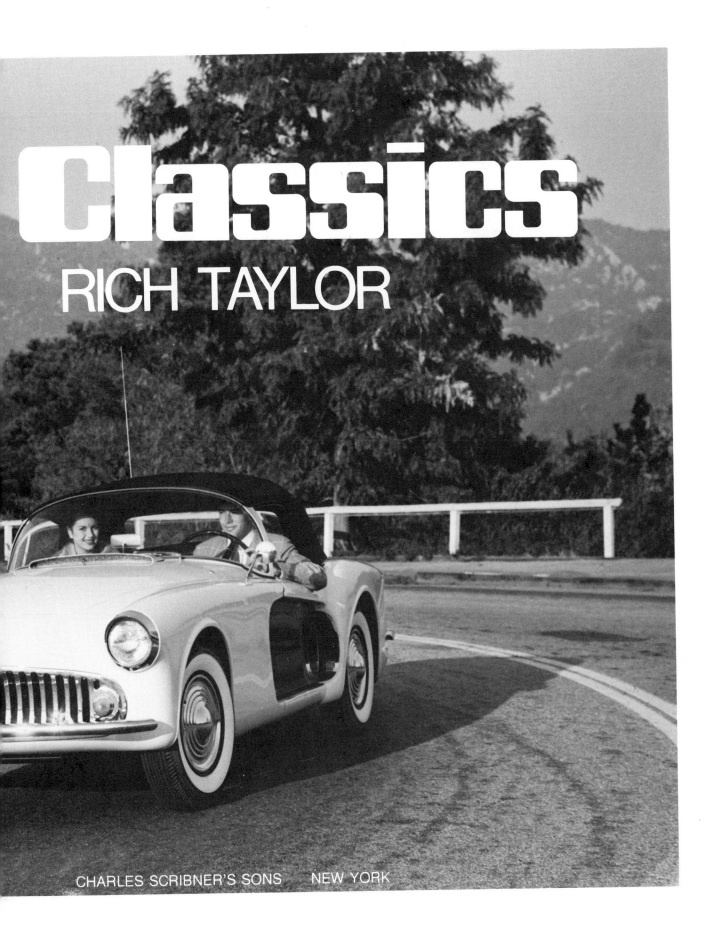

Classics

RICH TAYLOR

CHARLES SCRIBNER'S SONS   NEW YORK

Library of Congress Cataloging in Publication Data

Taylor, Rich, 1946–
    Modern classics.

    Includes index.
    1. Sports cars. I. Title.
TL236.T38   629.22′22   78–4450
ISBN 0–684–15525–7

1 3 5 7 9 11 13 15 17 19 Q/C 20 18 16 14 12 10 8 6 4 2

Printed in the United States of America

TO J. EDGAR OPEL
AND BOB BROWN

CONTENTS

PREFACE

The whole world is crazy. A decade ago, you could buy a marvelous SJ Duesenberg phaeton for less than $20,000. Today, $175,000 would be a good price for that car. And that's lunacy. It has nothing to do with automobiles and everything to do with the international art market, speculators, investors, auctioneers, and all the rest. But the primary fact remains that ten years ago you could buy legendary sports cars—1750 Alfas, Bugattis, 3-liter Bentleys—for less than peasants were paying for hopeless Chevy Impalas. A pauper with taste could ride like a king. No more; those days are gone for good. In another ten years, the only SJ Duesenbergs you'll see are going to be in museums, and you'll have to pay five dollars just to walk in and ogle. Already, virtually all the prewar cars available to people with less than a fortune to spend are either unusable and dull or overpriced and expensive . . . or all of the above.

Because of the increase in prices, many classic-car collectors have had to turn to postwar cars. And there they've met other car enthusiasts—the sports car buffs and the racers—who realize that just as World War I marked the end of the Edwardian era of expansion and World War II ended the colonial era, the Vietnam War ended an era, too. Since automobiles are of necessity reflections of society, they mirror its changes. The antique era pretty much ends around 1917; the classic era ends logically with 1941; and what we now recognize as an era of immense automotive vitality during the fifties and sixties ended on December 31, 1967, when the federal government established the first of its emissions and safety requirements.

That halcyon era closed for good with the stringent federal requirements for 1977. Many cars of that period were special, definitely worth saving, unique machines that will never be built again. And they *are* worth saving. That's what this book is about. Don't worry. I'm not going to tell you to go out and buy that cherry '54 Plymouth Cranbrook sedan the little old lady down the block is hanging on to because it's going to be a classic someday. Balderdash. That was a dumb car when it was new; it's a dumb car today. What's important—what distinguishes the cars of the last thirty years from everything that went before and everything that will come after—is performance. The world discovered acceleration, braking, handling, top speed (and of necessity, aerodynamic styling) during the fifties and sixties.

Think about it. When we came out of World War II, we were still riding around in DC-3s and Super Connies; now we're pushing Jumbo Jets and SSTs. The same thing happened to cars. The acceleration, braking, handling, and top speed of good sports cars from ten years ago are not only worlds better than almost everything that's currently in production but also a giant leap forward from the "performance cars" of the thirties. Most of the hot cars of the thirties perform roughly on a par with a good Volkswagen Beetle. A ragged slant-six Aspen will blow the doors off an SSK Mercedes, and most Chevy Impalas could successfully tackle any Duesenberg. There's just no comparison. *The* high performance cars were built between 1946 and 1976.

But that period is over. The federal government's regulations have now changed not only the engines but the shape of our cars, too. Something like the delicate, unprotected but gorgeous snout of the Maserati Ghibli simply cannot be sold in this country anymore. Things have changed in a big way in America, and at least when it comes to cars, we've regressed. I *like* pretty, fast, quicksilver sorts of cars, the kind that leave you all shaky and jazzed-up after a ride. I *enjoy* high performance, whether it's wringing the most out of a Lotus or hanging on for dear life to a Cobra in full flail. I think something will go out of the quality of life when those sorts of cars are completely gone, and I think that's reason enough for saving them.

I'm firmly convinced that the best single point about good postwar sports cars is that you can *use* them without fear of reprisal. So what if you blow the Chevy small block in your Bizzarrini sky high? There's only something like 25 million more engines just like it kicking around, and you can plug in another one for almost nothing. You can't do that with a Bugatti, nor would you ever take the chance of even driving down the street in a monster classic that's worth more than most people's houses. A Bizzarrini may not be cheap, but it is cheap enough for you to drive it, use it, and enjoy it without feeling guilty.

Enjoy. That's the key word. The cars in this book are all automobiles that provide an extraordinary amount of pure enjoyment for the price, cars that you can savor, get to know, enjoy, and, yes . . . love. They are the best we've been able to do so far in the realm of personal transportation, works of art that can take you way outside yourself. These cars are all very different, an incredibly diverse group of machines. But they share one important quality. Not a one of them is dull.

Modern Classics

INTRODUCTION

There have been some really fabulous automobiles bolted together over the last thirty years, both in this country and abroad, by large companies and small. They are not only quality pieces but fun to drive, useful, beautiful, and still reasonable investments for someone without ten generations of old money behind him. And many of them are being sadly neglected. Of course, there are also a lot of cars that've been slapped together over the last three decades that aren't worth the effort to tow them to the scrapper. But thousands of dummies are collecting them anyway, driving the prices up as high—and sometimes higher—than knowledgeable enthusiasts are paying for high-class cars that for one reason or another the speculators haven't discovered yet. The hard part is separating the wheat from the chaff, and that's one of the purposes of this book. I want you to understand *why* some cars are more valuable than others and what makes some worth more not only monetarily but in an aesthetic sense, too.

You have to admit that some cars can make your blood pound just to look at them. They're such fascinating mechanical objects; they do indeed have an inner luminosity, an intrinsic artistic merit—over and above the fact that not only are they still fast enough to really pull your pucker string up tight, but they're also unburdened by the damned emissions controls and safety add-ons that have wrecked the mechanical essence of nearly all new cars. One of the best things about older sports cars is that they're so *comprehensible.*

Almost anybody old enough to drive has

a gut appreciation of machinery that falls somewhere between Rudolf Diesel and James Watt. We *like* to watch the bits and pieces whir around; we *like* to see the mechanism in full swing. There's nothing romantic about a PCV valve, but damn, the double-overhead cams on a V-12 Ferrari are enough to send even perfectly rational adults into paroxysms of childlike wonder. And the sounds. You know all those little clicks and beeps and hums that computers make. That's all fake, you know. The completion of solid-state electronic circuits is a soundless operation. But even a century into the electronic age, we still don't trust machines that work without noise. We're still mechanical, not electrical, most of us, back there with Barney Oldfield in our response to inanimate devices. So computers come with little fake noisemakers in the circuitry to make the operators feel like something is really happening inside that big crackle-finish gray box.

But in a car the damn noises *mean* something—*that* is the tappet whacking the rocker arm, *that* is the gear drive to the oil pump, *that* is the piston slapping in the bore. You can understand it. Lever A moves rocker B which touches adjuster screw C. As a mechanism it's comprehensible . . . a mechanical device that can be understood in the most direct, visceral way possible. That's a big chunk of the appeal of these postwar cars. Some of them—the Gullwing Mercedes, for example—are about as sophisticated as any wheeled device ever designed. And yet, with an almost casual look, you can trace the purpose and beauty of every part.

Even more, though, a Gullwing Mercedes says *people*. It has a thousand stories to tell, from engineer Rudi Uhlenhaut doing the first test drives to John Fitch and Pierre Levegh at the tragic '55 Le Mans, from Karl Wilfert's drawing board to some forgotten Mercedes craftsman putting a labor of love into hidden internal parts that no one would ever see. It's not an easy car—in the sense that a Ford Maverick is an easy car—but, boy, the rewards are sure a lot greater. Something like a Gullwing is a bona fide, signed and authenticated objet d'art, as precious as anything in the Museum of Modern Art.

Unhappily, the traditional "hobby" aspect of car collecting is seriously threatened right now. On one side are the profiteers, on the other the collectors and true lovers of old cars. For their own defense, collectors have largely banded together into marque clubs, all more interested in "Maintaining the Breed" than making a fast buck. But they're the only ones keeping any sort of lid on the insanely rising costs of car collecting, and they're definitely in the minority. Inevitably, the profiteers will push too far, too fast, milk the market dry, and hope to scamper out the back door before the whole damn house of cards collapses around their ears. It's an old, old story, one that's ravaged everything from Renaissance bronzes to early American quilts. The best pieces will end up in museums, the fast-buck merchants will trade inferior specimens for a while, and then price levels will drop back down to something more realistic as only the enthusiasts are left to pick up the pieces.

People will always collect cars, though, inflated prices or not, for as many reasons as there are collectors. Some are just plain fascinated by the mechanical integrity of older cars, an element manifestly lacking in the average polyurethane-and-polypropylene new car. There is a directness, a sense of machinery, a *mechanicalness,* if you will, that distinctly marks some cars as very special. Other collectors are fascinated by the aesthetics of thoroughbred cars, the fineness of line that makes many collector cars—from Avanti to GTB/4—giant rolling sculptures. There is a tautness, a brittle, lithe surface development missing from mundane cars, that sets off the best. They can be collected like sculpture, placed literally or figuratively on a pedestal, carefully dusted and tended, exhibited, admired . . . and rarely, if ever, driven. To the collector of automotive art, it is enough that he owns an original by Pininfarina or Giugiaro. That it should be among the rarest, fastest, and most powerful of all cars is an added fillip, not a matter of primary concern.

There are collectors of luxury, too. Face it. The average federalized safety car—with its sponge rubber dashboard and recessed control knobs—has all the cheerful ambience of a padded cell. *Luxury car* is a misnomer when applied to something like a Mark IV or Eldorado, even more to an Audi or Volvo. But a Bentley Mulliner Continental Flying Spur carries with it a hedonistic aura that is worth more than all the safety padding in Detroit. The luxury in a true luxury car comes from the careful hand-craftsmanship, the opulent materials, the fine lines, the conveniences taken for granted, but even more from that intangible security—that correctness of taste—that Brooks Brothers and Bergdorf's have been purveying for years. Today's manufacturers are trying to educate car buyers into settling for less, and the tasteless egalitarian trend of American society is nowhere more evident than in the undermining of the proud old cars, the ones with the Right Labels.

The Right Label extends to sports and racing cars, too. It means pedigree; but more, it means a sense of rightness in every part that is characteristic of all good machinery. And in the mid-fifties and early sixties, some of the most fabulous sports/racing cars of all time appeared. They don't have the primitive appeal of a 1750 Alfa or Bugatti Type 35, but they do have a red-blooded masculinity that current racers sure as hell lack. They look like cars, with the engine in the front where God and Ettore Bugatti intended it to be. They roar and shake and slide and do all sorts of wonderful mechanical things that a McLaren would be embarrassed to admit to. In other words, they're racing machines . . . for real men. For racing.

The best part of old sports/racers is that what was world-championship performance in 1954 is still damn fast, but not unreasonably so. And they have—many of them—legal electrics and horns and things, so that they can indeed be licensed and occasionally driven on the street. The gulf between sports cars and sports/racing cars was not so wide twenty years ago. And even if they're not suitable for street use, old sports/racers can at least be run with the Vintage Sports Car Club and made to go remarkably fast on a race track. For hard-core enthusiasts, it's a perfect combination—an old and beautiful racing machine with some golden memories welded in with the space frame, that pervasive smell of Castrol R and hot metal palpably clinging to every bit . . . and a chance to go out and play racer besides. If you can afford it, every bit the very best toy since slot cars.

Of course, in the last analysis, what you're collecting with an old sports car is history, either your own or someone else's. And be-

sides the participatory history of vintage racing or even just everyday driving in a postwar classic, there's also the far more intricate history you enter with the purchase of the car. Virtually every car of worth, it seems, came into being under fascinating circumstances, whether born with a gilded butterfly in the carburetor or midwifed through bucks-down adversity. In either case, the men who conceived, financed, styled, and engineered cars of interest were, almost to a man, perforce, interesting themselves. Martinets like Enzo Ferrari, racers cum engineers like Rudi Uhlenhaut and Zora Arkus-Duntov, chicken farmers cum racers like Carroll Shelby . . . not a one of them hasn't driven through life at ten-tenths, balls out and foot to the floor. And that, because they've gone so much farther and faster than most of us, makes them incredibly interesting.

Buy one of their cars and you enter a whole new world of historical monuments. A surprisingly small world, because when it comes to cars, just a very few people—a handful, really—are the ones responsible for all the quality products. No exaggeration. It's something easily overlooked in that trivializing concern with proper engine numbers, authentic accessories, and all the other necessary but ultimately fatiguing information that small-minded car buffs feed on . . . the fact that cars are built not by corporations but by people . . . and that extraordinary cars are the products of extraordinary men.

Buy a superlative car and for free you acquire a direct perception into the thoughts of a superior mind. And *you* can take the very machine that he devised and—if you're good enough and brave enough—drive the hell out of it, just the way he wanted you to. For if the men who've built great cars have one thing in common, it's a love of hard driving . . . and hard living. They built cars for themselves, mostly, and then if they could, sold the kind of cars *they* would like to drive. No compromises.

There are pragmatic reasons for collecting any high-quality postwar car. Parts, for one thing. Fords excluded, the older a car gets, the scarcer the parts, until you get to brass-era antiques for which there simply aren't any spares at all. Not so with postwar cars. Parts for even the most exotic postwar production cars are usually available *somewhere;* it's just a matter of finding the right person who has the part you need. And that's where the marque clubs come in. Most clubs either deal collectively in parts or have members who deal in parts or can put you in touch with suppliers who still have or can get the parts you need. Obviously, Mustang body parts for a Shelby GT-350 are a lot easier to come by than engine parts for a one-off Maserati sports/racer, but usually the scarcity—read *price*—of that more exotic piece will make it worth your while to go to the added expense of fabricating a new part from scratch. All it takes is money.

Most people aren't going to get into machine-shop work or other complex procedures like welding aluminum or some nonsense, but almost anyone can handle routine maintenance, replacement of engine and suspension parts, light bodywork, and interior refurbishing. For the rest, it depends on how heavily you want to get involved, how much work your particular car needs, and how much time and money you have. The gut appeal of car collecting is, I think, that it's an active, participant hobby. Unlike stamp collectors or quiltmakers or orchid growers, car collectors can get into their hobby—literally and figuratively—and *go* somewhere. The absolute best part about owning Phil Hill's old Ferrari is not so much that it's Hill's old Ferrari and you own it but that you can take it to Laguna Seca for the annual old-car races and put in a few hot laps against the very same cars—and ofttimes the same drivers—that Hill raced when both he and your Ferrari were young. Because sure as hell, some other crazy like yourself is going to be out there pretending he's Richie Ginther or Augie Pabst or Ken Miles. And like as not, Phil Hill himself will be there with an old Ferrari, pretending he's Phil Hill.

If you have a bent that way, there're also swap meets—like Carlyle—and clubs—like the Milestone Car Society—that are devoted solely to postwar cars. In either instance, and in the case of hundreds of postwar marque clubs, too, the members are amazingly active in restoring, driving, and showing their cars, more so than the collectors of antiques and classics. At the 1975 Milestone national meet, for example, members were able to race around at 140 mph on the old Packard test track. That's something the members of the Antique Automobile Club would never want nor need nor be able to do.

The point of all this is that collecting postwar cars is a relatively new field, one that you can get into right now with a minimum of trouble and expense, all things considered. You can have some fun, drive some really neat cars, and perhaps even make a dollar. Among all sorts of car buyers, from Duesenberg collectors to stenographers financing Pintos, the enthusiasts putting money into postwar thoroughbred machinery stand to come out the best in the long run—in terms of enjoyment, excitement, practicality, and expense. Postwar sports cars, in other words, are what you call "the hot setup."

BUDGETS

If I were just getting into postwar sports cars, there'd be a few simple guidelines I'd set myself right from the start. First, I'd sit down and dispassionately figure out just how much I had to spend. There is *nothing* that promotes a family free-for-all quicker than driving up in what was going to be the new bedroom set. A way to keep this sort of hassle to a minimum is to make a budget for what you really think you can afford for a toy. Deduct 25 percent immediately for unforeseen expenses and repairs. What you have left is roughly what you can spend.

BE PRACTICAL

Then I'd take a good look around. Obviously, some cars are going to be more expensive to operate, to repair, and generally to own than others. Part of the cost, though, will depend on what you do with the car. A mid-fifties Italian sports/racer may be discouragingly expensive to repair, but if it's just going to sit on your mantelpiece, that's not really much of a worry. Conversely, if you expect to drive your postwar classic every day, be smart and get something strong and easily serviced, preferably with a reliable American V-8.

You should certainly be taking into consideration just what you're going to do with the car after you've got it. Will you have to carry all your friends and relatives, or will a cramped sports/racer be a better choice for getting away from the very same relatives? Give it some thought. Most car collectors—and car buyers in general—rush into what can really be a pretty major purchase with their hearts high above their heads. On the other hand, you don't want to go analyzing an old-car purchase the way you'd enter into buying a family station wagon. The whole point of having a collector car is that it's something special. I mean, so many things we deal with every day just don't *mean* anything to us. But your collector car can be anything you want. Anything. You can always get another bedroom set, but how often is a 289 Cobra going to come by at the right price? Remember what Rudyard Kipling said: "A woman is only a woman, but a good Ferrari's a trip."

NOVELTY

Some people are turned on by mechanical novelty. Give them quintuple underhead cams with a pancake eleven driving the front wheels through endless variable chains and they're in heaven. I say neato. Whatever turns you on. But at the same time, you'd better be the world's foremost expert on underhead cams and variable chains, because nobody else is even gonna know what you're talking about, and the damn thing *can't* run forever. For the casual enthusiast or the guy who really wants to use his car, I'd have to suggest either something European with a fairly mundane specification—like a Bentley or Mercedes—an exotic European that's common as beer cans in Georgia—like a Porsche, maybe—or something with a good ol' cast-iron Amurrican V-8, pushrods and all. That doesn't mean it has to be dull—Corvettes and Cobras are not dull—but it does mean you can *drive* it if and when you want without worrying about whether the goddamn anodized titanium block is going to melt and blow the water jackets out the exhaust pipe.

CONDITION

Another thing to consider is condition. Once you've decided that what you really want is the world's very best specimen, are you prepared not only to pay through the nose to get it but also to keep it that way? If you're thinking of concours and you really want to keep the car nice—which is the object, after all—do you have the means to keep it up? Not only the cubic dollars but the facilities. If you live anywhere in the snow belt, for example, do you have garage space for the car? Or, even better, a heated garage? Nothing, *nothing* deteriorates faster than a concours-quality show car. You can turn a 99-point champion into a 90-point also-ran in maybe two hundred miles of thoughtless driving. It's so easy you'd be amazed.

So the thing to ask yourself is just what are you going to do with the car and what condition will that require. And are you willing to pay for it. Economically, the very best buy is usually a "good original" car. This is one that's been taken care of properly all its long life, has low mileage and everything works the way it should. You'd be surprised how many of them are around, though admittedly it'll be easier to find a well-maintained Chrysler Newport, let's say, than a perfect original Porsche Speedster. Sports and racing cars usually get kind of . . . well . . . used up. But there are good ones around, and they're definitely the ones to buy.

PRICE DISPARITY

Unfortunately, they're also the ones that cost more. And also unfortunately, the car is probably in superb condition because nobody drove it. You start running the Mille Miglia on your way to work every morning in some old barrister's Sunday afternoon gem and soon you're going to have a rotten unrestored car, just like everybody else. Unfortunately even more, the disparity between concours cars and mediocre specimens is embarrassingly wide.

For example. Right now, a perfect—I mean *purr*fect—Sunbeam Tiger is worth over $7,000. Maybe more. I've got one with 38,000 miles on it—hardtop, mag wheels, repainted, brand-new interior, straight chassis, runs fine, looks great—that I just bought for $800. The difference? Well, it doesn't really show, but mine must be 50 percent Bondo from the beltline down. The important thing is, *I don't care.* I deliberately bought the car that way because I know, I just *know* from experience that if you give me a perfect car . . . I won't drive it. And I bought the Tiger to drive, not to baby. I already have more collector cars than I need, and I wouldn't take my Devin SS out on a rainy day for love nor money. The Tiger is my everyday car. Since it isn't perfect, I can park it in shopping centers, scream around winding back roads, do all sorts of fun things with it. And not worry.

With Corvettes, among others, the price disparity is even worse. You can get a decent original 1963 split-window for about $4,000. Concours '63s are going for $15,000 these days to hard-core collectors. That's a mighty big difference and one that bears some thinking about before you put your money down. Now, I'm not suggesting that you buy a roach, only that you don't throw your money away on an impossible-to-maintain gilded lily.

A word of warning. You could spend years looking for *the* car. If you have the time to spend, fine. But prices *are* going up all the time. And if you leave yourself some latitude, you'll be able to take advantage of deals that might come up, or grab that really good car that's similar but not just right. My experience with the Tiger is a good example. What I needed had to be big enough for two people and some grocery bags, had to be a roadster, pre–'68 emissions controls, reliable, and fun to drive. So I looked around . . . and eventually ended up with a Sunbeam Tiger. It's not the answer to all the world's problems, but it *is* diabolically fast, fun, reliable, economical—and I can leave it sitting out in the snow under an MG Mitten and not feel like a heartless cad because it's got cold feet. And wonder of wonders, as I sit here the little dear is appreciating at roughly $100 a month.

SHOPPING

Of course, if you know the car you want, the first thing to do is to join the club for that marque. Even before you think about anything else, join the club. There can't be anything left on wheels that somebody somewhere isn't collecting and that doesn't have a club formed in its honor. And nearly every club publishes a newsletter with classified ads, which are often the best place to shop for a car. Club members figure that if you're in the club not only are they going to have to keep seeing you at meets and hearing about the junker they foisted off on you, but also, since you've taken the time to join the club, you probably have more interest in preserving their precious baby than someone in off the street. Indeed, many car owners will sell only to other club members, often with the proviso that when the car is resold, it must be offered to club members first.

If the club classified doesn't list your car, there are other places to look. If you're searching for almost anything with wheels, check *Hemmings Motor News, Cars & Parts,* and *Old Cars.* Other places to look are *Road & Track* and the Sunday *New York Times.* Particularly in *Hemmings,* however, the advertised prices are *very* high. I seriously doubt that many cars are actually sold at anywhere near what's asked. The technique for buying an old car is roughly equatable with bargaining for white slaves in Morocco, and it's a wise man indeed who can walk away *knowing* he got a deal. Few will admit to the actual purchase price. As a general rule, however, it's hard to find an honest bargain in the big national classifieds.

A secret place to find thoroughbred cars is the local *Want Ad Press* or *Buy Lines* that have sprung up around the country. The bigger ones have sections strictly for collector car classifieds, and you can often find honest bargains in cheaper sports cars. There aren't many Ferraris or Lamborghinis, but I have inquired about everything from a Studebaker Avanti to a Bentley R-type Continental through my local *Pennysaver.*

AUCTIONS

What about auctions? Well, what about auctions? There must be some honest old-car auctions, but I haven't heard of one yet. Either the cars have unreasonably high reserve prices—so nothing is ever sold—or the purchase prices paid are "record setting," though the car has already been presold for less to a friend of the auctioneer. Outsiders are the ones who pay the really high prices and pay through the nose. This is strictly a game for knowledgeable experts, and even then it's a damn good way to get eaten alive. More than one of those $200,000 Mercers and Duesenbergs has been for resale ever since the auction, with no takers at half the price. Unless—and that's a very strong unless—you know *precisely* what you're doing, I wouldn't even go near an auction tent to scratch my nose. You'll end up owning the place.

Nor is it a good place to sell. By the time you pay commissions and fees, the higher price you might get has eroded away. And lately, it seems as though most auctions are running 80 percent and even 90 percent cars that don't meet the reserve price. That's a lot of trouble and expense to absorb to find out that no one wants your car or to find out that everyone's car is overpriced and you can't afford the one you want. Stay far away from auctions, and ignore anyone who tries to tell you different. If he's not a shill he's either misinformed or dumb. In either case, you really can't afford his advice.

L. Scott Bailey, the gracious publisher of *Automobile Quarterly,* is none of the above. In the Christmas 1974 issue of *Quatrefoil* he wrote what is at this moment still the definitive article on automobile auctions. Scott is a very conservative fellow, but behind his gracious veneer you can just see the indignation boiling over. "As it stands now," he wrote, "the auctioneer in the motorcar collecting hobby is all powerful. It is ludicrous to presume that he is a true value setter, since his raison d'être is to create by theatrics, sales that are not sales, prices that are not prices. The commercialization of the hobby is a fact. The values and prices of historic cars today are unrealistic, artificially created in a market that seems to listen only to the sound of an auctioneer's gavel." Like the man said, stay away from auctions.

RESTORATION

If you want a perfect car for show, restoration is your only recourse. Again, it comes down to the size of your pocketbook. A frame-up professional restoration on any car is going to take roughly the same amount of time, give or take the basic condition going in, the diffi-culty of locating parts, etcetera. But the value of the car coming out is going to depend on the intrinsic worth of the car itself. In other words, a $25,000 restoration applied to an MG-TD ultimately worth $10,000 is silly. The same restoration on a Ford GT-40 valued at $50,000 makes a lot more sense. This may seem perfectly obvious, but you'd be surprised how many collectors get carried away and start literally pouring money into a car that will just *never* be worth the expense.

If you intend to do the restoration yourself, that's another story. And once again, it depends on the ultimate goal of your project. But be careful. Normal tarting up—new carpets, upholstery, convertible top, a little bodywork and painting, refurbishing the running gear—is easily within the capabilities of most enthusiasts, at least on simpler cars. Something like a Gullwing Mercedes is so valuable—and so complicated—that no one reading this book should do anything more mechanical than turn the key on . . . or maybe wash the windows. Anything harder you should leave to the professionals. And that means money. A total rebuild on a Mercedes engine is roughly $5,500; paint will cost just as much, as will an interior, and so on. A quality total restoration on a tired 300SL could run $30,000, exactly what the car is worth right now. If you buy a basket case, make sure it comes cheap.

Never buy someone else's half-completed project unless you know exactly what you're doing. When they start unloading your new car from two dozen corrugated supermarket boxes and a U-Haul, that's the time to run away. Fast. Unless you already have considerable experience with similar cars—or you're an awfully fast learner—you'll have nothing more than a monumental headache when you're done, and the job will probably end up being finished by a professional restoration shop in any case. And even the pros would rather take a car apart themselves, just so they know where all the bits go back in.

SPECULATION

If you haven't realized by now, my advice is not to expect to make a lot of quick money owning your old car. The days of easy money, *big* money, are over for the private investor. It's a situation precisely parallel to the stock market. There are very few successful, big-time private investors left, because companies like the Kruse Brothers—who auction something like $30 million worth of cars a year—have been there long before you. Starting from ground zero, it's pretty hard to become a Tom Barrett or George Waterman anymore. There are no Bugattis left in barns. Even if there were, the barns are all in Yugoslavia or Albania or Iraq, and not only has Ed Jurist from the Vintage Car Store just bought them all the week before you got there, but if you try to take an old car across the border—it's a national treasure, after all—they'll either break both your thumbs or cut your hands off at the wrists, depending.

Over the long haul, real thoroughbred cars are obviously going to appreciate in value. The problem is finding one at a reasonable price in today's inflated market. This translates as "no quick profits." When you get to Ferraris and Gullwings, everybody knows exactly what he's got. There aren't any bargains. For those who just want to turn over a few dollars rather than buy cars to save for an extended period, there's only one thing to do—swallow your pride and start dealing in old tinware. Buy that perfect '53 Cranbrook wagon from *Buy Lines* for $500, and sell it through *Hemmings* for $1,300 to some damn Plymouth zealot with foam-flecked lips and a permanent stare. This can be a great way to stay in pocket money, and the total sums aren't so great that even if you guess wrong once in a while you'll lose your shirt. If you have the stomach for it. Otherwise, you'll just have to wait for enthusiasm and inflation to catch up with the car you've picked to hold for a while. If you absolutely *have to* make a quick profit on your old-car investment, may I humbly suggest a nice treasury note at 9 percent and a subscription to *The Milestone Car* instead. I'm afraid it's really the only guaranteed way to make money owning your old car.

IMPORTS

If you have a medium amount of money to play with, an option to consider is importation. You won't find that $500 Bugatti in Ru-

mania, but there *are* certain cars that can be had in Europe—shipping included—for substantially less than in the States. I would pretty much avoid British and Continental auctions. Most of the auction companies are international now, the dollar is very soft, and there are buyers with big sums almost everywhere. The auctioneers are not dumb. They will ship major cars to the country where they expect the best profit, and the Jaguar D-type you buy in London for $50,000 you might have bought the month before in Indianapolis for half that price.

A classic example of this occurred a few years ago. The Kruses sold a Grand Prix 1908 Benz at a Scottsdale, Arizona, auction (at which the famous $153,000 "Hitler" Mercedes was also unloaded) for $51,000. Just three months later, Lord Montagu of Beaulieu—just about the sharpest collector/investor in the old-car world—paid $85,000 for *the same car* at a Christie's auction in Geneva. This case may be extreme, but it does prove, I think, that car collecting is an international movement and that there are no fantastic bargains left overseas. There is only one way to do it. *If* you are traveling to Europe anyway and *if* you want to shop while over there and *if* you know precisely what you want and what it's worth at home plus shipping costs, *then* perhaps you can justify looking for cars abroad. Just don't expect to make a lot of money.

A further disclaimer. There are no bargains in developing countries. The cars are there all right. South America is absolutely chock-a-block with postwar collectible cars—all in abominable shape and worth a king's ransom even if you could get them out . . . which you can't. And in the Middle East, although there are millions of old American and European cars, things like '58 Impalas are worth $10,000 in these oil-rich days. End of fantasy.

THE 1967 MASSACRE

Unless you live in a cave, you must know by now that the boffins at the Department of Transportation actually run the U.S. automobile industry. And have, ever since December 31, 1967. Remember that date. Any car built after January 1, 1968, has to meet a surprisingly long list of specifications that most European countries don't require. What this means is simple: unless you are buying a new car that comes with U.S. spec equipment through a reputable drive-it-in-Europe plan, *do not buy* a 1968 or newer car overseas.

You can't have it. Literally. When your precious baby lands in Newark, the federal agents not only will check the trunk for stash and gold bullion, they'll look under the hood for the little plaque from the manufacturer that says your car is U.S. legal. If they don't find it, *they will keep your car.* Simple as that. You must post a bond equal to the value of the car *plus* the import tax so that you can take your car off the docks and have it changed to U.S. specs. Customs gives you ninety days to have the emissions and safety widgets you are missing put on your car. On a Ferrari or Maserati, this might mean a whole new engine, new body structure, bumpers, different tires, rims, interior, and God knows what all. In other words, a whole different car. Impossible. So at the end of three months, they come and take your car away and send it back to where it came from—at *your* expense. There's really not a thing you can do about it, either.

Now there are a bunch of late-model Italian exoticars that you'd swear look like '68s and '69s or maybe even '71s, that have a 1967 plaque under the hood. In other words, some factories kept making '67s right up until the government got wise. Hell, they could *still* be making '67s for all anyone *really* knows. The federal agents have caught on to this one now. You might get by with some wacky Abarth one-off or something, but in general, trying to bring in a post-'67 car is really asking for trouble unless it has a manufacturer's U.S. legal plate.

EXCEPTIONS TO THE RULE

As with any good bureaucratic rule, there are loopholes. The ones that interest collectors are the exceptions for racing, "experiment," and show cars. The Department of Transportation people are primarily concerned with safety and emissions on cars used by the public. So it is legal for museums, collectors, recognized engineering facilities, and racers to bring into the country nonconforming cars as long as they won't be used on the street. The DoT will *not* let you bring in that Ferrari Boxer you might think about racing *someday.* They will let you bring it in if you can prove it will actually be raced . . . or never leave your garage. And the government is pretty strict. At least one too-clever enthusiast brought in a Lotus Seven for "display," then loaned it to a magazine for testing. Sure enough, the DoT reads *Road & Track* too, and not only was the Lotus shipped back to England but the fine was $10,000. If you do *everything* wrong, it is possible to add up to $150,000 in fines for an illegal entry. Which is *very* expensive.

Of course, you *can* circumvent the feds, at least if you're willing to keep a low profile. Desperate enthusiasts have been known to ship parts over and assemble the "kit" in this country and also to bring illegal cars into Canada and then drive them across the border. But fair warning: the consequences of bucking the system are damned severe.

RIGHT-HAND DRIVE

You can get bargains on right-hand-drive cars both in England and over here. There's a reason. If you actually expect to *drive* your car, RHD is a pain in the ass. It's hard to pass, the gear lever is usually on the wrong side, and it can be a pest to park. On the other hand, it's easier to race on most courses and many desirable cars—not just British—are right-hand drive. If you're adaptable you can learn to put up with it without terminal trauma. However, don't expect that the RHD Morgan you buy in England is going to be worth as much as a comparable LHD + 4 in the States.

BUYING SIGHT UNSEEN

Hundreds of collectors every year spot cars for sale in England in *Motorsport* or *Veteran and Vintage,* send over thousands of pounds, and receive cars by mail, sight unseen. I've bought in England and flown a car home but never ordered one without seeing it first. The tension level when you go to uncrate your prize at the docks is said to be right up there with meeting the stage to collect your mail-order bride. I've a friend who bought a 1933 Morgan Trike this way for $2,700, which he kept for four years and sold for $6,500, so it can be made to work. The secret is the Royal Auto Club. For a small fee, a professional assessor will inspect the car of your dreams and write out an honest report on its condition. And, of course, any reputable seller will include recent photographs. A trick in this department is to ask that he take pictures just for you. Kodak dates its processing, so it's easy to tell if the pictures are brand-new or if they're old photos of a restoration that's since been ruined.

Dealers I would trust a bit less than private sellers. Many European dealers still seem to think the streets are paved with gold over here and price accordingly. Individuals don't seem as confused, though you often see absurd prices in ads placed by British sellers in American magazines. Always shop in British magazines for cars in Britain; that way you're reaching the local enthusiasts, not the international speculators. *Motorsport* seems to be the best marketplace, though it goes without saying that if you're shopping for $500 cars that will cost you $1,000 to ship across the Atlantic, you're wasting your time. Shipping costs can only be amortized over an expensive purchase.

SPEAKING OF SHIPPING

The very best way to ship is by air, and for motorcycles it's the only way. Unfortunately, bulky cars are prohibitively expensive to fly. The next best thing is containerized shipping. If you're lucky and persistent, you or your (you hope) reliable agent will be allowed to lock it up personally. You want to mail anything not tied down—tools, manuals, radios—separately, for small items will absolutely vaporize on the docks. You also want to photograph the car just before it is loaded, so any question of condition can be authenticated. And of course, insure the car. Trying to get paid off by an English insurance company for a car damaged on the New York docks is flat impossible, so I'd take the paperwork to my own Stateside insurance agent and have the car already covered for damage *before* it's

shipped. It's the only way to guarantee that you'll be able to collect.

INSURANCE

Insurance is one of the nice economies of owning a postwar classic. Companies like J. C. Taylor and Condon & Skelly specialize in insurance for older cars of all sorts and surprisingly new collector cars, as new as 1960. As long as you own at least one "regular" car for daily transportation, the specialist companies will insure your collector car for roughly 25 to 40 percent of what conventional insurance runs. And of course, a regular insurance policy will pay off at "book value," which goes back only ten years or less and shows no reflection of collector car values at all. The specialists allow you to set your own value—within reason—and will pay off to that amount. They'll even let you select your own restorer rather than require bids for repairs as do conventional insurance companies. Since most collectors drive very carefully in their old cars, the accident rate—and hence the premium—is much lower.

CALIFORNIA CARS

You'll often notice in classified ads that "Arizona car" or "California car" will bounce the price up considerably. Automobiles really do deteriorate faster in the Northeast, and in states like Pennsylvania, where rock salt is used on icy roads, the damage is devastating. Southwestern or West Coast cars, if they've been well taken care of, can look brand-new underneath after twenty years of regular driving. It can be worth the price to buy an "Arizona" or "California" car, particularly if you're shopping for "excellent original" cars. A trip to California to drive back a car can be a reasonable vacation as well.

ALUMINUM, STEEL, OR FIBERGLASS

Virtually all coachbuilt cars, most racing cars, and many sports cars are clothed with aluminum. Now aluminum has many advantages.

It's light. It's easily worked for hand production, essential for one-off customs. It doesn't rust or rot. If you know what you're doing it's easily repaired, though it does stretch. An inept bodyman can quickly make your aluminum body three sizes too big for the chassis without half trying. So although it's easily worked, qualified labor is expensive. Aluminum also bends easily. As the old saw has it, you can tell when a fly visits a Ferrari: he makes one dent when he lands, another as he takes off. Aluminum is also unstable in varying temperatures, shrinking away from the paint in the cold, expanding when it's warm. So paint is hard to keep on it. Also, many world-famous carrozzeria—Italian especially —use a lot of body filler to cover their mistakes. And aluminum with plastic is a lousy surface to keep in paint. Aluminum bodies are a mixed blessing, then, though many people swear by them for the rust resistance alone. If the car is going to be in a fairly stable climate, it's definitely *the* preferred material.

Steel bodies I don't have to tell you about. They're sturdy, cheap, easily worked, easily repaired, stable under paint . . . and, mostly, all there is. They rot away without care, but then so do your teeth. It's all a matter of maintenance. A well-kept steel body will last almost as long as aluminum, though rust is a constant problem in virtually every part of the humid Northern Hemisphere.

Fiberglass has yet to come into its own, fully thirty years after it was first used for cars. About the only plastic collector cars you'll see are Corvettes, Avantis, Kaiser-Darrins, Woodill Wildfires, Lotuses, TVRs, and most sports/racers from the last two decades. Fiberglass is weird. It shatters in collisions because of its high tensile strength, but repairs are relatively easy because it bounces back to its original shape. And fiberglass itself, as long as you have some sort of armature underneath it, is surprisingly easy to repair, even for amateurs. Of all body materials, it's certainly the easiest to modify, too, which is why so many Corvettes have been chopped up and ruined for collectors. Surprisingly, then, though Corvettes are among the most overpriced of postwar sports cars, if you expect to do your own restoration, they can be considerably cheaper in the long run because you *can* do your own restoration. And replacement body parts in plastic—which absolutely wreck the value of other collector cars—can be used with perfect confidence on a fiberglass body. So it's a pretty good deal, all in all.

COACHBUILT COLLECTIBLES

All Ferraris until 1956 and many of them afterward were coachbuilt. The same is true of Pegasos, Maseratis, and all sorts of strange and exotic beasts from Sunbeam Harringtons to Monteverdi Hais. But between the clear-cut extremes of true mass production and wholly unique one-offs, there is another large and nebulous area of "limited-production" and "batch-built" cars that are neither one nor the other. The first version of the Nash Healey— 130 built in aluminum by Panelcraft and assembled by Healey—represents the British approach pretty well. These bodies were built over a one-off jig used a hundred times. They stopped building cars when the jig wore out. On the other hand, Pininfarina runs a true mini-assembly line with all the modern conveniences, whether building Ferraris by the dozen or the thousand.

What difference does it make to you? Well, a lot. The price for a one-off will be considerably higher than for a standard body on the same chassis. And many times, it simply won't be worth it. A Corvette produced by the thousands is apt to be better debugged than a Ferrari one-off, for the simple reason that there's much more riding on the GM design. That's not to say it's a better car or a better design, heaven forbid, but simply that one-off construction implies that there'll always be something entirely new that the coachbuilder hasn't done before. The chance for error is much greater. On the other hand, a mass-production work of art—because it must appeal to a wide audience—is very nearly a contradiction in terms. But a coachbuilt body can be as innovative and brilliant as the stylist and client want. If the coachbuilder is reputable it can be better built than anything that was *ever* stamped out on the assembly line. Really, it's like anything else. Some are good, some are terrible. The Right Label counts for everything.

American

CHAPTER 1

Sports Cars

The American sports car is a curious beast. Back before the Great War, in the days of T-head Mercers, Stutz Bearcats, and motoring goggles, America built some of the best sporting machinery in the world. Even then, American sports cars exhibited the distinctive characteristics that have come to define the breed. Mostly, the early builders started with a big, powerful engine making as much horsepower as possible. This they stuck in a lightweight frame with—on the best cars, at least—decent brakes, superlative handling, and minimal bodywork. These were harsh, demanding, crude devices intended for going as fast as possible across those endless, plumb-straight Midwest dirt roads that stretched off to the intimidating horizon.

Our sports cars were never mass-market machines. Fledgling General Motors never built anything approaching the panache of the Mercer, and though a million small entrepreneurs produced tons of speed equipment for T-model Fords, the factory never tried to sell a truly high-performance sports car. The interesting American cars came from tiny, underfinanced companies, and none of them ever got to build many cars before the market and the money dried up. The same was true in the twenties, thirties, and forties. What American sports cars there were usually had been whacked out in somebody's backyard from a flathead Ford or Willys. There was little interest in spartan cars that would go fast, almost no interest in racing other than Indianapolis in May, and except for wealthy internationalists like Briggs Cunningham and the

Collier brothers, zero interest in European road racing, then in its Golden Age. There weren't even any racing publications in America, the equivalent of *Motor, Motorsport,* and all the rest that kept European enthusiasm for sports machinery, racing, and amateur events at a surprisingly informed level.

After World War II, though, there was a drastic change. The clubby, amateur, "run what ya brung" atmosphere of English racing was imported lock, stock, and stringback driving gloves along with the first MG-TCs and XK-120s. Soon, the T-baggers of the fifties were spending all their time reading Ken Purdy and mooning about Ferraris, Mercedes SSKs, and Morgan three-wheelers, moaning the fate that had located them in this automotively benighted country. But at the other end of the social spectrum, there were a whole passel of dry lakes hot-rodders who knew how to extract ungodly amounts of horsepower from Detroit V-8s, were pretty fair craftsmen when there was enough money to pay for the work . . . and were quick learners. It didn't take them long to figure out that if the horsepower they already had could be harnessed in one of those little bitsy European-type chassis and made to go around corners, they could whip ass anytime they wanted among all the stringback twits with the expensive Ferraris.

Presto: Renaissance of the American sports car, a direct result of the inevitable class warfare between the European-oriented socialite types and the indigenous hot-rod greasers. Curiously enough, the center for both types was in the automotive Disneyland of southern California, and it wasn't long before hot-rodders like Frank Kurtis, Troutman and Barnes, Chuck Daigh, Ak Miller, Phil Remington, Jim Diedt, and a dozen others were able to get a handle on chassis design and suspensions that borrowed a little from Indy cars, a little from European sports/racers, and a lot from good ol' Yankee knowhow.

These native-born California hot-rodders got mixed in with some exotic imports—like Ken Miles and Zora Duntov—and pretty soon a whole string of limited-production sports cars started coming out of L.A. and environs. And of course, the New England contingent—Phil Walters, Bill Frick, and John Fitch—wasn't far behind. The essential thing to remember is that except for the mild-mannered

'55–'57 Thunderbird—which even Ford called a "personal car"—*every* American sports car, including the Corvette, came out of the despised hot-rod/oval-track racing community. Detroit had nothing to do with them except to supply wonderfully sturdy engines.

All of which explains why, when you read this chapter, it'll be full of people you've never heard of who made handfuls of cars you might not remember in garages you'd be ashamed to be seen in. But that's irrelevant. The cars are superb, many of them, far and away the most visceral, masculine cars ever built in the world. Some of them cost a fortune to engineer; many of them came together one step ahead of the bill collector. But the thing they all have in common is a vigorous élan, a high performance that's really *high.*

I mean, the British can take something like an Austin A-40 that goes 40 mph, put a swoopy little body on it, hot-rod the engine till it's near the bursting point just sitting there, and make the result go 65. Big whoopee, as the Americans would say. Hell, they were taking Chevy V-8s out of sedans that would go 120 and building sports/racers that would do 200. We think *big* in America, always have, probably always will. That doesn't make us subtle. When you hear a Cobra light up, you just know that the car was conceived by an American—a Texan, by God—and it's gonna be just a little bit larger than life.

Even in the mid-sixties when Chevrolet and Ford got heavily into sports cars, it was still the California hot-rodders like Pete Brock and Phil Remington and ol' Carroll Shelby who produced the results. And the factories came to them, for the most part. With a massive influx of funds, the unassuming West Coast racers were able to take on the best in the world. Ultimately, that symbiotic deal became the only way an independent sports car maker could really stay in business in this country, by linking up with one of the big factories—Shelby with Ford, for instance—and in a sense, applying for aid to dependents. It just costs so much these days to come up with a new car that it can't be done by a true independent anymore.

There will probably never be another all-new, right-from-the-ground-up American production sports car. The Bricklin fiasco will see to that. The big problem is the federal government. After January 1968 the required and expensive federal crash tests, emissions tests, and other folderol have kept manufacturers with limited funds from getting involved in exciting cars. The only loopholes are modifications of standard Detroit products—and they're getting so they're not worth hopping up—or doing backyard kits for mundane chassis. That's why there's such interest in all those plastic kit bodies for Pintos and VWs. They are flat terrible cars, most of them, but they do fill a need. At least they *are* more interesting than anything else you can buy new for under $20,000.

And that, of course, brings us back to why someone would want an old American sports car. Well, it's simple. Because despite the best paternalist efforts of the federal government, it is impossible to eradicate that basic animal instinct in human beings that just *has* to test the limits. Every animal does it. Cats will hang from a limb just to see how far they can go before they fall. Dogs will attack bears to see if they can get away with it. Horses will leap fences that are too tall, daring to chop themselves up if they fail. Animals—people—*need* to extend themselves beyond their limits, if for nothing else but to see where their limits *are*. And you can do that with an old American sports car, if you want. Or at least you can think about it, 'cause you could do it if you wanted to. Or at the very least, you can be amazed at the other men who dared to open up one of these things in anger. And you can feel a kinship with them.

Besides all of which, this kind of car is just never going to be built again. Not with the responsiveness, the crispness, the *control*, the mastery of machinery that's possible with the early iron. And most of all, not only are these really bitchin' machines in their effortless power, beautiful and well built, but they are—many of them, and those not for long—surprisingly inexpensive for what you get. A good American limited-production two-seater should cost less than half of what you'll have to spend to get the same mind-boggling level of performance out of a European machine. A good Devin SS—built in beautiful downtown El Monte, California—would blow the doors off a Testa Rosa Ferrari that cost twice as much when they were both new and will still blow its doors off today. And still cost half

as much. In addition, and this is the best part, Ferrari parts are so overpriced as to make you faint. If you've never spent $100 for a set of spark plug leads or $90 for an ashtray, you haven't lived Ferrari. On the other hand, that Devin—and any American V-8 sports car—can be almost totally mechanically rebuilt with parts from J. C. Whitney and your corner NAPA store, parts that cost almost nothing and that will last forever. And that's the whole secret right there. American sports cars may not be sophisticated, they may not be subtle. But by God, they *work*.

Kurtis

Just as the Duesenbergs and Harry Miller were the kings of America's golden age of racing, the absolute ruler of USAC ovals for the first fifteen years after World War II was Frank Kurtis. The fabulously popular V-8 60 midgets were virtually his private class. Kurtis Kraft supplied something like 550 assembled midget racers and another 550 kits. Between 1941 and 1963 Kurtis built 128 cars for the Indy 500, winning every year from 1950 through 1955 and building more than two-thirds of the starting field right on up through 1957. The last two Kurtis chassis—basically 1950 designs—raced at the Brickyard in 1965. Hell, A. J. Foyt *still* has his Kurtis sprint car, and dozens of the antique front-engine Kurtises continue to run lesser USAC events. Kurtis built go-karts, land-speed record cars for Bonneville, experimental racers, and uncounted specials. He also built a fair number of sports cars, some meant as strict boulevardiers, some for Bonneville and the drag strips, some as road racers. And though they were financial disasters, they were all as successful at the track as the open-wheelers. Of all the constructors who've bolted together racing cars since Count Jenatzy, Frank Kurtis has built the most.

The first Kurtises were more hot rod than sports car, starting way back in the twenties

Granite-jawed Frank Kurtis shows off his first 1948 "Sport Car," one of thirty-four.

when, as a young bodyman, Frank rebodied wreckers into sleek boattail speedsters and sold them for a profit. He got into building racing car bodies in 1932, then graduated to complete cars. His USAC cars were always beautiful and sturdy. When they weren't faster than the opposition, they outlasted 'em. Kurtis built sports cars the same way. Probably the seminal one was a prewar, slab-sided roadster with a huge removable padded Carson top, a faired-in grille of chrome tubing, and a '41 Buick chassis. Like all his previous street cars, this one was built as a rolling advertisement for Frank's race shop.

After the war, Kurtis kept building midgets until '48, when supply finally equaled demand as midget racing began a swift decline. However, Kurtis had a good-sized shop in Glendale, California, that was getting idler and idler. So in place of building midgets he set the Kurtis Kraft crew to building a revised version of his curious old Buick-based show car, with an all-new 100-inch-wheelbase frame laid out to accept components from almost any American car. Over this went a strangely bulbous two-seater aluminum body reminiscent of his early Buick . . . right down to the padded Carson top. The suspension was basically V-8 Ford, and power plants ranged

from a supercharged Studebaker six to a Cadillac V-8.

Kurtis managed to sell thirty-four of his roadsters, in both assembled and kit form. The high point of the whole enterprise was a 1949 trip to Bonneville, where Wally Parks of fledgling *Hot Rod* magazine managed to get an Edelbrock-prepped flathead Mercury version up to a 142.5 mph average. John R. Bond, then technical editor of *Road & Track,* wrote after a ride in a Cadillac-powered Kurtis, "I must admit I've never before been shoved back into the seat quite so hard. The driver was a man of no little sports car experience and he swears it handles better than the Jaguar XK-120 . . . I'm inclined to agree."

About this same time, in late 1949, Earl "Madman" Muntz stopped by the old Glendale shop and promptly bought Kurtis's '41 Buick show car for $5,000. After a tour of the place, the madcap used-car impresario ("I want to give 'em away, but Mrs. Muntz won't let me!"), television manufacturer ("Stop staring at your radio, folks!"), and Kaiser-Frazer distributor bought the Glendale plant and all it contained for $200,000. And so, just like that, the original Kurtis Sport Car became the Muntz Jet, embarking upon an improbable career as a promotional vehicle for TV personality and car collector Herb Shriner, as well as a crop of other attention-seeking celebrity Muntz owners. The crazy Muntz Jet served as *the* Hollywood all-purpose personality runabout, just like the Dual-Ghia later on in the fifties and the Excalibur today.

Unfortunately, the sleek and lightweight Kurtis began to grow—literally and figuratively—under the hot arc lights of the Madman's publicity mill. After cranking out only twenty-eight cars in the Glendale factory, Muntz moved the whole operation—lock, stock, and overhead-valve Cadillac V-8s—to Evanston, Illinois. The car itself got a steel body instead of aluminum. And the wheelbase went out to 116 inches from a stretched box-section perimeter frame that looked like it'd been stolen off a two-ton truck. The Cadillac V-8 was swapped for a heavy flathead Lincoln V-8, coupled to a GM HydraMatic. But most of the running gear remained lightweight Ford, with a modified Hudson rear axle. Performance dropped markedly, of course, for the luxuriously appointed Muntz—complete with one of the Madman's super-duper radios in a fancy underdash console—now weighed damn near 4,000 pounds.

Road & Track tested the Jet in 1951, explaining that "the Muntz Jet was not intended as a true sports car, but rather as a deluxe high-speed convertible touring car in the American manner. As such, it offers the fastest acceleration and highest top speed of any American-built car available from the salesroom floor today (0–60 in 12.3 seconds, 108 mph top speed). For those who wish to travel rapidly, carry five passengers, be protected from the weather and who have the necessary change . . . this is the car." The necessary change was between $5,000 and $6,000, depending on options . . . pretty steep compared to the base Cadillac price of $2,940 for a four-door sedan in 1951.

Madman Muntz stayed in the car business until 1954. At that point his TV business went through some heavy competition from RCA and Zenith, and money got a bit tight. After building 394 Jets, the Madman stopped production. He claimed to have lost $1,000 on each car, mostly because he'd never gotten the production volume up to where it was a paying proposition.

Today, either the early Kurtis Sport Car or the Muntz Jet is a wickedly sensible buy

Earl "Madman" Muntz inspects the hardtop on the prototype four-passenger Muntz Jet of 1949.

Bill Murphy's 1956 Kurtis 500S was one of the first sports/racers to use a Buick V-8; this aluminum envel

. . . if you don't mind the styling, which is admittedly pretty weird. Still, the frame and running gear are incredibly strong, and both Cadillac and Lincoln V-8s are easy to repair, with parts plentiful. The suspension bits are Ford, so that's no problem either. Even better, no matter who built them, the Jets were assembled like jewelry by craftsmen who were basically racing car constructors and who worked to precision tolerances. As Michael Lamm wrote many years ago in *Special-Interest Autos,* "Here's a car that's over-constructed, but its basic plan is simple. So it's easy to maintain and restore. There's not too much that can go wrong, and parts are still available. From a collector's viewpoint, this is a good car to own if you're interested in a *driveable* collectible."

Amazingly, too, considering its pedigree, the Kurtis/Muntz Jet is still pretty cheap. A really good one shouldn't cost more than $5,000, though the inevitable speculators seem to think it should be twice that much. The Kurtis/Muntz Jet is a historically important and fun-to-drive convertible that indisputably was the first American sports car, in the modern sense of the term. And from a total

production of over 400, there're still a fair number of survivors.

After selling out to Muntz, Frank Kurtis continued building race cars, of course, and in 1950 started on his incredible Indy winning streak. In 1952 he constructed the famous Cummins Diesel roadster, the first Indy car with an offset drivetrain and a "laydown" engine. His Indy "production" version was the equally famous Kurtis 500A, the Indy winner in '53, in '54, and in revised 500C form, in '55. Even more interesting, though, Kurtis was inspired by the straightforward success of the 500A to make a road-racing version in 1952. He called it the 500KK, and it was nothing more than an Indy car with two seats, fenders, and lights.

The original concept of the 500KK was that the race-bred chassis—a tubular space frame with trailing-arm suspension and solid axles at front and rear—could be purchased as an inexpensive kit for only $1,300, to be clothed with any sort of fiberglass or aluminum body the backyard builder had available and powered with anything from an anemic Henry J flathead to a hulking Chrysler hemi. To accommodate these disparate engines,

laced the Allard-inspired sheet metal of the early cars.

frames were available to order in anything from a 92- to a 100-inch wheelbase.

As it turned out, most people were understandably a lot more interested in having a complete Kurtis car than an intimidating bare frame kit. So Frank Kurtis started building up complete cars—model 500S—covered with a rudimentary aluminum body patterned somewhat after the Allard J2-X and somewhat after his own 500A Indy car. Kurtis said, "I'll build a car like the Allard. But it will *handle.*" And it did. Bill Stroppe raced a Mercury-powered 500S. So did Bill Murphy, but his car later got a Buick V-8. Jack Hinkle dropped an Indy Offy in his and proceeded to absolutely clean house throughout the Midwest.

Mostly because of all this road-racing publicity—and because he was the hottest name in oval track racing during '53 and '54—Kurtis managed to sell about forty dual-purpose 500KK frame kits and 500S roadsters at $5,000 each before he phased them out in 1955 in favor of the strictly competition 500X. An even dozen of these were built, but it was hard going to convince a snobbish sporty car T-bagger that an aluminum-bodied space frame with an archaic suspension taken directly

from an Indy roadster would go around corners better than the big Ferrari and Maserati sports/racers that were all the rage. Kurtis was butting his head against a wall. So he went the other way.

The 500M was the 500S chassis with a fancy Thunderbird-like fiberglass body and a Ford V-8. It was meant strictly as a boulevard showpiece, though a couple were raced, with indifferent results. Once again, an outside contractor came along and bought up the right to make the 500M with Frank's help. About two dozen were built before the money dried up, at which point Kurtis gave up on sports cars and resumed his infinitely more successful career as a racing car constructor. He retired to Arizona in 1963, but Kurtis Kraft is still around, now run by Frank's son. They build racing ski boats today.

Of all the Kurtis sports cars, probably the best one to consider actually owning—outside the Kurtis/Muntz Jet—would be a 500S. Not only are they more plentiful (if a world supply at this point of maybe one dozen can be considered plentiful) but because of their rock simple construction and granite strength, there can't be an easier car in the world to work on. About the only bits you'd *ever* have to replace would be engines, and since almost anything you fancy will fit and be legitimate, too, you can just toss in a Caddy V-8 every twenty years or so and drive the thing right into the next century. Prices are all flooey right now, with good examples going for any-

Kurtis's 500S, basically a two-seater Indy car.

A Kurtis 500S with a fiberglass body plus Ford V-8 became a Kurtis 500M.

where from $8,000 for a good original to $15,000 that some speculator on Long Island has been asking for one with a Chevy V-8 from the wrong era, a Corvette rear end, and a whole bunch of other restoration gaffs. Someplace in between is probably about right.

Most collectors who have a masterpiece from the atelier of Frank Kurtis are just beginning to realize what they've got, I think, and the big price boom is just around the corner. And Kurtises just don't come on the market all that often. When one does, be prepared to jump quick. You won't be sorry. In spite of their seemingly naive design, the cars of Frank Kurtis were as fast, point to point, as anything in their day, Ferraris and Maseratis included. And they are *much* sturdier. Except for a disappointing string of bad business breaks—and the fact that he was maybe five to ten years ahead of the market—Frank Kurtis could have been A. J. Watson *and* Carroll Shelby rolled into one . . . an incredible combination, when you think about it.

Super Sport by Crosley; 26 hp and 1,250 pounds.

Crosley

Over the years, the American automobile industry has attracted a wacky collection of freethinkers, all the way from Ned Jordan to Liz Carmichael. Most of them expected to beat Detroit with a cheap, economical "people's car." Keller, Playboy, Davis, and a host of forgotten cars—including the 1975 Dale and Tri-Vette—have kept this dream alive right up until the present day. But only one man made it work even a little. Middle-aged Powell Crosley, the pride of Cincinnati, was a self-made multimillionaire from other sources—dull things like tire inner liners, radios, and refrigerators—before he ever thought about cars. But once he got started, Crosley built nearly 70,000 funny little cars that would have been more at home on the narrow back alleys of Napoli or Paris than the corn-lined, straight-arrow asphalt ribbons that radiated from the Marion, Indiana, factory.

Of course, most of Crosley's peculiar minicars were no more than that—funny little cars. But alongside the baby station wagons, sedans, convertibles, and trucks that constituted Crosley's standard line, from 1949 through 1952 he also built a whopping 2,498 sports cars. Yes, true sports cars.

And the tiny Hot Shot and Super Sport were even phenomenally successful racing cars. For starters, they were ultralight. Overall length was only 136 inches, on an 85-inch wheelbase. Curb weight was a piddling 1,250 pounds. The front brakes were very effective spot discs, and the sturdy ladder frame with stone-simple leaf *and* coil spring suspension handled amazingly well, all out of proportion to the car's size, price, and sophistication. The Crosley Hot Shot, in other words, was one of those happy accidents of automotive design, 100 percent better than anyone ever intended it to be.

Lloyd Taylor, a West Coast engineer, was responsible for the basic Crosley engine. The most unusual feature was that the block and head were made as a one-piece unit copper-brazed together out of sheet steel stampings. The bore was greater than the stroke, and an overhead cam, full-pressure lubrication, and five main bearings made it both sturdy and incredibly lightweight. At 138 pounds, the 45-cubic-inch Crosley four was just about the lightest engine ever to power any car, King Midgets included. Later on, for the Hot Shot and Super Sport the block was switched to cast iron, and the engine weight climbed to a big 150 pounds complete, which was *still* ridiculously light. In stock form, it produced a whimpering 26 hp at 5,400 rpm.

In standard form, the Hot Shot—which came without even doors—and the Super Sport—*avec portes*—were bog slow, even by 1949 standards. Top speed was around 75; the standing quarter-mile took almost 25 seconds. Obviously, the Crosley suffered from a horrendous shortage of *cojones.* Happily enough, though, its little mill was one of the most hotroddable engines ever built. Almost immediately, a substantial industry grew up to supply speed equipment for Crosleys. Most important was Braje of Los Angeles. Fitted with two motorcycle carbs, a hot cam, headers, and a Vertex magneto, a bored-out Crosley would make a reliable 55 hp at 8,000 rpm. SCOT sold a Roots-type supercharger that would bring the horsepower up to 75, and the best engines could consistently turn 10,000 rpm without trouble. In road-race trim, a decent Crosley was good for nearly 100 mph.

It's hard to believe, but in 1950 a Hot Shot won the Index of Performance at Sebring and would have garnered the same coup at Le Mans the next year (sponsored by Briggs Cunningham) but for a duff voltage regulator. In '51 too, a Crosley-powered Bonneville streamliner went 98.79 mph, and a similar engine in a racing hydroplane managed a 52-mph record. The best Crosleys were small-bore amateur sports/racers, however, and right into the sixties Crosley specials of all descriptions ruled the H-modified class in the hands of forgotten luminaries like Chal Hall, Harry Jones, and the immortal Martin Tanner. These unbreakable little mills appeared in public under everything from sectioned Devin bodies to hand-built aluminum masterworks to scruffy homemade panels that looked as if they'd been rolled on the way to the track. For the indomitable Crosley engine it seemed to make little difference what the body looked like, or whether it had the aerodynamics of a 707 or a bread van.

There are still quite a few stock Crosley Hot Shots and Super Sports around, and even more with modified engines. A fair bunch of Crosley-based H-modifieds have survived too, appearing for sale every once in a while in *Autoweek.* Any one of them, particularly in

Martin Tanner at speed in his Martin T3, the ultimate Crosley-powered special.

modified form, would be an absolute blast to own, and some of the specials were so small and light—700 pounds was competitive in the mid-fifties—that you could literally use one for a "mantelpiece racer." Or put a piece of glass over it and make a coffee table. Or hang it from the ceiling like the Smithsonian's Spirit of St. Louis. It'd be fun to own, and there's not a cheaper postwar collectible around which to build a collection.

The Super Sport's price hovered right at $1,000 for its four years of production, and a perfect restored car is worth less than twice that today. Old H-modifieds go for roughly the same. The best thing is that not only are spare parts readily available, but also whole new engines. In fact, even vintage Braje speed equipment is still being made. Crosley was a losing proposition for most of its life. Powell Crosley spent something like $5 million of his personal fortune from 1939 to 1952.

In July of '52 Crosley sold out to General Tire, which later changed its name to Aerojet-General. Aerojet sold all the Crosley spare parts to a shop in Florida that's still got them available through the Crosley club, and continued making engines for government generators and small boats. After half a dozen different owners, stock Crosley engines are *still* being manufactured by Fisher-Pierce and sold as the Bearcat 55 for inboard powerboats. Replica Braje speed equipment, produced in batch lots by John Aibel of the Crosley club, coupled with a brand-new engine, would keep either an original Super Sport or racer running for years and years. For most old cars, vintage speed equipment—Ardun heads, Edmunds manifolds, and such—is almost impossible to find. The little Crosley, of all the improbable roller skates, is one of the few cars from the fifties that can still be reliably hotrodded with *all-new* parts.

Driving a stock Crosley is almost identical to piloting an Austin-Healey Bugeye Sprite. The two cars are Siamese twins in everything except horsepower, and a Braje kit makes that about even, too. The Sprite is slightly more comfortable, the Crosley a better handler. Otherwise . . . just about the same. The interesting difference is that one was designed by a former racing driver in a country mad as hatters for small, spartan roadsters; the other by a Midwestern refrigerator magnate with

a mania for cheap cars and an ingrained faith in simplicity. BMC was able to peddle 50,000 of Healey's Sprites, many of them to the United States. Crosley sold one-twentieth of that. His cars are at least as good, and historically more important. For among other things, the unassuming Hot Shot was America's first mass-produced sports car since the Stutz Bearcat. And a helluva racer, too.

Nash-Healey

If the truth be known, by the time Madman Muntz was done with it, Frank Kurtis's Jet was honestly more of a Grand Tourer than a sports car. And although Kurtis Kraft was familiar to every kid over eleven for its Indy winners, hardly anybody knew they also made blindingly fast sports cars for sale. Crosley was a lot better known, of course, but even in the car-starved years after the Hitler War, it was pretty hard to take a $1,000 Hot Shot— 26 hp and no doors, for Chrissake—very seriously. But the Nash-Healey had a chance. It really did. A substantial advertising budget bought full-page ads in *Life* and the *Saturday Evening Post,* Kelvinator needed something to liven up its car line, Lord knows . . . and the car itself was actually pretty good, even if it was only a Nash.

Well, even if it had a Nash engine. Most of the rest of the Nash-Healey was pure British, which in 1951 was no bad thing for a sports car to be. The most important component of the car was probably Donald Healey, an internationally known English rally driver whose main claims to fame were his outright win of the Monte Carlo Rally in 1931 and considerable development work on prewar Triumphs. After the war, he and his son Geoff continued racing but, more important, left Triumph to become constructors in their own right, working out of a tiny old factory in Warwick.

They started with a pair of Riley-engined models, neither of which was all that much to write home about. A stock Elliot Saloon *was*

Leslie Johnson finished an amazing third at Le Mans in 1952, eleventh in 1953, in this Nash-Healey.

clocked at 104 mph . . . claimed to be the fastest sedan on the postwar British market. But that didn't make it pretty, well made, or particularly appealing. In 1949, though, Healey introduced his famous Silverstone, a dual-purpose sports/racer with streamlined body, cycle fenders, attractive styling, and the same 2.4-liter Riley four the early cars used. Because of really superb handling and relatively light weight, the Silverstone became the most beloved clubman's racer of all time.

In late 1949 Donald·Healey traveled by ship from London to New York. As fate would have it, he got into conversation with a fellow passenger, George Mason, president of Nash-Kelvinator. Whether Healey's shipboard romance was premeditated or not, by the time they reached New York, Mason had agreed to bankroll a prototype Nash-engined Healey for the 1950 Le Mans 24 hours. A 234-cubic-inch Nash Ambassador six with special aluminum head and stock 3-speed plus overdrive transmission soon appeared at Healey's Warwick shop and was shoehorned into a Silver-

stone chassis. A log manifold with two SU carbs was clamped on the side of the old-fashioned but sturdy pushrod six, one of the ugliest aluminum bodies ever hammered out was slapped over the long-suffering Silverstone frame, and the whole Healey entourage embarked for la belle France.

Incredibly, this initial cobbled-up Nash-Healey took fourth *overall* after 24 hours at the most prestigious race in the universe. Driven by the jolly duo of Tony Rolt and Duncan Hamilton, the fastest funnymen on the circuit, the Nash pottered home behind two cycle-fendered Lago-Talbot Formula One Grand Prix cars and Sydney Allard in his own J2-X. George Mason was understandably overwhelmed, though Nash took virtually no promotional advantage of their Le Mans success. They rightly figured that most Americans neither knew nor cared about European endurance racing, Le Mans included. In the first flush of success, however, Mason did give Healey the go-ahead to start production of a street version.

The Silverstone chassis stayed the same, but the abominable body had to go. Healey and Nash stylists combined to come up with a supersmooth envelope body that incorporated a stock Ambassador grille and hood scoop, Rambler bumpers, and Statesman taillights. Otherwise, everything was strictly British specialty car. Healey ordered Panelcraft to pound out 130 one-piece aluminum bodies, perhaps *the* most impractical ever built in terms of maintenance and repair, but handsome nonetheless. And the Nash-Healey was in production. Just like that.

The first show car debuted at the Paris Auto Show in late 1950, so most of the production cars were 1951 models. Surprisingly, the pretty and aerodynamic standard car was not much raced by the Healey factory, and only a last-minute effort got them to Le Mans in '51 with another backyard racer, this one an immensely ugly coupe. Rolt and Hamilton managed to trundle it into sixth, missing the next notch up by a miserable eight seconds after twenty-four hours. This was the first year of the all-conquering C-type Jaguar, followed by two Aston Martins and the two disguised Talbot GP cars. Once again, the Nash-Healey had done phenomenally well at Le Mans, with zero effect on sales.

In the spring, Donald and Geoff took a virtually standard roadster to the Mille Miglia. Running with the fast iron as number 406 out of 428 starters (the Mille Miglia always started the fastest cars last), they managed to trail the big Ferraris and Lancias into a respectable 30th overall, in driving rain. Which wasn't bad at all. To take advantage of the publicity, twenty-five of the Panelcraft bodies were given a new grille, new bumpers, and an Alvis six. The result was called the Healey 3-Liter, for the British market. But firsthand experience had already shown that the thin aluminum body was just too expensive and impractical for use by unfeeling Americans, and Mason had Pininfarina—who was already styling the standard Nash line—redo the Healey into an all-steel roadster with very sophisticated lines. The headlights quirkily lived within the grille, but otherwise, Farina's body was a spectacular improvement.

Building the second-generation cars was anything but easy. Nash sent the engine and

The 1951 Nash-Healey was smooth and pretty; this is the factory Mille Miglia entry in Brescia.

Pininfarina's steel-bodied Nash-Healey of 1952.

drivetrain to Warwick, where Healey put them into a modified Silverstone frame and shipped the now complete chassis to Turin. Pininfarina added a body and interior, then packaged the whole thing and mailed it back to Kenosha. In late 1952 the engine was bored out to 252 cubic inches and given American Carter carbs, and in 1953 an award-winning Pininfarina coupe was added to the line. Eventually a total of 506 Nash-Healeys came together before Donald Healey broke his contract in 1953 in order to sign with Austin and develop the much more successful Austin-Healey. The last Nash cars were considered to be 1954 models, but by then the stodgy Nash-Hudson combine really didn't know what to do with a low-volume hybrid sports car with a British chassis, an Italian body, and an American engine. According to insiders, the Pininfarina Healeys—which sold for roughly $5,000 new—cost Nash over $9,000 each. And that's no way to run a car company.

In 1952 Donald Healey entered two of his typically ugly Nash specials at Le Mans. Leslie Johnson and Tommy Wisdom brought old Number 10 into an amazing *third,* behind the two factory prototype Mercedes 300SL Gullwings. But for some reason, even with back-to-back performances good enough to win the Rudge-Whitworth Biennial Cup, the Healey was pretty much ignored. Perhaps it was those homemade bodies that did it. Few racing pictures of the Le Mans cars exist, for the pretty

Talbots, Astons, Cunninghams, and Mercedes got all the photographers' attention. Judged not by aesthetic standards, the Nash-Healey racers were a tremendous success, especially considering the low-key, half-hearted way they were constructed and prepared. It was Geoff Healey's custom, for example, to drive the race car from Warwick to Le Mans for the race, and then take it for a vacation to Italy afterward. And in 1951 there was no practice for Rolt and Hamilton, for the car didn't arrive until race day itself. With this casual attitude, it's a wonder the Healeys were even let out on the track with the Jaguar, As-

Bridgehampton, 1953, and Pininfarina's award-winning

ton, and Mercedes factory entries, let alone beat them.

At least one of the racing cars still survives, owned by a Nash-Healey collector in Maryland. And a surprisingly high percentage of the Pininfarina cars are still around. Because of their fragile aluminum bodies, there are far fewer of the Panelcraft cars available. They aren't all that expensive, however, and good Panelcraft roadsters are only worth between $4,000 and $6,000 today. Pininfarina cars go for correspondingly more, up over $7,000. For American tastes, the later cars are probably more desirable, though the aluminum cars have much better performance—classic performance, even. The winning C-type Jaguar averaged 93 mph at Le Mans in 1951; the third-place Nash-Healey averaged 92 mph in 1952. Top speed for a well-prepped Healey is over 140 mph, and most of the speed parts are standard bits from other cars of the period. A. C. Sampietro, Healey's resident genius, even cast up a handful of double-over-head-cam heads for the old Nash six, and a few Nash-Healeys were supercharged with Paxton blowers.

The chassis and running gear are simplicity itself on any Healey, so for driving and

Nash-Healey coupe is the car of honor on the original course laid out through the village streets.

restoring there's no problem. An American club just for Nash-Healeys is quite active, and the Nash club can supply engine, transmission, and overdrive parts. The Pininfarina bodies are good, maintenance-free units, though the early aluminum cars are virtually impossible to repair if damaged. I know. I owned a '51 Nash-Healey a couple of years ago, a perfect Arizona car so clean it still had the decals on the shock absorbers. Some kid ran into me in Manhattan, and a professional aluminum craftsman quoted me $15,000 to repair the body. If I hadn't found a parts car, that would have been the end of the poor beast.

I drove cross-country in my Panelcraft roadster before it was hit, however, and I found that with the overdrive engaged, cruising at 75 mph was perfectly comfortable . . . and delivered 23 mpg, besides. I grew to love that car for its fine handling, good brakes, and fussless dependability . . . wish I still had it. I wouldn't hesitate to buy another one, and in my fantasies I've often considered building up a modified Le Mans version and going over to Lime Rock to see what it would do against the expensive toys of the Vintage Sports Car Club T-baggers, assuming that they'd condescend to having their pedigreed Ferrari doors blown off by a Nash. Hell, if it worked in 1952, I don't see why it wouldn't work today.

Cunningham

Briggs Cunningham always did everything right; better than right, even. After his mandatory stint at Yale, Briggs spent the Depression years of his movie star–handsome youth figuring out how a man of leisure could occupy himself when the rest of the world was grim. His father had invested heavily in Proc-

John Fitch and his Cunningham C-2, after running second, finished eighteenth at Le Mans, 1951.

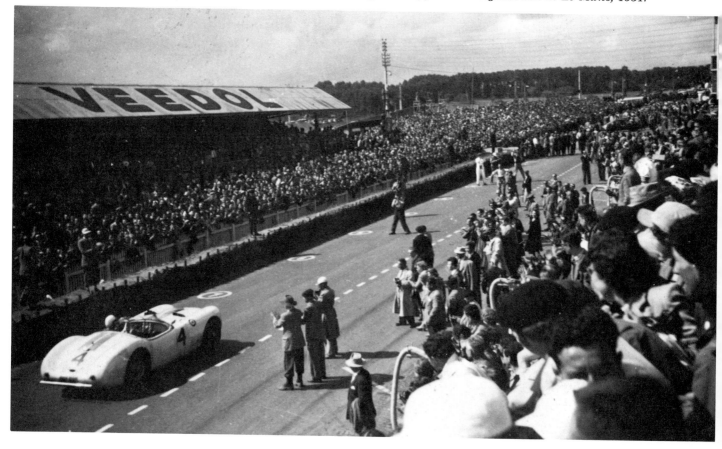

ter & Gamble at an opportune moment, so there were no financial obstacles to his enjoyment of the perfect life. He honeymooned in Europe with a girl who'd been his childhood sailboat racing crew, happily drifting from port to port on a six-meter racing boat they had shipped over from Long Island. For dockside transportation he picked up an Alfa Romeo 6C and a blown SS Mercedes.

Back home once again, Briggs made himself into a championship-caliber small boat racer and bluewater yachtsman, an expert golfer, and a crack seaplane pilot. He also hung around the famous Collier brothers and their Pocantico Hills Automobile Racing Club of America, the only place in this country at that time where one could see amateur road racing with Dixon Rileys, Bugattis, MGs, and suchlike. By 1936 young Sam Collier and George Rand were racing Briggs's K3 Magnette in Ireland, and in 1940 Miles Collier raced Cunningham's well-known Bumerc—a Buick Century with Mercedes SSK body—at the World's Fair Grand Prix.

After flying antisubmarine missions for the CAP during the war, Briggs himself took the old Bumerc to Watkins Glen in 1948. He finished second. The next year, he temporarily led the race in one of the first Ferraris to enter the United States. Cunningham was hooked on racing. Around the same time—in mid-1949—he met Bill Frick and Phil Walters (Ted Tappett to his cronies). Frick-Tappett Motors was dropping Cadillac V-8s into '49 Fords and Studebakers to make, logically enough, Fordillacs and Studillacs. Cunningham conceived the idea of taking a Fordillac to Le Mans, but the French turned him down because it wasn't a true production car. Frick and Walters told him to take a stock Cadillac instead.

And so he did. Frick reworked two cars: a Series 62 coupe and an identical Cadillac chassis fitted with a body that was long ago unanimously granted the title of Ugliest Racing Car Ever Built, after which they retired the trophy. Next to "Le Monstre," as the French crowd gaily dubbed it, Nash-Healey racers were works of art. To the amazement of all, though, the Cadillac finished 10th at Le Mans in 1950, with Le Monstre immediately behind. "This is a lead-pipe cinch," said Briggs. When the crew returned from France,

Frick and Walters had become the nucleus of the B. S. Cunningham Company of West Palm Beach, formed for the sole purpose of bringing an all-American winner to Le Mans.

The C-2 was the first real model; the C-1 was only a prototype chassis. Three C-2s were built and brought to the Sarthe for '51. Basically, you can think of the first Cunningham roadsters as white and blue Ferrari 166 Barchettas inflated enough to hold a Chrysler hemi. They were, uhhh . . . forceful cars. John Fitch and Phil Walters got one into second place for over five hours, but all three C-2s eventually retired, though the Fitch/Walters car did complete one last lap to finish 18th overall and first in class.

John Bentley tested a C-2 for *Motor Trend* and got 0 to 60 in 6.3 seconds . . . in first gear. Second was good for 100 mph, and the top speed was up around 150 with Le Mans gearing and a 2-speed rear axle. Roadholding was not the car's strong suit, however, what with Ford, Chrysler, and Cadillac suspension bits and a homemade DeDion rear end. But the Chrysler's 270 hp and truckish torque covered a multitude of sins, rapidly towing the Cunningham from slow corner to slow corner. It was a perfect Le Mans car, built to order for the old circuit, which put a premium on power, with one straight of over 3 miles and others nearly as long.

For 1952 it was necessary to have at least twenty-five production cars similar to the racers built for homologation by the FIA. The C-3 started out to be a dual-purpose car, but it was quickly turned into a high-speed luxury roadster on a racing chassis. Built by Vignale in Turin, the similar C-4 coupe was picked by Arthur Drexler for the Museum of Modern Art's landmark "ten best cars" show in 1953, and by a handful of wealthy enthusiasts as just about the best solution for U.S. motoring. For a mere $9,000 to $11,000 (they cost Cunningham nearly $15,000 to build) you could have a bridge-girder chassis proved at Le Mans, a reliable Chrysler hemi, and superb accommodations. And all nicely encapsulated within an aesthetic tour de force that was favorably compared by Drexler to Pininfarina's perfect Cisitalia coupe, *the* definitive postwar design. Unfortunately, the street cars were built solely to satisfy a sanctioning requirement. And though there might have been a

The 1952 Cunningham C-4 coupe by Vignale.

market for the exquisitely built C-3 roadster and C-4 coupe, once eighteen coupes and nine roadsters were delivered from Vignale, the quota was filled and production stopped.

The Cunningham racing car for 1952 was the C-4R, incorporating an all-new frame, a trick suspension developed by Chrysler factory engineers, fancy Al-Fin drum brakes, and a 325-hp version of the hemi. Two roadsters were built and also a radical coupe, the C-4RK. The K stood for Kamm. Indeed. Cunningham's coupe was the *only* postwar car actually designed by Dr. Wunibald Kamm himself, strictly in accordance with his flat-tailed aerodynamic theories. It has been the prototype for the chopped-off shape of every racing coupe designed since then. From the front it was mean and nasty, picked out with added-on scoops, louvers, and driving lights; from the side it was remarkably sleek, with little slit windows, side pipes, and fenders just high enough to clear the big Firestones on Halibrand knock-off mags; from the rear it was . . . nothing. The tail sloped away to an absolute vertical box. It was too good and fast

to call ugly. Maybe . . . purposeful. Unfortunately, Cunningham insisted on using home-grown talent in his American racing cars, and USAC star Duane Carter stuffed the coupe into a tenacious Le Mans sandbank after Phil Walters had carefully brought it up to third overall. Cunningham himself drove one of the roadsters for almost 20 hours out of the 24, and finished in fourth overall, not bad for a guy in his forties. The C-4Rs were even good enough to come back for repeat performances in '53 and '54, garnering seventh and tenth, third and fifth.

At the same time, the Palm Beach crew started on the C-5R for 1953, building a very Kurtis-like chassis with a straight front axle, torsion bars, Halibrand Indy wheels, and incredibly big 17-inch-diameter Al-Fin drum brakes. With a sharp-tailed roadster body suggested by Michelotti, the C-5R managed to top 155 mph between Tetre Rouge and Mulsanne. But once again, it was to no avail. The new C-type Jaguars had disc brakes and simply motored away from the faultlessly running Cunningham. John Fitch and Phil Walters drove exactly the race they had planned in advance, within .02 mph of the average they expected would let them win . . . and finished *seven laps behind* the winning Jaguar of Tony Rolt and Duncan Hamilton. Walters said later that if Cunningham should ever have won at Le Mans, 1953 was the year.

The following year, they decided to take a different tack and rebodied a 4.5-liter Ferrari chassis. This hybrid retired at the halfway mark with engine problems. So for '55, the Cunningham armada came back with the C-6R. This had a resleeved Indy Offy of 2942cc, a completely different tube-frame chassis, and a very pretty body copied from the all-conquering D-Jag. Unhappily, the C-6R was mediocre at best, dropping out of the tragic '55 Le Mans while running 13th. Later it was repowered with a 3.8 Jaguar XK engine for U.S. racing, but this too was pretty much a failure.

After five years running as an enormous tax loss, the B. S. Cunningham Company went out of business because, Number One, it was impossible for a private entrant to compete head to head with the factories in international racing and, Number Two, the IRS would no longer let Briggs write the whole

John Fitch and Phil Walters shared the winning Cunningham C-4R roadster at Sebring in 1953.

Dr. Wunibald Kamm designed the C-4RK coupe, the only car ever built with a genuine "Kamm" tail.

Phil Walters at Sebring with the Michelotti-designed Cunningham C-5R, second at Le Mans in 1953.

thing off. The team went on to minor success with Jaguars, Corvettes, and Maseratis after Briggs became the New England Jaguar distributor, but that was strictly a sideline, not an obsession. Cunningham handily skippered *Columbia* to the 1959 America's Cup victory and later built his wonderful museum in Costa Mesa, California. The most successful of his racing cars are now living out their retirement years there, and Briggs himself divides his time between the East and West coasts, a legendary figure in both yachting and motoring circles.

And what about the cars? Well, miraculously, most of the racers survived and, of the eight built, Cunningham still has half. An even better percentage of C-3 and C-4 street machines are out there, and just last year someone was offering a rolling chassis—never

been bodied—through the San Francisco *Examiner* for $1,500. If I'd been able to figure out a way to get it through the door, it'd probably be in my living room right now. I admit to having ridden in a C-4 only once. It was a scruffy black-and-cream coupe off a dealer's lot in Newport, Rhode Island, and I was a college kid. It was surprisingly big inside—wide enough for three people on the front seat— and seemed huge for a sports car, wider and higher than any Ferrari. And much more spacious inside. The Chrysler hemi—even with a 3-speed—moved off with an impressive production of both torque and clatter, and I remember that the steering was lighter than I expected. I wouldn't mind having it today, that's for sure. There's nothing on one that could break, and even if it did there'd be no problem fixing it. And Chrysler hemis you can still buy brand-new. But fifteen years ago, that Cunningham was carrying an astronomical price tag, something like $2,000, as I remember. If you can find one for less than $15,000 today, snap it up. It'll never be any cheaper, and Briggs won't be building any more.

Of all the trials he won and tests he set himself, the only real failure in Cunningham's career was the Le Mans attempt, ironically his grandest obsession and the saga for which he is best known. With sharp-eyed hindsight, it's easy to pinpoint where Cunningham went wrong. Rather than develop one initial chassis—which was more than adequate—he had Frick and Walters design and engineer a whole new car for each Le Mans, often getting the racers to France with no testing. In 1953, for example, the obvious solution would have been to stick with the successful concept of the C-4RK, improving the brakes and other details to be competitive with the C-type Jaguars. Also, abandoning the reliable Chrysler V-8 for an Offy after all their experience was silly. Most important, Cunningham insisted on having American drivers in his cars. And though John Fitch, Phil Walters, and Briggs himself were all fine Le Mans pilots, oval-track star Carter, among others, was just out of his depth. Experienced European endurance racers might have brought home a winner, or at least backed up the expert Fitch/Walters duo. In the final analysis, it was nothing but fate that kept Briggs Cunningham from hearing the "Star Spangled Banner" played at Le Mans. God knows, he did everything right. Better than right, even.

Woodill Wildfire

It's hard to realize now, but fiberglass—or GRP for Glass Reinforced Plastic, as it was called then—was developed only during World War II. And though Owens-Corning began the experimental Scarab III for Bill Stout in April 1944, it was 1950 or so before GRP had any real influence on automobiles. Typically, fiberglass was promoted as a "miracle" material that could be easily worked in anyone's backyard and used to build anything from swimming pools to cabin cruisers in a matter of hours. Typically, too, California was the cutting edge of fiberglass experimentation. The Lancer and Skorpion—developed in Costa Mesa for a Crosley chassis—were just about the first plastic kit bodies for cars. They

Designed by boat maker Bill Tritt, the 1952 Glasspar was one of the first fiberglass body kits.

appeared in 1949 and disappeared into oblivion nearly as fast.

These early experiments were the forerunners of what is now Big Business—supplying fiberglass body kits to fit production chassis. A lot of people tried it, but most of them spent their way out of business before they were ever really *in* business. The most successful of these fiberglass pioneers was Bill Tritt, from Montecito's Green Dolphin Boat Works, and he never really broke even on his car stuff. But in 1950 Tritt and three partners started Glasspar, still a big name in fiberglass boats. And what they made on boats they spent on experimental plastic cars. Tritt's first fiberglass automobile body was done on commission in 1950, for the wife of a friend, Major Kenneth Brooks. Mrs. Brooks's army husband had appropriately presented her with an olive drab Jeep for around-town shopping, but she was too embarrassed to drive it. So Tritt molded up a very pretty two-seater roadster reminiscent of the Jaguar XK-120. This was duly mounted on the Jeep chassis and painted a particularly attractive light leafy green.

This car—which they called the Brooks Boxer—garnered them considerable attention across the country. The Connecticut-based Naugatuck Chemical Division of U.S. Rubber, which supplied Tritt's fiberglass resins, agreed to buy the first batch if Tritt would go into the production of kit bodies. The most important result for U.S. Rubber was that *Life* devoted a full-length feature article to the car made of "miracle" plastic. Eventually Naugatuck bought Mrs. Brooks's car and renamed it the Alembic I after the division's benzine ring corporate logo. Naugatuck—which also made Naugahyde from the skin of the elusive Nauga—used the Alembic as a show car for years.

In February 1952 Glasspar formally announced that they had kit bodies—replicas of the Boxer/Alembic—available for $650. About two months later, Tritt received a visitor from nearby Downey, California. He was Woody Woodill, who'd taught aeronautical engineering at the University of Southern California during World War II. When he came to see Tritt, Woody was the youngest Dodge dealer in the country, with a companion Willys agency next door. More to the point, he had decided to build a sports car for himself,

something along the lines of the XK-120, but didn't want to worry about getting parts. He was looking for a pretty new body to put on a Willys-based chassis. He bought two from Bill Tritt.

Woodill had Shorty Post, a well-known West Coast chassis builder and customizer, weld up a ladder-type frame out of steel tubing. Post used a Jeepster front end, Willys driveline, and Tritt's body. He added a false hood scoop, different windshield, and Willys Aero taillights set in extended fenders. Jeepster bumpers and fake wire wheels finished it up in time for Petersen Publishing's Los Angeles Motorama in November 1952. The car received enough attention that Willys borrowed Woodill's car and had it shipped back to Toledo. They began talking about producing a little something to compete with Nash's Healey. It was all set. Unfortunately for Woodill, at the very last moment, Henry J. Kaiser bought Willys, and Dutch Darrin's similar Kaiser-Darrin was chosen to be the corporate sports car. Woodill was back on the sidewalk again.

But Woody had had a taste of the Big Time, and it was good. So he built another handful of cars for California customers, using Tritt's body. And he decided there was a market for chassis and body kits scaled to the do-it-yourselfer. Woodill was also smart enough to realize that most backyard hot-rodders were Ford addicts, so Post's frame was reworked to take the transverse-leaf spring suspension from early V-8 Fords, along with any sort of V-8 engine. Woodill's frame kit was so complete that for $228 you even got a shortened driveshaft and radius rods to mate with standard Ford components.

The modified Glasspar body cost a whopping $995, but it came with all the little details—hinges, locks, and upholstery—that most other kit suppliers, including Glasspar, left to the builder's imagination. Says Woodill, "We went *to* the market. The others left too many things for the builder to do. He had to be too mechanical." A Wildfire—Woodill's name for the completed kit car—could be built in fourteen hours. He went on "You Asked For It" to prove it by assembling one for the cameras.

Most of the Wildfire kits were put together by professional race shops—even Frank Kur-

Woody Woodill's 1956 Wildfire, with Cadillac V-8, tubular chassis, and modified Glasspar body.

tis built some with Cadillac engines—or dealers. Buick V-8s were used too, but most got Ford flatheads. Total cost was around $2,000 if you built it yourself, though Woodill Motors sold complete cars for $3,260 with Willys power plants. Professional shops got $4,500 for V-8–powered cars. Woody Woodill claims he sold 300 kits and a dozen complete cars between 1953 and '56, when demand dried up in the face of the T-bird and Corvette. But Bill Tritt says he supplied fewer than 100 bodies. So no one really knows how many Wildfires there were, or are, for that matter. Not very many. Woodill even had a line of optional extras, including a fiberglass hardtop, continental kit, side curtains, tach, radio, and a fastback coupe top. Of course, each individual builder could do anything he wanted to the basic kit, and some of the results were pretty weird. Even Woodill's factory cars had different grilles, windshields, and engines, depending on customer whim.

In their heyday, Woodill Wildfires were quite the thing around L. A., surprisingly enough. Woodill supplied three roadsters for the Danny Kaye movie "Knock on Wood," one for "Written on the Wind" with Dorothy Malone and Rock Hudson, and yet another three for the famous Tony Curtis/Piper Laurie rac-

ing melodrama "Johnny Dark." Their brash good looks, foreign flavor, and zappy performance made them popular with film companies and film stars alike. None was ever raced with much success, for neither the frame, suspension, nor brakes were up to the task. But as a distinctive boulevard buggy for California sports, it had no peers; particularly at the price.

Because of the homebuilt nature of the Wildfire kit, the quality obviously varied considerably. Any that are still left around today *must* have been bolted together pretty well to make it for over twenty years, all things considered. Prices are up around $3,000–$4,000 now, depending on which engine it's got and what kind of shape it's in. Owning one would be fun, I think, not so much because it's the kind of exotic car that every peasant knows but can't afford—like a Cobra or Ferrari—but something that's so alien to the average person, or even the average car enthusiast, that you could tell him it was anything from a 1946 Jaguar to a 1976 Lamborghini and he'd believe you. Tell people it's just a boat-builder's kit body on a Willys chassis and they're bound to be disappointed. The peasants won't care that you've got the first successful fiberglass-bodied sports car, the prototype for the early Corvette. And they won't remember "Johnny Dark" or Piper Laurie . . . or even crazy old Woody Woodill. But that's *their* loss. Peasants.

Kaiser-Darrin

Howard "Dutch" Darrin legitimately belongs in that select group of early-day American automobile stylists that includes Gordon Buehrig, Tom Hibbard, Ray Dietrich, and Raymond Loewy. He really does. But unlike most stylists, who tend to be shy, retiring types, Dutch was the original extrovert, always out there blowing his own horn. He was the sales genius behind Hibbard & Darrin. But more than anything, he knew how to sell *himself*.

Still, Dutch really *was* a pretty decent designer. Everything he touched had a distinctive, high-nosed flair, accented by the famous "Darrin Dip" in the beltline that was his trademark. Darrin cars aren't pretty in the sense of classically right. In fact, some of them are downright tasteless. But Dutch always did give his cars a very strong visual identity, what industrial designers call high product visibility. Even when a Darrin design whipped past you at 75 on the Harbor Freeway, it stood out sharply amid that mass of machines all blended together into an amorphous, high-speed blur.

There was Hibbard & Darrin in the Paris of the twenties, Fernandez et Darrin in the Paris of the thirties, Darrin of Paris in the Los Angeles of the forties. At one time or another, Dutch consulted for damn near every automobile company, from Moon to Packard, Stutz to General Motors. He made and lost several fortunes, made himself into a championship polo player who courted his wealthy clients on horseback, became a worldly-wise bon vivant equally at home on the French Riviera or Sunset Boulevard. Honestly now, how many other automobile draftsmen would have the nerve to claim that they left Paris for good because Darryl F. Zanuck personally promised them that the polo was better in California?

Darrin's swan song was Kaiser-Frazer. It's beside the point to go into the myriad death throes of that ill-conceived corporation or to dwell on the high-handed ways they often treated Darrin. Dutch, as was his norm, was not actually an employee of Kaiser-Frazer but an outside styling consultant brought in to pep up the line when K-F's own draftsmen had failed to come up with anything suitable. He designed the regular Kaiser line around 1946, had a fight with Henry J., left, came back, and worked on a crazy door that slid forward into the fender to open up the rear seats, slid into the back fender to reveal the front seats. It was patented in 1949 but, rightly enough, never saw production.

In 1946 Dutch also designed one of the first cars ever built from fiberglass, a smooth convertible totally devoid of trim. The sliding door and fiberglass body ideas both simmered in his mind until 1951—at which point he had another fight with K-F management. K-F promised to put an electric sliding door into production, but when they didn't, Darrin started out on his own to justify the concept.

Darrin had a custom body shop in Hollywood, so he got a used Henry J chassis and began a spare-time project, a fiberglass roadster with a sliding door. Henry J. Kaiser first saw it as a prototype in 1952 and anted up funds to build a few more. Like George Mason at Nash, who expected the Nash-Healey to lure buyers into the showrooms, Kaiser was looking for a line leader that was more exciting than anything Ford or GM offered. As it turned out, of course, Mason and Kaiser were perfectly right. There *was* a market for an American sports car, a market that the Corvette and Thunderbird masterfully exploited, thanks to the groundwork done by the Nash-Healey and Kaiser-Darrin.

Ah yes, the Kaiser-Darrin. Henry J. and Edgar Kaiser liked Darrin's car so much that they went into limited production of prototypes, each one different from the last. During 1953 they built sixty-two similar cars with bodies supplied by Glasspar, the Naugatuck Division, and Owens-Corning—the Big Three in fiberglass molding at that time. After Darrin was all done with it, Kaiser's engineers couldn't avoid raising the fender line to bring the headlights up to legal height, which predictably caused Dutch to lose his temper once again, but to no avail; the changes stayed.

The 1954 Kaiser-Darrin had a distinctive Darrin Dip, sliding doors, and Clara Bow grille.

Darrin did win one battle in his long war with K-F. In an *Automobile Quarterly* article long ago, Dutch himself wrote, "They came around and held a big meeting to decide what to call it. They concluded 'DKF' for Darrin, Kaiser, Frazer. I said this was pretty silly, the DKF was a German motorcycle, the DKW a German car. There were about thirty executives there, and they took a vote. It was unanimous for DKF. Then Henry Kaiser quietly reminded them that he hadn't voted. You could have heard a pin drop. And Henry said, 'I say we call it the Kaiser-Darrin.' Then Henry smiled—broadly—and winked at me."

Strangely enough, as K-F finished with the different prototypes, each was destroyed. Only one is known to survive, rescued by a Kaiser PR man. All were built on Henry J chassis, many with Edmunds speed equipment. In 1953, though, just as they were about to go into production, Kaiser bought Willys, so the production cars got the more powerful F-head Willys six fitted into the Henry J chassis. All this took time, however, and it was December 1953 before production started. By then, the Saint Louis Corvette plant was in volume production and Corvettes had been seen in auto shows for nearly six months.

Even worse, Henry J. Kaiser was in deep trouble with the Defense Department and Senate subcommittees. The end of the Korean War meant the end of big aircraft contracts and ultimately the end of Kaiser-Frazer. Kaiser was supporting the huge Willow Run factory on government aircraft orders, and when they went away, so did Willow Run. The world's largest factory was closed, and what few Darrin roadsters there are were built in an ancient plant in Jackson, Michigan. After only nine months, Kaiser-Darrin production stopped with number 435, and K-F collapsed within a year.

Typically, Dutch Darrin himself was the country's top Kaiser-Darrin dealer, working out of his Hollywood body works. After the company went broke, he bought a bunch of factory leftovers in 1956, dropped in overhead-valve Cadillac V-8s, and tried to make a real performance car. Some Willys cars were supercharged, too. McCulloch was right down the block from Darrin's shop and already had a successful unit that was easily adapted to the old Jeep six.

In stock trim, the Kaiser-Darrin produced an anemic 90 hp from 161 cubic inches and a top speed of around 100 mph. With the supercharger, you got 135 hp and about 115. The 365-cubic-inch Caddy, on the other hand, gave 285 hp and more thrills than the flimsy Henry J chassis could stand. Briggs Cunningham had one of these monsters, and his wife was timed at Palm Beach at 148 mph. I'll bet she had her eyes closed, too, because the handling just wasn't up to that kind of horsepower. Significantly, the Cunninghams only raced the thing that once, as far as I know.

Amazingly, about 320 out of 435 Kaiser-Darrins still exist, a better than 75-percent survival rate. This is thanks mostly to the active Kaiser club, I think. Kaiser-Darrins cost only $3,700 new, and good ones are bringing $9,000 and up nowadays. To be honest, Kaiser-Darrins, with stock Henry J running gear and a Willys engine, aren't all *that* exciting to drive. But the chassis will last virtually forever, it's easily maintained, and the fiberglass body is easy to fix. Most Kaiser-Darrins are California cars, besides, so as a group they're in better-than-average shape.

The cutesy rosebud lips, narrow sliding doors, and high-prowed fenders of the Kaiser-Darrin always seemed pretty strained to me. But then, I admit to an irrational prejudice against Kaiser products of any sort. Hard as I try, I just can't get excited about an old Jeep motor in a Henry J frame under fiberglass. Still, I suppose it's aged pretty well, all things considered. It doesn't look like modern cars, but then, it didn't look like anything else on the road in 1953, either.

The Kaiser-Darrin is one of those rare things, an automobile that really looks like nothing else. Oh, maybe there's a hint of Harley Earl's LeSabre about it, but not so's you'd notice unless somebody told you. Really, it's unique. *Un type,* as Dutch would say. Not only that, it's a historically important car, a real milestone on the way to the Corvette. And speaking of milestones, the Kaiser-Darrin is, of course, a recognized Milestone Car Society pick. Most of all, though, the Kaiser-Darrin is the last and probably purest expression of Dutch Darrin's highly individual vision of what automobiles should look like. Not better or worse, particularly, just, uhhh . . . different.

Excalibur

At the very time Woody Woodill and Dutch Darrin decided that Kaiser-Frazer just had to have a new sports car, Brooks Stevens had exactly the same idea. Now Woodill was just a crazy young Willys dealer from California who'd never had much to do with Kaiser, and Dutch Darrin was just a crazy old stylist from California who'd broken up with Henry J. Kaiser more times than Liz Taylor has broken up with Burton. But Brooks Stevens was a well-known industrial designer, creator of the highly profitable Willys Jeepster and a freelance styling consultant at Kaiser-Fraser, working on the passenger cars. In other words, he was in a hell of a lot better position vis-

Stylist Brooks Stevens proudly shows off his '52 Excalibu

a-vis Kaiser than were either Woody Woodill or Darrin.

Stevens was also the Midwest regional director of the SCCA and an occasional amateur racing driver. So his idea of what constituted a sports car was a lot different from Woodill's or Darrin's . . . or Henry J. Kaiser's, for that matter. Stevens wanted a sports car that was truly dual purpose, that would be admittedly basic in terms of creature comforts but could actually be raced with a reasonable chance of picking up some silver cups. If Darrin was proposing a boulevard sports car, the spiritual forerunner of the Thunderbird, Stevens was proposing a quasi-racer, the spiritual descendant of the Frazer Nash and Allard.

Being pretty much oriented toward little

European racers—he was racing an MG-TC and a Jag XK-120 at the time—Stevens naturally saw his sports car as a small, lightweight roadster. No Cunningham excesses for him. Fortunately, of course, his design contacts were all at Willys and Kaiser, neither of which were exactly contenders in the postwar horsepower sweepstakes.

Kaiser's little Henry J was the perfect platform on which to erect a small-bore sports car, as Dutch Darrin had already figured out. So Stevens's 1950 proposal sounded remarkably like Darrin's. And old man Kaiser had the same reaction to both. He encouraged both Stevens and Darrin to go ahead and build a prototype, without actually spending anything himself. If something developed out of

ne of three surprisingly successful SCCA racers despite their plebeian Henry J origins.

the first car, then he'd think about committing Kaiser-Frazer funds to the project. But until that time, both Stevens and Darrin were on their own.

Stevens was pretty well off financially, so he set up a little corner of his styling center/ old car museum/industrial design firm as Ecurie Excalibur. Then he hired a few local panel beaters and went into the sports-car business. Excalibur started by building three identical roadsters. They took the stock Henry J frame—which was about as conventional a piece of hardware as you'll find—and started modifying it. Sporty knock-off wire wheels—unusually wide for the era—were splined onto new hubs and fitted with Dunlop racing tires. Metallic linings found their way into the stock Kaiser brake drums. Stiffer shock absorbers appeared, along with some extra chassis stiffening.

But the real secret of the Excalibur's success was that Stevens—like Kaiser-Frazer for the production Kaiser-Darrin—threw out the uninspired Henry J engine and replaced it with the 161-cubic-inch F-head six from the Willys. With three SU carbs, dual exhausts, and normal SCCA prodifying, the old tractor engine would make around 125 hp. Stevens positioned it a full 28 inches farther back in the frame than the Henry J mill had been, giving excellent 50/50 weight distribution. Even with a stock 3-speed plus overdrive trans, the Excalibur would go 120 mph down the straights and through the corners faster than anything else in SCCA Class D.

Since the Willys engine was now roughly where the front seat had been in a Henry J, Stevens put his driver just before the rear axle, or roughly in the back seat of a Henry J. Like MGs and other European sports cars, the seats had separate bottoms but an upright one-piece back that gave a classic, wheel-under-the-chin driving position. Everything was all right so far, considering the state of the art in America circa 1951. But the most curious thing happened. Stevens—who styled the pleasant Jeepster and later the smooth Studebaker Hawk GT—came up with the weirdest body ever clapped on a chassis except for maybe Cunningham's Le Monstre. And the worst part was that Stevens was a stylist, so all the awkward lines were delineated in excruciating detail.

Classic illusions—running boards, no doors, streamlined

Copying his personal MG-TC, Stevens gave the Excalibur cutaway doors. But like a Chain-Gang Frazer Nash or something, only the one on the driver's side opened. A tall, square trunk was flanked by thin fenders with nascent tailfins complete with air-exhausting slots in the trailing edge to help cool the brakes, just like the Ferraris of the period. Only thing was, there were no air intakes at the leading edge of the rear fenders to supply brake-cooling air to be exhausted.

Instead of an envelope body—or four separate fenders, for that matter—Stevens gave the Excalibur a unified rear body but a narrow nose with separate clamshell front fenders. It was sort of a squared-up Allard J2-X, but with curious aerodynamic front fenders that might have been stolen off a 1929 Schneider Cup biplane. The hood height was determined by the radiator height, but the rectangular nose was set considerably lower. Where the nose and hood met, the two-inch gap formed a full-width air scoop. The final touches were huge headlights tucked into the grille out of the airstream, stainless steel step plates on the vestigial running boards that covered the

ycle fenders—Elkhart Lake, 1954.

side exhaust pipes, and a curvacious wind-shield that protected the passenger not at all but that carefully kept the wind off both the driver and the rearview mirror. *Distinctive* is about the nicest word anybody ever used concerning the styling of the first Excaliburs.

But the goddamn things could *go*. The only cars in Class D that could touch the Willys-powered Excaliburs were Ferrari 2.9s with about twice the horsepower, three times the sophistication, and quadruple the selling price. Throughout 1952 and '53, Ecurie Excalibur raced from Elkhart Lake to Sebring, almost always winning their class and usually beating the Class C Jaguars, too. An Excalibur even beat the world-class Cunningham C-4RK at Albany, Georgia, in 1953. You could look it up somewhere.

Drivers Ralph Knudsen, Jim Feld, and Hal Ullrich rotated between the blue Excalibur, the white Excalibur, and the red Excalibur until the end of 1953. At that point, Stevens pitched Henry J. Kaiser for the final time on putting his roadster into production, at an estimated price of $2,000. Instead, showing uncharacteristic good taste, Kaiser voted for

Darrin's precious design on a similar hybrid, Willys-powered Henry J chassis. Stevens was not amused. He'd spent two years and umpteen dollars campaigning the Excaliburs to show Kaiser what they were made of, and here he'd lost out to a car that had never been near a race track and looked like Clara Bow in full pucker, besides. The Excaliburs retired in October 1953.

In 1958, however, Stevens—egged on by his teen-age sons—pulled a spare chassis out of his museum and cleaned it up for another go-round. F-head Willys sixes were hardly the hot setup by then, though, so the Stevens crew dropped a 3.8-liter six from a Jaguar XK-140 into the Excalibur. And if that wasn't enough, they rigged up a GMC supercharger, which raised the car into SCCA B-modified, cleverly out of the way of the all-conquering C-modified Scarabs. With a much cleaner all-new envelope nose and no running boards, the car was a million percent better all-around. And better yet, in 1958 there was almost nobody else *in* B-modified. The restyled Excalibur/Jaguar was SCCA National Champion. Not bad for an eight-year-old design, and a Henry J, besides.

For 1963 young Steve Stevens built a Studebaker Hawk–based coupe with an R-4 engine, McCulloch supercharger, and—courtesy of his dad—even weirder details than the original Excalibur. The Excalibur Hawk had limited success, for by the time it appeared front-engine styling exercises were just simply no longer competitive on the race tracks of America, not even with Studebaker engines breathed upon by the garlic-scented atmosphere of a blower from Andy Granatelli. Out

Ferrari-inspired 1958 Excalibur SCCA champion.

of the failure of this Excalibur Hawk, of course, Stevens was inspired to create the Mercedes SSK/Studebaker-based Excalibur SS, which evolved into the expensive Corvette-powered replicar that the Stevens firm still manufactures today.

I've often wondered what would have happened if Henry J. Kaiser had chosen Stevens's racy Excalibur over Darrin's defiantly nonracy K-D 161. Would Kaiser-Frazer have survived? Would the Corvette have had more of a spartan, stripped-for-competition feeling? Would production American sports cars have been more like European versions, with minimal bodywork, small engines, and excellent handling? Or, more likely, would things have turned out just the same, except there'd be a few hundred Kaiser-Excaliburs instead of just three? If only the Excalibur had been pretty instead of funny looking, who knows what might have happened. I wonder if Brooks Stevens ever wakes up in the night and asks himself these questions.

Arnolt-Bristol

Stanley Harold "Wacky" Arnolt II was one of those rare guys whose college nickname is totally appropriate. A monster of a man, a Big Ten football star for Wisconsin, Arnolt accentuated his size by wearing high-heeled cowboy boots and a tall Stetson, Texas oilman–style. Which made him stand out more than just a little in Warsaw, Indiana, I promise you. But Arnolt was larger than life, anyway. Wacky started out in 1939 with not much more than his cowboy hat and his boots. He got his first break building Arnolt Sea-Mite marine engines for the government during World War II, and by 1950 he was the biggest industrialist in northern Indiana, with factories all over the country. And he'd discovered sports cars. So typically, he started his own foreign car store in Chicago, became the BMC importer for the entire Midwest, got into racing, and generally had a good time. And made it all pay, besides.

Wacky's passion for fast cars carried him to the Turin Auto Show in 1952, where he saw a pair of styling studies on the Bertone stand. At that point, Bertone was in a monumental postwar lull. In fact, the two studies on display represented the last few million lire that Bertone could get his hands on. Wacky Arnolt came homing in like Pooh Bear to a honey pot. He marched up to Nuccio Bertone, looked over the sample coupe and cabriolet, and offered to buy a hundred of each. Poor Nuccio fainted dead away and had to be carried from the hall, for in one breathless sentence Carrozzeria Bertone had been saved from impending bankruptcy by a car-crazy American. Some people have even claimed that Wacky's heaven-sent order was the turning point for the entire postwar Italian coachbuilding industry. It certainly didn't hurt.

Bertone's coupe and cabriolet were built out of MG-TDs, so Arnolt went straight to Abingdon and arranged for them to ship complete MG chassis to Turin, where they were fitted with slab-sided coachwork and shipped to the States. The distinctive MG grille was retained, but otherwise the Arnolt-MGs—particularly the coupe—looked like miniature Ferraris. Mechanically, of course, they were straight MG, meaning slow but fun. Even at $3,195—$1,000 more than a TD roadster—Arnolt was able to sell everything Bertone could make. . . . a total of 100 Arnolt-MGs.

Inspired by the response to his MG, Arnolt began to think bigger. He got together with the Bristol Aeroplane Works, which built (in addition to fighter planes for the Royal Air

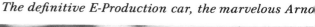

The definitive E-Production car, the marvelous Arno

Force) a limited production of high-performance 2-liter coupes and convertibles, roughly from the same mold as contemporary Jensens and Astons. The Bristol engine had started out as the power plant for the prewar BMW 328. Bristol inherited the design after the war and had designer Fritz Fiedler set up production in 1945. His engines ended up not only in Bristols but in postwar Frazer-Nash, A. C., Lister, Cooper, and E.R.A. cars as well.

When Wacky Arnolt stopped by in 1953, Bristol was making a two-seater coupe on a short, light chassis with a wheelbase of only 96 inches. From a performance viewpoint, it had limitless potential. Fiedler's old six, with curious horizontal pushrods that went across the head, could be made to produce over 150 hp in racing trim and, even as fitted to Bristol's conservative 404 coupe, was rated at 130 hp. For body stylists, however, it was a nightmare. The ancient six was extremely tall and awkwardly placed. Bertone, fresh from his stunning success with the Alfa Romeo Giulietta Sprint and BAT series, performed a minor miracle for Wacky Arnolt's new car. He threw away Bristol's stodgy coupe body and came up with a lithe roadster that looked like nothing else before or since. The swooping fenders had lovely razor-edge lines that curved into an open mouth carrying the headlights and a simple grille. Bertone's front had all the smiling ambience of Ollie the Dragon. The rear end was equally smooth and, even better, the resultant car weighed only 1,800 pounds, which was next to nothing.

Wacky meant it as a street car, but his

The first of Wacky Arnolt's sixty-five MG coupes.

Arnolt-Bristol was quickly adopted by small-bore racers. The old BMW/Bristol six had been around so long in high-performance circles that speed equipment was easy to come by, and the engine was thoroughly known. In 1954 Freddie Wacker tied for the E-modified national championship with his Arnolt, and in 1955 and again in 1956 a factory squadron of A-Bs finished first, second, and fourth in the 2-liter class at the Sebring 12-hour. They repeated the win with lightweight aluminum cars in '60, too. Needless to say, Arnolt's little toys were the scourge of SCCA E-production for years.

Wacky Arnolt had Bertone draw up a coupe version in 1955, but only three were actually built; the roadsters were much more popular. Totally unchanged, the Arnolt-Bristol remained in limited production until 1964, by which time some 130 had been sold. Considering that there was only one showroom—in Chicago—and that the whole operation was run in an extremely low-key manner, it's a wonder Arnolt was able to stay in business as long as he did. Compared to most other limited-production sports cars available at the time, however, the Arnolt-Bristol was extremely well put together, incredibly robust, beautiful . . . and it went like hell. All in all, it was a peculiarly happy design, well balanced, a delight to drive, and more than equal

Bristol, at Harewood Acres, Ontario, 1956.

Nuccio Bertone's masterful solution to the problems of a tall engine and a narrow track.

to similarly sized Ferraris and Maseratis . . . and at only half the price.

Indeed, through some fiscal legerdemain, Wacky Arnolt was able to buy chassis from Bristol, ship them to Bertone, get them bodied and shipped to Chicago, and still sell the finished roadster for *less than half* what Bristol asked for their own cars on the same chassis in England. Over the years, the price crawled from $3,995 to $4,250 for the "race-ready" Bolide and up to $4,995 for the more expensively decked-out Deluxe. The Bristol 404 was $9,946. By comparison, the similarly sized but considerably more plebeian TR-3 went for around $2,600, and tiny Alfa Giuliettas started at $3,800. Even a stripped Corvette cost $4,000, and most of them went for more like $5,000.

Somehow, I always imagine Arnolt-Bristol drivers as fortyish and well-off but slim, urbane, and impeccably tweedy, the sort who would trounce some young hot-shoe in a Corvette on his way to a party and then calmly steal the kid's girl once they got there. It was a car for experts, for people who could *do* things with a minimum of fuss and ostentation. It was, as Wacky's ads had it, "The choice for discriminating drivers."

An Arnolt-Bristol is still a discriminating choice. In a peculiar sort of way, despite its mixed Anglo-Italian heritage, it remains an American sports car well suited to U.S. driving conditions. In fact, Arnolt-Bristols were never sold either in England or on the Continent, in spite of considerable publicity in the States. The Bertone bodies are one piece of aluminum that can be damned expensive to repair, but then most similar limited-production Italian cars are the same. At least it won't rust or sag because of poor chassis support, the bane of most Italian bodies. The Bristol frame has to be one of the strongest ever slipped beneath a Bertone custom. Bristol still builds spares for the engine and running gear, so there's no more problem there than with any new car. In fact, you can probably get faster service out of the prestigious, conscientious old-line Bristol works than out of most more plebeian modern manufacturers. And Wacky's equally flamboyant son, Mike Arnolt, has all sorts of spares for sale in Warsaw, Indiana. There's an active Arnolt-Bristol club, too.

Unfortunately, Arnolts are popular with their owners—many of whom bought the car new and never had the heart to sell it—and just about everybody who still has one knows exactly what he has and what it's worth. Over three-quarters of the total production is still on the road, according to the A-B club, but

Rarest of the rare, only three Arnolt-Bristol coupes were built in 1955. Two still survive.

prices are awfully high. Today they can be anywhere from $6,000 to $10,000, depending. I suspect there's not a bargain to be had in an Arnolt-Bristol anywhere, unless you find some old racer that's been leaning against the garage wall since 1960. And even then it will probably be expensive.

Arnolt-Bristols are about the best dual-purpose sports cars from the fifties. They were the first cars since the Type 35 Bugatti that you could actually drive every day and race on the weekend without major modifications or carrying a mechanic to the office with you. Ferrari built street-legal cars that were mostly for racing, and another whole line of cars for street use that could sometimes be raced if properly set up. But none of them was a true dual-purpose car. The same is true of almost everything else, even if Porsche Speedster fanatics will argue differently. But the Arnolt-Bristol really could be *competitively* raced without an extensive "prodification" first, and it was a perfectly acceptable high-quality day-to-day sports car, besides. A car, all in all, for the real connoisseur . . . twenty years ago and today, too.

Edwards America

Sterling Edwards was Briggs Cunningham without the benefit of a consuming passion. Heir to a gigantic wire cable company south of San Francisco, he was and is a well-known socialite in northern California. "An upstanding civic leader," as the *Examiner* might say. But back in the early fifties, Edwards was damn good on a race track, too, particularly for someone once called in print (rather inaccurately) a "Beverly Hills sportsman." At the beginning, then, he was just another of the wealthy young blades attracted to the sound and fury and parties of road racing. But like a very few, really—Cunningham, Reventlow, Masten Gregory, Phil Hill, Fon Portago—he was one of the postwar moneyed elite who actually got deeper into race cars than polite society would deem proper.

Professional drivers—guys who tried to make a living at it—never did understand what would possess a society millionaire to deliberately risk missing out on his inheritance. Ray Crawford was another of this wealthy breed. And Bill Vukovich—who drove for the cash—told him once, "If I had your money, I wouldn't go near a goddamn race car." Every wealthy racer has faced the same thing. And some of them, like Cunningham and Reventlow, eventually decide the scramble for good cars, for good rides, is a plebeian pursuit better left to others. So they cash in a few bonds or whatever and become constructors. Rather than scramble for rides, they make their own.

Edwards got into it all quite early, early enough that he won the very first race held at Palm Springs, back in 1950, driving a special built by Emil Diedt and Luigi Lesovsky. This pair of old-line car builders put together a ladder frame with large-diameter tubing longitudinals reminiscent of the later A. C. Cobra. It had fully independent suspension, a pretty aluminum body by Jim Diedt, and a little 1500-cc flathead Ford V-8 60, converted to overhead valves and built by Eddie Meyer to his notoriously powerful midget specs. It was designed by Indy car designer Norm Timbs, with help from Phil Remington, who worked for D & L.

After a fair bit of success in West Coast racing, the first Edwards Special was retired, but not forgotten. Phil Remington soon pulled a fiberglass mold from the original body buck, with a few minor modifications. This smoother plastic body was clapped onto a basically stock Henry J chassis, with a Chrysler hemi shoehorned under the hood. This car appeared in time for Pebble Beach in 1952. But though the big hemi was willing to tow Sterling down the straights at a frightening pace, the poor overworked Henry J chassis just wasn't up to any sort of cornering. Edwards got his doors blown off. Literally. There was so much frame flex that the doors opened on sharp corners and eventually disappeared into the bushes. Very embarrassing.

Now some people at this point would have dug their heels in and started throwing away immense sums trying to build a winner, but Sterling was much smarter. He decided to go in two directions. For his racing—since cost

Sterling Edwards provided the cash, Phil Remington the expertise for the Edwards America.

1953 Mercury taillights give a clue to the chassis underneath, fitted with a big Lincoln V-8.

was pretty much no object, after all—he bought a pair of lightweight Jaguar XK-120Cs, a C-Jag and, later on, a whole handful of Ferraris. He never achieved national prominence as a driver, but he did do pretty well in West Coast racing and was a familiar figure at the track until 1955. Then he put together one really good season with a pair of big-bore Ferraris and quit.

Edwards continued to build cars, however, which was the second part of his project. Instead of building immediately obsolete racing cars, he went into the high-performance, luxury GT market with a line of really lovely street machines. Starting in 1952, Edwards Engineering established headquarters in a tiny shop next to the wire cable factory. Phil Remington, Chuck Tatum, and old Joe Conlon were the entire staff. And the car was a typical California amalgam of hot-rodded parts, but all superbly finished and carefully assembled.

The chassis for the first street car was pretty much that of the second special, a reinforced Henry J powered by a big Oldsmobile V-8. This was no better than the old special, so the next street car had a Mercury frame with a Lincoln V-8. With big Kelsey-Hayes wire wheels and comparatively wide tires for the time, handling was pretty good for a street machine. And the big Lincoln gave 205 hp. All-up weight was only about 2,800 pounds, so straight-line performance was good, too.

The body for the Edwards was one of the best early fiberglass bodies. Edwards himself styled it after Virgil Exner's famous Chrysler D'Elegance. It was nearly slab-sided except for a vestigial rear fender bulge. A massive, Ferrari-like grille, a beautifully lightweight removable hardtop, and a squared-off rear end made the Edwards honestly one of the best-looking American cars of the day. Bob Rolofson called it "a modern Lincoln Continental . . . first elegant styling since 1941." He wasn't far wrong, either.

During 1954 and '55, Edwards Engineering supplied a grand total of six hand-built, luxurious, four-passenger GT cars, both coupes and convertibles. The price was a healthy $8,000, which sort of limited the market. Still, Edwards lost a fortune on each one. And even then they used a lot of proprietary parts. One of the nice features for a restorer, in addition to the easily repaired fiberglass

body and stock Lincoln V-8, is that much of the hardware on the Edwards came off contemporary American cars, which isn't as horrid as it sounds. The taillights are '52 Mercury, the dash is Oldsmobile, the wire wheels are Chrysler Newport, all blended harmoniously. So really, it would be a surprisingly practical, eminently striking car to own.

Price? God only knows. Sterling Edwards has been restoring his own pair of cars over the past few years, and there are two others known. The final two might still be tucked away in private garages somewhere, most likely in the ritzier sections of south San Francisco, the Monterey Peninsula, or Palm Springs. I've never heard of one on the East Coast, though undoubtedly one could have made its way back to Newport, Watch Hill, or Palm Beach. The going rate would be anything you could get it for . . . $20,000 certainly wouldn't be too much to pay for a good one, I shouldn't think. The Edwards America was undeniably classy, expensive, *very* exclusive, fast, and possessed of plain old unadulterated *style* in big gobs. Not unlike Edwards the man.

Corvette

Big corporations are strange. Wrapped in bureaucracy, they ponderously move forward across a long gray line of committee decisions. And yet, if he has his finger on the corporate pulse and knows just the right buttons to push, a single individual can make the largest company in the world do handsprings. Happily enough, the Corvette has been blessed over the years with a succession of enthusiasts who could absolutely play *tunes* on General Motors's pushbuttons.

The first was Harley Earl, the legendary creator of GM Art and Colour, the man who determined the shape of more than 50 million automobiles between 1926 and 1960. Throughout the fifties he supplied futuristic "dream cars" for the GM Motorama, a traveling circus that each year previewed the new GM line in a dozen major market centers across the

Thanks to stylist Bob McLean, the '53 Corvette was the right size for a "proper" sports car.

country. In 1951/'52 Earl provided the LeSabre and XP-300 show cars, which introduced, for better or worse, tail fins, wrap-around windshields, and "Dagmar" bumpers. Indeed, the outlandish LeSabre was probably the most influential styling study ever built by anybody, anywhere.

For the 1953 Motorama (which he was already thinking about in late '51) Earl thought he'd try and pick up on the current sports-car rage. Just down the hall from his office in GM styling, U.S. Rubber had Bill Tritt's Alembic roadster on display in the auditorium, where Earl had to pass by it at least twice a day. The Naugatuck Division of U.S. Rubber was unabashedly wooing GM, hoping to get a fiberglass body onto a real production car, not just on backyard homebuilt cars like the Woodill and Glasspar. At the same time Earl was admiring the Alembic I and worrying about an encore for the next Motorama, his son Jerry was pestering him for a cheap new sports car to take to college. Everything coalesced in Earl's mind and in the winter of '52 he started working on a high-style fiberglass roadster that would theoretically retail at the same price as a mundane Chevy Sedan or MG's popular TC. The target price was $1,800.

As head of all GM styling, Harley Earl could choose the projects he'd work on himself, and also the personnel to help him. For the Motorama sports car, he assigned a young Cal Tech grad named Bob McLean, with degrees in both industrial design and engineering, to lay out the basic car. McLean turned out to be totally crazy for sports cars. He decided, since he had carte blanche anyway, to get as close to the real thing as possible, still using stock suspension and drivetrain pieces. The choice of engine was easy. If the car was to be inexpensive, it had to use Chevrolet parts. And the old Stovebolt, the Blue Flame Six, was the only engine Chevrolet *had.*

The legend is that McLean started his full-size plan by drawing the rear tire, putting the seats as close as possible, leaving minimal leg room, and then snuggling the engine as close to the firewall as he could get. This gave him a wheelbase of 102 inches, which meant a whole new frame. Harley Earl's acceptance of McLean's full-scale renderings—with the all-new frame—ultimately meant that while the finished car would have excellent weight distribution and classic sports-car proportions, it would never retail for the MG price Earl had originally envisioned. McLean's sports car was priced at Jaguar prices before it ever got off the drawing board.

In May of '52 Earl presented a full-size plaster model of McLean's proposed Motorama car to Ed Cole, the flamboyant new chief of Chevrolet engineering, and to Harlow "Red" Curtice, the conservative president of GM. Another GM staff member who attended the top-secret showing told Karl Ludvigsen that Cole "literally jumped up and down" when he saw the new car. Red Curtice told Earl and Cole that they could not only have their Motorama car but that Cole could start making plans for production if the public's response was as enthusiastic as his own.

Cole was at least as adept as Earl at getting what he wanted out of GM Corporate, and Maurice Olley, one of the best development engineers in Detroit, prepared the chassis for production in less than a year, lightning fast for GM. He and Cole managed to boost the six's horsepower from 115 to 150 and made a million other refinements to what had become Engineering's pet project. By January 1953 not only was the Motorama car finished and on display at the Waldorf-Astoria, but similar engineering prototypes were already running around GM's Milford, Michigan, proving grounds. For the Motorama, the car finally picked up a name—Corvette. Corvair had been the earlier choice. "It is named after the trim, fleet naval vessel that performed heroic escort and patrol duties in World War II," quoth the official Motorama press release.

As hoped, the Motorama car was a stunning success, so Curtice ordered the Corvette into limited production in June 1953. Up until the last minute, there was talk of building the production car of steel formed over disposable Kirksite dies, even though the show car was GRP. The novelty value of fiberglass was so great, however, that it became a major selling point instead of a drawback. In addition, Ed Cole later explained that it would have cost something like $4.5 million to tool up for volume production in steel; in plastic it cost only $400,000.

Although they built 300 cars beginning in June, it was December before Corvette production really got going in Saint Louis, with bodies supplied by Bob Morrison's Molded Fiber Glass of Ashtabula, Ohio. Morrison had ironically underbid U.S. Rubber for the $4 million initial body order. In a curious promotional offer, the first Corvettes were reserved for VIP customers—celebrities, socialites, leading local businessmen. More than one plumber with $3,490 burning a hole in his

The definitive Corvette of all time, the 1957 with 283 V-

pocket found he had to get the local mayor to buy his Corvette for him. It was July 1954 before just *anyone* could walk in off the street and buy a Corvette, and yet, curiously, Chevrolet was soon forced to shut down even their limited production facilities because, to be blunt, they couldn't give the damn things away, VIPs or no.

In their haste, Cole and Olley had used Chevrolet's deadly dull Powerglide automatic transmission in what was meant to be a sports car. The automatic transmission was quicker to adapt to a floor shift and they didn't have room under the hood for a column shifter

el injection, and 4-speed transmission . . . quick, fast, and sleek enough to bring tears to your eyes.

linkage. But even Americans were smart enough to know that sports cars didn't have Powerglide—or Blue Flame Sixes designed in antiquity, for that matter. Chevrolet built fewer than 4,000 Corvettes in 1953 and '54, and could sell only 2,863. The other 1,076 were still sitting on loading docks in January 1955.

Corvette production totaled a big 700 in 1955 and came close to being cut to zero from then on. But another enthusiast with just the right GM connections personally took over the Corvette and almost immediately made his name synonymous with Corvette. This was Zora Arkus-Duntov, expatriate Russian, de-

signer of the famous Ardun conversion for flathead Ford V-8s, Allard engineer, and part-time racing driver. He cleaned up the early car's handling and did much of the development testing when Ed Cole stuffed the new 265-cubic-inch V-8 into late 1955 production 'Vettes. At the same time, the Corvette was saved from extinction by Ford's introduction of the two-seater Thunderbird. The T-bird virtually forced Chevrolet to continue with a competitive model.

For '56 the Corvette was happily restyled under Bill Mitchell's direction into a surprisingly clean package, bigger than it needed to

Chevrolet advertising in 1957 claimed, "It is our intention to make the Corvette a classic car. one of those

By 1962, Bill Mitchell had restyled the classic 'Vette into this curious compromise with four headlights and

e and happy milestones in the history of automotive design,"one of the most prophetic ads ever written.

rodynamic, high-lift tail . . . but 360 hp from a fuel-injected 327 V-8 covered a multitude of sins.

be, but handsome. In contemporary racing pictures, the Corvettes positively loom over D-Jags, Testa Rossas, and the like. But by 1956 John Fitch and Walt Hansgen were able to keep a factory car together long enough to finish ninth overall at Sebring, and Duntov himself drove a special V-8 with a prototype of the famous Duntov cam over 150 mph at Daytona Beach. Dick Thompson, the Washington, D.C., D.D.S. who literally built a second career behind the wheel of various Corvettes, also won SCCA C-production in '56 in a semifactory car. Technically it was owned by Thompson, but actually it went back to Duntov for rebuilds after every race.

Although they went to quad headlights for 1958 and a high-lift tail designed by Bill Mitchell for 1961, the Corvette stayed basically the same from '56 through '62. However, two important changes came in 1957. John Dolza and Zora Duntov designed a fuel-injection unit for the bored-out 283 V-8 that ultimately allowed Chevrolet to advertise "one horsepower for every cubic inch." Harry Barr, who was chief engineer of Chevrolet Division, revealed in *Special-Interest Autos* that the average fuel-injected engine was actually good for 291 hp on the dyno, but Campbell-Ewald was intrigued by the advertising possibility of 283 hp from 283 cubic inches, so that's the way it was reported.

At the same time, the now-famous Borg-Warner T-10 4-speed became an option. Linked up with the 283-hp V-8, it made the '57 'Vette good for 130 mph with a 4.11 differential, getting through the quarter-mile in under 15 seconds at over 95 mph. In 1957 that was superb performance, I promise you, and the Corvette became justly popular with both real racers and street rodders. It still weighed too much, the cockpit was cramped, the standard brakes weren't up to the speeds, and handling was vague by comparison with most of the imported competition. But as *Sports Cars Illustrated* pointed out, a $3,600 fuel-injected Corvette "is the fastest-accelerating genuine production car *SCI* has ever tested. In fact, up to 80 mph, it's not so far from the data posted by the Mercedes 300 SLR coupe, which is generally regarded as the world's fastest road car."

In 1957 too, Dick Thompson and Gaston Andrey won the GT class at Sebring, Thomp-son won SCCA B-production, and hundreds of private owners raced everything from local rallies to NHRA with varying degrees of success. Even the factory got into the act with the ill-fated Corvette SS, a weirdly styled, magnesium-bodied extravaganza for Sebring that lasted only twenty-three laps before succumbing to terminal poor preparation. Aside from John Fitch, who inherited the SS almost on race day, the car was basically a styling and engineering project masterminded by Duntov in his spare time. That it was too much of the laboratory and not enough of the race track was painfully evident. And right after Sebring, before the SS ever got sorted out, the Automobile Manufacturers Association ban on racing—which went into effect in June 1957 and killed direct factory support of racing from the American manufacturers—immediately put it back in the lab for keeps.

Despite the factory ban, standard Corvettes virtually owned A and B production until the Cobras came around in 1964, though to be fair they were about the only make in the big-bore classes, too. Few Americans were going to pay twice as much for a GT Ferrari when they could race a Corvette with equal chance of success. The high point of early Corvette competition was in 1960, when durable Briggs Cunningham took a three-car team of blue and white coupes to Le Mans, getting John Fitch and Bob Grossman into eighth overall. In a way, it was a good indication of how far the U.S. sports-car market had come. Only a decade earlier, when Cunningham had wanted to race an American sports car at LeMans, he'd had to build his own.

The single biggest problem with owning an early series Corvette is not the price. A good '53–'62 is now worth anywhere from $5,000 to $15,000, depending. For the car you get, that's a helluva bargain. Even when they were new, V-8 Corvettes should have sold for twice what Chevy asked, and it's a fact that the Corvette ran deeply in the red until after 1958. Production climbed slowly, and it was 1960 before Chevrolet built 10,000 'Vettes in a year. So the cars are relatively rare, and since many of them were raced and broken or customized and cut up, there aren't all that many left. The price is not the obstacle.

The problem with 'Vettes is this very

same popularity with racers and customizers and just plain snot-nosed hot-rodders. It is hard—I mean really *hard*—to find a Corvette from any era that hasn't been mucked about and crudely stuck back together at some point in its life, and irrevocably ruined in the process. If there's a favorite car for inept modifications, it has to be the fiberglass-bodied Corvette. George Barris alone must have ruined a couple of thousand all by himself, and he was *good.*

What this means is that when you go to buy an early 'Vette the engine will probably be a late-model 327 or 350 instead of a 283, it'll have a 4-speed and fuel injection from a '63, mag wheels, disc brakes, Thrush pipes, and God-knows-what-all hop-up parts. The nose clip will probably be a cheap aftermarket replacement that's been resined on, and the paint will be all crackly. The very same accessibility that is the Corvette's greatest strength has become its biggest weakness as far as collectors are concerned, and even most of the cars you see at Corvette Club concours are modified in some way.

My only advice is to be super careful when you buy. The definitive early Corvette is the '57 with 4-speed and fuel injection. It's prettier than the later cars, just about as fast, and more fun to drive. Unfortunately, as the early-series Corvettes went along they got heavier and uglier. The 327 engine was standard in '62, but otherwise there were few significant changes over the early cars. The '53/'54 is historically important as the first mass-production American sports car and the first from a major maker with a fiberglass body, but it's not really much of a car. By '57, though, the styling had been refined and the chassis finally whipped into shape. It's by far the best car of the Harley Earl/Ed Cole era.

It marked, indeed, the end of a fine era at Chevrolet, an era when the factory was directly and openly involved in racing and when the lessons learned at Sebring directly affected the cars you could buy. The '57 Corvettes are remarkably direct, straightforward machines, probably the most honest cars to come out of Detroit between the '40 Ford and the Pontiac GTO. Thanks to a trio of strong-willed GM executives who were precisely keyed in to the enthusiast market, the '57 Corvette came together in one brief shining hour

when between them, Harley Earl, Ed Cole, and Zora Duntov could have gotten *anything* out of General Motors as long as it was for the Corvette.

Thunderbird

The Thunderbird was a Corvette without Harley Earl, Ed Cole, and Zora Duntov; in other words, a purely corporate solution to the sports car problem, a committee creation in what should be a highly individualistic sphere. The Corvette was just what the GM trio wanted it to be; the Thunderbird was what Ford Motor Company thought would sell. And that made all the difference. From a purely business point of view, of course, Ford was right. In 1955 Ford sold 16,000 T-birds against 1,700 Corvettes. In '56 it was 15,000 to 3,400; in 1957, 21,000 to 6,300. And of course, though the Corvette stayed basically the same from 1958 through 1962, averaging fewer than 10,000 cars a year, the four-passenger "Squarebird" sold a whopping 48,000, 72,000, and 81,000 in 1958, '59, and '60, respectively.

Very early on, Chevrolet decided to concentrate on the hard-core "purist" market, leaving the "personal car" spectrum to Ford. For Chevrolet the Corvette was meant to be a prestige line leader, even if it had to be sold at a loss. The Thunderbird was intended to break even, so the four-passenger Thunderbird was put into its own division in 1958, where it was expected to—and did—show a profit. Interestingly enough, although the Squarebird was enormously popular in its day, it's pretty much a glut on the market today. The two-seaters are going for anywhere from $5,000 to $10,000, and good '61–'66 T-birds—the ones that look like motorboats—are worth $2,500 to $5,000. But a totally restored Squarebird from '58–'60 is worth $3,000 tops. It might even be some sort of sleeper as a low-dollar investment, because it just can't get much lower.

The two-seater Thunderbird was planned in direct reaction to the Corvette. The first GM

Motorama 'Vette went on display in January 1953; work on the Thunderbird started on February 9. Lewis Crusoe, general manager of Ford Division, desperately wanted to beat Chevy. George Walker was chief of styling, and together he and Crusoe hatched the "all things to all men" personal-car concept that they expected to appeal to a wider audience than the Corvette's racing-oriented performance market. Working on a 102-inch wheelbase—coincidentally identical to the Corvette's—Ford's passenger-car stylists modeled the Thunderbird in the same studio with the regular Ford line. Crusoe wanted a strong family resemblance that would help sell Fords, and there was much trading back and forth of motifs. As it turned out, the T-bird shared taillights, headlights, and instruments with the cheaper sedans, but that was all.

The chassis of course used existing FoMoCo components whenever possible. The 292-cubic-inch Mercury V-8 was standard. Most of the suspension bits came off the Ford station wagon attached to a conventional Ford frame. Rather than fool around with low production volumes and fiberglass, Ford went to Budd Body Co. and had conventional steel bodies stamped out at the Charlesvoix plant. Once they got up over 15,000 units a year, steel was just as cheap . . . and a known quantity, besides.

Because of the lead time necessary for carving dies, it was nearly eighteen months after Crusoe decided to get going before the first Birds were built. And also because of the steel body and passenger-car components, the little T-bird came out weighing 3,600 pounds—as much as the full-sized Ford convertible and some 800 pounds more than the cleverly designed Corvette.

In a straight line, though, performance was actually pretty good. A T-bird would get up to nearly 115 mph and go through the quarter-mile at 85 mph in around 17 seconds. This was *very* respectable performance for 1955, more than enough to justify the car's sporting pretensions. When it came down to handling, though, it was strictly a boulevard sports car, even worse than the Kaiser-Darrin and Woodill Wildfire. But T-bird buyers didn't notice; they never went fast around corners anyway. The Thunderbird, by comparison to the Corvette, was not only very attractive, it also came with such handy amenities as roll-up windows and a weatherproof top that the original Corvette sadly lacked. For 99 percent of the market, the Thunderbird was a better car.

It was also considerably cheaper. Because of the much greater production run, Ford undersold the Corvette by $500. A base T-bird went for just under $3,000, head to head with the Buick Century convertible and only a little

George Walker was in charge of styling the smooth and unpretentious '55 Thunderbird.

By 1957, the T-bird had grown up into a sleek and powerful "personal car" with a porthole top.

more than something like Studebaker's Golden Hawk.

The Thunderbird was definitely an upper-middle-class sports car, with none of the questionable virtues that racing weirdos found so attractive about the Corvette. It was a good car, handsome, durable, and a fair bargain. The same rear oil seal and transmission problems that plague all Fords of that era are there, but that's nothing that a little patience can't cure. And of course they *do* rust. Late-fifties Fords are hopeless rust-outs, with T-birds no exception. But a good California car can be a joy, particularly if what you're after is a solid investment, a usable car, and a dash of style.

My own choice would be a '57 because I think the styling got better as it smoothed out. The subtle fins of the later car, the porthole top, and the egg-crate grille are all lovely touches that bring a real breath of life to the Bird. In its day it was a sports car for indoor sports, a genteel and pretty carriage to give your mistress for around-town showing off. The best year for postwar Ford styling in general was 1957, followed closely by '55 and '56,

and the Thunderbird shared the glory. Ford did a lot of NASCAR racing in '57, too, and the T-bird was available with a McCulloch-supercharged 325 hp from 312 cubic inches. So drag racers found they could order up a pretty exciting package, all things considered. Indeed, particularly in 1957, the T-bird managed to transcend its committee origins. But of course, way back in 1955, the same committee was already planning the homogenized four-seater Squarebird for 1958. That's the trouble with committees. They never know when to stop.

Dual-Ghia

Ghia is not Pininfarina. Nor even Bertone or Scaglietti. The problem with Ghia has always been that it was run either by artists who were

The long-wheelbase Thomas Special, put into production in 1953 as the Chrysler GS-1.

Virgil Exner's short-wheelbase Thomas Special, styled in his basement at home.

no businessmen, or businessmen who were no artists. So either they drew pretty cars and lost money or made money but drew dull cars. From 1915 to 1946 Giacinto Ghia—who was an artist—struggled to compete with the other carrozzeria in Turin. After he died, Gigi Segre—who was a businessman—got Ghia into making bicycles and trailers, which wasn't very exciting but paid the bills. So by 1950 Ghia was, for the first time, actually in better shape than the other more famous Torino coachbuilders.

And Chrysler, in America, was looking for a stable Italian coachbuilder to whip up some show cars with which they hoped to change their bland image. Ghia wasn't going to do any of the designing, however. Oh no. For that Chrysler had Virgil Exner (commonly known as Virgil Excess), the man who designed the 1947 Studebaker "coming or going?" model and gave the tail fin to America. Exner was Chrysler's "idea" man, the stylist who was supposed to turn the company completely around. He started with a couple of show cars to show what could be done, but because Chrysler was stretching every last stamping out of its old dies, it was 1955 before any of Exner's ideas really showed up on the production cars, and he'd been with Chrysler since mid-1949.

No matter. There was a veritable flood of Ghia-Chrysler show cars, at least one or two a year, to keep the Chrysler—and Exner—name out in front of the folks. Most of them were pretty horrible, if the truth be known, heavily into weird two-toning, tail fins, ham-fisted surface development, and obnoxious detailing. Virgil Excess was never accused of subtlety. With two exceptions. In 1952 and '53 he came up with two groups of similar cars that, given the times, were pleasantly understated. Almost painfully so. They were as good as anything being done anywhere, actually, and better than anything that came out of Detroit before the Bill Mitchell era.

Now the secret may be that the first two of these good cars weren't done for the company at all but for Chrysler vice-president C. B. Thomas. And they were called, logically enough, Thomas Specials. Thomas himself called them SSs for Styling Specials, though. They were *huge,* of course. For the first one Exner used a shortened 119-inch version of the standard Chrysler New Yorker chassis. The second one was on the even more immense 125.5-inch chassis. But Chrysler did have the superb 180-hp hemi V-8, and though the chassis was dead conventional, it was no worse than anything else in America. Which isn't saying much, but *still.*

On this uninspired basis, Exner designed two variations of a 2 + 2 sports coupe: one a fastback, the other a notchback. They were designed in Exner's home basement in Birmingham, Michigan, built by Ghia—and of course, exhibited by Chrysler on the all-important auto show circuit. As these things happen, the importer of Chryslers into France saw the Thomas Specials at Ghia. When it became obvious that Chrysler had no intention of putting either one into production, Gigi Segre and the distributors got together and made a deal. The result was a production run of 400 gargantuan coupes, based on Exner's long-wheelbase Thomas Special.

The chassis of the GS-1 (Ghia Special) was stock New Yorker. But at that time, all the American manufacturers listed "export" suspension kits, which mostly meant heavy-duty shocks and springs. So at least the GS-1s did get these heftier bits, a lot more solid than what was sold in this country. The bodies were, of course, fantastic. Almost identical to the Thomas Special in every way, the GS-1 had a bigger, oval grille, heavy stock Chrysler bumpers, and ribbed aluminum rocker panels. Otherwise it was pure Exner, which in this case was just great. The Thomas Specials were maybe the cleanest designs he ever did, and the GS-1s weren't cobbled up to any great extent. The front bumper was pretty bad, but you'd take that off anyway.

The GS-1s are strange cars. They're not Facel Vegas, because they're not small and nimble. But they're not big Chryslers, either, because they were exquisitely built and finished and luxuriously appointed throughout. Really, the GS-1s are unique. Most of them came with the heavy Dayton wire wheels that Chrysler offered as an option in those years, and a few of them got overdrive 3-speeds instead of the stock automatic. In any case, they're about the only cars conceived in Detroit that you can think of as true luxury GTs—at least from the fifties—and though they are big, they don't look it.

The Dual-Ghia, with a Dodge hemi and Italian body, was a favorite of Frank Sinatra's "Rat Pack."

Surprisingly enough, there's a hint of Bentley Continental about them—slab sides, rounded front fenders, headlights inset next to the grille, long long hood, light and airy greenhouse. And, of course, a genuine 120-mph top speed, effortless performance, and a really luxurious—but not ostentatious—interior. GS-1s are also surprisingly expensive, at least to me. Dick Merritt, *the* Ferrari expert, tried to sell me one for $7,500 two years ago, and it wasn't anywhere near concours. So $15,000 might be what you'd have to pay for one in good condition. There are less than a dozen in America, but quite a few more closeted in France and Switzerland. That would be the place to look first.

As with any hybrid special, the GS-1 has a lot of advantages over purebred European exoticars. Such as parts and service available right around the corner. And because there's a stock Chrysler chassis under it, not just the engine/transmission, the GS-1 is even better that way than something like an Allard or Facel. It's actually a pretty good deal, all things considered. The car is rather grand—certainly imposing—it's extremely rare and a real eye-catcher. In fact, if you want the convenience and reliability of an American chassis without all the hassles attendant on real hybrids or purebreds, but with more style than any American car has *ever* had, the GS-1 is just about all there is. It's no racing car, but a rare, desirable, and neat collector car nonetheless.

After the GS-1s, Ghia built another series of Exner-inspired cars just for the States. Remember the Dual-Ghia? That's what I figured. But they really weren't bad cars at all, even if they did seem to appeal to an inordinately tasteless group. I mean, just because Frank Sinatra and Dean Martin had matching Dual-Ghias customized by George Barris, this doesn't mean the cars themselves were dumb. The Dual-Ghia was the Excalibur of its day, or maybe the Stutz Blackhawk replicar. What Hollywood celebrities drove who were, you know, *beyond* Rolls-Royces and Ferraris. But that's no reflection on the cars themselves.

The Dual-Ghia came about much the same way as the earlier GS-1. A Detroit trucker named Gene Casaroll, owner of Automobile Shippers and Dual Motors, decided, like everybody else, to go into the car business. He liked Exner's 1952/'53 Firearrow series, a coherent group of show cars built around the same styling theme, with squarish grilles, no bumpers, slab sides, and tall, angular fenders.

They were, really, the next logical mutation of the Thomas Specials. Casaroll saw the Firearrows at the Detroit auto show, talked to Chrysler, and bought the right to build replicas. Chrysler had no intention of ever going into the limited-production luxury GT market—which was a mistake, they could have cleaned up—so they were perfectly happy to get paid for something they didn't expect to use anyway. Exner, of course, received nothing other than a pat on the head.

Casaroll got together with Ghia and by 1955 he had a running prototype in Detroit to show at the Grosse Point Yacht Club. But it was mid-'56 before the first cars appeared, priced at $7,646, which wasn't all that bad. The Dual-Ghia was really the Firearrow convertible built on a shortened Dodge frame with a reasonable 115-inch wheelbase. Overall length was 203, pretty short for an American chassis. The V-8 was Dodge's hemi, in either 230 hp or 260 hp trim. And you could have only a Powerflite automatic. But what the hell. With 260 hp, *Motor Trend* got 0 to 60 in 8.2 and a top speed of 124.

The body was all-steel, the interior all-leather, with every possible gadgety option Casaroll and Ghia could think up to tack on. The Dodge frames were sent to Torino, shortened, bodied, and sent back to Detroit where Dual Motors finished the chassis. Between 1956 and '58 Ghia built a whopping 117 cars: two coupes, the rest convertibles. Nearly all of them went to California. Eddie Fisher, Peter Lawford, and David Rose were the sort who paid through the nose for Dual-Ghias. And honestly, they were bargains at the price.

Number One, Ghias were much more exclusive than any Ferrari. Number Two, they cost enough to let everyone know you were bucks-up, but Number Three, you could still get your hemi serviced almost anywhere. So, Number Four, you didn't have to be afraid to actually *drive* the car, or lend it to your latest girl friend or boyfriend or whomever. All things considered, the Dual-Ghias were perfect cars for their intended audience, and they played just as well in Detroit as in Hollywood. Almost overnight, Dual-Ghias became *the* American status cars. Sammy Davis, Jr. had to settle for a Jaguar when Casaroll refused to sell him a Dual-Ghia.

After a two-year hiatus, Casaroll got back

Ghia's L6.4 looked like Exner's '61 Plymouth.

The L6.4 grille echoed the first Dual-Ghia.

into production in 1960, with the L6.4. The front was similar to the original car, but now the back had been restyled with a surprisingly smooth, extremely horizontal look that presaged Virgil Exner's finless '61 Plymouth. The greenhouse was Chrysler-like, but otherwise the fabulous L6.4 (325 hp, 4,500 pounds, 210 inches long, and $15,000 delivered in Detroit) was a unique piece. It looked like nothing else, but at the price it was pretty hard to sell. Exactly twenty-six of the later cars were built between '60 and '63, and quite a few of them were tastelessly customized with fakey tooled leather interiors and stainless-steel roofs.

Casaroll had gotten into the car business mostly as a hobby, and it was no big deal for him to get out again. He simply went back to spending all his time making money, instead of part of his time wasting it. The Dual-

Ghias never made a profit—cars like that rarely do. But they were big, boisterous, luxury carriages, and Chrysler's current Cordoba is really kind of a cut-down, bourgeois version of the Dual-Ghia personal luxury car. Normally I hate the whole concept: there is nothing worse than a Mark IV unless it's a Thunderbird, and I'd never take either on a bet. But the Dual-Ghia had more class than that, enough to rise above its plebeian origins, enough to take even Virgil Exner's excesses in stride and still wind up as a decent, flamboyant carriage with definite character. It's not my cup of tea particularly, but a lot of people swear by it. The second-series cars are going for at least as much as they brought new, and there's a waiting line to get in. Frank Sinatra is no fool, and his Dual-Ghia was a grand mobile billboard screaming "Money, Class, *Status*" so loud even the proles could understand. Even if you don't agree with it, that is one of the primary functions—hell, maybe *the* primary function—of cars in America. And the flamboyant Dual-Ghia did it *very* well. No argument.

Jim Orr in his Scaglietti-bodied '52 Ermini, the car from

Devin SS

Bill Devin was a genuine Okie, one of those migrants who moved to California in 1939 after Oklahoma blew over into Texas. He got into hot-rodding and spent his dissolute youth hanging around grease racks and El Mirage lakesters. No matter. He graduated to his own Los Angeles Chrysler-Plymouth agency and a road racing Crosley Hot Shot. This led inevitably to a short-lived partnership with crazy Ernie McAfee—who was a fearless big-bore sports/racing hero in the mid-fifties—importing Italian machinery. Devin and McAfee sold Siatas and Erminis and all sorts of weird stuff like that, including a 4.1 Ferrari to Masten Gregory, a GT-250 to Phil Hill, and a handful of exotics to Briggs Cunningham. When McAfee split, Devin decided to go into business for himself.

He borrowed Jim Orr's Scaglietti-bodied Ermini 1100—which was about the prettiest little car floating around L. A. in 1952—and pulled a mold off it. Then he started selling a fiberglass replica for kit cars. Devin's body fitted chassis from 78- to 106-inch wheelbases and tread widths from 40 to 52 inches. This unusual body versatility was cleverly accomplished with a battery of modular molds that could be fitted together in sections to expand or reduce the proportions of the basic body as needed.

In the mid-fifties the Devin body was the only one to have. The quality was excellent, the lines were superb, and it could be made to fit anything from a Crosley special to Dean Moon's famous Moonbeam Bonneville car. A bunch of Minnesota racing zealots built up three Corvette-based, B-modified "Echidna" racing cars in late '57, about the same time Ak Miller was bolting together Devin-covered road racers and Pikes Peak hillclimb cars with Corvette and Oldsmobile engines. The

which Bill Devin pulled his original mold.

lightweight Devin body was a logical choice for anyone, and the bare-bones model only cost $295, no matter what the dimensions. A bargain at twice the price.

Inevitably, there were imitators. Within a few years, Byers, Victress, Almquist, Kellison, La Dawri, and a slew of others were making similar fiberglass kit bodies, so Devin decided to go them one better and build a whole *car.* Let 'em try and match *that,* he said. Coincidentally, he got an order from a builder in Ireland named Malcolm MacGregor, who was putting together a sophisticated chassis to fit Devin's body. After much transatlantic correspondence and a couple of trips, Devonshire Engineering was set up in Belfast to make a really high-quality chassis to take a Corvette engine and Devin body.

MacGregor's chassis was a true objet d'art. The main structure was welded up from 3-inch-diameter steel tubing, with loops at the cowl and behind the seats to serve as rudimentary roll bars. This triangulated perimeter

frame even afforded side-impact protection, and the whole thing was immensely strong. Into it went a standard Corvette V-8 with Bill Devin's own low-profile intake manifold and four-barrel carb to make 290 hp from 283 cubic inches. The transmission was the excellent Borg-Warner 4-speed. At the front, huge Girling disc brakes and Dunlop wire wheels were carried on parallel wishbones; at the back was a coil-spring independent rear end with DeDion tube, 11-inch Girling discs mounted inboard next to the Salisbury differential, and dual parallel trailing arms. At the time it was as sophisticated as any chassis available.

Over all this went a really excellent modified version of Devin's standard body, fitted in his El Monte shop with Stewart-Warner gauges, leather buckets, and a wood-rimmed wheel. It even had usable trunk space. About the only uncivilized touches were side curtains and a build-it-yourself sort of traditional British top. But hell, even Shelby's Cobra had side curtains, and ten years later, too. Devin's paintwork was excellent—usually bright red—and needless to say, the fiberglass finish was outstanding. And the price. The tab for this exceptionally well designed and constructed bolide was a mere $5,950, ready to run. And that was for Cobra-like performance—0 to 60 in 4.8 seconds, 0 to 100 in 12—in early 1958. That's with a *stock* Corvette engine. By comparison, the *much* heavier, drum-braked, live-axle Corvette would do 0 to 60 in 6.6 seconds, 0 to 100 in about 17.5, and cost about $5,000 in fuel-injected trim. Just the wire wheels and DeDion rear alone were worth the difference.

If anybody ever deserved to succeed, it was Bill Devin. His cars were screaming bargains, hand-built masterpieces at comic-book prices. Californian Pete Woods won an SCCA C-modified national championship in his Devin SS in '59, and he was only the most successful of a whole crew of Devin SS racers. The cars were strong, fast, beautiful, well made . . . and Devin couldn't *give* the things away. It makes you wonder about the whole free enterprise system. Every car magazine in the country—and many general-interest books—gave the Devin SS rave reviews, and the cars were advertised copiously and often. And *still* the whole goddamn project went

Ed Grierson in his Devin-bodied Echidna leads a Ferrari Berlinetta at Elkhart Lake in 1959.

down the tubes without a trace. Incredible.

Only fifteen Devin SSs were built between 1958 and '61 before the Devin crew gave up and quietly went back to building body kits and waiting for orders that never came. The price had gone up to $10,000 by 1960, which *still* was cheap for what you got. A group of enthusiastic engineers at Chevrolet tried to fix up the sort of deal Carroll Shelby later pulled off at Ford, but the AMA ban was still on and the high-performance market still in its infancy. Devin himself tried to find backers so he could build 100 replicas to qualify for homologation as a GT car, but there were no takers for that scheme either. In the end, the superb Devin SS just sort of dried up and blew away.

But Bill Devin wasn't an Okie for nothing. He had staying power. In 1959 he took basically the same fine concept and scaled it down to take a Volkswagen engine in the rear. A new body with a higher rear deck and no front grille was evolved out of the original Devin body. This was fitted with a super-sturdy square tubing frame bonded into the fiberglass undertray, which in turn took a stock VW front and rear suspension, engine, and drivetrain. Fitted with a bucket seat interior, it came as a cheap $1,495 kit with all the lights wired, windshield, bumpers, etc. A complete *car* was only $2,950. The Devin D was just about the first—and finest—of the VW-based kit cars, forerunner of the whole dune buggy industry.

If the Devin SS was a Shelby Cobra six years too early, the Devin D was a Meyers Manx equally before its time. Once again, Devin's perfect idea fell flat on its face, and though the kit-body business continued to perk along, there never was much demand for Devin Ds, not even when he tossed in a turbocharged Corvair engine and drivetrain beginning in 1962. Devin claimed 0 to 100 in 13 seconds with a reworked Corvair in his Devin C, but by the mid-sixties the old Devin/Scaglietti/Ermini body was a decade out of date, the price had zipped up to over $4,000 for the Corvair-powered Devin C—at a time when John Fitch would sell you a much more practical Corvair Sprint for less than $3,000—and, well, the Devin had become just too little too late.

Which is a helluva shame. Really. The Devin SS, in particular, is maybe the best all-round sports car *ever* built in America, Cobras included. But because they aren't as well known, there's virtually no market for Devins today, a situation that's bound to change when people wise up. And I think they will pretty soon. There *are* some Devin SSs around. I for one just bought one of the beasts. *I love it.* I have 1958 Devin SS #SR3-1, which is the first car of the definitive third series. It's got a piddling 9,800 miles on it and is, curiously enough, right-hand drive. According to Devin, he built a handful of offside cars for racing, and that's what I've got.

The thing is great. The fiberglass must be half an inch thick most places, and the chassis is so solid nothing has cracked in twenty years. Mine has three Rochester two-barrels on an Edelbrock manifold, headers, and outside exhausts. In shiny refrigerator white with blue stripes—what else could I have painted it besides American racing colors?—the thing looks as classy as any Testa Rossa. Plus, of course, it'll absolutely blow the doors off anything less than a sharp 427 Cobra. It's even comfortable to drive, easy to work on, and cheap to maintain. The brakes are fantastic, the handling even better. It's very

nearly the neatest car I've *ever* driven, and it didn't cost me $30,000, either. Hell, if I break something, Bill Devin even has a garage full of spares. And of course, Chevy's got another 25 million small-block engines if I happen to need a new one.

Really, I can't think of a car I'd rather have, all things considered. Which is why I have it, I guess, and why it's definitely *not* for sale. Think about it. Where else am I gonna find another beautifully hand-built roadster with enough *cojones* to whip anything except 427 Cobras . . . and maybe even them on a winding road . . . at a price I can afford? Judged on a performance-per-dollar

Devin SS: hand-built masterpiece, comic price.

John Brophy's right-hand-drive Devin SS at Tucson in 1962; capable of giving fits to Ferraris.

basis, the Devin SS just doesn't cost enough. And that, when you get right down to it, was Bill Devin's problem.

Ned Jordan—Somewhere West of Laramie, *that* Ned Jordan—was the cleverest automobile marketing man ever to scan a showroom. And way back in the twenties he said, "The manufacturer of a truly high quality product is under obligation to the salesman to keep his price higher than that of his competitor to make it *easier* to sell. You will get the order for a quality product as soon as the customer says to himself, 'It must be better because it costs more.'" Bill Devin never heard of the Jordan Playboy.

Scarab

Lance Reventlow's Scarab was the ultimate hot rod. Not that he had grease under his nails, far from it. Reventlow's main claim to fame pre-Scarab was merely being born . . . to Barbara Hutton, the flamboyant Woolworth heiress and the "richest woman in the world." Reventlow, Sr.—*Count* Reventlow—was husband two or three, somewhere along in there. Anyway. Just about the time Lance turned nineteen in 1955, he started racing sports cars, with a notable lack of success. In his second season, 1956, he got a bit better, in a Cooper 1100. And for 1957 he campaigned a Maserati in Europe without being either really good or really bad.

He had that impatient temperament so common in the very rich, not surprisingly, and for 1958 Lance Reventlow decided to build his own cars. They would *have* to be better than the Maser he'd been driving, and of course that would make him a winner. Absurdly simplistic. But incredibly, it worked. The Scarab *was* better than anything else, and Lance *did* win. He was still an inexperienced driver, as he was the first to admit, so most of the winning combination was obviously the car. But what a car. Just as the Costin-designed Vanwall is probably the most beautiful

open-wheel racer ever built, the Scarab is *the* sports/racer of all time. It has a brawny elegance, a perfect rightness of line that succinctly proves that old dictum, "If it looks right, it probably *is* right."

What Reventlow did was simplicity itself. He went around with a *big* bag of money and bought the best car-building talent on the West Coast. He got Ken Miles—long before his Cobra days—to draw up a space frame based on his famous Flying Shingle MG but big enough to take a Corvette V-8. Curiously enough, for a jet-set internationalist born in London to an American mother and a European father, Reventlow had developed a Briggs Cunninghamish desire to win major road races in an all-American car. Growing up in L.A. will do that to you, I guess.

From Miles's drawings, Dick Troutman and Tom Barnes—just about the finest freelance race-car constructors anywhere—built the first Scarab in Warren Olson's garage in picturesque West Los Angeles. Phil Remington—who had a hand in *everything*—was the chief fabricator. Eventually, there were three beautifully finished racers, each a work of art. And Miles's design was right at the limits of 1958 racing technology. The front suspension

The most beautiful sports/racer ever; Chuck Daigh in t

was conventionally independent, the rear was DeDion, there were four-wheel aluminum disc brakes, adjustable rear hubs to facilitate chassis tuning, and a Halibrand quick-change differential. Almost everything was hand built by Troutman, Barnes, and Remington, including the exquisite aluminum—not an ounce of plebeian fiberglass—body with its tall headrest, taller rollbar, tapered tail, and covered headlights. Halibrand mag wheels gave it that final bit of forcefulness. And the fuel-injected 5562cc, 385 hp Corvette V-8 was the hot setup in 1958. Chuck Daigh—like Troutman and Barnes an old West Coast hot-rodder and dry-lakes habitué—was working for Stu Hillborn. He designed a set of special Hillborn injectors for the small block. Then Reventlow got him to build the engines. And finally, he hired Daigh full time as the team's all-rounder and number-two driver. He turned out to be much faster than Lance and a crack tuner, besides. Daigh did most of the sorting out that makes a winner from the raw material of a good but unproven design.

The 1958 season was truly legendary. Scarabs won almost every major North American road race and broke track records at Riverside, Willow Springs, Nassau, Thompson,

Scarab at Laguna Seca, 1958.

Lance Reventlow's lovely Scarab at Pomona, 1958.

Montgomery, Santa Barbara, Minden, Laguna Seca, and Meadowdale. It was uncanny. The only times either Daigh or Lance didn't beat the track record were at Palm Springs and Danville, where they had mechanical problems even before the race. The Scarabs dominated American racing like nobody until Roger Penske and Mark Donohue a dozen years later, with the very important proviso that Reventlow was personally picking up the tab, unlike the sponsor-flush Penske era when everything was a corporate advertising write-off for Sunoco, Goodyear, or Chevrolet.

In 1959, having won all there was to win in the States, Reventlow determined to go Formula One racing. Which was a dumb idea from the very beginning. Troutman, Barnes, Remington, and Daigh, though they were all hot-rodders supreme, were emphatically *not* up to running head to head with Enzo Ferrari and Colin Chapman . . . or even John Cooper. And just as the front-engine, Offy-based Scarab F/1 car appeared in Europe in 1960, the unorthodox Coopers completed the first stage of the "mid-engine revolution" that totally revamped racing. The Scarabs were doomed before they ever left California.

Sadly, they knew it, too. Despite a lot of nationalistic blather in the American press and a really hard push by the Reventlow team, the Scarab Formula One cars were hopelessly outclassed in Europe. After a truly dismal sea-

Harry Heuer's Meister Brauser Scarabs were three years old when they came to this Times Grand Prix at River

son in which they were lucky to qualify, let alone last through a race, F/1 was changed to 1.5 liters for '61 and the cars became truly outlandish white elephants. Their best finish was a tenth overall. Reventlow and his first wife, Jill St. John, kept at it as a tax write-off for the government-allowed five years, building a mid-engine sports/racer that later proved fairly successful for John Mecom's Texas team when driven by A. J. Foyt. But once the tax loophole was shut, Reventlow gave up the Scarab team, racing, and Jill, too. He later remarried and became a part-time polo player. But Lance Reventlow never raced again. So it goes.

The original Scarabs—those beautiful toys—stayed in racing longer than Lance. He had the original left-hand-drive car converted for his own street use and sold the right-hand-drive racers to the Peter Hand Brewery, owned by Harry Heuer. The Meister Brauser team consisted of Heuer and rival beer heir Augie Pabst, who won the '59 USAC road racing title. For 1960 they garnered SCCA B-modified one–two. Pabst split in 1961, so Heuer won B-modified. By '62 the Scarab was down to C-modified and still competitive, though Heuer himself had a Chaparral and brought in hired guns to run the old Reventlow car. The Scarabs stayed in contention right up un-

side in 1960, but Augie Pabst was still third overall.

dated shape by now. All of them, though, were ungodly fast, hair-raising machines with enough torque to push over walls. Most of them were incredibly strong, too, because the combination of choppy airport circuits, high speeds, and really brutal engines would just rip delicate cars apart. A converted sports/racer, whether one of the virtually priceless Scarabs or somebody's flathead Ford with a Devin body, would still make a wildly unique street machine for sunny days. The price for such a mongrel shouldn't be too much, and the performance will be stupendous. Not a blue-chip investment certainly, but a lot of cheap, dirty fun. Unlike the Scarabs, which were damned expensive.

Chaparral

When the overextended Reventlow/Scarab Formula One fiasco started to go down the drain, Troutman and Barnes bowed out. They had more racing experience than anyone else on the team and knew without having to have it spelled out that Reventlow was soon going to be spending more time on a polo pony than in a Scarab. During November 1960 the well-known pair bumped into Texan Jim Hall in the pits at the Riverside Grand Prix, and about six months later Hall agreed to bankroll a Scarab-like sports/racer, only this time one that could be offered for sale.

He couldn't have picked a better team, of course. Troutman and Barnes learned their trade building rock-solid Indy cars for Frank Kurtis. Way back in 1952, though, they'd built a Ford-based special that was absolutely devastating in the hands of Clay Smith, the equally legendary tuner and builder of USAC cars and Pan-American road-race Lincolns. Later, Chuck Daigh had driven it with equal success. The Scarabs were designed by Ken Miles; T & B were just builders. But for Jim Hall's new car—which he called a Chaparral after the road-runner bird of his native Texas—they went back to their original special to inspire a super-sophisticated chassis

til the big mid-engine modifieds simply outclassed them, and then they simply faded away. You'd be hard put to find a Scarab today, though all three *are* around. Reventlow's personal car was given to the Briggs Cunningham museum a few years ago when his estate was settled after a fatal 1972 private plane crash, and Augie Pabst still has his.

Although the Scarabs were far and away the best of a genre—the West Coast road-racing hot rod—they weren't the only ones. Throughout the fifties and early sixties, American road-racing grids were almost universally made up of "specials." Many of them are still around—probably in pretty dilapi-

competitive with the Lotus 19s, Cooper Monacos, and Birdcage Maseratis that pretty much
ruled big-bore fields at that point.

The Chaparral came out like a simplified
Scarab. The bored-out, 318-cubic-inch Corvette small block V-8 used up a whole passel
of standard West Coast hop-up gear and gave
a reliable 325 hp. It was plunked in the middle
of a tubular space frame to give perfect 50/
50 weight distribution. The driveshaft was
only about a foot long and connected to a Halibrand center section. It had an independent
rear suspension with coil springs, inboard
Girling disc brakes, and rear trailing arms.
The front suspension was conventional fabricated wishbones, also with Girling discs. The
fuel tanks rode next to the driver, forming
the body sides. An oval-section body, not really
much different from the original 1952 T & B
Special, covered the innards over with hand-
hammered aluminum. It was clever, simple,
and effective. But best of all, the whole thing
weighed 1,700 pounds ready to race, a significant 300 pounds less than the Scarab.

Front-engine sports/racers were dying a
lingering death in the early sixties and disappeared for good with Bill Thomas's Cheetah.
When the Chaparral appeared in June 1961,
however, it was more than competitive. The
car seemed so good that Hall's buddy Hap
Sharp was inveigled into buying one, and
Troutman and Barnes built two for Harry
Heuer as mates for his still competitive Scarabs. They built another for a British racer and
one for Skip Hudson. The selling price was
a healthy $16,500—cheaper than a Ferrari and
not bad for a guaranteed race winner.

Funny thing, though; Jim Hall's first Chaparral really didn't win many races. Jim won
at Elkhart Lake/Road America in '62 and
then went on to build the mid-engine Chaparral 2 to compete head to head with the mid-
engine Lotuses and Coopers. He spent 1963
in Europe doing Formula One, and by then
the T & B cars were way out of contention
in international-caliber racing. Harry Heuer's
car did a lot better, winning SCCA C-modified
in 1962 and '63, running well in the fledgling
USRRC with a fifth at Monterey and, in its
final appearance, taking a fourth at Atlanta
in the 1964 USRRC. After that, the Meister
Brauser Chaparrals—like Hall's—were retired. They're still out there, waiting for some-

Jim Hall's first Chaparral leads Daniel Gurney's Lotus 1

In 1962, the Troutman and Barnes Chaparral was

t Riverside in 1961.

odified but was still only marginally competitive.

one who wants a really sophisticated, aluminum-bodied sports/racer for a pet.

Of all the Chevy-powered specials, the most desirable are the Scarabs and Chaparrals, both coincidentally enough from the magic fingers of Troutman and Barnes. Any of them is going to be expensive—$25,000 to $30,000, I'd guess, since there's no blue book on obsolete, hand-built racing cars. But if any American sports cars are filled with historical importance, it's this handful of aluminum works of art. There really aren't very many signed originals by Troutman and Barnes— maybe a few dozen cars in all, built over a thirty-year career—but virtually every one of them has been an outstanding success and an artistic tour de force. What more could you want in a collector's item?

Bocar

If the beautiful Scarabs of Troutman and Barnes were good for one thing, it was to convince every would-be racing wizard that his backyard special would turn out to be just as good. And once he'd made his name on the tracks, it would be a short jump to limited production of replicas, for which the world would beat an expensive path right to his door. Hell, Colin Chapman had done it, and Cooper, and Eric Broadley. Even old man Ferrari started out that way. So in 1958, the simplistic solution was to beat the Scarabs, thereby replacing Reventlow as the big gun in American racing, and then steal all the marbles.

Bob Carnes, a crew-cut engineer from Denver, thought pretty much that way. In April 1958 he started to build "the fastest, safest sports car in the world." This was another way of saying Scarab-beater. Needless to say, *everybody's* heard of Lance Reventlow and his Scarab, and *nobody's* heard of Bob Carnes's Bocar. But it wasn't for lack of trying. Over roughly a two-year period, Carnes built something like two dozen cars, evolving step by step from a crude Chevy-powered roadster with a body that looked like sin to a highly sophisticated Chevy-powered road burner too outlandish to be simply ugly.

In between, Carnes built two models that were not only wickedly fast but fairly pretty, too. The first of his "production" cars was called the XP-4, correctly indicating that there had been three previous failures before he got this one right. The XP-4 had a super-short 90-inch wheelbase, tubular space frame with your choice of Corvette or Pontiac V-8, Girling disc brakes, and Jaguar wire wheels. The fiberglass body was nicely made; the cars went very fast. But their looks would stop a truck and the short wheelbase gave them an unfortunate tendency to spin like tops every time you got on the gas.

Immediately there came the XP-5. About a dozen of these were built and sold. Which was really quite a few. Although the wheelbase was still 90 inches, Carnes added Frank Kurtis–inspired solid axles carried on dual trailing arms and torsion bars to both ends of the space frame. He also junked the heavyweight Pontiac V-8 for the ubiquitous and *much* lighter 283 Corvette. These Bocar XP-5s did all sorts of things, from racing up Pikes Peak to USAC and SCCA road courses. They

Crewcut Bob Carnes in his Denver shop with the Boca

The supercharged, 170-mph Bocar XP-6.

Weirder than any car has a right to be, the 180-mph

XP-5, an XP-6, and his "assembly line."

Bocar Stiletto of 1960.

never beat the Scarabs, but they were successful and relatively inexpensive ($11,000) for the amount of performance they delivered.

Finally, in 1959 Carnes added 14 inches to the wheelbase of the XP-5, put on gigantic Buick brakes, and added a wide but smooth fiberglass body distinguished by quad headlights hidden under plexiglass covers. The same 283 Chevy went under the hood, but this time with a monstrous GMC 4-71 supercharger that would drive it well over 170 mph and through the quarter-mile at a gut-wrenching 112. Amazingly, the long-wheelbase XP-6 handled well in spite of an overabundance of sheer horsepower, and Carnes thought he finally had it made. No such luck. At $11,700, he couldn't give the things away.

As an encore, he built a handful of Bocar Stilettos, among the weirder-looking fiberglass wonders of a wonderfully weird era. They weren't any more salable than the XP-6, and Carnes faded out of racing. The Bocars, however, kept right on going, and drivers like Harry Heuer, Augie Pabst, and Paul O'Shea used XP-5s and XP-6s as alternatives to their prettier but crankier Scarabs. Even a few years ago, time-ravaged Bocars were still showing up at SCCA regionals and drivers' schools, clattering around in C-modified with a lot of other has-been race cars.

I haven't seen one in person lately, but they're still out there. A good original XP-5 was sold for $2,000 through *Hemmings* last year, and a guy from Illinois named Rick Metz is restoring it. It's just the car for someone who appreciates really solid construction, dirt-cheap pushrod engines with amazing performance, and championship-level handling. Bocars don't have the exquisite looks of a Scarab, but they're not all sequestered away in private collections, either. Of all the late-fifties American sports/racers still battering around, the Bocars are among the best built, most available, and easiest to maintain. They aren't worth more than a few grand these days, and the stringback T-baggers at the VSSC will probably pee their pants when they hear that GMC blower kick over as you rocket into the hook at Lime Rock at 170. *Wheeee-O.*

Sting Ray

In December of 1958, the shiny new vice-president of GM styling, Bill Mitchell, was allowed to "buy" for one dollar the chassis of the Corvette SS "mule" practice car. This was basically identical to the overcomplicated SS chassis Zora Duntov had disastrously entered at Sebring in 1957. Mitchell promptly had stylist Larry Shinoda draw up a strange fiberglass body for this old SS chassis. Mitchell's idea was to make the entire body into a huge inverted airfoil for better road adhesion, so the beltline was dramatically high, the top of the body almost flat. It was a complete departure from anything Chevy had done before, which is what Mitchell wanted. He was trying to erase Harley Earl's look and replace it with something all-new of his own.

This new body was perfect for Mitchell's purpose. He called it the Sting Ray and gave it to Dr. Dick Thompson to race in SCCA C-modified. Zora Duntov officially spurned this presumptuous amateur effort, though the car *was* maintained by Ed Zalucki and Dean Bedford from Corvette Engineering and Ken Eschebach from Mitchell's own Styling staff. After a year of teething troubles—the brakes never *did* work right—Thompson won an SCCA national championship in 1960. After that, Mitchell brought the car back to Styling and turned it into a show car. He exhibited it at major car shows all over the country, building up public enthusiasm for the new and radical Sting Ray shape.

At the very same time Mitchell's Sting Ray was winning C-modified, Zora Duntov was putting together XP-720, a prototype for the production Corvette he hoped to have ready for 1963. Duntov reduced the wheelbase to 98 inches and cut costs by using passenger-car front suspension bits. He got 53 percent of the weight onto the rear wheels. With the money he saved on the front end, he had enough to engineer a whole new independent rear suspension hung over a transverse leaf spring and located by huge stamped radius rods. Though he wanted discs, Duntov ended up borrowing huge 11-inch drum brakes from the big sedans to further cut expenses. After much careful cost accounting, the production version of the XP-720 chassis cost about the

Dr. Dick Thompson, in Bill Mitchell's "inverted airfoil," leads Walt Hansgen's Lister-Jag.

same as that on '62 Corvettes, though its independent rear end was a damn sight better for handling and control under acceleration and braking. Duntov's improvements were all free, so to say.

The XP-720 got Shinoda's Sting Ray body, almost identically. The first prototype had the now-familiar pointed fastback roof with a split rear window, but from the beltline down it was remarkably close—though marginally smaller all around—to Larry's original Sting Ray on the older, larger chassis. Even the high nose (which Mitchell and Shinoda *knew* created unwanted lift and wrecked high-speed handling) was transferred from Dick Thompson's racer direct to the production car. For the next four years, countless SCCA racers cursed Mitchell for the Sting Ray's dramatically flaring nose.

Mitchell became something of a maniac on the subject of this nose. The original car—running as a modified—needed only minimal headlights, tiny little bulbs, to meet the letter of the rules. To keep the same sharp-browed shape on a street car, they had to go to retractable headlights. They did. An indication of Mitchell's corporate power is that Duntov got his greatly improved independent rear suspension *only* by proving that its higher cost would be offset by a cheaper front suspension. Mitchell's headlights cost a bundle to engineer—they went through five complete redesigns before they got them just right—created dangerous aerodynamic lift, and were horrendously expensive to manufacture. But there was never any question whether the Sting Ray would have retracting headlights for '63. Ironically, in wind-tunnel testing, the slippery new shape turned out to have almost exactly the same aerodynamic drag as the old one. Mitchell's styling was an aesthetic, not functional, tour de force.

No matter. Everybody was proved right in the end. Corvette sales bounced from 14,000 in '62 to 21,000 in 1963. Prices were only a little over $4,000 base, and for another $600 you could have a 4-speed and 360 fuel-injected horsepower. Rough road handling wasn't too good, quality control was abominable, and the ride was surprisingly stiff for what was essentially a boulevard sports car. But even the myopically nationalistic British *Motor* called it "the equal of any GT car to be found on either

The Sting Ray racer in the team's Michigan shop.

side of the Atlantic." Strangely enough, the one thing *every* roadtester hated was the split rear window, a motif Mitchell fought desperately to get through Duntov's scrutiny in XP-720 form. It's the one feature, too, that really distinguishes the '63 "Split Window" from later Sting Rays. Still, it was deleted by popular demand for '64 over Mitchell's protests.

For most car magazines in 1963, the Sting Ray—particularly in fuel-injection, 360-hp form—was the fastest, quickest street car they'd *ever* tested. *Sports Car Graphic* got 0 to 60 in 5.6, 0 to 100 in 14 seconds, the quarter-mile in 14.2 at 102 mph, and a top speed of 151. With no trouble at all, Duntov's baby would suck the headlights out of Aston Martins, XK-Es, Ferraris, and all sorts of exotica that cost two to three times as much. The Sting Ray was so good for the price, in fact, that most people assumed that all the hyperbolic acclaim was just rabid journalistic blather. But it honestly wasn't. The early-series Sting Ray was head and shoulders above anything else around as a total package. And over the next four years it got even better.

Detail changes such as variable-rate springs, a one-piece rear window, less chrome trim, and 375 hp from the fuel-injection engine were made for '64, but little else changed. In 1965, though, Delco four-wheel discs appeared as standard, and after mid-year you could get the 396-cubic-inch, 425-hp big block

A '63 Sting Ray model during aerodynamic tests.

and go *really* fast. What the Corvette didn't need was even more weight on the front end, however, and the fuel-injection small block was still available through 1965. In 1966 a tacked-on hood bulge wrecked some of the car's smooth looks, and though the big engine was now out to a full 427, the car just wasn't as finely balanced, visually and mechanically, as the 375-hp fuel-injection '65 with four-wheel discs. For 1967, the 427 was smoothed out with three two-barrel carbs that *Car and Driver* admitted were "as smooth and responsive as fuel injection." But the big go-fast option was the incredible L88, a pure racing engine available to anybody who wanted one. Chevrolet didn't dare put a rating on it, but most experts estimate it at somewhere around 560 hp at 6,500 rpm. More than anything, the L88 was meant to make the Sting Ray competitive with Shelby's 427 Cobra for SCCA, A-production. It wasn't. At 3,200 pounds plus, the 'Vette was just too damn heavy. And unless you were a professional street racer, the L88 was just too much to actually *drive*. You kind of pointed it and prayed.

Genuine L88s are superb collector's items already, of course, particularly those that had the optional race package but weren't raced. Don't laugh. More than just a few speed-crazed thrill seekers managed to upset everyone from their minister to the local constabulary by crumpet collecting in what was just about the hottest factory machine ever to hit the Tastee-Freez parking lots of America. Particularly with outside factory Thrush pipes—the famed "off-road exhaust system"—the L88

was *it*. If you can find one that hasn't been beat to a pulp and you're really ready for what you're getting into, it'll easily be the fastest, quickest, meanest street car you ever sat in.

If you don't cotton to the idea of driving a Le Mans racer/Pro Stocker every time you go down the block, and if your ego isn't measured by the decibel level of your exhaust, I think *the* Sting Ray to have is a silver-metallic-with-black-interior 1965, 375-hp, fuel-injection coupe. Or maybe a '65 roadster with factory hardtop. You'll have more power than anyone really needs, four-wheel disc brakes, and the definitive Sting Ray body style, before GM started to muck around with hood bulges and side pipes. Get one with the optional genuine knock-off mag wheels and I guarantee not only will every teenybopper in the neighborhood start to look at you different, but your wife will think you're crazy, your mistress will tell you your jaw looks a little crisper, and your secretary will blush when she hands you file folders. *Besides* all of which, the damn thing can get fixed at any local Chevy dealer, there's an underground parts network that can build you a whole new car out of spares if need be, it should cost only about $7,000 for a really good one, *and,* if that's not enough, I hereby go on record as stating that if that goddamn bear doesn't double in value over the next five years, you can bring it back in 1984 and I will personally give you your lousy $14,000.

The '63–'67 Sting Rays were built under Bunkie Knudsen's tenure at Chevrolet, but they were Zora Duntov's cars. Knudsen was no Ed Cole, and though Bill Mitchell had enough swat to force the Sting Ray body over, he was really more interested in the super-smooth second-generation Corvair and the new Riviera/Toronado/Eldorado big body. He couldn't be bothered to interfere with Duntov on a day-to-day basis. In early 1965, however, Pete Estes replaced Knudsen as the head honcho at Chevy, and like the consummate corporate gamesman he is, Mitchell rushed to present a portfolio of new ideas that would let Estes put *his* mark on Chevrolet.

For a long time, the new Corvette was planned to be a mid-engine Ferrari LM replica with a "sugar scoop" rear window. But it just wasn't economically feasible within the shared components structure of GM. So Bill

Missing some chrome trim, the prototype '63 "Split Window" at the Milford Proving Grounds, 1962.

"Off-road" exhaust, 396 big block, hood bulge, and knock-off mags: Duntov's ultimate 1965 Corvette.

LT-1 meant the high-performance 350 V-8, almost a match for the 427 L-88 Stingray in 1972.

Mitchell had reliable Larry Shinoda design the outlandish Mako Shark, a personal/show car for Mitchell that eventually served as a preproduction styling prototype. The "Coke bottle" pinched waist of the Mako, removable hardtop, razor-edge fenders, long nose, short deck, and tiny cockpit all went into the production car. It was meant to debut in '67, but Zora Duntov had the introduction put off a year as he frantically tried to correct at least a few of the serious performance handicaps Mitchell's crazy body created.

For starters, the new car weighed considerably more, air penetration was even worse than in the original Sting Ray, the nose *still* lifted at speed, the retracted headlights blocked the radiator . . . the list went on and on. Sometime in there—in late '67 or so—Duntov's "special consultant" status on the Corvette was seriously undermined by Estes, and he no longer had the necessary corporate power to force through the track-oriented features he'd always insisted on. Without Ed Cole to protect him, Duntov was getting eaten alive by Mitchell's Shark. The Mako-based Corvette got bigger, heavier, softer, and more expensive . . . a two-passenger personal car like the Thunderbird in everything except name.

Happily enough, in late 1967 outspoken Steve Smith of *Car and Driver* wrote a scathing editorial on a Corvette the magazine was supposed to test, telling in minute detail why they'd sent it back to Chevy after deciding it was "unfit for a road test." Said Smith, "With less than 2,000 miles on it, the Corvette was falling apart." Predictably, things really blew up at Chevrolet. The upshot was that Duntov was once again given full responsibility for the Corvette, and Chevrolet Engineering had its collective insignia stripes publicly ripped off one by one.

Still stuck with Mitchell's pinched-waist body—hell, it's *still* stuck with it—the Corvette rapidly got better again. Called the Stingray from '69 on, it was available with the whole raft of racing options Duntov had developed over the years, plus some really incredible engine choices. The L88 was still there; Duntov timed his personal car from 0 to 100 in 8 seconds. Fast enough to make your ears bleed. There was also a mechanical lifter version of the new 350-cubic-inch small block called the LT-1 that was nearly as quick. Plus, absolutely the ultimate in street exotica, a dry-sump, aluminum *block* version of the 427 L88 called the ZL-1. What it did mostly was take 100 pounds off the front end. But offering them for sale also allowed Duntov to homologate the aluminum big block for competition and, incidentally, make it worth Tonawanda's time to cast up a batch. Ironically, because of heat transfer and detonation problems with the aluminum block, the iron block L88 could be made to give higher specific output over a long period.

Reliability was—and is—by far the biggest problem with any 'Vette from the '68–'78 period. *Consumer Reports* annually gave them the worst marks of *any* car, and as Allan Girdler pointed out in a *Car Life* road test years ago, "Things fall off, or don't work, or rattle." Unfortunately, it's still true. *Road & Track* discovered through one of its owner surveys that "the worst thing about Corvettes . . . is the workmanship—or lack of it." According to that magazine, only 18 percent of Corvette owners were unhappy with the quality of their '63–'67 cars, but 40 percent complained about their later cars.

Ironically, now that the Stingray was more of a boulevard car than ever, despite the big engines, the 427 Cobras finally got a bit long in the tooth for racing. Jerry Thompson won the A-production national championship in his Corvette at the ARRC in 1969, the first time since '62 that the 'Vettes hadn't been stomped by Cobras. As the competition disappeared, quixotically, the Stingray got better and better as a pure racing machine. The street cars, though, started in the luxury/personal car direction they occupy today—no longer fast, quick, agile, or particularly desirable in comparison to the early cars. Emission controls, bumper standards, and all the other federal paraphernalia have made them simply not very good, surprisingly expensive, and, ultimately, dull.

The Stingray package never *was* as good as the earlier cars. The current chassis isn't *that* much different from the disc-brake 1965 chassis . . . and the body is a lot worse. Total Stingray production has been much greater than that of the early cars, however, so from a collector's point of view they're not as interesting either. In '69 alone, Chevrolet pumped out more Stingrays than there are Corvettes from '53 to '60 inclusive. The only '69 to have—indeed, the only Stingray to have—would be a '69 L88. The ZL-1 would be fun to park in the garage, but it's just too much car for puttering around. As the ultimate you'll-never-guess-what-I-just-bought, a ZL-1 is probably a bargain if you can find a good one. Same with the L88, which would be a much more drivable package and worth only $7,000 to $9,000 right now. I'd get the removable hardtop myself, only because I like roadsters. The coupe is probably the one to have. Personally, though, you can go zapping away from stop-

lights and making your ears bleed all you want. I'll stick to a nice 1965 fuel-injection coupe with enough punch to dust off everything except you and your crazy L88 and the occasional 427 Cobra. I mean, enough is enough.

Cheetah

Bill Thomas wanted just one thing: to be Chevrolet's answer to Carroll Shelby. With everyone going Cobra-crazy in 1963, Thomas figured that just what GM needed was a similar competition-oriented, very high visibility car builder to blow Ford into the weeds. Unfortunately for Thomas, Chevrolet figured they needed a resident racing guru like they needed a poke in the eye with a sharp stick. Charismatic ol' Shel was definitely *in* at Ford, but hard-working Bill Thomas was so far *out* at Chevy he wasn't there at all.

Based in kar-krazy Disneyland, California, Thomas built up an enviable reputation over the years as *the* Chevy man. He specialized in things like sticking Corvette V-8s into the back seats of Corvairs and building a lightweight Sting Ray with a fiberglass Chevy II body and 400 hp called Bad Bascom. But best of all, he built the Cheetah. This was supposed to be Thomas's Cobra, but though it *was* capable of blowing the doors off the ol' chicken farmer's Anglo-American creations, Chevy wanted no part of it. Thomas tried like hell to build 100 and get them homologated for 1964, but the most he could bolt together was sixteen before the money tree withered away and he went back to race-tuning Corvairs. Nearly all the Cheetahs still survive, however, and they have to be just about the ultimate front-engine Chevy specials, Scarabs with another five years of technology under the skin. The Cheetah was not only more complex than the Devin SS, the Scarab, or Troutman and Barnes's Chaparral, but also faster and a lot tougher.

The Cheetah was the last gasp of the big-bore, front-engine, V-8 sports/racers that had dominated American racing for nearly two decades, but it was set up to be as close as possible to a mid-engine car. In fact, with 55 percent of the weight on the rear wheels, it *was* a mid-engine car, though with the driver behind the engine. Fact. Thomas set his 400-cubic-inch, 400-hp fuel-injected V-8 so far back that the Corvette 4-speed shared a U-joint with the differential. There was no drive-shaft at all. Conveniently enough, Thomas was able to do this with stock Chevy parts, because the Sting Ray's independent rear end bolted right up to Thomas's tubular space frame. He threw out the Corvette transverse leaf spring and used coils and his own trailing arms. But otherwise, there were a surprising number of stock Sting Ray bits in the little 1,500-pound Cheetah.

A really innovative touch for a road racer in 1963 was a full roll cage, which Thomas tucked inside a masterfully sleek coupe body on a short 90-inch wheelbase. He used a conventional independent suspension at the front and huge sintered metallic Chevrolet NASCAR drum brakes. Said Thomas, "If they'll stop a 4,000-pound stocker from 160 miles per hour, they ought to stop my little coupe." They did, too. And that's about all there was to the Cheetah; a huge mother fuelie engine, great brakes, super suspension with huge American Racing mag wheels and fat tires . . . and a lovely truncated aluminum gull-wing body. Later cars got fiberglass bodies, which is just as good, if not better.

In its heyday, the Cheetah was already obsolete for the modified class it was forced to run. If they'd been able to build that required 100, they could have run production GT against the Cobras, Sting Rays, and Berlinettas and absolutely cleaned house. As it was, chauffeurs like Jerry Titus and Ralph Salyer were forced to race against King Cobras, Cooper Monacos, Dan Gurney's Lotus 19B, and the overwhelming Chaparral 2s. Incredibly, though, Titus usually ran right up with the leaders; rarely first, but often second or third. By comparison with the *real* sports/racers, his dual-purpose coupe—tiny as it was—looked hugely out of place. It was probably the cheapest car on the track, too, for Thomas sold the Cheetah for only $10,000 in either race or street trim. Not only that, it was street-legal, more than you can say about any of its race-track competitors.

In the few years of the feverish mid-sixties when the Cheetahs raced, they built up an enviable underground reputation among West Coast cognoscenti that still lasts today. For obvious reasons, few if any of the Thomas Cheetahs got into outside hands. No Sunday drivers from Cleveland bought Cheetahs for churchgoing, and there aren't any in the hands of dumb high-schoolers who'll trade you theirs for a pack of prophylactics. Anybody smart enough to own a Cheetah knows precisely what it is and will want what's right. Today, that's $15,000. But look at it this way: you'll spend at least as much for a good Cobra, it'll be one out of 1,100 instead of one out of

Ralph Salyer in his Cheetah at Daytona, 1964; the last gasp of the front-engine sports/racer.

16 . . . and if you ever do meet some guy in a squat, mean-looking, hunkered-down coupe with outside exhausts and enough torque to turn rock to gelatin, he's *still* gonna blow your Cobra into the weeds. Hell, if Chevrolet had let him, Bill Thomas would have had a fighting chance at Shelby himself. His cars were that good.

Corvair Sprint/Stinger

Since we're among friends, I can speak freely and tell you that if you don't have much money but like interesting cars, Corvairs are *the* answer. And none of that paternalistic, Nader-inspired crap about rear engines and swing axles. "If you can't drive it, Sonny, park it," as my great-aunt used to say. Moreover, the national Corsa Club is incredibly active, even doing things like helping sponsor an SCCA D-production, championship-quality Corvair Yenko Stinger. Corvairs are *still* competitive autocross and Solo II cars, and a network of firms like IECO and EMPI make more after-market Corvair stuff than you would imagine possible. No other fifteen-year-old car is as painless to own except a Volkswagen, and who the hell's collecting *them?*

Another nice thing about Corvairs is that they're so easily tweaked. And for the purist types who would never modify a collector car, there were demon tweaks available right from the *factory,* or better yet from bona fide car builders like Bill Thomas, Don Yenko, and John Fitch. You can justifiably collect Corvairs in everything from nine-passenger van to full-blown road-racing trim, and the most expensive street Corvair in the country is worth less than $4,000. Aside from the Crosley Hot Shot, Corvairs are also about the only American collector cars that are spectacularly economical to run, easily averaging 20 to 25 miles per gallon. You won't get that from a Cobra, not that you'd care, but if you expect to *use* your collector car, good gas mileage can be a real boon in these troubled times. All

things considered, a Corvair is such a sensible buy that it would make a reasonable *first* car, let alone playtoy.

Even more than his landmark ohv Cadillac V-8 in '49 or his small-block Chevy V-8, the Corvair was Ed Cole's baby. Cole's sidekicks Harry Barr and Maurice Olley were the ones in actual charge of Corvair development, which started way back in 1955/'56 when GM felt the need to come up with something to counteract the incredible market penetration of the compact Rambler, Volkswagen, and lesser imported cars. It was something that the Big Three all felt. Characteristically, though, Ford's Falcon and Chrysler's Valiant were scaled-down full-size American cars; Cole's Corvair was a scaled-up European car.

Bob Benzinger was pretty much in charge of Corvair engine development from the very beginning until 1969 when production stopped, though it was Cole's idea to try a flat six. According to legend, Cole's private plane, a Beechcraft Bonanza with an air-cooled Continental flat six, provided the inspiration. In September 1957 Red Curtice gave his blessing and the Corvair—air-cooled rear-engine, rear-wheel drive, unit body, all-independent suspension—was on its way. All these characteristics were unheard-of engineering innovations within GM at that point, and when the Corvair finally appeared in late '59 it was the first American production car with a rear engine, the first in years with air cooling, the first GM unit body, and the first high-volume all-independent suspension in the United States. Much of the development thinking (like unit-body construction) that went into the Corvair ended up in other GM cars—and even some things that wisely didn't make the Corvair (like an aluminum block without liners) were resurrected for Cole's ill-fated Vega a decade later. At Chevrolet they don't talk much about the Corvair these days, but many of the manufacturing techniques that are commonplace now were first developed for Nader's nemesis.

Corvair styling was handled by Ned Nickles for the first series and by Ron Hill for the second. Poor Nickles has, among other things, the dubious distinction of being the one who put the portholes on Buick fenders back in the late forties. Ron Hill had a lot to do with middle-period Cadillac Eldorados. But sur-

John Fitch Corvair Sprint, still a bargain GT.

prisingly enough, they both came up with good, smooth bodies for their first mini-car. The first-series Corvairs are pretty boxy, but that was what a rear-engine economy car was *supposed* to look like in 1957 when it was styled. By 1962 when Ron Hill started on the second series for '65, it was already pretty evident that the Corvair would never compete with the Falcon and Valiant but was going to be more of a mini-Corvette. So the second series is all-around smoother, cleaner, prettier, and better. In fact, it ranks right up there with the second Camaro as the cleanest of all Bill Mitchell–era GM cars. It's more flamboyant than the first series designed by Nickles under Harley Earl, but both Nickles and Earl were near retirement and were designing a cheap transportation module. Ron Hill was still under thirty when he designed the Corsa for '65, and Mitchell has always been pretty young at heart. And, of course, they were designing a small sports car.

Built in a new addition to the huge Willow Run plant, with engines from the Tonawanda, New York, engine factory, the first Corvairs appeared October 2, 1959. They got a mixed reception at best, from public and experts alike. Although production totaled some 250,000 in 1960, rising to 329,000 in '61 and

dropping off slowly to 207,000 in '64, those standard Corvairs were not really very good cars. They had poor weight distribution—like 40/60; worse with air conditioning—a front sway bar only as an option, 80 hp, rudimentary rear swing axles, slow steering, stiff rear springs, and a 3-speed transmission. But the basic package was right. By 1962 you could get a TRW-turbocharged 150-hp Spyder with 4-speed, Positraction, heavy-duty suspension, and metallic brakes right from the factory for less than $2,500. With more than one horsepower per cubic inch in a 2,600-pound package, the Turbo Spyder ran 0 to 60 in under 10 seconds and would go about 110 mph, tops.

At this time John Fitch came up with his first Corvair Sprint. Now Fitch has nothing if not credentials. He looks for all the world like a tweedy Ivy League sociology professor but he's probably the most experienced American racing driver of them all. Fitch was a P-51 fighter pilot in World War II, a factory Mercedes driver in the Fangio/Moss era, the mainstay of Briggs Cunningham's teams in everything from Cadillacs to Jaguars, developer of the Corvette SS, designer and manager of Lime Rock Park, and just about the classiest person ever associated with automobiles on this side of the Atlantic.

In 1961 John Fitch took a Corvair Monza coupe back to Falls Village, Connecticut, and started making changes—*little* changes—that would make it go, stop, and, mostly, handle. Things like speeded-up steering, metallic brakes, a four-carburetor, 130-hp engine, air springs, and a rear camber compensator. He put on a distinctive appearance kit—vinyl roof, racing stripes, headlight stone shields, Lucas flame-thrower headlights, wood-rimmed steering wheel—and then he set it loose over the twisty little roads of western Connecticut. And at least in Fitch's expert hands, the little Corvair Sprint, as he called it, would blow the doors off anything even near its modest price.

Eventually, Fitch had a dozen or so helpers packaging Sprints and Sprint kits for Corvair drivers all over the country. Thousands of unassuming Monzas were turned into Sprints by either Fitch or private owners, for though the package was never intended for racing, it was a dynamite street GT. With the Turbo Spyder, Chevrolet went Fitch one better in the horsepower department, though the Sprint was still a much better all-rounder. The nice thing is that the Sprint bits could be adapted to the turbocharged car if desired, or alternately you could turbocharge a Sprint with no trouble at all.

Probably the ultimate pre-'65 Corvair would be a genuine assembled-by-John-Fitch-himself Sprint coupe with a little aftermarket engine work from the local Corvair specialist, but without the unreliable Turbo. With that combination you could easily get a reliable 150 hp in a chassis that can really make use of all that power. It's a better car than something like the contemporary MGB or Triumph TR-4 and just as ecologically sound and financially feasible. Compared with a 'Vette, it won't push your buttons very hard, but what performance it has is everyday, driving-to-the-A & P performance, not just once-a-year, stand-on-it-when-the-cops-aren't-looking performance. That has to count for something. The other nice thing about the Sprint—or indeed any early Corvair—is that they built well over a million basic Corvairs, so parts cars and run-of-the-mill spares are easy to come by. A good early Sprint shouldn't cost more

than $2,500 these days and is a very refined little bomb, indeed. If you're not into pavement-ripping, bellowing–V-8-type supercars, the Sprint's the answer.

In 1965 when Chevrolet changed to Ron Hill's larger, heavier, nicer Corvair to compete with the Mustang, all the aftermarket Corvair people jumped up and down and smiled a lot (except John Fitch; he's much too dignified for that). In factory trim, the new 164-cubic-inch Corsa put out 180 hp in turbocharged form, but since the new Corvair at 2,800 pounds weighed another 200, performance in a straight line changed almost not at all. Around corners, though, the Corsa was a whole new ball game. Zora Duntov got interested in the Corvair's swing axles and replaced them with a real fully independent rear suspension similar to the Corvette's. A U-joint at each end of the half-shaft kept the tire perpendicular to the road over bumps and eliminated the tuck-under that had hard-driven early Corvairs cornering on the outside rear sidewalls instead of the tread. There was now enough room to stick a decent amount of tire under the fenders, and a suspension designed to use it. The cars still weren't rac-

Flat black paint, fiberglass roof, Hands wheels, and 155 hp . . . a $3,000 Grand Tourer in 1965.

ers, but with a few modifications they could be super-successful autocross and rally cars.

The interiors and exteriors of the '65–'69s were so good as they came from the factory that Fitch found little to improve. The second-edition Fitch Sprint used the four-carb factory engine altered to get 155 hp. The Turbo was giving 180 hp at this time, but it was also a nickel rocket. Fitch's was better. He was able to make the suspension work a lot smoother, tighten up the steering and shifter, make the interior a little more luxurious, and—with the addition of a fiberglass roof extension, pints of flat black paint, and some really pretty Hands cast-aluminum wheels—make the outside of the Sprint look really mean. Fitch's second-generation Sprint wasn't the quantum improvement on the factory car that his first had been, mostly because the factory had borrowed many of his ideas and put them into their cars already. For less than $3,000 in 1965, though, Fitch would sell you a real European-style, built-in-Connecticut sports coupe that acted like a cheap Porsche. The price is still about the same for a good example today, and the performance hasn't dimmed a whit in the last decade.

In 1966 Fitch and illustrator Coby Whitmore got together to come up with the Fitch Phoenix, a $9,000 Corvair with a dramatically tense steel body welded up by Intermeccanica in Turin. It was intended to be a limited-production, high-class American sports coupe for refined types who thought Corvettes and Cobras too gauche. Unfortunately for Fitch, Americans absolutely *adore* gaucherie, and the expensive Phoenix never got to rise from the ashes of an introduction in Abercrombie & Fitch (no relation) among all the other expensive gadgets.

About the time GM corporate was deciding to abandon the Corvair in the face of government pressures and declining sales (fewer than 400,000 late-series cars were built in all, and only 9,000 of the 180-hp turbocharged Corsa engines in '65 and '66 before they were discontinued), Don Yenko decided to go Corvair racing. Yenko, the squire of Canonsburg, Pennsylvania, is one of the biggest Chevy dealers in the country, Donna Mae Mims's boss, and one of the wildest-eyed racers who ever got behind the wheel of a Corvette. He won B-production twice in the early sixties, when it was just about the most competitive

Jerry Thompson winning the 1967 D-Production national championship in his Yenko Stinger.

Cunningham's brute, the 1952 C-4RK, powered by Chrysler and styled by Dr. Wunibald Kamm.

Cited by the Museum of Modern Art, the beautiful Vignale-bodied Cunningham C-4 coupe.

Feminine and precious, Dutch Darrin's Kaiser-Darrin owes nothing to any other car.

The most collectible of all Corvettes, the 1957 hardtop with fuel-injected 283 and 4-speed.

One of the most delightful small-bore machines ever built, the Bertone-bodied Arnolt-Bristol.

Lance Reventlow's personal 1958 Scarab was not only an overwhelmingly competitive sports/racer but

Bill Mitchell's personal 1959 Sting Ray was not only SCCA C-modified national champion in 1960 but

everybody's nominee as the most beautiful racing car ever built and the one they'd most like to own.

everybody's favorite Corvette and the prototype for the 1963 production Sting Ray.

Loewy's 1963 Studebaker Avanti had tightly controlled surface development and a supercharged V-8.

The 1965 Shelby Cobra Daytona Coupe; intuitive and surprisingly lovely aerodynamics by Pete Brock.

Ford GT-40 Mark II, a 427-cubic-inch Le Mans winner, not subtle but with surprising grace.

Of all American sports cars, easily the best investment is Shelby's awesome 427 Cobra.

An all-American interpretation of the Pininfarina style—Bill Mitchell's 1973 Camaro RS LT-Z/28.

SCCA class. He also showed up at Sebring and Daytona and, well . . . everywhere, really, in a variety of big-bore machinery.

Anyway, in 1965 Yenko ordered 100 Corsa coupes (I told you he was a *big* Chevy dealer) and modified them into homologated D-production racers. The things were mostly fiberglass, with full-race suspensions and gutted interiors: the works. A Yenko Stinger is to a Corvair as a GT-350 is to a Mustang—lighter, faster, noisier, harsher, and tremendously more exciting. Yenko even gave them the same paint treatment—white with blue racing stripes—that the Shelby cars used. In order to get rid of the 100 Stingers he'd built, they were offered in 160-hp, 175-hp, and 190-hp versions, depending upon whether you just wanted to go fast around the block or were ready to tackle Bob Tullius, Jim Ditmore, and Jerry Titus in D-production.

Anyway, in 1966 Jerry Thompson and his buddies Dick Rutherford and Don Stoeckel of RST Engineering decided to go Stinger racing. Between RST and Yenko, the weight came down to 2,000 pounds and horsepower went up to 200+. Thompson qualified on the pole and won the first six races he entered but got beat in the ARRC by Jerry Titus in a Porsche 911. The next year, though, Thompson won the national championship. His car was later bought by Jim Reeve of Atlanta, who finished near the top of D-production in '71–'78, winning second at Atlanta's ARRC in '73, fourth in '75, and leading in '76 before he broke.

Yenko, on the other hand, made fifty more Stingers in 1969 and then moved on into turbocharged Vegas and all sorts of weird concoctions. For Corvair racing freaks—those who want to go Solo II, for example—a Yenko Stinger is the only answer. Good Corvair engines will make damn near 300 hp these days, and the cars still weigh 2,000 pounds. Prices are up to $4,000 or so for an unraced street Stinger, a bit less for a tired racer, more for a truly competitive mount. Reeve offered his championship car for $6,000 in 1976, but that's for a competitive D-production racer, not a collector car. In any case, it's just one more example of how versatile the basic Corvair concept really is. Particularly if you're a mini–hot-rodder at heart, the perfectly tweakable Corvair is the only answer. It's also the only true small-bore GT ever built in America.

Meyers Manx

Don't laugh. *Dammit.* People are *always* laughing at the Meyers Manx. Don't you be one of them. I mean, of *course* the little dears are cute and lovable and all like that. But so is Mary Tyler Moore, and nobody laughs at her. And besides, Bruce Meyers is maybe the single neatest guy who ever passed through the U.S. car business. Albeit, kinda like Halley's Comet—flashing on through almost before we had a chance to see him—but a true shooting star, nonetheless. And the Meyers Manx is one of the all-time great alternate life-style success stories. It took the moribund Kalifornia Kustom fiberglass body industry—about the only one who was doing well was Bill Devin, and he wasn't doing *that* well—and turned it into a double-throw-down big-budget success story. Of course, as these things have a way of happening, poor Bruce Meyers, who started it all, ended up bankrupt, divorced, and on the beach. But somehow, that seems to be the way we reward resident geniuses.

Meyers fits right in there with Bruce Brown and Hobie Alter and Ed Roth . . . they all found fame and fortune by catering to southern California's kid kulture in the sixties. The standard-issue surfboards and motorcycles and custom woodies were all a part of Meyers's background, too, along with a lot of experience building fiberglass boats and fooling around on the beach with anything that had big tires on it. Eventually, around 1962, he designed himself a little fiberglass body to take VW components and in 1964 went into production with a modified kit that bolted on to a shortened Volkswagen chassis.

Now today, everybody in the world makes a body kit for shortened VW pans. In fact, in most areas it's harder to find a crashed VW with a good chassis than almost any other single automotive item. Strange but true. Bruce Meyers started it all. He was the first to shorten a VW and stick it under a fiberglass body, and the world literally beat a path to his door. The Meyers Manx, the single-most-versatile vehicle ever designed, could be turned into anything from a pack horse to a racing car simply by choice of engine and wheels.

For example, nobody, *nobody,* used a

California classic: Bruce Meyers's 1964 Manx.

stock VW engine in a Manx. Ted Trevor of Crown Manufacturing made conversion kits that let you bolt in anything from a full-house Porsche six with 5-speed and 200 hp to a Turbo Corvair with 180. You could have a car for off-road, on-road, autocross, anything. Put great hulking sand tires on it and you could win the Baja 1000. Put road-racing tires on it and you could pull a measured 1.G under both braking and on the skid pad, which was better than a Formula One car in the mid-sixties. Unbelievable. But *Car and Driver* did it in 1967, and their instruments worked. No hanky-panky. Plus One Gee in both critical directions. Needless to say, the Meyers Manx made a dynamite autocross car.

Acceleration was whatever you wanted to bolt in. What the Manx didn't have was much top end. You could get 0 to 60 in 6 seconds with a Porsche motor, and spectacular quarter-mile times. But up over 100 or so, the bluff front of the Manx ran into all those little air molecules and that was that. If you were willing to wait it out, you could go pretty fast eventually, but the aerodynamics weren't too good. And with an 80-inch wheelbase, the handling got a mite twitchy. Still and all, in a smiles-per-dollar contest the Manx could beat almost anything with more than two wheels or three letters.

Bruce Meyers started his Manxery in 1964

and finally went bankrupt in '71. In between he built some 7,000 little cars. But other people built some 100,000 little cars, most of them pulled from molds taken right off a Meyers Manx. No court in the world would touch that kind of lawsuit, 'cause who's to say how something as simple as the Manx design should be protected? So the sharks ripped Bruce Meyers apart, all quite innocently snuggled within the close confines of the law. A lot of people made a lot of money off the Meyers Manx. One of them was *not* Bruce Meyers.

Once the feds got wind of the whole dune buggy movement—"Jesus Christ, Charlie, there's guys out there *building* their own cars"—the handwriting was on the wall. All those state laws that require wide, wide tires to be covered over with fenders are aimed at dune buggies. And stupidly enough, California and Hawaii, the two states where the sun-loving Manx was most at home, have the most stringent anti–dune buggy laws. So basically, the whole dune buggy movement—and B. F. Meyers & Co.—just dried up and blew away. There are still people selling fiberglass body kits; those will probably be with us until the government says, "No more." But the true Manx-type dune buggies are rapidly fading and soon, as with most everything else that's been fun lately, they'll go the way of off-road motorcycles, road racing, supercars, and hard rock.

Meyers lost money mostly because there were lots of people willing to crank out inferior kits at lower prices. The *real* Manxs are infinitely superior to the imitations, and if you decide to go sniffing around for a dune buggy, try to get a genuine Meyers Manx. For that matter, try to get one that's been professionally built. There's nothing worse than a completely cobbled-up dune buggy, and most of them were. The best of the lot are the Porsche-engined ones, I think, with disc brakes and intermediate-sized street tires. You don't need a dune buggy for climbing Pikes Peak, and the road to Ensenada is paved now. Set it up for pavement and go have fun.

A Meyers Manx is the nearest thing left to a sports car. A *real* sports car. Side curtains, hard to get into, drafty, noisy, but blessed with wish-quick steering, effortless performance, and a potential limited only by your own reflexes. Around $1,000 ought to be enough to pay for one, though the really spectacular jobs can cost over $5,000 and be perfectly well worth it. After all, you're getting not only a car but the physical embodiment of a whole southern California sociological movement, one of the most fabled fun cars of all time and a museum-quality example of simplicity in design that ended up in shows from the Pasadena Art Museum to the Tokyo World's Fair. Not to mention half the movies made in the sixties, most spectacularly *The Thomas Crown Affair.* A Manx isn't a collector car in the traditional sense, but it *is* one of the most significant cars of our time, and someday, some way, people are going to start wanting them around again. And at that point, you may as well be the guy with one tucked in his garage. Don't laugh. Crazier things have happened. Take Bruce Meyers and his Meyers Manx, for example . . .

Avanti

Most people just don't know what to make of Avanti Motors. Not Studebaker, now. We're not talking about Studebaker. Everybody had *them* precisely pegged. No, this is Avanti, which is very different. When Studebaker-Packard finally flunked out of the car business in 1964, a pair of irrepressible Studebaker crazies—Nate Altman and Leo Newman—dumped their worthless Studebaker-Packard dealership and bought the rights to produce the Avanti. They also scooped up a warehouse full of parts plus the original Studebaker wagon factory, a ramshackle brick conglomerate on the wrong side of the tracks in South Bend, Indiana. And after an eighteen-month hiatus to get organized, they started making their own version of Studebaker's ill-fated line leader.

A practical, elegant, blue-chip investment: Nate Altman's timeless Chevy-powered Avanti II.

This original 1963 Avanti, designed by Raymond Loewy's firm for Studebaker, has to be the best America

Normally, this sort of thing would be like building a freeway straight to the South Bend poorhouse. But that discounts Nate Altman, the most ingratiating salesman to pass through the automobile industry since Ned Jordan. Altman single-handedly took Avanti Motors—which even its strongest boosters will admit started under the worst sort of cloud—and made it one of the great industry success stories, starting flat-footed with nothing but a stack of debts and everyone's good wishes. And he did it in just a few years, besides.

How? Well, the Avanti body is one of the great all-time classics, maybe the best visual statement put on wheels in America since World War II. Unlike Bill Mitchell's clean Camaro/Firebird, which is really a U.S. interpretation of the internationalized Italian style, the Avanti is purely American. Pininfarina could never have produced a body with the nervous, histrionic surface development of the Avanti. Raymond Loewy is the designer

of record, but Bob Andrews, Tom Kellogg, and John Ebstein—all of whom were working for Loewy—are the guys who actually turned out the Avanti shape—in just two weeks, working in a rented house in Palm Springs.

Bob Morrison of Molded Fiber Glass made—and still makes, for that matter—the Avanti bodies. And the chassis is a modified Studebaker Lark Landcruiser station wagon, which honestly isn't as bad as it sounds. Studebaker's chassis was infamous as the "rubber frame," but it wasn't hopeless at all. I mean, the Avanti won't outcorner a Lotus or even a Camaro, but it *will* manage over-the-road, typical American driving as fast as anything you can name. It's not a car to go play games with on Sunday morning but rather an everyday, easy-to-live-with GT that's got more style than almost everything else around. And a pretty good dash of reliability, too.

Early Studebaker Avantis are much prized by Studebaker collectors. For which,

visual statement in decades, a modern masterpiece.

the hell with them. Nate Altman's Avantis are *much* better cars, and as far as Avanti connoisseurs are concerned, just as collectible. The axiom seems to be that *any* Avanti is worth at least 75 percent of its price new, and good Avantis are worth just about what they cost at the dealer. In other words, a 1963 Studebaker Avanti that cost $4,500 in 1963 is still worth $4,500; a 1978 Avanti II that cost $16,000 is still worth $16,000. The price parity is just a balancing out of inflation and collector-car appreciation. And though a new Avanti isn't four times better than an early one, it is at least twice as good.

Avantis since 1966 have used the same Loewy body and Studebaker frame, with a modified version of the Studebaker interior that's much more comfortable, and a small-block Chevy engine and transmission in place of the Studebaker parts. This has many advantages. The 327/350/400 Chevy is about ten times the engine the old 289 Studebaker is.

And as EPA requirements have gotten stricter, Chevy has kept in line, so the latest Avantis meet *all* the U.S. safety and emissions standards, from side-guard door beams to 5-mph bumpers, which is something almost no other collector car can boast. Even better, it was all done without mucking up the cars. A desmogged Avanti II is still capable of 0 to 60 in under 9 seconds, the quarter-mile at 85 mph in the low 17s, and a top speed of over 120. These days, that's high performance indeed.

The Avanti is one of those rare cars that's all things to all people. The Smithsonian Institution had one on display as an example of Loewy's fine design sense, so it's a bona fide work of art. Andy Granatelli took a few to Bonneville in 1963 and ran 170 mph in a stock-supercharged R-3 and 196 in a double-supercharged monster called *Due Centro*. With Koni shocks and wide tires on the optional mag wheels, you can make an Avanti II handle nearly as well as anything ever made in Detroit, despite a severe front weight bias. And on a day-to-day basis, for transporting the supine body from pillar to post, an Avanti has all the dull luxury of a Mark V. On long trips the remarkably spacious Avanti interior, usually upholstered in Connoly leather or some equally exotic fabric, is as comfortable a place to be as can be found on four wheels.

In other words, far from being a virtually unusable mantelpiece racer, the Avanti II is one of the few collector cars you can buy used or new, for a reasonable price, that you can treat just the way you would some clapped-out Impala. It will take all the abuse your kids might want to heap on it and ten years down the road *still* be worth what you paid for it. Very few cars will do this. There is really no such thing as a practical, everyday, blue-chip collector car, but the Avanti comes closer than anything else I can think of. If you have a family, or a hedonistic wife, it just might be the buy of the century. For a totally hand-built, limited-production (they've never made more than 400 a year) sporting GT, the price is ridiculously low. And because of the active Avanti club, there will *always* be a healthy market for the car when you want to give it up. What more can you ask?

Cobra 289

One bright September morning in the Year of Our Lord 1961, the smog-besotted heavens parted over the purple hills of the great Los Angeles basin to the vibrato murmurings of the Hollywood Strings. The Hand of Fate descended from the cumulus pillows in all its chrome-plated glory and touched down at Dean Moon's speed equipment shop, where it tapped Carroll Shelby on the shoulder. "Lissen, you damn chicken farmer," said Fate. "Strictly 'twixt you, me, and this stack of tires, Ford's got a super new little V-8 that'd fit perfect in some British sports car, and Bristol Aeroplane ain't gonna make no more engines for that little A. C. Don't say I didn't warn ya."

"Well, Ah swan," said Shelby. "You mus' be mah fairy godmother. Ah kin tell by yo' chrome-plated mittens."

"Well, it don't make no nevermind who *I* am. You just call Evans, *Dave* Evans, unnerstan', at Ford Motor Company. Tell 'im Fate sent ya. Oh, and one last thing. Call it a Cobra." Thus is immortality born.

Carroll Shelby, on the other hand, was born in Leesburg, Texas, with a broken plastic spoon in his mouth. East Texas, like Indianapolis, is the place where lots of famous people are *from* but where nobody *is*. Ol' Shel was a pretty unlikely superstar. He fought his way out of East Texas—a former dump-truck operator and failed chicken farmer—to become a highly paid "amateur" road racer. In his distinctive bib overalls—honest—the likable, gregarious, stoop-shouldered Texan with the funny accent became a crowd favorite. And he went fast. After a remarkably successful transatlantic career in sports cars, he linked up with John Wyer at Aston Martin to help win a Manufacturers' Championship in '59, won at Le Mans with Roy Salvadori, and did some minor things with the abortive Aston GP car. In 1960 Shelby developed heart trouble and was forced to retire after driving out the season munching nitro pills in the cockpit. By this time, he owned the Goodyear racing-tire distributorship for the West Coast, the Carroll Shelby school for racing drivers, and a little corner of Dean Moon's L. A. speed shop. In other words, he was pretty much at loose ends when the Hand of Fate tapped him on the shoulder.

Nobody's fool, Shelby called up Dave Ev-

When Carroll Shelby visited A. C. in 1961, this is the car they had—the Ace 2.6 Zephyr six.

ans at Ford. And sure enough, a couple of weeks later a pair of shiny new Ford V-8s arrived at Dean Moon's with Shelby's name scratched into the packing cases as if by a huge chrome fingernail. These were just about the first of the new thin-wall, 221-cubic-inch Ford V-8s ever seen outside the factory, and the only reason Shelby got them was that Evans had gotten the idea Shelby was a *very* big Texas oilman. Ray Brock, the editor of *Hot Rod*, stopped by about then to see Evans and his sidekick, Don Frey. They told him about their "oil-rich" Texan. "Sheeut," said Brock. "He's from Texas right enough, but he sure as hell ain't got a goddamn dime."

But by then Shelby had already called up Charles Hurlock at A. C. cars in Thames Ditton and had him shoehorning a Ford V-8 into a tremulous A. C. Ace. Now this was actually a pretty good idea. The Ace was just about the best-handling middle-sized British sports car, a real quality piece. And even though it had been around since before the wheel, it was still winning SCCA championships in the mid-sixties. A couple of engines had been used in it, including A. C.'s own anemic 2-liter, the rompin', stompin' Bristol/BMW 2-liter, and even a 2.6-liter English Ford Zephyr six.

The American Ford V-8 was obviously stronger than any of them but, amazingly, was lighter and smaller, too. This nice little.V-8 had come about because for 1962 Ford had to compete with the new Chevy II, Pontiac Tempest, Buick Skylark, and the rest of the "compact" market segment that had just started up. So they needed a compact engine for their compact Fairlane. Now when planning for this project was going on in 1959, the smallest V-8 Ford had was the 292 version of the extremely heavy big block that had been designed way back for 1954. It was a first-generation overhead-valve V-8 with all the limitations of early-fifties technology. So when the new smaller engine was put together, Ford used thin-wall lightweight castings formed around preheated core boxes instead of the older baked cores. All this meant was that manufacturing tolerances could be more closely controlled and the walls of the block needed less meat to allow for production variations.

The old Ford V-8s had a Y-shaped block the better to support the crankshaft bearings,

and this was eliminated too. The new baby engine came out at a short-stroke 221 cubic inches, 143 hp, and a total, all-up weight of 470 pounds, ready to run. At the same time, a 260-cubic-inch, 164-hp version was put together and, almost immediately, the famous 289 displacement. Conveniently enough, the 221 fit into the 225 Hydroplane boat racing class, the 260 into the 266 class . . . and either engine into an A. C. Ace with room to spare.

Even though he didn't have much money, Shelby had a good reputation in racing circles. And in 1961 Ford *loved* anything that had to do with racing. Way back, Henry Ford—*the* Henry Ford—was a genuine balls-to-the-wall racer who even set the Land Speed Record in Old 999's twin, the Arrow. He went only a big 91 mph back in Ought Four, but *still*. He was a racer and understood that racing *sells*. Fords were always good performance cars, particularly the flathead V-8, which absolutely ruled the hearts of America's hot rodders from '32 till '53 and beyond. But Henry Ford II never had that gut feeling for machinery his grandfather enjoyed and is emphatically not a racer. So during the fifties, when Henry II and his whiz kids were rebuilding the Ford Motor Company, racing was a pretty small part of their plans. Performance was measured at the showroom, not the race track.

In November 1960, however, Lee Iacocca replaced Bob McNamara as head of Ford Division when the chief whiz kid went to Washington with JFK. Iacocca later said, "It had really built up inside of me that we were going to go racing on all fronts." Iacocca believed totally in the youth-oriented "total-performance" image that Ford publicized throughout the sixties, and he got Ford into racing—and performance cars—in the biggest way possible. Iacocca was not a racer, but he *was* interested in high-performance cars, if only for their sales potential. As soon as he thought Ford had exhausted the promotional opportunity available through racing, he quit. But for a few glorious years there, in the boisterous sixties, Fords, Ford engines, and Ford money virtually kept international racing alive.

Incredible as it seems, between 1962 and 1967 Ford Motor Company not only developed the Twin-Cam British Ford engine that went into many Lotus models . . . and all the Formula Ford engines . . . and the aluminum

Shelby's 1962 assembly line—complete with covered-up Scarab—in the old Reventlow shops.

block, double-overhead-cam Indy-Ford . . . and the Cosworth-Ford V-8 for Formula One . . . but also the V-8 Falcon Sprint Rally cars and the Mustang, not to mention the single-overhead-cam 427 dragsters and NASCAR stocks, too. Between them, Carroll Shelby and the Ford Motor Company came up with the 289 Cobra, 427 Cobra, Cobra Daytona Coupe, GT-350 Mustang, Sunbeam Tiger, GT-40/Mark III, Mark II, and Mark IV J-car. All, really, in less than five years. Incredible. Never before in the world had one small group of men come up with so many diverse and successful, totally different racing cars, *all* of which are collector cars of the first magnitude today. There's not a rotten one in the bunch.

Within a few weeks after Dave Evans sent Shelby those engines, he was covering Ol' Shel's expenses. And almost four months to the day after he called Evans, Shelby was test-ing the first prototype Ford-powered A. C. In April the prototype was part of Ford's New York Auto Show exhibit, and mostly because of the excitement it generated in the "buff books," Iacocca just about bought Shelby outright in August. At that point a Ford engineer, Danny Jones, spent months sorting out the whole Cobra concept into a more workable, drivable package. And all of that was Ford money, too.

Shelby's first employee was young Pete Brock, Larry Shinoda's assistant on the Corvette Sting Ray project and later Datsun's all-conquering competition head. As soon as Shelby signed the papers with Ford, he had Brock and Phil Remington of Scarab fame start building Cobras in Lance Reventlow's old shop in Venice, California. By Christmas of 1962 they had built the required 100 Cobras to be homologated as a GT car, and Billy

Krause became the first factory driver. By car 76, the 260-cubic-inch V-8 grew to a 289. The price was only $5,995, which, though $2,000 more than a Corvette, was only $200 more than the A. C.-Bristol. How much Shelby had to pay for the A. C. rolling chassis isn't known, but since A. C. was fairly desperate and the volume was pretty high, considering, it probably wasn't all that much. Of course the engines came cheap, since Ford was bankrolling the whole venture.

Even so, the Shelby operation was never profitable. Ford underwrote the whole thing—production cars and racers—right up until 1968 when the last signature-model Shelby Mustangs were built back in Ionia, Michigan. In Iacocca's mind (rightly so), Carroll Shelby with his Cobras and racers and Mustangs was just a minimal advertising expense that more than repaid whatever Ford had in him through youth market goodwill alone. Shelby also allowed Ford to be involved in big-time international racing without incurring the unfortunate "overdog" image they finally bought themselves at Le Mans. Shelby-American also gave Ford experienced racing personnel for next to nothing.

For his part, Shelby gave good value for money. He got Ford into some winner's circles they wouldn't have visited otherwise and kept the Cobra name out in front on the street. It was a perfect symbiotic relationship. You have to remember, however, that though Shelby was undoubtedly the one who made out best from his involvement with Ford in the sixties, he was only one of many similar subcontractors.

Under Iacocca, Ford got more heavily into racing than any manufacturer in history. For USAC and Indy, Colin Chapman built Lotuses, and everyone from A. J. Foyt to Mickey Thompson has used the famous production-block-based Indy-Fords in a wide variety of machines right up until the present day. Backing up the independent but factory-supported folks like Chapman, Ford itself had a full-time USAC racing and engineering staff under the control of Dave Evans. For NASCAR and USAC, John Cowley was in overall charge of a program that funded everyone from Holman and Moody on the East Coast to Vel Meletich/Parnelli Jones in California. Such exotica as the single-overhead-cam 427 came

out of the factory stock-car program. Ray Geddes had a full-time staff in charge of sports car activities, which included Le Mans and the big European endurance races, rallies, and road races. And all of it was under the control of Leo Beebe, who became the head of all Ford's racing efforts.

As far as Ford was concerned, ol' country boy Carroll was just another little fish in a medium-sized pond. Shelby knew it too, but he was also smart enough to try to get bigger without upsetting anybody higher up the corporate ladder. What he did was concentrate on his Cobras and wait for Ford to ask him into the GT-40 program, which they did. They came to him, and Shelby made himself indispensable to Ford. But that's a whole other story distinct from the Cobra saga.

After Carroll himself, Pete Brock, and Phil Remington (whom they literally inherited from Reventlow when Shelby took over the old Scarab works), Ken Miles was the first important addition. Unlike Shelby, expatriate Englishman Miles—the man who designed the Scarab—wasn't easy to get along with, but he was probably the best car developer in America. While Shelby and Remington cranked out production cars, Miles and Brock concentrated on whipping the newly homologated GT racers into shape. The first time the Cobras appeared in international competition was Daytona in '63. Skip Hudson blew his clutch and broke his ankle. Dan Gurney, using an aluminum version of the small block that eventually became the Indy-Ford, blew his Welch plug and broke his engine and Dave MacDonald limped home fourth. At Sebring, where they had the 289 V-8s for the first time, out of five entries Cobras finished 11, 29, and 41. It was not, as they say, an auspicious debut.

The Cobras got better. Independent Bob Johnson won SCCA A-production; the factory cars of Miles, MacDonald, and Bob Holbert won the manufacturers' half of the new USRRC; and Holbert and Miles finished one–two in the drivers' championship by running their production cars in modified races too. Things were going so well that Shelby bought two mid-engine Cooper-Monacos and stuffed a 350-hp small block in each. MacDonald won *both* big West Coast autumn races, Riverside and Laguna Seca. Earlier in the year, too, Ninian Sanderson and Peter Bolton brought an

A happy Ken Miles winning the 1964 USRRC GT-class at Elkhart Lake in his factory 289 Cobra.

A. C.-entered Cobra into seventh at Le Mans.

By midsummer of 1963, the small-block Cobra was pretty much in definitive form. The standard engine was the same 289-cubic-inch, 271-hp high-performance version used later in the Mustang GT, though Brock and Miles developed a whole line of Shelby signature-model options that ranged all the way up in exotica to quadruple Weber carbs that helped to make 370 hp for the full-race version. The transmission was Ford's standard 4-speed Borg-Warner T-10. Differential ratios ranged from a tooth-puller 4.56 for drag racers that limited top speed to about 120 to a 2.72 that was theoretically good for 180 mph if you had the horsepower to pull it. Normal was a 3.54, top speed an honest 150. This healthy performance was available mostly because the A. C., with an aluminum body on a 90-inch-wheelbase tube frame, weighed a feather-weight 2020 pounds in street trim, complete with gas, oil, and water. This wasn't down in Bill Thomas Cheetah country, but it *was* lighter than the exotic Scarabs.

Aside from its build-it-yourself British top and side curtains, the Cobra looked pretty sophisticated. The flat nose of the A. C. Ace had been extended into a nice oval mouth with an egg-crate grille. Fat tires on wire wheels made it seem pretty mean, even though it was super-short—only 167 inches overall—and archaically narrow. Under that smooth body was where the A. C. showed its age. Even with 12-inch Girling discs on all four wheels and a new rack-and-pinion steering box unique to the Cobra, the basic A. C. layout had been around since the early fifties, and its suspension belonged on a Model T. That's not fair, really. The Cobra *did* have an all-independent suspension carried on lower A-arms at both front and back. It's just that the upper A-arms at both ends were formed by a single transverse leaf spring that looked like it belonged under an old Ford. The basic layout was pretty much that of the Corvette Sting Ray in the rear, though not as sophisticated in its geometry as Zora Duntov's carefully contrived suspension system.

No matter. With just as much horsepower and 1000 pounds less, Cobras were more than competition for racing Corvettes. At Nassau in 1963, though, a bunch of factory Corvette engineers decided to take their Christmas vacation in the islands and just happened to bring a handful of ultralight Corvette Grand Sports with them. The 'Vettes ran away and hid from Shelby's factory Cobras, running 10 seconds a lap faster. General Motors was still officially out of racing, however, so they gave Shelby little hindrance after that. But the point *had* been made, and everybody got it.

In the marketplace it wasn't even a contest. The Corvette was a real car—a mass-produced carriage with a heater, roll-up windows, a workable top—all those things that wives and girl friends demanded. The Cobra was nearer to a stripped street racer than anything else, probably the most unabashedly masculine production car since the SSK Mercedes. The modern, comparatively effeminate Corvette sold between 22,000 and 27,000 cars each year from 1963 to '67. By comparison, Shelby sold 655 Cobra 289s and 356 Cobra 427s—*total*. It was no contest. But then it was never meant to be. Enthusiasts dreamed up a Corvette–Cobra battle, but Ford and Chevrolet were fighting in different wars on different battlefields with different weapons.

Beloved of true wind-in-the-face, rain-in-the-ear, hard-core enthusiasts, the Cobra is the wildest street car ever built. Even in mild everyday tune, a 289 will run 0 to 60 in under 6 seconds, 0 to 100 in under 13. You pay for this performance, needless to say. Today a good 289 Cobra is worth upwards of $15,000, and special parts are correspondingly steep. But if any American car can be considered a blue chip, the Cobra is the one, and prices are guaranteed to go right out of sight.

Despite the obvious appeal, racing promise, and tremendous amount of publicity that Shelby, Ford, and the Cobras received in 1963, Leo Beebe, the head of Ford Special Vehicles (i.e., racing cars), got together with Iacocca and Henry the Deuce after Le Mans 1963. They decided that the Shelby Cobra, much as they loved Ol' Shel back in Dearborn, was just a dead-end street. And in a manner of speaking, they started plotting to put Shelby out of the car-building business.

But the plot goes even deeper. You see, sometime in February 1963 Enzo Ferrari let it be known through intermediaries that he would not be averse to selling out SEFAC and Ferrari Automobili to Ford Motor Company. Things went smoothly until June, when he actually met some of the people from Ford with whom he'd have to deal. No way, said Ferrari. I'm not selling my personal fiefdom to a bunch of hick bureaucrats. The Ford executives came away determined to beat the old sumbitch. As a footnote, there was no love lost between Ferrari and Carroll Shelby, either. Way back in '57 or so, Shel had been offered a seat in one of Ferrari's racers. On Il Commendatore's terms, of course. Instead of rolling over to play dead like most drivers when they faced Ferrari, Shelby got insulted. And then mad. "Ah'm gonna whip yo' ass someday," he said. And Shelby promptly took his patron, Tony Paravano, across town and bought a quarter-million dollars worth of racers from Maserati. Ferrari didn't need an interpreter to get the message.

Anyway, in late 1963, after they'd won just about everything they could in the States, both Ford and Shelby started thinking about whipping old man Ferrari's ass, just like they'd promised. There were two separate programs going on in '63 and '64 that eventually came together into one unified Ford racing effort. Out in Venice, Pete Brock, Shelby's resident design wizard, drew up what has to be the best-looking GT coupe ever designed. Built to fit the standard 289, front-engined Cobra chassis, Brock's aluminum coupe swept back from a surprisingly small radiator opening flanked by covered headlights to a super-smooth, low-cut top with extreme Kamm-chopped tail. It had outside exhausts, huge mag wheels, and enough spoilers, NACA vents, and aerodynamic aids to start a flight school.

Brock's coupe added nearly 25 mph to the top speed of the Cobra chassis, and with 370 hp it was good for 180 mph with Daytona gearing. The coupe first appeared at Daytona and became known, obviously enough, as the Daytona coupe. Six were built, and of all the Shelby cars they're certainly the prettiest, the nicest, and just about the best. The more sophisticated Ford GT-40s and mid-engine derivatives were raced by Shelby but weren't designed and built by his crew. The Daytona coupe, though, was a pure Brock/Shelby/Miles/Remington invention, one that, in fact, Ford engineers told them wouldn't work because Brock's intuitive aerodynamics would lift the tail at high speeds. Needless to say, the engineers were wrong.

Bob Holbert and Dave MacDonald led the '64 Daytona Continental with room to spare, until their coupe melted at a pit stop when the crew managed to pour gasoline on the hot differential. The highest-placed Cobra was fourth. At Sebring soon after, though, the Cobras finished 4–5–6–8–10 behind three prototype Ferraris that were expected to be faster than the GT cars. Both races were part of the FIA Manufacturers' Championship, which the Cobras came within an eyeblink of winning. The high point was fourth at Le Mans by Gurney and Bondurant. The low point was the Tour de France, where all three Cobras retired and lost the championship. In the United States, though, Miles won the USRRC, winning seven of nine races (Ed Leslie won the other two in *his* Cobra) and Bob Johnson won A-production again.

The next year was even better. The international team pretty much dominated long-distance racing, and though the Ferrari prototypes usually won overall, the Cobras took the GT class. By July 4, 1965, at Rheims, the championship was decided. In the States, the Cobras once again won the USRRC and, with the new regional championship system of the SCCA, took four out of six championships in A-production. For at least a year, Shelby ran Cobra coupes and GT-40s concurrently, and Phil Remington actually spent most of his time developing the new mid-engine factory racers. Judged against the GT-40—which was ungodly expensive and complex—the Cobra coupe was a cheap, simple, and effective solution to a succinctly stated problem. While the Ford GT-40 racing people were worrying about making the gearboxes last and whether their trick vented seat backs would work, the Cobra people were worrying about where to fit all the trophies on their mantelpieces.

But by '66 the handwriting was on the wall. The Cobra in street form was just too much for most people to handle, and besides, they wanted things like windows and tops. And at the track the day of the front-engine sports car was pretty much over, at least in international competition. Ironically, the front-engine Stingray Corvettes came into their own as racing cars only after Shelby had abandoned the field, and it's a fascinating speculation whether, if the Cobras had been kept in production, an evolutionary Daytona coupe might not now be winning the IMSA and SCCA races that John Greenwood's Corvettes contest.

Lew Spencer's beautiful Cobra Daytona Coupe, designe

Cobra 289 production stopped in May 1965 at Thames Ditton, and from then on Shelby sold only the 427 version. But A. C. kept making a hybrid, using the 289 engine in the all-new 427 Cobra chassis. A. C. sold them in England as the A. C. 289. Production of the English version continued until November 1968; 200 were built. The world total of 289 Cobras, then, is 855, three-quarters of which went to the States. Probably 80 percent of them are still around, and because of skyrocketing values, the supply should stay pretty constant.

Compared with the Cobra 427, the little 289 is handier, lighter, cruder, prettier, and makes a lot more sense on a day-to-day basis. For most people the 427 has to be a mantelpiece racer, mostly because it's such a handful. But the 289, though it's faster than almost anything except its big brother, is a bit more docile. It's still a man's car. The clutch needs a real set of calf muscles, the steering asks for forearms if not of steel at least of something stronger than pot metal. The hair-trigger throttle has to be eased on with superb control or else you'll find yourself spinning all the way from your driveway to the local drugstore.

On the other hand, if you can handle it, when you get its ears back, belly to the ground, and start that mother movin', a well-set-up Cobra is an absolute blast. You can get the rear end out anytime you want, of course, and if you're good enough, sit there steering with

Pete Brock, at Sebring in 1965.

the throttle. The brakes are great, the acceleration is tremendous, and if it gets a little wobbly when you're tottering on the edge between ten-tenths and eleven-tenths, that's part of its charm, too. And a built-in early warning system to get you to back it down a few notches before you start going sky-ground, sky-ground, sky-ground.

A Cobra is not for the "mature" enthusiast. It's a car that fits with a *Vogue*-thin blonde in $70 jeans, not a lumpy matron in Pendleton tweeds. The spiritual descendant of the Stutz Bearcat and Jordan Playboy, it's a car to drive, for sure. What a car to drive. And it's a fancy car to be seen in. But more, it's a magic car, a car in which to dream wild dreams, to chase down what those wonderful old Jordan ads called "the world's far edge . . . somewhere beyond the unfathomable sky—beyond the purple hills—where lies laughter and joy and smooth delight."

Ford GT-40/Mk II

Leo Beebe and Henry Ford II got together the morning after Le Mans in 1963. The lone Ford

to finish had been a British-entered Cobra way back in seventh, and they decided that if Ford Motor Company was going to lay its international prestige on the line, it had to be in something more substantial than a Cobra. This was the birth of Ford's Special Vehicles department. The most important man in it was Roy Lunn, who came from Ford of Britain. He had helped bring Aston Martin their one Manufacturers' Championship—including the famous Le Mans win in '59 with Carroll Shelby and Roy Salvadori. Roy Lunn, in other words, had credentials.

Lunn also had carte blanche to win Le Mans for Ford. The immediate and obvious requirement was for a mid-engine car, which meant all-new from the ground up. Shelby's busy operation was scarcely equipped to engineer and build a car from scratch, nor were captive American Ford shops like Holman-Moody. Indeed, Lunn determined that there was really nobody in America who could fabricate a mid-engine sports/racer. He went to England. Colin Chapman was already working with Ford and Dan Gurney on a pair of Indy cars. He was the obvious choice, except that he was also a strong-willed eccentric whom most of the American Ford people considered a pompous pain in the ass.

John Cooper was dismissed as merely a has-been Formula car builder on the skids, which as it turned out was a remarkably perceptive evaluation. The rising star of British constructors was obviously Eric Broadley of Lola; at the annual London racing-car show he had exhibited a 42-inch-high, monocoque mid-engine coupe built around a Ford 260 V-8 he'd scrounged from Jacques Passino at Ford. In mid-1963, it was probably the most advanced racing car in the world with an American engine. Coincidentally, it used the same Ford small block that Lunn planned to use anyway.

The plan came together at once. Broadley was signed to an exclusive contract to build revamped copies of his mid-engine racer, Carroll Shelby agreed to handle them at Sebring and Daytona, and John Wyer (former general manager and racing manager of Aston Martin, with whom both Lunn and Shelby had worked) was given a contract to race the cars in Europe. Construction of the first car started in November 1963 at Lola's Bromley shop, and

Eric Broadley's 1963 Lola-Ford prototype.

there were two ready by April. Lunn dubbed it the GT-40, because it was a GT coupe only 40 inches high.

At the mid-April Le Mans trials, Jo Schlesser wrecked one car and Roy Salvadori broke the other when the back end began to aerodynamically lift on Mulsanne, up around 200 mph, and put Salvadori into the notorious sandbank at Mulsanne corner. The entire 1964 season was that way for the GT-40. In all the endurance races started, not one car finished. Phil Hill set the race lap record at Le Mans, but otherwise it was a pretty dismal year. At the end of the summer, Eric Broadley quit to concentrate on Formula cars and the American Ford personnel went home, leaving the whole operation of Ford Advanced Vehicles to John Wyer in England.

In Dearborn in the fall of '64, Roy Lunn started work on a successor to the GT-40 called the Mark II. Basically, he took the 427 NASCAR motor (single four-barrel carb, 500 hp) and stuck it in the back where the little 289 had formerly lived. The big block weighed 200 pounds more but gave Lunn an additional and reliable 125 hp and twice as much torque to play with. As in any engine swap, the details took up more time than the big pieces. The heavier, more powerful engine meant faster speeds, which required better aerodynamics and much bigger brakes, which necessitated tougher suspensions, which meant even more weight, which required bigger brakes, ad infinitum. Even with most of Ford Motor Company working on the Mark II, it took almost

a year and a half before it was good enough to race.

In the meantime, just a few months after Lunn started on the Mark II, the annual social ball on the racing calendar, the Bahamas Speed Week in Nassau, was held. Even though most people went to party, Ford—and particularly Leo Beebe—went to race. John Wyer sent two poorly prepared GT-40s over from England, both of which promptly crashed because of a mechanic's assembly error. It was not Ford's finest hour. Now you have to understand about Leo Beebe. He had met Henry Ford II in the Navy during World War II and had become sort of his right-hand man. In 1965 he was the head of Ford Special Vehicles, a pseudonym for the racing department. Until Indianapolis the previous May, Beebe had never seen an automobile race, so he rarely criticized what the experts like Wyer and Lunn were doing. When he did, it was only to preface his observation with, "I don't know anything about racing, but . . ." After the Nassau debacle, he called a meeting of all the Ford racers in a local hotel ballroom. Said Beebe, "I don't know anything about racing, but there is one thing that has become increasingly apparent to me in the past few months. *You don't either.*"

In January 1965, Carroll Shelby—who *did* know something about racing—took over all Ford road racing. Wyer had a three-year contract, so J.W. Engineering was put to work building 100 replica GT-40s for sale to the public. This would allow Ford to homologate them as "production" cars. Priced at $18,500, the Wyer-built Mark III was sold over the counter to anybody who could pay the entrance fee. Fitted with Cobra-ized versions of the 289, these GT-40s were rated at 306 hp.

It goes without saying that a street GT-40 is pretty much a contradiction in terms. A GT-40 is a racing car, pure and simple. The street version is a racing car with harder tires. Anything that weighs 2,300 pounds on a 95-inch wheelbase, is only 40 inches high, takes a contortionist to get into, and goes like a bat out of hell is a racing car. The production cars used ZF 5-speed transaxles to give all-independent suspension, and of course the whole subchassis was really one huge aluminum monocoque. The nose and tail hinged up as one-piece units for access to the internals.

The GT-40 Mark III, a 164-mph, 40-inch-high, $20,000, mid-engined race car for the street.

Ford experts figure that about 75 or so GT-40/Mark IIIs are still around, virtually all in the hands of collectors. They do change owners, though, and the going rate for one in good shape—hell, almost all of them are low mileage, it's not the sort of car you drive very often—is a nice round $50,000, give or take a crumb or two. As a collector car, the GT-40 is considered just about the ultimate Ford, and already—less than ten years old, some of them—they're worth more than any other Ford model ever built. Twenty years from now, who knows?

Myself, I'd rather have one of Pete Brock's lovely Cobra Daytona coupes, at the same price. The GT-40 is a helluva car, sure. It's as modern as tomorrow, as tough a piece of pure, unadulterated single-purpose machinery as has ever been built. John Wyer's quality control was pretty shoddy, but that can be rectified with a little bit of restoration work. Unfortunately (and I know this is heresy), to me the Mark III looks like a Fiberfab Avenger, the sort of thing some benighted buff would bolt together in his basement on a Volkswagen chassis and never get the doors to line up right. So personally, I'll take that Daytona coupe for my mantelpiece.

While John Wyer was fulfilling the dreams of wealthy Ford nuts, Carroll Shelby was winning races. In February 1965 two GT-40s painted in Shelby's racing livery—dark blue with white stripes—came first and third at the Daytona Continental, with one of his

Cobra Daytonas in second. At Sebring, Ken Miles and Bruce McLaren finished second to the pure racing Chaparral of Jim Hall and Hap Sharp but were still the first of the GT cars. At Monza, McLaren and Miles were beaten by two Ferraris; at the Targa Florio, the single GT-40 was wrecked. At the Nurburgring, the best GT-40 finish was an eighth, behind a Cobra Daytona coupe.

Despite what was becoming a staggeringly massive inflow of dollars and man-hours, the GT-40s were doing worse, not better. By comparison, Shelby's Daytona coupes had cost almost nothing to put together. And they were not only equally competitive but more reliable. By Le Mans, the first two Mark IIs, top speed over 210, were ready. In addition, there were four GT-40s and five Cobras in the Ford fleet. At the end of 24 hours, Phil Hill had the fastest qualifying lap, Bruce McLaren had the race lap record, and the single remaining Ford was a terminally ill Cobra that placed eighth behind a raft of Ferraris. Once again, Ford's massive international racing program—which had now become something of a corporate fetish—had ended as nothing more than a monumental corporate embarrassment.

For 1966, the racing effort turned into a scary, monomaniacal determination to win at Le Mans. Period . . . no excuses. Hang the cost in dollars, hours, or people. The word came down from the very top: Henry the Deuce *will* win Le Mans. Virtually every Ford department started in June 1965 to prepare for Le Mans in June of '66. The unwieldy team was split among Alan Mann racing in England, Shelby-American, and stock-car stalwarts Holman and Moody. Kar Kraft, Ford's in-house specialty constructor, built all the cars in Dearborn; Shelby-American finished them up in California. Shelby's Ken Miles did most of the development testing, too. All summer and fall, Ford threw good money after bad, trying to build a Mark II that would last. With over 500 hp and top speeds near 220, the problem with the big 427 cars wasn't performance but reliability and consistency—which were more important qualities at Le Mans than raw speed. By February, for Daytona, they'd found what they needed.

Mark IIs—led by Miles and Lloyd Ruby—finished 1–2–3–5 at Daytona in '66. At Sebring, Alan Mann, Shelby, and Holman-Moody each had two cars to care for. Once again Miles and Ruby won, this time in a topless version of the Mark II called the X1. This was its only appearance, leading a pack of Fords in a 1–2–3 sweep. At Spa, Scarfiotti and Parkes in a Ferrari beat the Mark II fair and square,

though GT-40s were third, fourth, and fifth. And finally, Le Mans. Ford brought a veritable army to the Sarthe, some 100 people, eight racing cars, Holman-Moody's portable machine-shop tractor-trailer, and over 40,000 pounds of spare parts . . . more than enough to rebuild every car half a dozen times.

Ford's 1966 Le Mans win was an anticlimactic redundancy, which Beebe managed to screw up even then. Leo Beebe placed Mark IIs 1–2–3 at Le Mans, steaming across the finish three abreast. And still lost. Up until that moment, you see, Ford—despite the millions they had spent on racing—enjoyed an underdog image versus Ferrari. This was nonsense, of course. Ferrari's whole corporation wasn't much bigger than Henry Ford's office. Still, Enzo Ferrari was known as an autocrat, an iron-willed tyrant who dictated team tactics, chose winners, and generally ran international road racing any way he felt. And his cars had virtually owned Le Mans for umpteen years. A lot of people were happy to see Ford kick his ass.

On the Ford side, Ken Miles was an extremely popular driver with the public, an

Ford's GT-40 Mark II was the best endurance racer ever. This is Paul Hawkins at Le Mans, 1965.

outspoken sumbitch who made his way in the world on sheer talent, not on his abrasive personality. It was also well known that he had done most of the development testing on all the Ford racers and that the eventual success of the Le Mans program was due largely to him. He had also won Daytona and Sebring, paired with Lloyd Ruby, and dominated Le Mans with Denis Hulme. But about an hour before the finish, with Miles/Hulme comfortably in first and Bruce McLaren/Chris Amon trailing close behind, Ford racing director Leo Beebe decided to have a dead heat at the finish rather than let Miles win. Bitterly, two laps from the end, the fiercely proud Miles slowed down and let McLaren catch him, and the two went around side by side. As they crossed the finish line, Miles locked up the brakes. He let McLaren win by yards, his form of public protest against what he thought was a dumb, petty decision on Beebe's part. It was also one that robbed him of the distinction of being the first driver ever to win all three big endurance races—Daytona, Sebring, Le Mans—in the same season.

"If we had realized the whole world would take us on over it, we would have let Miles win," said Jacques Passino, too late to stop an avalanche of criticism that made Ford look ridiculous in its hour of glory. As the brouhaha continued, it became crystal clear just how much Ford had spent to win Le Mans's clouded victory. Coupled with their treatment of Miles, it all combined to give the company a real "overdog" image that did more harm than good. Simply letting Miles win would have been easier, fairer, and ultimately much more profitable. Leo Beebe had finally learned about racing; he still wasn't too good at PR.

After Le Mans, Beebe became marketing manager of Lincoln-Mercury and Passino took over the racing program. Passino decided to go back to Le Mans in '67 and *really* show 'em. Accordingly, Kar Kraft started building up a second-generation Mark II they called the J-car because it fit into Group 7, appendix J in the FIA rule book, the Can-Am cars. The plan was to run the Can-Am as a trial, then contest the big endurance races. Ken Miles, of course, was the development driver, the poor professional who gets to go out in a brand-new, totally untried car on an empty track and go as fast as possible to try to make

something break. On August 17, 1966, at Riverside, something did. Miles and the prototype J-car came crashing down the back straight at upwards of 200 mph, a blazing fireball shooting off flaming bits hundreds of yards into the California desert. Miles was dead before he hit the ground, his body torn from the car despite his seat belts and roll cage.

Miles was missed. No one else could sort them out, so the J-cars were pretty much dropped. The Mark II was still the favorite. At Daytona, the highest-placed one was seventh, behind a private GT-40. For Sebring, however, Phil Remington thoroughly rebodied the killer J-car, and though it was only a few miles per hour faster than the Mark II and weighed an incredible 3,100 pounds, Ford decided to use both. A rebodied J-car—now called the Mark IV—led a Mark II into first and second at Sebring. With this bit of promise, Passino went back to Le Mans . . . with six cars. And that's the year Dan Gurney and A. J. Foyt won—in a Mark IV. Gurney had been trying to win Le Mans for eight years and never succeeded. Foyt had never seen the place before the previous Tuesday. Between the two of them, though, they managed to bump the race average up almost 10 miles per hour to 135, set a distance record, and even win the Index of Performance.

Unlike the previous year, Le Mans '67 was a popular win for Ford. They promptly retired at the top, though John Wyer did come back in '68 and '69 with Gulf sponsorship to win with reworked GT-40s he called Mirages. After that, the Porsches and then Ferraris took over again. By 1968 in the United States, though, performance cars had died. A Ford GT-40 with emissions controls and safety door guards was a ludicrous proposition, as was a Cobra with impact bumpers. So rather than waste their time and energy battling a hostile government, Ford Special Vehicles and Shelby both shut down. The cars simply went away, just like that. America won't ever see their kind again: immaculately designed and executed works of art, crafted solely for the wonderfully existential goal of winning at Le Mans.

Racing demands the ultimate nihilism, the ultimate cynicism—the ability to see death and mechanical breakage all around you, to see years of planning, thousands of

man-hours, millions of dollars thrown away—
and merely shrug your shoulders in that age-
old expression, "So it goes." But racing has
its golden moments, too, the bright, sunny
highlands of the mind when the strong-col-
ored cars, as perfect as man can make them,
thunder through White House and beneath
the Dunlop Bridge, scattering silence before
them like the beat of angels' wings. Americans in American cars were there. Once.

Shelby Mustang

Carroll Shelby is a born entrepreneur. It's just
that before linking up with Ford in 1962 he
never had enough money all at once to really
make his mark. When the Cobra exercise
started, he had his Goodyear tire franchise
and his racing drivers' school. Three years
later he still had them, but he was also building two kinds of Cobras and GT-350 Mustangs;
putting the finishing touches on Sunbeam Tigers; developing the Ford GT-40 and Mark II
racing cars; partnered with Dan Gurney in
All-American Racers, the Eagle Formula One
and Indy programs; selling a whole line of
Ford performance equipment; thinking about
his charitable school for wayward boys and
girls, Carroll Shelby's special Texas chili mix,
deodorant, hair oil, and God knows what-all.
Somewhere in there he even found time to
write his autobiography. He also had a new
wife, a couple of new houses, and more money
than anybody except maybe Henry Ford.
Starting flat-footed from zero at age thirty-
eight, Shelby launched himself into Success
with a capital S. His autobiography ought to
be distributed in coronary wards as inspiration: there *is* life after forty with a bum ticker.

Easily the most popular of Shelby's cars
are the GT-350s. *Car and Driver* called theirs
"a brand-new clapped-out race car," and that
about sums it up. The situation was this: Ford
and Chevrolet were going head to head on the
race tracks, though nobody would really admit it. The Cobras had Corvettes beat all hol-
low in A-production, but the old 283 and 327

"A brand-new clapped-out race car," Shelby's GT-350 was

'Vettes dominated B-production. Besides, Cobras were too spartan and cost too much for
most guys to buy, so the only choices for American sports were the Fitch Corvair Sprint and
Corvette.

Now Ford didn't really have anything that
would make a good B-production car (nor a
sports car, for that matter), but they did have
the Mustang. It wasn't much, but it was something you could jack around pretty easily to
make into a vague semblance of a sports car.
Not only that, but in the mid-sixties the SCCA
was never quite sure how to tell a sports car
from a sedan. The most famous example—
aside from the Shelby Mustang—was the
Porsche 911. Now everybody *knows* that
Porsche practically invented the term *sports
car*. But the 911 had a vestigial back seat
which, if you gave it slightly thinner seat
cushions, left just enough head room so that
the SCCA would consider it a four-passenger
sedan for racing. Porsche 911s absolutely
whipped ass in the Trans-Am and SCCA sedan

meant as a low-cost street GT.

classes for two years before the board of governors finally wised up and changed the rule.

Shelby, ironically enough, was going the other way. Everybody knew the Mustang was nothing more than a Falcon with a long hood, which made it a sedan. So Shelby got hold of a Mustang fastback and pulled the damn back seat right out. And just so that nobody would think his Mustang wasn't a two-seater sports coupe, he put the spare tire right there where the back seat used to be—*pop*. And the SCCA said, "Sure 'nuff, 's got only two seats. Must be a sports car." So to prove the point, Jerry Titus from *Sports Car Graphic* jumped in one and won the B-production national championship for 1965, and Walt Hane won again in '66, too. And Freddie Van Beuren won in 1967, in *his* GT-350. The Shelby Mustang was a sports car, sure enough.

Now to make a B-production champion out of a Mustang takes a little work. The Shelby Mustang is quite a bit more automobile than a regular old Mustang, though not so dif-

ferent that you can't tell them apart. Shelby just went through the standard car and started pulling out unnecessary bits. Early on it became pretty obvious that there would have to be two Shelby Mustangs, for road and for track, as it were. The street car was obviously closer to the standard Mustang, so the easiest way to describe the Shelby version is to tell what's different. Starting with the 108-inch wheelbase, semi-unit-body Mustang fastback, Shelby stuck a big cast-aluminum sump on the standard Ford 271-hp, 289-cubic-inch V-8, along with a high-rise manifold, four-barrel carb, and fabricated headers. This gave him 306 hp at a nice 6,000 rpm. For the competition version, they just popped one of the race engines from the 289 Cobra into the Mustang and got a nice easy 350 hp; hence the name GT-350. Actually, you could get close to 400 hp from the small block with a little work, if you didn't mind that it blew up soon after.

The standard Warner 4-speed was plenty good enough, so it was left alone, though the race cars did get aluminum cases. At the rear, Shelby spliced in a limited-slip differential and heavy-duty rear axle from the bigger Fairlane, along with super-duper 10 × 3-inch drum brakes with metallic linings. The front brakes were Ford's optional Kelsey-Hayes discs with competition pads. Probably the most important change Shelby made to the Mustang was relocating the front suspension mounting points for better handling. Then he put in Koni shocks all around, trailing arms at the back, and a front sway bar. There was

Irving Hertz's gift to collectors, the Shelby GT-350H.

even a tubing chassis brace that went right across the engine compartment and tied the shock towers together.

The GT-350 also got fancy wide-rim mag wheels, big 15-inch tires, speeded-up steering, scoops carved into the rear fenders to cool the brakes, a fiberglass hood complete with scoop held on by NASCAR hood pins, little plastic windows in place of the standard Mustang airvents (on the '66s only), a cleaner grille, and a Yipes-Stripes paint scheme based on Shelby's race colors, either white with blue or blue with white.

Inside, the street cars got extra instruments, a wood-rimmed wheel, racing-style quick-release 3-inch seat belts, and optional rear seat cushions to replace the ones Shelby took out. Between Shelby-American, Ford, and a zillion other accessory places, you could also get anything you wanted for a Mustang, from a bolt-on supercharger to Thunderbird-like sequential taillights. The Mustang was a personal car not only in the conventional American sense—a smallish car with personality—but also in that you really could make almost anything you wanted out of it, from a transportation module to a Double-A/Pro Stocker.

Mostly, what people made of a Mustang was a hashed-up mess. The average early Mustang around today is owned by a seventeen-year-old, has big air shocks, extended shackles, reversed chrome wheels with Mickey Thompson tires, and three-inch-deep pink angora carpets. Even the average GT-350 probably has an eight-track tape deck cut into the dash and quad speakers dangling from the headliner. The major problem with finding one to keep as a collector car is finding one that doesn't look as though it's been rolled down a cliff and then resprayed by "We Paint Any Car . . . $49.95."

In your search through the garages of teendom, you may come across what is obviously a GT-350, but painted in black with gold stripes. Ah, yes. For those of you who don't remember, a minute of silent prayer for Irving Hertz, God rest his soul. In 1966, believe it or not, Hertz had Shelby build 936 GT-350s—no kidding—just like their standard, he-man street cars, except that most of them had Ford's regular 3-speed automatic with floor shifter. For $17 a day plus 17¢ a mile, which was pretty steep in 1966, anybody over twenty-five with a driver's license could play Ken Miles. More than one Hertzkar became a true rent-a-racer in B-production, and at least one GT-350H (for Hertz) had the dubious honor of racing its engine at Sebring in '66 in somebody's Cobra while the car sat in the pits.

All in all, Shelby-American built 562 GT-350s in '65 and another 2,378 in '66, rent-a-racers included. They range today anywhere from around $3,500 for a mediocre example to $7,500 for one that looks like it just rolled out of Shelby's shop at the L. A. airport in 1966, priced then at $4,500. In 1967 Shelby built another 3,225 GT-350s on the new, bulkier 1967 Mustang base. They also cost roughly $4,500 new and are worth about the same today as the early cars. Except they're just not the same. The early Shelby Mustangs are light, quick, hair-trigger cars. *Car and Driver* called the GT-350 "a real *guts* sports car with hair on its chest—all the way down to its navel."

By comparison, the '67 cars are soft, boulevard pony cars with a bunch of fake fiberglass scoops, spoilers, and "appearance options." The best feature on the '67s was a built-in rollbar on both coupe and convertible, which just isn't enough to make them worth seven grand. The later GT-350 still used the 289, but the 1967 GT-500 got a 428-cubic-inch boat anchor from the overblown T-bird. This was not the same engine as the fine NASCAR-derived 427 but a conventional (read *heavy*) Detroit V-8 that pretty much ruined the wonderful responsiveness of the original Mustang. Quarter-mile times dropped to under 15 seconds at 95 mph or so, but you didn't see any running SCCA road races. The early GT-350s were pretty decent race cars and exquisite street cars; the later GT-350s and 500s were customized Mustangs for people who never drove fast enough to tell the difference.

In '68 and after, Trans-Am racing Mustangs like the Boss 302 took over Ford's street-performance "image car" niche. Shelby sold his name, the Cobra name, and everything but his mother-in-law to Ford and went on to other, bigger things . . . like Carroll Shelby's Special Texas Chili Preparation. The last "Shelby" Mustangs were actually built by Ford Motor Company in Ionia, Michigan, after the L. A. shop had been dismantled. In other words, the later Shelby cars had nothing at all to do with Carroll Shelby. They are mere decal racers, decorated Mustangs with fancy paint jobs.

Unknowledgeable investors have driven the price of '67-and-up "Shelby" Mustangs to the levels asked for the genuine 1965 and '66 cars. Which is great—because it lets the enthusiasts who can appreciate the gutsy appeal of the *real* Shelby Mustangs buy the cars they want for prices that are considerably lower than if the speculators had zeroed in on them and driven the prices up to foolish levels. Sooner or later, though, the world's supply of genuine '65/'66 Shelby cars is going to be exhausted, and the prices are going to absolutely skyrocket. A word to the wise . . .

Sunbeam Tiger

"International" is about the only category the Sunbeam Tiger *really* fits into, but since the initial impetus came from California and the cars were sold only on this side of the Atlantic, I suppose it's an American car more than anything else. And seemingly like everything else that's interesting from the mid-sixties, the Tiger came out of Carroll Shelby's shop. It seems that one fine day in 1962 West Coast motoring journalist Bill Carroll—who was also a pretty fair country-boy driver—had taken his buddy Ian Garrad out to visit Shelby. Now Garrad was the California head of Rootes Motors, makers of such forgettable bolides as the Hillman, Singer, and Sunbeam Alpine. I take that back. The Sunbeam Alpine was a nice little E-production sports car that looked kind of like a shrunken '57 T-bird, with a capacious cockpit, sturdy frame, pretty body (originally designed by American stylist Ken Howes, who *had* worked on the Thunderbird), but with a serious dearth of *cojones*.

Anyway, Carroll—Bill Carroll, that is—took Garrad for a real white-knuckles blast up along the Pacific Coast Highway in Shelby's latest project, which just happened to be an A. C. Ace—which like the Sunbeam Alpine

was a nice little English sports car with no guts—hiding a 260 Ford V-8 under the hood. When he got back to the shop and dared to open his eyes again, Garrad allowed as how he was damn impressed with this Cobra. Shelby said something like, "Wha don' yo' stick one of them things in that there li'l sheeut box a yourn?"

Garrad was no dummy and, egged on by Bill Carroll, he dreamed he saw a whole new high-performance market stretching out before his now wide-open eyes. What Garrad realized, you see, was that the Sunbeam Alpine didn't weigh but a couple of hundred pounds more than the A. C. Ace. But it had roll-up windows, a nice, optional hardtop, a heater that worked, and a whole bunch of other handy gadgets that Shelby's car lacked. Even better, A. C. Bristols cost $5,700. Shelby's car would have to cost even more. But Garrad was practically giving away his little Alpines for $2,495, and no matter what it cost to drop a Ford V-8 into a Sunbeam, the result couldn't help but be a couple of grand cheaper than the more spartan Cobra. Garrad thought he'd found Sutter's Mill all over again.

Bill Carroll suggested that his friend Ken Miles—who still had an independent shop down the road from Shelby's—might be the one to make the trial conversion. Shelby said he'd like to take a shot at it, too. So Garrad nodded yes to both. Miles and Carroll could do a quick and dirty conversion to see how cheaply it might be done; Shelby would do a more expensive, more refined conversion aimed at real production. And so it happened.

Miles simply took a Fairlane V-8 with automatic transmission and dumped it in where the Alpine's puny 100-hp, 1725cc four had lived before. Mostly he put an extra 200 pounds right over the front axle, so even though the car went like the very hammers of hell in a straight line, it took three men and a boy to turn the steering wheel. Profiting from Miles's experience, Shelby chopped out the firewall so he could mount the V-8 farther back, put in the 4-speed and positive rack-and-pinion steering that he was also adding on the Cobra, and in general made a more professional, albeit more expensive, job of it.

Garrad sent Shelby's car to Rootes in England, and they in turn sent it to the Jensen Brothers to figure out a stronger rear axle. Jen-

Sunbeam's Ian Garrad conceived the 120-mph, $3,500 Tiger, a true "poor man's Cobra."

sen dug up a hefty Salisbury axle with a super-tall 2.88:1 differential ratio for quiet high-speed cruising. They also decided to chop away at the firewall even more and eventually got the weight distribution down to an almost perfect 51/49 in the production cars. Of course, you have to change the left rear spark plug through a hole beside the gas pedal, but what the hell. Jensen also added a hefty sway bar to the front and a Panhard rod to locate the rear axle.

Jensen's Tiger prototype then went back to Shelby, where the front sway bar grew even bigger, the engine got a wide oval air cleaner to fit under the low hood, and the bigger radiator got a necessary remote header tank. By the summer of '63, the first production cars were coming over to California, where Ol' Shel's crew cleaned them up, made sure the V-8 Fords were working right, and gave them back to Garrad to sell. For a piddling $3,499. Sheeut. Garrad really *had* discovered a gold mine. *Car and Driver* loved the car, and its readers voted it Best in Class in the annual *C/D* Readers' Choice poll. *Sports Car Graphic* called it "amazing value for the price . . . eveything you'd expect from a high-performance GT or sports car costing twice as much." Even staid old *Road & Track* thought it "a

Grand Touring car that is really grand for touring."

The standard Tiger came with the original 260-cubic-inch, 164-hp version of the Fairlane V-8, with a Warner T-10 4-speed. The performance—on regular gas—with the stock two-barrel carb was pretty spectacular for 1964 . . . or even 1978. In a 2,500-pound car, the Ford V-8—even with that incredible 2.88 rear end—would do 0 to 60 in 7.5 seconds, 0 to 100 in 23, and get through the quarter at 85 mph in only 16 seconds. Top speed was over 120 mph. And at 60 mph, because of the tall differential gearing, the engine was only loafing along at 2800 rpm. Of course, Shelby was never satisfied. Almost immediately, you could order through Rootes a 289-cubic-inch, 306-hp version that used the Cobra V-8. This car was good for damn near 150 and would go over 100 mph in the quarter. Shelby also started making tighter gear sets for the differential, and as soon as the SCCA classified the Tiger into B-production (dropped to C-production later on), full-race 370-hp Cobra engines found their way into the unsuspecting virginal confines of innocent Sunbeams.

The big problem with the Tiger on the race track—and the street, for that matter—was tires. The standard Sunbeam wheels were dinky 4.5 × 13-inch steel jobs that held Dunlop 5.90 × 13-inch rim protectors. There were some 5.5-inch mag rims available, but even those weren't much help. Without cutting and bulging the fenders, the biggest street tires you can get under any Sunbeam Tiger are 185-HR × 13 CN-36 Pirellis on 5.5-inch rims. They are just not capable of standing up to 200 hp or so. Racing Sunbeams today use really hefty rubber and flared wheelwells, but in 1964 you weren't allowed to go big enough on tires to transmit the power to the ground. And that was that. Tigers won some SCCA B-production races, but Shelby was more interested in promoting his own GT-350 in the same class. Although Tigers have won some fairly big races over the years, Garrad's good idea has never been a national champion.

The Sunbeam factory got interested in Le Mans in '64, however, and they had Brian Lister of Lister-Jaguar fame put together three brutish coupes. The engines were full-house 260s built up in England from Shelby parts, the chassis were heavily reworked, the suspensions were modified to take four-wheel disc brakes, and the fenders were cut away to allow really big tires and knock-off mag wheels. Fiberglass fastbacks covered huge fuel tanks and all the other normal Le Mans gear. In this form, the fastest Tiger coupe was officially timed at 158 mph down Mulsanne. Unfortunately, the Tigers were off 20 mph from Pete Brock's aerodynamic Cobra coupe, and the British-built engines in the Sunbeams went off like Roman candles in the race itself, spraying pretty showers of hot metal all over themselves and the course. Sunbeam didn't come back to Le Mans again.

Despite the lack of racing success, Garrad sold street Tigers as fast as Sunbeam could bolt them together. At the price—almost identical to that of the underpowered Triumph TR-4/TR-250—the Sunbeam Tiger was probably *the* performance bargain of the sixties. Particularly in 1967, when the 200-hp, 289 V-8 became standard in the Tiger II, there was just nothing on the American scene that could touch it for all-around performance. And taking advantage of the Cobra parts situation, an enterprising Tiger owner could go hunting much more exotic machinery with a real promise of success.

Unhappily, just about the time the Tiger went into production with its Ford engine in '64, Chrysler Corp. bought Rootes, eventually turning it into Chrysler U.K. Chrysler's 273-cubic-inch small block was just big enough so that it wouldn't fit under the Alpine hood without a major redesign of the whole chassis. And Chrysler just wasn't about to put that kind of money into a project with limited returns. Sportingly, the Tiger was kept in production for nearly three years after Chrysler took over, though the "Powered by Ford" emblems on the fenders were understandably changed to read "Sunbeam V-8." For 1968, however, the whole Rootes line was changed around and the Tiger was dropped. The Sunbeam Alpine V survived another year, then was replaced by a truly miserable dog of a car styled like a half-scale '65 Plymouth Barracuda and also called the Alpine. Chrysler's decision to drop the Alpine/Tiger in '68/'69 led directly to the removal of Rootes from the U.S. market and ultimately to the fight for survival that Chrysler U.K. has recently been losing.

Unfortunately, that makes the Alpine/Tiger an orphan. Fortunately, the engine and driveline parts are still used in Fords, and a number of specialty firms carry almost all other body and chassis bits. So the Tiger is a pretty painless car to own. Being a flimsy Rootes chassis and unit body to boot, the underpinnings are overly susceptible to corrosion, in the Northeast. Otherwise, though, Garrad's little cars are damn nice. At 156 inches overall, a Tiger isn't a very imposing

Lister-Sunbeam Tiger coupe at Le Mans, 1964.

car. In fact, it's downright unassuming. It's some sort of ultimate Q-ship sports car that will absolutely trounce almost anything you're likely to meet these days.

The definitive Tiger is the '67 Tiger II, with 289 V-8, egg-crate grille, factory removable hardtop, and mag wheels. Surprisingly civilized, it's a truly long-legged GT car that has the same sort of nervousness around town that the best Italian Grand Tourers have. Speeds in the gears are 40, 60, 80, and 120+, so most U.S. driving is handily accomplished in second. At the 55 speed limit, the biggish V-8 is just idling along, and with the 50/50 weight distribution and ample power, fast cornering works pretty well, too. "It's a car with dignity and asks to be driven that way. That doesn't mean slowly, necessarily, but that there's sufficient power on tap to embarrass the incautious. But if you treat it right . . . the Tiger can offer driving pleasure of a very high order." High praise indeed from the objective pages of *Road & Track*. And still true today.

For an underground classic that not too many people know about, Sunbeam Tiger prices are quite high, I'm afraid. A perfect restored example is worth $5,000 to $7,000 these days, and even good original California cars start at $2,500 and go up. And like Corvair and Corvette owners, Tiger club members seem to have a hot-rod streak. The average Tiger has accessory mag wheels and maybe fender flares; the extreme cars have outside exhausts, full-house Boss 302 V-8s, four-wheel discs, 8-inch-wide aluminum wheels, and God knows what all.

Like Corvairs, too, the Tigers are *very* competitive Solo II and autocross cars once you fit wide tires and wheels, and the Tiger club seems to be at least half amateur racers. That also seems to keep the prices up. On the other hand, even though Tiger prices are equal to or double Garrad's original $3,499 figure, Cobra prices are triple to quadruple their original price. In its day, the Sunbeam Tiger was called the poor man's Cobra. That's exactly what Ian Garrad planned it to be that day at Shelby's shop, of course. And it remains that today.

Griffith/Omega

When all those fancy imported car dealers saw what unassuming Carroll Shelby—a Texas *chicken* farmer, for Chrissake—had been able to do with the Cobra and then what Ian Garrad had done with the Sunbeam Tiger, everybody and his brother decided the freeway to riches could be traversed as quickly as possible in little English sports cars powered by hulking Ford V-8s. People were sticking Fairlane engines into *everything* back then in '62 and '63, from MG Midgets to Daimler limousines. If it was English and had a Ford V-8, it had to be another Cobra, right?

The most ambitious of these schemes was started by a Long Island entrepreneur named Jack Griffith, one of those irrepressible movers and shakers who are congenitally driven to bite off more than they can chew. Griffith was a Ford dealer, and his buddy Dick Monnich was the importer for TVR. You can guess the rest. The TVR was a funny little British specialty car, designed by Trevor Wilkinson, that had been around since 1954. It had a tube frame, an indescribably ugly fiberglass body, a teensy little wheelbase, no overhang, and a perfectly acceptable MG engine that gave it performance about on a par with all the other little Elva Couriers, MGBs, TR-3s, and suchlike scurrying about the landscape.

Griffith's scheme was easy. As David E. Davis tells it, "Griffith substituted his own surname for the TVR badge, and a great, chuffing 289 Ford V-8 for the MG part, thus changing it from a passive little car that did nothing wrong to a manic little car that did nothing right." The V-8 in Griffith's Griffith sat right over the front wheels, by God. On a wheelbase of only 85 inches, the 1,400-pound Griffith 200 pretty much pivoted on the front wheels to go around corners, with the insignificant weight of the rear just sort of fluttering out behind.

The stock Ford's 210 hp gave better than one horsepower for every 7 pounds of car, so the Griffith would run 145 mph and 0 to 60 in something like 6 seconds. I've driven a Griffith *once,* and vowed never to set foot in one again. My racing Yamaha motorcycle at 150 mph on the high banks of Daytona is safer than a Griffith sitting in your garage. If there was ever a killer kar, this is it. Flimsy, over-

Frank Reisner's first hybrid, the 1962 Buick V-8–powered Apollo GT styled by Ron Plescia.

powered, really vicious handling that will spin you out just accelerating away from the curb . . . there has never been a more dangerous production vehicle. For $4,500, Jack Griffith was doing a land-office business in rolling death traps and it's a lucky thing for him Ralph Nader wasn't on the scene yet or he'd still be peeking out 'twixt iron bars. If you ever need an expert witness, you can quote me.

Griffith built about 200 Griffith 200s, shipping bare chassis from Blackpool to Hicksville and shoehorning the engines in himself. Sometime around the autumn of 1964, Griffith got religion. He decided that if he was gonna do it, he'd do it right. So he got hold of Frank Reisner, another of these American automotive independents, a free-wheeling free-thinker who set out to carve himself a niche in the automotive realm by building classy sports cars in limited numbers at high prices. A Hungarian-born American who emigrated to Turin in 1958, Reisner rightly figured that the best place in the world to build a limited-production, high-performance sports car was down the street from the little independent craftsmen who supply parts to Ghia, Vignale, Scaglietti, and all the rest of the Italians making big limited-production, high-performance

sports cars. He called his Turin-based manufactory Intermeccanica, to make it sound more imposing than it looked.

Reisner, with his engineering degree from the Detroit-oriented University of Michigan and his specialty shop in Turin, was a natural for putting together American power plants in Italian-style chassis. About the first project he got was for something called the Apollo GT, a doughty-looking fastback designed by Ron Plescia, Milt Brown, and Newton Davis of something called International Motor Cars in Oakland, California. These three had the same delusions of grandeur that sparked everybody from Woody Woodill to Carroll Shelby, but sad for them, the Apollo wasn't very good. It used the unlamented 215-cubic-inch Buick aluminum V-8 that's now giving trouble in the Rover and Morgan +8, with an expensive all-steel body built by Intermeccanica. Reisner produced some ninety Apollos, not all of which were delivered and many of which he subsequently ate.

The Apollo did attract Jack Griffith, though. Once he'd decided to do something better than the TVR—which wasn't saying much—Griffith started throwing money around and generally acting like big time. He had Reisner engineer and build a very nice, sturdy ladder frame out of square tubing, to which they attached 289 Ford V-8 running gear. The rear axle was modified to take disc brakes, so Griffith could advertise four-wheel discs. Long Island stylist and illustrator Bob Cumberford drew up a very sleek and pretty coupe body that looked like the offspring of a Lotus Elite mated with a Ferrari GTO. It was long and low and very pointy, with set-in headlights and a high tail. Lovely.

Reisner built three dozen in steel, with welded-up unit body/frame assemblies, beautiful black leather interiors full of switches and gauges, and all that other neat stuff. And he shipped them off to Griffith on Long Island for the installation of Ford V-8s and transmissions. Somewhere along in here, which by now was 1966, Griffith had sold his lucrative Ford dealership and was using the money to bankroll the project with Intermeccanica. Except then he started to run out of money, and Ford backed out from its commitment, and there was poor Jack Griffith sitting on the beach in Hicksville with thirty cars without engines, no connections left in Detroit, a passel of outstanding lawsuits, and pockets full of sand. Jack Griffith had spent his way out of the car business as fast as he'd bought in.

Bob Cumberford had a lien of some sort on Griffith's leftover cars, and so did independently wealthy *Car and Driver* technical editor Steve Wilder. So Wilder and Cumberford inherited the ill-fated Griffith. Now they were sort of smart. The in-est of all *in* people at Ford (aside from Carroll Shelby, who already had a Ford-powered sports car) was the Charlotte, North Carolina, team of Holman and Moody. They were a lot more than NASCAR racers, and for a suitable fee they agreed

The sleek 1972 Intermeccanica Torino roadster.

to reopen the lines of supply to Ford and fit the Mustang drivetrain the Griffith GT had been designed for.

Wilder tried hard to make a go of it, but even his reserves of old New England money were not limitless. He changed the name to Omega to avoid Griffith's wrath, and got Holman and Moody assembling cars as quickly as they could. But it was no go. Even though Wilder tried all he knew, the money tree grew bare before the car-buying public ever became aware of the Omega. Reisner was left with 142 engineless cars sitting on the Turin docks, with nobody to ship them to.

"Hellfire," said Reisner, "I can do this better myself." So he did. He set up his own distributorship in New York and got a commitment out of Ford to supply drivetrains straight to Turin. He stuffed engines into those Omegas sitting on the docks and changed the letters on the hood to read "Italia." As of December 1966, young Hungarian-American Frank Reisner of Torino was finally in business building an Italian car with Dearborn components for American markets. Intermeccanica had turned out to be a pretty apt title after all. In 1967, Reisner added a convertible version of the two-seater Italia, which he logically called the Torino. The price in the States was $8,500. In the first three years, Reisner sold more than 500 cars. By the time Intermeccanica was driven out of the American market in 1974 by federal emissions and safety rules, over 1,000 Italias and Torinos had been bolted together.

Happily enough for Reisner, by 1969 he had enough extra cars to start selling them in Europe, too. His distributor in Germany was an ex-racer named Erich Bitter who arranged to show the cars to Opel. Opel was impressed. Now in the great scheme of things, there have been only two universal engines in the last twenty years. One was Ford's 260/289/302/351 V-8 as used in the Italia; the other was Chevrolet's earlier and ubiquitous—but surprisingly similar—small block 265/283/302/305/327/350/400 V-8 as used in Opels, among other things. In 1969 Opel and Reisner got together, and at the Geneva Auto Show in 1971 jointly introduced the Intermeccanica Indra. A sleeker Italia, the Indra was built just for the German market with a 327- or 350-cubic-inch version of Chevy's small block

The final mutation of stylist Bob Cumberford's svelte Omega, the Italia GT coupe.

stolen from Opel's line leader, the Diplomat. All the running gear was Opel, too. The Indra was a great success with wealthy German sports, and Reisner put together a whole new empire in Europe to replace the always shaky American market which, despite the fairly large number of Italias sold, pretty much ignored Intermeccanica.

Which is just downright stupid of the American market. Like every other lightweight European sports car with a huge American V-8, the Omega/Italia goes faster in second gear than many people will want to go at all. Zero to 60 in under 6 seconds and a top speed so high it's completely academic—130, 140, 150 . . . what difference could it possibly make?—exceptional braking from four-wheel discs, really thoroughbred Italian handling with mild oversteer for twisty little roads. And an all-steel body/chassis that's incredibly strong. Of all the specialty cars in the world, Reisner's Italia is among the most thoughtful, a car for which a long gestation period and numerous developers served to get all the details sorted out right. And that makes it very different from most specialty cars, even those from Turin.

Omegas use the drivetrain from the 271-hp, 289 Mustang; Italias use virtually identical 302-cubic-inch Boss Mustang parts or 351 Cleveland high-performance engines. In any case, the motors are as common as dirt, just about as expensive, and well-nigh indestructible. The steel body is more durable than aluminum if you're careful to keep it from rusting, and the straightforward interior, since it was hand-built initially, is easy enough to hand-restore the second time around. Probably the biggest problem with an Italia is electrics. Despite its American overtones, Frank Reisner's cars were still built in Italy and therefore suffer from severe constipation in their "spaghetti electrics."

It is standard procedure for many Ferrari and Maserati shops to completely rewire their customers' cars with American components—this is called "taking the pasta out"—so the intricacies of the Italia will pose no problems for any mechanic familiar with Italian machinery. Other than that, the Griffith GT/Omega/Italia/Torino/Indra of Jack Griffith/Robert Cumberford/Steve Wilder/Frank Reisner should be as lovely to own as many less interesting cars built by duller people without the larger-than-life tribulations of the Italia's creators. It's a good car, perhaps even a great car, and nine or ten grand will get you one. Just as beautiful and just as fast as any Ferrari, it's also a lot more practical . . . not to mention a *lot* cheaper.

Camaro Z/28

Sometime in the early autumn of 1968 or thereabouts, Bill Mitchell and Irv Rybecki sat down and started thinking about 1970 models, particularly the Camaro, which at that point was the brightest star in Chevrolet's galaxy. The Corvette was off in left field somewhere, but the "sporty car" market segment was a whopping 13 percent in 1967, with Ford's Mustang outselling the others two to one. And then there was the Trans-Am series, SCCA's modest proposal for the Sport of the Seventies. Chevy already had Roger Penske and Mark Donohue—the Captain and computeroid—to win the championship for them in '68 and '69. They were sitting on top of the greatest goddamn gold mine in the history of the world, and the only thing they needed to take home *all* the marbles was a high-style Camaro instead of that sharpened brick with the hideaway headlights they were selling.

Of course, when Mitchell and Rybecki were planning, they had no way of knowing that the bottom was about to fall out of the Trans-Am, the SCCA, and the sporty car market. They got all pumped up to spend millions of dollars retooling the Camaro, only to find out everybody else had gone home and they owned 100 percent of nothing. But that was later; after the fact. In 1968 a shiny new Camaro was just the thing that any bright-eyed, far-sighted auto division had to have.

Now Bill Mitchell has his faults, heaven knows, but he's maybe the sharpest guy in Detroit ever to screw a 00 point into his Rapidograph. And he had carte blanche to restyle Chevrolet's style leader. He could do anything, spend anything, as long as it was sporty,

beautiful, and most of all, *young.* The whole idea of the Camaro was to lure first-time new-car buyers into the fold so they could graduate over the years to a Nova, a Chevelle, and eventually that Impala Custom wood-grained station wagon that awaits us all on the other side of a split-level in the suburbs and our very own Little League nine. In other words, the Camaro was a Very Important Package.

Mitchell rose to the occasion. The restyled Camaro came out of the best era of GM styling, the same years that produced the Olds Toronado/Buick Riviera/Cadillac Eldorado and, later, the Vega/Astre and Seville. But the Camaro is the best. In fact, the 1970–'73 Camaro is probably the best-looking American automobile since Gordon Buehrig's 812 Cord. Bob Bourke's '53 Studebaker Starliner is right up there, and so is Loewy's Avanti, but Mitchell's Camaro is better.

Better, not more original. The Avanti is *un type,* a unique design that owes nothing to any other car. The second-series Camaro, on the other hand, was admittedly and openly inspired by Pininfarina's oeuvre in general and his fabulous Ferrari Short Wheelbase Berlinetta in particular. You can see it if you look . . . in the long hood and short deck; the single side window; the light, pointing front

Mark Donohue, the best driver/engineer since the war,

fenders; the trim, tapered quarter panels; the small, high-set, ovalish grille. Mitchell's Camaro is the SWB Ferrari inflated to double size and adroitly homogenized for the American market.

But there's not a false line on her. The Camaro is easily the most tightly controlled body to come out of Detroit, happily spared the Avanti's visual legerdemain and blessed with a smooth envelope of a body that fits with dignity and noblesse oblige into the most demanding of roles, that of the high-performance, sporting Gran Turismo. The more I study it, the more I'm convinced that this shape is nothing less than a restrained, tasteful, consummately expert body, the best that this country has to offer. Indeed, given the urethane noses and hefty bumpers that stylists must now contend with, it seems clear that the '70–'73 Camaro will remain the high point of this phase of American car design. Just as the Cisitalia 1100 is the one car by which Pininfarina will be remembered and the Maserati Ghibli is the masterpiece of Giugiaro's oeuvre, so the second-series Camaro will be the one people mean when they talk about the Mitchell style.

Happily enough, the '70–'73 Camaros can be more than just works of art; they're also pretty good cars. Not plain-Jane Camaros, of course. Any Detroit production car is merely a platform on which to erect options. The Camaro is no exception. So there is only one Camaro you can even consider collecting. And that's the fabulous Z/28. Now, in 1968 and '69 the Z/28 was really something. These early Camaros are lighter and tighter than the second-series cars, and the 302-cubic-inch Trans-Am engine is a true high-performance road-racing engine with all the sweet, turbinelike desire to rev that makes a racing engine, well . . . a *racing* engine.

On the other hand, after 1970, the Z/28 engine got a lot more civilized. But the 350-cubic-inch, mechanical-lifter small block in the later cars still makes 370 hp at 5600 rpm—which isn't half bad—and the car itself is so much better that there's no comparing overall packages. With either the close-ratio 4-speed—which is what most people ordered because they thought it was better—or the wide-ratio 4-speed—which really *is* quicker except on the race track—the Z/28 will blow the doors off most cars around. Quarter-mile times are in the low 14s at over 100 mph—which is *very* fast—and top speed was pretty much academic, depending upon what differential was used. With a medium-tight 3.73,

whelmed the Trans-Am competition in 1968 and '69 in this first-series Camaro owned by Roger Penske.

Chevy's answer to the GT-350, a 1969 Z/28.

Ferrari for Americans, the 1972 Camaro Z/28.

you could still get 130 mph without sacrificing acceleration. And though that's not as fast as an SWB Ferrari, a good Camaro Z/28 only cost $4,500 in 1970.

If you did it right, and lots of folks did, the optioned-out Z/28 is one helluva car. It goes fast in a straight line. It will pull .94G braking, according to *C/D* tests. It will pull .85G on a skid pad, which is also damn good for an American car, even one with antiroll bars front and rear. And with an all-up weight of 3,600 pounds—distributed 56/44—transient handling is more than acceptable, if not spectacular. And the car is only 188 inches long on a 108-inch wheelbase, which is also pretty small and handy for a car built in Detroit.

There *are* things wrong with the second-series Camaros, but even your wife isn't *perfect.* And given price, city of origin, availa-

bility of options to improve all the bad parts, and so on, the Camaro is a double-throw-down tour de force. I've a friend who's the editor of a major motorsports magazine, a bachelor, independently wealthy. He has, among other things, a collection of road-racing motorcycles that's one of the best in this country, and perfect taste in cars. He's also an incorrigible Italophile, running off to Maranello to sample the latest Ferrari the way you go down to the corner for Wonder Bread. In 1973 he decided that U.S. emissions laws and bumper standards were going to wreck automobiles as we know them, so he decided to buy *the* car to drive for the rest of his life.

It may sound a bit bizarre, but I have no doubt he'll still be driving it, perfectly kept, twenty years from now. He's that kind of perfectionist. It's a Camaro Z/28, of course, stock, except that he took off the factory Yipes-Stripes paint job and rear spoiler, which he rightly feels mucked up the car's exquisitely clean styling. The whole thing, Ziebarted and air conditioned, with all the right performance options and none of the junk, left him enough change out of $4,000 to pay for gas and insurance to drive it from New York to California. The point of the story is, this guy could own any car he wants, near enough. And as a drivable collector car, he chose the Z/28 . . . after nearly driving *me* bananas calling up in the middle of the night to discuss Maserati gear ratios and Ferrari oil-leak problems. He chose the Camaro not because it was cheap, but because, all things considered—like service and parts and performance and style and all-around panache—it was the best car for his purposes that he could find in the world. And weekly, someone offers to buy it for more than it cost new. Which, if not a lasting test of value, is a pretty good indication of popularity.

I've ridden more than a few miles in his Z/28—he won't let me drive it—and I'm always impressed by how *civilized* it is. In subtle silver metallic with a black interior, it has all the class of a Ferrari. And the Ferrari-owning women that he dates seem to appreciate the quiet, unhurried, masculine feeling the machine generates. I mean, all those women just *can't* be hanging around waiting for the right man to come by, ready to spot him encased in two tons of steel. But more than once

The mature Mitchell style, as smooth and clean as it's possible to be.

I've seen him work magic in Laurel Canyon or Beverly Hills, picking up ladies on the strength of his choice in cars. Me, I can't even do that when I'm in a Monteverdi. But it says something about Bill Mitchell's innate sense of style that his Camaro is definitely a star in what's a lot more than just a Hollywood Class-B status league.

Firebird Trans Am

John Z. DeLorean was once the brightest star in the American automobile industry. And in 1968 he was at the height of his powers. DeLorean was only in his early forties but was already vice-president and general manager of GM's Pontiac Division. He was an enthusiast, and he surrounded himself with a bunch of young engineers who were also into racing and sports cars and high performance. His right-hand man was Bill Collins, who later designed the DMC-12.

DeLorean also had crazy Jim Wangers, the best automotive PR man since Ned Jordan. Wangers is the one who single-handedly turned the Pontiac GTO into a teen-age cult car, to the extent of personally writing a top-forty surf-n'-strip song called "L'il GTO." He must be the only ad man in Detroit who had a rock-and-roll hit single. Then there was Herb Adams, one of the most engaging personalities in racing. Adams is the one who gained immortality by building his wife's 81,000-mile Tempest into a competitive Trans-Am car and giving it to Bob Tullius to race. Later on, he had a chrome-plated Oldsmobile—yeah, the whole car—that actually won an IMSA road race. Adams has a weird sense of humor, as you might gather, but he's a hell of an engineer.

There was a really good engine man named Tom Nell at Pontiac then, too, and there was even an independent Trans-Am racing team run by Terry Godsall and Jerry Titus. Jerry was one of the nicest men who ever sat in a racing car, and the world kind of stopped for a second when he was killed at Elkhart Lake in 1970. There were sundry others at Pontiac in those days, too, but the point is that DeLorean had assembled a tightly knit group of men who got things done.

Now that's a relative term, of course. At General Motors, every car design is made to serve at least double duty through the miracle of badge engineering. The Corvette belongs exclusively to Chevrolet, but every other GM car is shared among at least two divisions.

Canadian John Cordts ran a Trans Am in 1971.

So DeLorean was hampered by the corporate structure. But still, the most promising GM car in 1968 was the Camaro/Firebird introduced in 1967. Chevrolet got the sales edge with an earlier introduction, Roger Penske's Trans-Am team and the fabulous Z/28 street machines. To counteract this combination, DeLorean had to come up with an overnight image, one that would give the Firebird instant credentials among the younger drivers at whom it was aimed.

The first Firebird "Trans Am" appeared in the spring of 1969. The idea was to capitalize on Jerry Titus's racing success in a lim-

ited-production version of the Firebird. At the same time, and more importantly, the street Trans Am would allow Pontiac to homologate a whole bunch of trick aerodynamic spoilers and scoops that Adams and Nell had developed for the race car but that couldn't be used because they weren't "production." Now all this took time. Some of the easier changes appeared on the 1969 Trans Am—like staggered shocks, heavier antisway bars, seven-inch-wide wheels, and a rear spoiler—but the Camaro/Firebird was being redesigned for 1970 and a half. So rather than create a lot of expensive spoilers for a body that was about to go out of production, the Pontiac crew stuck with mechanical improvements that would transfer to the new car without change. Most important was a 400-cubic-inch V-8 with functional hood scoops that was rated at 345 hp. It wasn't a racing engine like the 302 V-8 in the Z/28, but it would drive the Trans Am over 130 mph with ease. There were 697 white-with-blue-stripes Firebird Trans Ams built in 1969.

The new second-series Trans Am appeared with the second-series Camaro/Firebird in the spring of 1970. This new Trans Am weighed considerably more than the old one—almost 3,800 lbs.—but it was a better car in every way. It was still white with blue stripes, but the body was a gussied-up version of Bill Mitchell's Berlinetta-inspired Camaro, with easily the smoothest styling ever produced in Detroit. The Firebird had a twin-nostril nose like an old-time Ferrari, and it was as lovely

The first-series Trans Am had plastic bolt-ons, a 400 V-8, heavy-duty suspension, and special paint.

as a big car can be. Herb Adams stuck a full-width spoiler under the chin that wrapped up and merged with the front wheel wells. A similar spoiler faired-in the leading edge of the rear wheel wells, to streamline the car when used with wide racing tires. Across the trunk there was a tall spoiler (shared with the Z/28), and the Trans Am got distinctive exhaust outlets, wheels, and functional air vents in the front fenders.

But the most necessary bit on the whole Trans Am was a functional, rear-facing scoop that bolted directly to the carburetor mouth and stuck out through a hole in the hood. This scoop had a trap door that opened under full-throttle acceleration to blast cool outside air into the engine. It was a Mickey Mouse gimmick on the street, but Titus's race motor gained gobs of horsepower from this homologated production component. The Trans Am limit was 305 cubic inches, and the racing car used a 302 Chevrolet V-8 that was somehow legal under SCCA rules. But the street cars had either 400-cubic-inch Pontiacs or "High Output" 455 monsters that made power steering a necessary option.

The Pontiac Trans Am was the last American Super Car and far and away the best. Even with emissions controls and safety widgets, the car got faster and better looking every year. And each year it handled better, too. Herb Adams and his guys gave the Trans Am front and rear sway bars, heavier springs and shocks, and progressive-ratio power steering that gave the car the best road feel in America. A good Trans Am from any year with any engine would run the quarter-mile in under 15 seconds at well over 90 mph and do zero to 60 in 7 seconds. Top speed was over 120 mph with normal 3.42 gearing. The best part, however, was the .85 G cornering, better than almost any imported sports car of any price, and absolutely remarkable for a car that weighed 4,000 lbs. ready to run.

The Trans Am was in production without change from 1970 till 1979, and it's the only performance car I know of that didn't get slower, uglier, or ridiculously expensive during that period. And indeed, on top of everything else, the Trans Am never cost more than $7,000 or so, even if you loaded it down with every option in the book. There were some black and gold Trans Am Special Editions with T roofs that always leaked that were pretty tacky, and the later cars had an optional Firebird decal that glued on the hood that was as tasteless as anything ever pasted on any car. But overall, the decade of Trans Am production was remarkably consistent, with nary a clunker in the bunch.

There was even one bright spot. In 1973, Pontiac introduced an optional engine that Tom Nell had been working on for a couple of years. This was a race-prepped 455-cubic-inch V-8, with exotic touches like four-bolt main-bearing caps, shot-peened rods, a high-lift cam, forged pistons, and cast-iron headers. It was the kind of unburstable engine that a die-hard enthusiast might bolt together out of aftermarket high-performance parts, and it was good for somewhere over 300 hp, SAE net, complete with emissions controls. Pontiac made only 1,100 of these engines in 1973 before the program was discontinued, and they were sold as the Super Duty 455. The SD 455 was a collector car from the minute it first appeared, and you could buy one new and sell it the next day for more than you paid for it, the demand was so great. A good SD 455 will cost you $8,000 these days, more than any other car from the Camaro/Firebird series, including the fabulous first-series Z/28s. If somebody offers you a clean, original SD 455, snap it up. It's not a subtle car, maybe not a great car, but it's easily the best-handling car ever built in America, it goes like scat, it's not that bad looking, and Pontiac's quality control was always pretty good. For everyday street use, one could do worse than drive a Pontiac Trans Am, and the SD 455 is the best of the lot.

"Last of the super cars," and still desirable.

Pantera

You say you *really* like expensive mid-engine GTs from Italy like the $30,000 Maserati Bora, $50,000 Lamborghini Countach, and equally pricy Ferrari GTC Boxer? But all you've got is $10,000? Is that what's troubling you, buddy? Well, step this way to Uncle Richie's Expensive Italian Sports Cars, Inc. . . . Money Talks, Ain't Nobody Walks. And feast your eyes on this little honey. Bright red. Yes indeedy. I'd say that there is just about the brightest goddamn *red* you'll see outside an aorta. Yessir. And low. Only 43 inches to the top of that sleek little roof. You can stick your hand out the window and tippy-touch on the ground. Yessir.

Big magnesium wheels, swoopy all-steel body, Z-F 5-speed transaxle with independent suspension, four-wheel disc brakes, 150 mph top speed. Mid-engine. Handles like a dream. And for you, today only, I'll make a special deal. Super-low mileage this one, only raced on weekends. Ha ha. That's a little joke there. For you, $9,500, and you drive it away this afternoon. What's the name? Well, DeTomaso. How 'bout Ghia? Ford? Would you believe Lincoln-Mercury? No, huh? I'm telling ya, you don't know what you're missin'. So what if it ain't a Ferrari, nobody's gonna know except you and your accountant. Yessir . . .

Honest. Probably the biggest bargain in the whole world of cars is the Pantera. It really is the equal of any expensive Italian hand-built GT in performance, handling, looks, workmanship . . . everything but price. Back when even Ferrari Dinos were going for $14,500 complete with Fiat engines, a blockbuster Pantera cost $9,800 brand spanking new. I'm firmly convinced that Ford Motor Company lost oodles on each one and only kept bringing the cars in 'cause they wanted to get old man Ferrari's back up. And develop a pedigree for their entire plebeian Ford line. I'm not kidding. In all seriousness—and the Pantera is a serious car—it was and is the biggest status bargain in history.

Like most exotic cars, the Pantera has an exotic saga behind it. It starts, I guess, with Alejandro DeTomaso. Born in Buenos Aires, he came by his curiously Hispano-Italian name legitimately. His mother was a Ceballos, descendant of the sixteenth-century Spanish viceroy in charge of Argentina. His father was a second-generation Italian who came within a whisker of being *el presidente* of Argentina before dying tragically at age thirty-nine. Alejandro left the country for good in 1955, his exit hastened by his nearly getting stomped to death by government goons after active and vociferous political opposition to Juan Perón.

DeTomaso raced factory OSCAs and Maseratis and won the Index of Performance at both Sebring and Le Mans in '58. He then started to build his own Formula cars in 1960, financed by his wealthy American second wife, Isabelle Haskell. After a number of eminently forgettable racing cars—including a beautiful prototype designed by Pete Brock—DeTomaso had his one bright idea. Taking a big handful of Isabelle's money, he designed a chassis similar to that of the 5-liter mid-engine sports/racer that Brock had bodied, and powered it with the ubiquitous 289 Ford V-8. Then he drove over to Turin from his shop in Modena to meet with Gaspardo Moro of Ghia.

Now Moro had inherited Ghia after the deaths of Gigi Segre and Gino Rovere, the two who had made Carrozzeria Ghia the most famous of Turin's free-lance designers after Pininfarina and Bertone. Ghia was actually owned by Rafael Trujillo, son of the Dominican Republic generalissimo. And Trujillo was just about out of money. Manager Moro had been staggering along trying to keep body and soul together. And then, heaven sent, over on the other side of Turin, Nuccio Bertone had a fight with his star designer, Giorgetto Giugiaro, *il bello bambino* of Italian stylists. Young Giugiaro had come to Ghia and revitalized the failing shop with his genius designs. So when DeTomaso drove in, Giugiaro naturally got the assignment to put a body on the Ford-powered chassis.

Giugiaro's new body was presented at the 1966 Turin Auto Show, *the* show for coachwork. And was it ever a hit. Called the Mangusta, the DeTomaso/Giugiaro mid-engine coupe stood only about *this* high and had gigantico mag wheels and fat tires—bigger on the back than the front, like a real racing car—and this angular, swooping body that was so right it looked like it'd grown in place. There wasn't any part you could single out

Giorgetto Giugiaro's masterful 1966 Mangusta is one of the greatest designs of our time.

and say, "There, *that's* what makes it so beautiful," but the whole thing was pretty enough to make you weep. The surface tension in the body development was so precise, so effortless, you got the feeling there was no other possible shape that would fit that space. It was, to be sure, an art object. But more, it was an organic, growing, *living* thing that changed as you walked around it, that made your heart beat faster just to look at it. Giugiaro's Mangusta was "toward a natural automobile" the way Frank Lloyd Wright's Taliesen was "toward a natural architecture." Giugiaro handled plastic volumes better than any Italian since Michelangelo.

DeTomaso made quite a few Mangustas in a sort of limited-production assembly line at Ghia's OSI subsidiary. And he got a little money together, and his brother-in-law, John C. Ellis of the Rowan Controller Company, a New Jersey electronics firm, got a little money together. And in 1967 DeTomaso Automobili bought Ghia. Outright. Trujillo got $650,000 in cash, at least some of which was used for bail money to get him out of a Caribbean lockup. Ellis turned around and sold his controlling interest in Ghia to Rowan Controller.

Giugiaro stayed around for a while after the DeTomaso takeover, then went off on his own to start Ital Design. Rowan and DeTomaso kept building Mangustas, acquired a controlling interest in Vignale—another old

Every detail on the Mangusta seems like the only answer to that problem, a perfect car.

Ford's 1971 Pantera isn't nearly as perfect as the Mangusta, but it's still a styling tour de force.

Turin coachbuilder—and pondered their next move. All this took another two years, during which Ford Motor Company wrapped up the Cobra and GT-40 programs and got into Trans-Am sedan racing. And found they really didn't have a corporate image builder to replace the brutal roadsters and knee-high coupes Ol' Shel and Honest John Wyer had been making. Ford still needed something to keep them dead-center or even a little left of center in the total performance market.

Ever since the Ferrari-buying fiasco of 1963, Henry Ford had been interested in having something in Italy to go with his new Italian wife. And of course, the Ford Styling guys were absolutely drooling to get their hands on some of the old-time prototype builders and metal craftsmen in Turin where they could get their latest brainstorms hammered out into real, working one-off cars rather than just Dearborn clay styling mock-ups. To put the icing on the cake, just as Eric Broadley had back in '62 with his Ford-powered Lola coupe, here was this crazy Argentine with a really gorgeous, Ford-based mid-engine coupe already sorted out and in production. It was an opportunity too good to miss.

In 1970, Ford Motor Company bought Rowan's share of DeTomaso, including Ghia and Vignale. Ray Geddes, who had been Leo Beebe's right-hand man on the Le Mans GT-40, Mark II, and Mark IV, was installed in Turin as vice-president of DeTomaso, Inc. And

he had the Ghia stylists embark on a crash program to restyle the Mangusta. The nose got lower and pointier, flip-up headlights replaced the former quads hidden in the grille, big side vents grew behind the cockpit, the glass areas melded into shapes easier to handle for production, and the car as a whole got, well . . . not as perfect.

The revamped Mangusta, called the Pantera, ended up in Lincoln-Mercury showrooms in mid-1971. The transmission was still the fabulous Z-F 5-speed, the brakes were 11-inch discs, the wheels were beautiful Campagnolo, genuine magnesium extravaganzas an inch wider on the rears than on the fronts, the coil-spring suspension was independent at front and rear, the unitized body/chassis was all steel, the interior was black leather, and the engine was the 310-hp version of the good old Cleveland 351 V-8. At 98 inches, the Pantera wheelbase was just nicely sized for a good compromise between high-speed stability and nimble handling, the all-up weight of 3,100 pounds gave quarter-miles at 14 seconds and 100 mph, and the top speed was a booming 150 in overdrive fifth. Even second was good for 70 mph, which left three more to go on the high end.

At only $9,800 delivered, the Pantera was an unbelievable bargain. It was everything a Maserati Bora should have been at half the price. The first Panteras were also not quite all Ford thought they should be, however, and cooling problems, engine problems, weak chassis, and lots of typical Italian spaghetti drove Lincoln-Mercury dealers crazy. For a while, Ford had the West Coast shops of Bill Stroppe just about rebuilding every Pantera that came into the country, tossing in a good $2,000 of modifications and then giving back lucky Pantera buyers a lot more car than they had a right to expect.

Geddes quickly got the message, and the Pantera rapidly got better. It grew a black rubber nose, the better to meet federal impact standards, and the chassis was considerably reworked. Along about 1973, Ford really had a car to be proud of. From the very beginning, they knew it would never meet the Federal bumper standards after 1974, so they planned to have the 5,269 they eventually built be all gone within four years after they'd started. Sure enough, just as the Pantera really got *good,* it flat went away.

So did DeTomaso. Ford bought his share of the company in 1974, and Alejandro went off to buy Moto Guzzi and Benelli and become a motorcycle tycoon. Ford kept the Vignale and Ghia shops together making prototypes and show cars. And the small flock of Panteras slowly flittered off from Lincoln-Mercury dealers. Even new, you could buy what was really one of the most exclusive, high-performance, high-style cars in the world, hand-built just like all those Ferraris and Maseratis and Lamborghinis, for less than an optioned-out pseudo-Thunderbird. It just didn't seem right, somehow, and a lot of people never *did* get the message. Which is why a perfect Pantera is still worth less than $10,000. Yessir. Sure you don' wanna look at this little honey again?

Cobra 427

I could see *it, the ultimate vision. I could see his body stretched out and pressing down tighter and tighter upon the V-8 engine until his thoracic cavity was practically bolted onto it. Its fiery combustions were his neural explosions and his neural explosions were its fiery combustions. His body and that roaring engine block were one and the same creature, sailing—at 140—160—180—200 miles an hour —2000 miles an hour—sailing!—at last, the winged American centaur, the American dream, at last: soaring over God's own good green Great Plains of America bareback aboard a 300 horsepower Chevrolet V-8 engine!* —Tom Wolfe, "The Mild One."

Carroll Shelby went Wolfe one better. *His* neural explosions were one and the same with a Ford V-8 with *500* horsepower. Shelby's Cobra 427 is the quintessential *American* sports car for the quite simple reason that it is nothing more than a lightweight set of wheels upon which to set a great hulking V-8 engine. The whole car, in a very real sense, is merely an engine accessory, no more important than a spark plug. Driving a Cobra 427 is the closest it is possible to come in this life to riding bareback aboard a thundering V-8 engine, and it's not something you forget too quickly.

The Cobra *looks* like a car. Bright red, red and shiny in the soft green summer light, like a fire department hose truck on a hazy Saturday morning when they're washing it down. Sure. And it's startlingly *small.* Honest to God, the damn thing is within an inch or so in every dimension of being a Volkswagen *Rabbit.* Got that? This is a 2,100-pound Volkswagen Rabbit carrying somewhere over 500 horsepower. Gives you pause, doesn't it? That's only 4

Sir John Whitmore at Oulton Park in 1965.

pounds per horsepower for those of you who weren't keeping count.

This, then, is some different car from a goddamn Rabbit. Those huge mag wheels, for one thing. Real knock-off hubs, too. And the tires. Car oughta *handle,* with incredible rubber like that on the road. Jeezus. This thing looks mean, no matter where you look at it from. Sort of scary, too—like it would just as soon take a munch out of your leg as sit there. Just kind of eyes you, quiet like. But you can see the muscles tensing under that smooth skin if you get too close. Mean. Don't *lean* on it. It'll probably bite your arm off at the elbow if you get too close.

Door handle's on the inside. Careful, don't startle it. Slide your right leg in first, snake it under the wheel, then . . . plop. No room for your knees, right? Driving position reminds me of a prewar Alfa. Wood-rimmed wheel right up near your chin, hip-hugger bucket seat that fits only if you take your wallet out; pedals too close. And that long, red hood stretching . . . grasping . . . out in front. The top of the windshield cuts right across your line of vision, so you sit up extra tall and look over the glass, like driving an Invicta with Brooklands screens. Christ. Can't see a damn thing.

What's this? The tunnel is big enough to hold a driveshaft carved out of a telephone pole, and that curving gear lever has all the heft of a Louisville Slugger. The Cobra is not a, uhhh . . . dainty car. You know the minute you clamber in, it's going to take some muscle to move that shift bat from notch to notch, and the steering's gonna take two hands. No showing off. Even the clutch pedal might need two feet, and God only knows about the brake. Anyway, you get yourself all nicely settled in for a long spell. Survey that double row of white-on-black Stewart-Warner gauges—the very best. Kind of aircraft. You know? Key's over there on the left, behind the wheel. Neutral? Waggle to make sure. Ready? Contact.

Holy Mother of God! Sheeut. No. It emphatically has *not* exploded. Those great rolling swells of noise, like the unrelenting Galveston surf, are what it's *supposed* to sound like. What? I can't hear you. What? It's okay. Oh. And the vibration. Honest, this is no exaggeration. Just sitting here at idle, the fenders are rocking maybe two full inches up and

Johnson's Cobra 427 posed at L.A. International Airport

down in time to the engine. Hell, the whole *car* is rocking back and forth on the suspension like a crazy thing. *You're* rocking back and forth in time to the engine. That big 427 just sits there and *throbs,* right in cadence with your heartbeat, like a Double-A Fueler. You can feel the motor right in behind your sternum—throb *throb* throb *throb* throb *throb.* Jeezus.

Lock your knee onto the clutch. Jam the old Roger Maris signature model into first. Eeaasee down on that throttle, gently up on the clutch and throb*throb*throb*throb* off we go in a faint squeal of tire smoke, just the slightest little twitch sidewise. And that's with no gas at *all.* Run it up to two grand in first. Get it all pointed nice and straight down the highway. All lined up. Now. Hold on tight, tense your back muscles and . . . *floor this sumbitch.* Yaaahoo! Shiiift. 4000–5000–6000. Shiift. 100 . . . 110 . . . 120 . . . Shiiift. Yaawoll. Ecstasy. You can't *hear* anything, and the vibration's so bad you can't *see* much, and your eyes are pouring out tears past your ears, and the wind's whistling, and your goddamn knuckles are clenched so tight the wheel's gonna crush in your hands. That pounding V-8 plays up and up and up on the little nerves in the ends of your fingers and toes, and your pucker string is wound up so tight you won't be able to crap for a week. Jeezus.

in 1965: 500 hp, 2,100 pounds, capable of flying from 0 to 100 and back down to 0 in under 14 seconds.

The blood's all up in the back of your head, and your eyes are seeing little red dots swimming around like baby amoebas on your corneas and throb*throb*throb*throb* the blood is charging through your body like gas in a neon sign, maybe 5,000 volts. Hell, if it was dark out, you'd be goddamn lit up. Hooha. The trees are streaking by into a tight green tunnel with a black ribbon, narrow as hell, right at the bottom. And you're balanced on the black ribbon, yellow dots streaking under your ass. Hoohaa.

Your neck is already stiff from fighting the wind and the damn engine is just goin' on and on and on. This incredible, painful, tortuous, wonderful envelope of noise. Somewhere up around 160, it starts to feel a little wound up tight, a hard metallic clamor that seems like it would *have* to shatter *something.* Your eardrums, maybe. The glass on the instruments. Hell, the damn windshield.

Enough is enough. Take your foot off the gas and let it roll. And roll and roll. The bark from those big pipes comes sucking back in, crashing and booming. Touch, just *tooouch* the brakes. And whomph. Like running into a gigantic pillow. This huge Claes Oldenburg soft sculpture of a pillow comes down across the road, ten-foot-high lipstick stain on the corner, and you run right into it. Whomph. And there you are, feeling kinda foolish, sit-ting in the middle of the highway, perfectly still, with only the incessant throb *throb* throb *throb* battering its way through your senses. The key. KEY. Silence. Jeezus. This is *it.* I mean, this is IT. Right?

A 427 Cobra is the most incredible experience in the whole world of automobiles. There are a few—damn few—racing cars that will accelerate faster: Turbo Porsche 917s, Can-Am McLarens, top fuel dragsters and funny cars. But when it comes to street cars, this is it. This is the ultimate. Listen to the numbers. A Jaguar XK-120—*the* hot car of the early fifties—would do 0 to 100 in 25 seconds. A Ferrari 275 GTB/4 will do it in 15 seconds. A good—now I mean a really *sharp*—fuel-injected Corvette from 1964 or so would go from 0 to 100 in just about 14 seconds. Which is very, very quick, I promise you, too fast for most people to handle.

Now listen carefully. A decent 427 Cobra—not the best, not the worst—a *decent* 427 Cobra will go from 0 to 100 mph and *back down again to 0* in less than *14* seconds. Think about it. A 427 Cobra will do 0 to 100 in less than 9 seconds. And 100 to 0 in less than 5. *Consistently,* time after time. Hell, all *day* and all *night* if you want it to. While that goddamn Ferrari is still struggling up to 100, the Cobra will already be sitting perfectly still, pipes crackling and brakes sizzling, having already been up to 100 and back down again.

How do you end up in this place? What would possess you to unleash such a wicked bit of savagery on the unsuspecting world, this brutal Frankenstein's monster of a car? Well, it was pretty easy, really. When Chevrolet decided to stuff their big-block 396 and then the 427 into the Corvette, Ford felt that Shelby had no choice but to match it. To Sebring in '64 Ken Miles brought a 427 Cobra prototype, which he understandably managed to crash, rebuild, and retire. While it lasted, however, the damn thing was positively awesome. Shelby never let on whether his personal Hand of Fate had anything to do with it, but the Cobra 427, once they got it sorted out, was just about the fastest front-engine racing car of all time, far and away the scariest handful ever sold for street use.

Much too much. A good 427 Cobra—they made 356 between mid-'64 and the autumn of '67—is now worth at least $25,000. But that's hardly relevant. To the overachiever who has to have the fastest, the quickest, the best, the big Cobra could cost four times as much and still be cheap for what it can do. The 427 is The Ultimate. But what a handful. Even though the leaf-spring suspension was switched to coils and the frame was beefed up, most of the dimensions from the smaller Cobra—hell, from the A. C. Ace . . . from the 1953 Tojeiro-Bristol, really—remain, includ-

The ultimate American collector car, Carroll Shelby's 427 Cobra, a Frankenstein's monster that sold for $6,00

ing that embarrassingly short 90-inch wheelbase. So a 427 Cobra will swap ends, and sides and middles and fronts for that matter, faster than anything, certainly faster than most people—including racers—can catch it. Scare-y.

This is not to imply that a 427 Cobra won't handle. There is so much rubber on the road that you can go whipping around high-speed corners so fast your spleen will end up in the passenger seat, and if you're good—I mean really *good*—the 427 Cobra is faster, point to point, than virtually anything else on the road. Period. Its ultimate limits are much higher than those of the smaller 289, and it will go, and go and go some more, till you just can't believe you're still on the road, whistling

1967 and can't be had for four times that today.

through a 90-mph corner at 140. However, and that's a *big* however, if you don't know what you're doing, the Cobra will turn around and bite you faster than you can scream for help. Like a canny dog, it senses whether or not you're really in command, and if you're not—watch out. Once it starts to go, there's no catching it. No gradual falling off, no reassuring understeer, just . . . nothing. And there you are, upside down in a pine tree. The Cobra 427 is not a car for the inexpert or the intemperate. It emphatically does *not* suffer fools lightly.

So you end up with a tremendously ironic contradiction. The 427 Cobra is the quickest car you can buy. In first gear alone, it'll easily break the speed limit and half again as much. But there's almost nobody around who's good enough to really push it. I only know one 427 Cobra owner who had the balls to drive the thing on the street anywhere near its limit on a regular basis, and he just got out of a private Westchester hospital after a year of plastic surgery to give him back a nose, cheekbones, and a jaw. When you hit something at 160, a Cobra 427 does not offer many places to hide. A Cobra needs constant attention, constant corrections, and a constant awareness of just what potentially lethal business it is that you're about. So it becomes the ultimate mantelpiece racer, a puissant machine of such verve that it needs a superman to drive it really well.

Personally, I can't imagine racing one. Just acceleration in a straight line overtaxes the limit of most drivers' reflexes. Corners are much too much even to think about. The combination of 200 mph in a chassis that's basically engineered for about 90 mph tops is not for me. I would *not* want to open one up in anger, thank you. I don't even like to think about it. The Cobra 427 is a damn brute is what it is, and too much car for almost anybody. Of course, that's the beauty of it, too, and the reason I'd give my eyeteeth to own one. Think of it. Bareback aboard a 500-horsepower Ford V-8 engine. The winged American centaur . . . soaring over God's own good green Great Plains. Jeezus.

British

CHAPTER 2

Sports Cars

In order to understand British sports cars, you have to realize that all the stereotypes fit. I mean, Englishmen really *do* have stiff upper lips under Guardsman mustaches, and forge empires on the playing fields of Eton and drive on the wrong side of the road and are a tough and hardy lot not made of sugar candy. They can be as relentless as the pounding surf at Devon, as foolish as the pier at Brighton, as magnificent as Westminster Abbey. They can be stupendous and stupid at the same time, a marvelous bundle of consistent contradictions. *All* the stereotypes fit: the good, the bad, and the tasteless.

There are more brilliant racing car designers in England than anywhere else, and despite its small size and limited resources, England has built more grand cars of all types than all the rest of the world combined. It's uncanny. Even stranger, an overwhelming majority of those grand British machines have been stripped-out sports cars. You'd think that places like sunny Italy would be where the spartan little roadsters with lousy weather protection would come from, and rainy, gray England would be the home of snug, comfortable coupes. Not on your life. Pininfarina and Bertone and Giugiaro are all busy drawing up sleek little GT coupes, and the stiff-upper-lip British are all soldiering on in drafty, wet, uncomfortable roadsters with no heaters, leaky tops, and flapping isinglass side curtains.

This isn't a recent happening. When Americans discovered sports cars back in 1946, the British were already three generations into an unbroken tradition of spartan, front-engine, upright roadsters that shows little sign of dying, even today. And unlike British sedans (which for the most part are worse than any car has a right to be) their sports cars are, given Ye Olde Englishe character that's so ingrained, really quite magnificent. If American sports cars—and cars, period, for that matter—are characterized by thumping great V-8 engines and simply shattering straight-line performance, British sports cars are characterized by archaic styling, conservative engineering, and an uncanny ability to get quarts of performance out of a pint pot. The best ones are ungodly fast for their size and light on their feet, have excellent brakes—and, though spartan, are lovable in a simple, outdoorsy sort of way.

America is basically a nation of Anglophiles, impressed as hell by Pitt Club accents, obscure titles purchased in the last century, and the old-line assurance that is bred into one at the right schools. So we've been favorably predisposed to accept British sports cars. Consequently, they are extremely popular, the prices are generally high and rising, and given the vagaries of modern commerce, parts are easily obtained at reasonable prices, all things considered. Because we are Anglophiles, I think we apply different criteria to British cars than we do to our own.

The people who Buy British—and I'm one of them, always have been, always will be, I suppose—aren't buying competence or performance in the empirical sense. We're buying a prop more than anything else, a physical embodiment of a state of mind. I *know*, for example, that rated on an absolute scale, a Bristol/Morgan/Jaguar/Aston is not a *great* car, not the way a Lancia/Mercedes/Ferrari is a *great* car. But I don't care. There is something about the very Britishness of their going that makes the way other people look at you, the way the rain beads on the hood, the elegant way you feel when you're sitting in one considerably more important than how fast it will go in a quarter-mile or how many tenths of a G it will pull on the skid pad. There are dozens of great British sports cars. It's all a state of mind.

More than any other group of cars, British sports cars are also the definitive collector cars. After all, they're *made* to have charm and elegance and a winsome, other-times, other-places appeal. And though they can be exciting and ego-expanding to drive, they give almost as much pleasure just sitting there, wire wheels shining, big spring-spoke steering wheel glistening, leather upholstery giving off that nostalgic musty, clubby odor like a dark, oak-lined drawing room on Portman Square. Face it: the average collector car spends most of its time sitting in a cozy garage rather than rushing pell-mell from A to B. And British cars absolutely excel at sitting still. I am *not* being facetious. The true test of a Corvette is at Island Dragway. The true test of a Ferrari is in the midst of a high-speed, swooping turn on the Autostrada del Sol. But the true test of a Morgan is sitting casually at the curb in front of Harrods, drawing a cooing crowd of Chelsea girls. Or, if you insist, in the midst of a gentle four-wheel drift—yes, they still have those in England—around a low-speed corner, with some bright little dolly in the passenger seat squealing and laughing.

The thing is, there are no, well . . . upper-class cars in England. The few remaining upper-class Englishmen all drive Ferraris or Monteverdis or Mercedes, or are doing some inverse-status thing with a black Mini Cooper or something. The only people who buy Silver Shadows are Rotarians from Iowa or Arabian sheiks with no taste, just cubic money. And as for the rest, why, British sedans are definitely, one might even say defiantly, lower-middle (or upper-middle, some of them). But they are still undeniably socialist bourgeois, cars that some lovable old pipe-smoking daddums like Harold Wilson could drive without feeling ostentatious.

The same is true of British sports cars. I mean, there's an implicit assumption in a bare-bones roadster with a leaky roof and hopeless side curtains that let rain and snow and slush in all over you. And that's that you'll never be wearing anything good enough that it will matter whether it gets wet and stained or not. Right? British sports cars are, with only minor exceptions that prove the rule, strictly for cloth-cap chaps, the middle-class backbone of England with their workaday clothes. And for cloth-cap Americans, too.

Our hopelessly bourgeois tastes are perfectly matched to British sports cars. Triumphs, Morgans, MGs, Healeys, even Astons and Frazer Nashes are for the sort of enthusiasts who get out themselves and tinker on Sunday mornings, not the sort who have legions of mechanics to call upon. And since we like to wade in there with tools and greasy rags and such, that mechanical approachability can be a real godsend if you've ever been staggered in the face of a Ferrari valve job or died trying to disassemble a Mercedes fuel injection system. When you're doing your own work and paying your own bills, there's something to be said for mechanical simplicity, straightforward design, and honest—not elaborate—construction.

All in all, British sports cars are most of all, well . . . British, with all the good and bad that implies. Primarily they're youthful cars, built for kids who don't dress up, who do their own work, don't have tons of money, and still want as much excitement per dollar as possible. The cars aren't spectacular, most of them, but they *are* fun, quick, lively—lithe, even—with a steadfastness that's missing from so many of the queer and flighty cars there are in the world. And they are beloved; that's the other thing. You can have a short, passionate affair with a Ferrari, or a successful marriage with a Porsche, but it's hard to *love* either one.

Morgans and Jaguars and Astons, however, have the kind of looks that never fail to leave you breathless, the teasing kind of humor that keeps you unfailingly on your toes, the wonderful unpredictability that makes a lifelong love something to look forward to. At the very least, it won't be dull. She'll be charming, quirky, a little crazy, and the toast will be burned more often than not. But you'll love her just the same, silly faults and all, for the wonderful moments you'll share. A man could love a car like that. A *British* sports car.

MG-TC/TD/TF

These days, it's almost impossible to convey the mystical reverence in which British cars—particularly sports cars—were held in the halcyon days of inflation right after World War II. The anemic, upright, topless roadsters that tentatively wobbled their way over here may have been old hat in Europe, but in America they were an absolute revelation. The most revered of all came from MG, though in 1947 you would have been hard pressed to find somebody to tell you what MG even *meant.*

Maurice Ginsberg, Monkey Glands, and Mighty Good were the wise-ass answers that socialite Miles Collier, the prewar MG importer, had been in the habit of giving peasants rude enough to ask what the initials in the "sacred octagon" on the radiator stood for. This condescending habit was picked up by snobbish owners of postwar MGs, too. In actual fact, by 1945, when MG restarted production (one of the first European car companies to do so) the initials didn't really mean anything. The new M.G. Car Company had very little to do with the old Morris Garages firm of the twenties and thirties. Cecil Kimber was dead, you see, and Kimber *was* MG.

The MG saga is so well known that it's practically carved in stone in Westminster Abbey. But it's a good tale nonetheless. In high-speed summary, William Morris, the Henry Ford of the British automobile industry, controlled not only his own Oxford-based Morris motorcar empire but a number of ancillary businesses. One of these was The Oxford Garage, which later expanded to become The Morris Garages. Cecil Kimber, scion of a wealthy family who in the best Victorian tradition cut him off without a cent because of his untoward interest in motorcycles, came to work for Morris in 1921. He took over The Morris Garages within the year. Immediately, Kimber began modifying the rather dull line of standard Morrises with lightweight bodywork and revamped suspensions to produce classic British hot rods. He did this for three years before, with typical English logic, he produced Old Number One. Perhaps the sixth or eighth MG, it's the one still fondly remembered as The First. In any case, Kimber kept on modifying Morris chassis right up until late 1927, when the M.G. Car Company started guaranteeing its own cars. Most of the components still came from Morris, though. In 1929 the whole shebang was moved to Abingdon-on-Thames, and in 1930 MG became a separate corporation under the control of William Morris and Cecil Kimber, directors.

This is hardly the place to try to untangle the orgy of Depression-era MG models. Suffice it to say that from 1930 till '35 Kimber brought his cars to unbeatable records in nearly every under-2-liter racing class. He also had expensive overhead cams on everything right down to the smallest 750cc Midget, which is why they went so fast. In 1935, however, William Morris—who was now Lord Nuffield—went public with MG and Wolseley. They became Morris Motors, and Leonard Lord (later Lord Lord) was put in charge. Nuffield also disbanded Kimber's prolific MG racing department, for though he'd racked up an enviable record, he'd also spent most of the profits. Leonard Lord started rationalizing models, dropping the duplicates and overlappers and introducing the comparatively mundane but cheaper-to-build TA Midget in 1936. The TA had, blasphemy of blasphemies, a flathead *pushrod* four of 1292cc.

The TA soon became the TB, then was abruptly dropped for the duration of the Hitler war. Sir Miles Thomas took over as Nuffield's part-time assistant, over Cecil Kimber's head, and Kimber left MG in a huff. He was killed in a freak railroad accident in London in 1945, but that was already years after his former assistant, George Propert, had taken his place in Abingdon. And shortly after Kimber's death, Propert had MG back in postwar production making just one model, a mildly revamped TB called, logically enough, the TC. That's when America entered the MG picture.

Just about the only market *left* in 1945–'49 was in America. And Americans were fanatically car hungry. You could sell *anything* that had wheels and fresh paint, and Propert wasn't the only one in England who realized that it would take years before bombed-out Europe could absorb even a fraction of the new-car production the factories were capable of making, even on short rations of steel, rubber, and glass. Their only hope was America. Happily enough, the Hitler war put large sums of money into the hands of large numbers of American kids for the first time in his-

Flapping isinglass side curtains, a hood full of shins, and wobbly wire wheels . . . MG's immortal TC.

tory and also gave them the independence to spend it any way they liked. The MG-TC was made for them.

It wasn't particularly cheap. TCs cost $1,895. By comparison, you could get a Ford Deluxe coupe with a flathead V-8 for under $1,300 in 1948 and an all-new, slab-sided V-8 Ford for $1,500 in 1949. The V-8 Ford, just about the cheapest decent car you could buy, was a particular favorite with kids because it was also quick, fast, nimble, and easily hotrodded. The TC, different as it was, appealed for similar reasons. The performance of the two cars in stock form was nearly identical, 0 to 60 in roughly 20 seconds, at which point they also finished the quarter-mile abreast. The V-8 Ford was much quicker above 60, though, and had a consistently higher top speed, 85 compared with 75.

Despite their superficial similarities in drag-strip performance, the TC and Ford V-8 were worlds apart in almost everything else. The relatively huge Ford—about the size of a modern compact Nova, Fairmont, or Volvo—weighed over 3,000 pounds and was some 195 inches long. The little TC Midget—1,900 pounds and only 139 inches long on a 94-inch wheelbase—was virtually identical in overall size, weight, and horsepower to the current MG Midget, still the smallest car on American highways. By comparison with the Ford, though, the MG was a blinding revelation when it came to responsiveness and handling. The superbly balanced TC had almost no overhang and a nearly perfect 47/53 weight distribution. In 1947 when the first one came over here, it was the only car on American roads that didn't have a vast majority of its weight on the front wheels.

Even though it used a rigid front axle—which most American manufacturers, even *retardataire* Ford, had discarded by 1949—and skinny tires on spindly wire wheels, the TC would go charging around corners in one invigorating high-speed swoop instead of the series of bobs, nibbles, and heart-stopping front-end slides that characterized understeering American sedans. And instead of insensitive steering that took four or five turns lock to lock, the one and a half turns of the surprisingly direct TC had naive Americans convinced they were all Juan Fangio himself.

Mostly, the MG-TC was just about the

John Fitch's stripped TC at Watkins Glen, 1949.

most lovable car ever built, and a million American heartstrings twanged the first moment one appeared. So what if the impossibly long, boxy hood concealed mostly shins, or the wobbly wire wheels had all the precision of potato chips, or whatever the weather was doing outside was also happening inside, top and side curtains notwithstanding. The TC said SPORTS CAR in bright red or British racing green, and it took America by storm. We'd just never seen anything like it. It was so small and spindly and . . . winsome. A marvelous pull-toy that had you looking for the tow rope with the Brobdingnagian toddler tugging at the other end.

MG sold as many TCs as they could make, and even made enough of a profit to start the inevitable "improvements." In 1947 the Y-model four-seater appeared with a conventional independent front suspension, so it was only right that the same suspension should get bolted under the two-seater. By the time they'd finished, Sid Enever's crew had a whole new car. This was the TD, and it was greeted with howls of derision. As Don Vorderman wrote in *Automobile Quarterly,* "It looked awful in the photographs, but when the first batch arrived from across the pond, looked even worse. The TC's perfect proportions were gone, replaced by an expedient, easy-to-build blandness . . . but in our hearts we knew Abingdon had been right—it really *was* a better car."

And it was. With pressed-steel wheels that were as uniform as Pringles New-fangled Potato Chips, a reasonable turning radius, seats that were higher, and tires that were lower, the MG no longer looked like an early-thirties sports car. More like a *late*-thirties sports car. In January 1950 when it debuted, the TD was also the cheapest sports car you could buy anywhere, at just $2,157. While the hidebound TC zealots pooh-poohed the latest, more rational folks bought them by the bushel. TDs stood up to incredible abuse, and everyone I knew ran his regularly to ungodly revs for an archaic pushrod four with insufficient main bearings. It was rare that something broke, and when it did you could usually fix it in your driveway on Saturday afternoon.

There was even a high-performance Mark II version of the MG-TD, with lots of engine hop-up goodies. Anyone serious about it, though, had already redone his engine with American aftermarket pieces, and virtually every accessory manufacturer in the country made *something* for the MG, from Judson's supercharger to Marion's famous MG Mitten. Good TCs and TDs would reach 100 mph in full-fendered race trim. A California aerodynamicist calculated that the MG's blunt nose required 100 hp to cross the century mark, so double the stock horsepower was relatively commonplace, at least on the track.

The Bugatti Type 35 is claimed to be the winningest model ever built, with some 3,000 plus victories. The only reason the TC/TD/TFs don't claim the prize is that nobody has been able to *count* how many races they won. It's a safe bet that worldwide, in events great

The MG-TD was honestly better in every way than the TC; hill climbing at Virginia City, 1952.

and small, the T-series Midgets are the most successful club racers ever built, and with Ford V-8 60s, Volvo fours, and small-block Chevies, among the most outlandishly modified. A TD is currently running in VSCC events with four-wheel disc brakes from an MGA Twin Cam and a motor from an MGB. And it works. You can in fact do almost *anything* to a T-series and it'll come obediently back for more, sort of like a large, good-natured Saint Bernard that lets the kids pull his tail for hours on end without complaining.

The unfortunate MG-TF succeeded the TD for 1953. This was a Morganesque MG, with square radiator but headlights in the fenders. It was neither as pretty as the TC nor as easy to service as the TD. And of course, by the time it was dropped at the end of 1955, the whole MG concept was positively *archaic* for a company that had to sell cars by the thousands, rather than by the dozen like Morgan or HRG. The Morris/MG Nuffield combine merged with Austin in 1952 to form British Motor Corporation, and there was a lot of pressure to abandon the twenty-year-old T-series and get on with the job of building real cars. So in the summer of '55, the last "classic" MGs rolled out of Abingdon.

In all, MG built about 12,000 TCs, 30,000 TDs, and 10,000 TFs. It only *seems* as if twice that many are still around. The survival rate *has* been astonishingly high. *Road & Track* called the T-series "the sports car standard of comparison," and many of them were never neglected but simply restored again and again. Parts are among the most available of all imported car bits, and a perusal of the classifieds in any national car magazine will disclose dozens of firms, large and small, who can literally build you a brand-new T-series from parts.

Ten years ago, I sold my TD—hell, *everybody* I've ever met owned a T-series at some point or other, it's the universal sports car—mostly restored, for $1,000. The same car today is worth $4,500, and concours TDs are up over $6,000. TCs have always been more popular with collectors, and perfect ones go for $10,000, though you can get a decent one for under $4,000 if you look. TFs were nowhere twenty years ago; they're still nowhere today. God knows what one is worth, though prices are basically identical to TC/TD prices.

An MG-TF rallying at Rockville, Maryland, 1954.

But I doubt that any TFs actually sell for anywhere *near* that much. As a car to actually drive, the TF is probably better than either of the earlier models. But somehow it lacks the charm and precision of even the homogenized TD. It's an old-fashioned sports car edging toward being new-fangled, and the edges are a bit blurry as a result. The TF is an MG without a point of view and consequently overpriced in anybody's market. As Uncle Tom McCahill so charmingly put it in a 1955 MG-TF road test, "The Austin-Healey is the best MG buy in years."

The TC and TD, on the other hand, *made* the postwar sports car market . . . starting from scratch, with no outside help. *Created* it. Why? Because the cars, in their way, were great. Purely and simply . . . great. I admit to having been thoroughly hooked on my old TD, and the three years I owned it are among the happiest in my automotive memory. It broke my heart when I sold it, but somehow it was a kid's toy that didn't fit in with a graduate-school income, a brand-new wife, and a cross-country drive carrying everything we owned in the world—which no longer included an MG, more's the pity.

Triumph 1800

Watch out for the Triumph 1800s from right after the war. Yessir. Those funny-looking, bulbous roadsters with the windows in the trunk lid have bounced from ground zero or below right up to downright expensive in what seems like the last week and a half. Of course, strictly between you and me, they're not *real* cars, but still. They're as cute as a Cockney button, more fun than a poke in the eye with a sharp stick, and distinguished enough that you could tell your mother-in-law it's a Bentley and she'd believe you. Those old roadsters don't have enough punch to start a garden party, but they're solid, stolid, and believe it or not, they have a great pedigree.

The engine, for example, is the old prewar S.S. unit, father of the Jaguar. You see, things got very confused around Coventry just before, during, and after Hitler's war. And Jaguar, Standard, and Triumph were cheek by jowl in Coventry, so they consequently got confused. Triumph Postwar, especially, has nothing at *all* to do with Triumph Prewar. They are two completely different companies.

The story goes like this. As every British schoolboy knows, Triumph Cycle Company, Ltd., of Coventry was put together single-handedly by an expatriate German named Siegfried Bettmann way back in 1895. By 1921 not only was his Triumph the most popular motorcycle in England but he'd bought the Dawson Car Company, too. Triumph/Dawson cars never were very good, and when Bettmann retired in 1934, the motorcycle business was pretty much supporting the four-wheel division. Dismayed by his hopeless successor, Bettmann bought the cycle division back in 1936 and ran it until the war.

Triumph Motor Company—bereft of the two-wheel monies—pottered through the thirties and, despite the best efforts of Donald Healey, who started rallying Triumphs in 1928 and joined the company in 1934, and Walter Belgrove, who was Triumph's exceptionally quirky stylist, they never sold very many cars. The final blow was Maurice Newnham, a classic bodge-up of a managing director who canceled all the pseudo sports cars that were Triumph's only moneymakers and concentrated on a bunch of doggy sedans. Under his insipid leadership, Triumph went into receivership in July 1939.

Thomas Ward, Ltd., of Sheffield bought what was left of Triumph and made weapons until the Luftwaffe flattened the Coventry plant in 1944. Ward then sold what they had left—which was mostly the name on the bombed-out door—to Sir John Black of Standard Motor Company in November. Sir John was a close friend of Bill Lyons at Jaguar and had supplied the engines for the S.S. line throughout the thirties. He specialized in rescuing companies on the brink. Triumph was definitely his biggest challenge yet, but Sir John plunged right in. Donald Healey was long gone, of course. So in the summer of 1945, Sir John had designer Frank Callaby of Standard design a new roadster while H. J. Mulliner created an aluminum-bodied, razor-edge sedan. According to legend, the first roadster was built for Sir John as a personal car, since he was having a tiff with Bill Lyons and refused to be seen in his S.S. 100 any longer. Besides, Standard needed to make quite a few more engines if they were going to stay solvent, and Jaguar wasn't anywhere near ready to take them all. The new Triumphs were meant to sop up the overflow.

The engine that Sir John had was the old 1776cc overhead-valve unit that Lyons used in the S.S. 1.5-liter . . . both before and after the war. It made a puny 65 hp at 4400 rpm. Installed in the pretty but upright Mulliner saloon, toting a dry weight of 2,500 pounds and pushing a flat front through the atmosphere, the overstressed four was hopeless. It wasn't much better in the roadster, though the aluminum body—they couldn't buy steel, it was in such short supply—kept the weight down to 2,200 pounds. Top speed was an optimistic 75 or so, and the acceleration—0 to 60 in about 28 seconds—plain embarrassing.

But the rest of the car was surprisingly good. Callaby had drawn up a conventional ladder frame with hefty tubular rails that stretched out to a 100-inch wheelbase for Standard's own Standard 14. He used it under the two Triumphs, too. The front suspension was a simple independent setup with transverse leaf spring; at the rear was a rigid axle on semiellipitcs. Oh. Just so you'll know, Standard 14s are those old-fashioned black saloons that bumbling police inspector Terry Thomas is always wrecking in Roy Boulting comedies from the early fifties. Triumph's sedan was out of the same dull mold.

The Triumph roadster, on the other hand, was spectacularly individual. It borrowed ele-

Triumph's distinctive 1948 1800 had a Vanguard engine and rumble seat in the trunk.

ments from here, there, and everywhere, but the total body has a unique, quirky charm all its own. From the front it has all the ambience of a hyperthyroid chipmunk with a full cheek load. The grille is very skinny and vertical and slopes backward. But the fenders are exceedingly fat—bulbous, even—and project way in front of both wheels and radiator. A hell of an effect, really—sort of like Raquel Welch, buck naked, hmmmm . . . wearing nothing but a big silver Navaho pendant right in the middle of her tawny cleavage.

The Triumph 1800 also had an impossibly long hood—so you'd know it's a sports car—funny, narrow suicide doors, and a tall, rounded ass that's higher than the cowl. The trunk is so high because it's really a rumble seat, with one of the goddamndest gizmos ever seen on a production car. The lid swings back to reveal the twin jump seats and, at the same time, the front of the rumble seat cover swings forward to become a dual-cowl windshield. Like on a Twenty Grand Duesenberg or something. Yep. Right there in the trunk lid are these two square chunks of glass that turn into a windshield. Damndest thing you ever saw in your life.

The big problem with the Triumph roadster—aside from the fact that they sold only 1,700 in England and 300 in the States before it died in 1950—was that puny engine. So in 1949 Sir John had them splice in the 2088cc

four from the standard Vanguard, which, though it wasn't much, was better than nothing. The really good part for collectors is that this very same Vanguard engine turned up later in the Triumph TR-series and stayed virtually unchanged—except for some temporary fiddling with the bore to get it under the 2-liter class limit—right up until the TR-4A in 1967. By which time it was up to 2138cc and 104 hp direct from the factory, and considerably more from your corner racerman store. So it is eminently possible—and *almost* kosher—to stuff a TR-3 or TR-4 mill into an early Triumph 2000 and make a real *car* out of it. Which is something Triumph was never able to do.

You think Morgans are old-fashioned? Ha. In 1956 HRG was still building a car they'd designed in the mid-thirties to be a nostalgic reincarnation of the cars of the early *twenties*. It was sort of an early-day replicar for "die-hard enthusiasts, who shunned the 'softly sprung' over-adorned pseudo sports cars of the thirties," according to Anthony Pritchard. You remember those softy cars of the early thirties: JAP-engined Morgan Trikes, Chain Gang Frazer Nashes, 4.5 Invictas, Aston Inters, MG K-3s, Lagonda 4.5s—cars for sissies, right? Listen. You put iron-man Parnelli Jones in one of those "pseudo sports cars" for about an hour and he'd think he'd just run the Baja 1000 on a bicycle.

So who were these crazy masochists for whom classic sports cars weren't demanding enough? You've heard of Archie Frazer Nash, builder of Frazer Nashes? Well, before he built Frazer Nashes, he built G. N. cycle cars, funny little 700-pound miniature automobiles with V-twin motorcycle engines. The N stood for Nash, the G for H. R. Godfrey. The same G reappears in Halford, Robins, and Godfrey—or HRG. Got it?

Halford/Robins/Godfrey got together in early 1935 and designed a vintage sports car right down to the quarter-elliptic front leaf springs, solid axle, fold-flat windshield, wire wheels, working bonnet strap, cutaway doors, and elbows-out driving position. The engine was set so far back that the radiator was almost completely behind the front wheels. All in all, the 1935 HRG looked like nothing as much as a circa 1923 G. N. cycle car minus the chain drive and with fatter tires. Or more precisely, like a 1935 Frazer Nash TT Replica, which in turn was based on the G. N., too. Messrs. G. and N. always did think somewhat alike.

Throughout the thirties, Singer-engined HRG roadsters appeared sporadically from the Tolworth shops near the Kingston Hill bypass. During World War II, Godfrey and his free-lance engineering crew did government work like everyone else, and in 1946, instead of coming out with an all-new car, they decided to carry over the prewar line completely intact. The littler model had a 1073cc, 44-hp Singer four, the "big" model had a punched-out 1496cc, 65-hp Singer. Both had an overhead cam and were surprisingly sturdy little power plants. In the 1,400-pound HRG, the 1.5-liter engine was good for 90 mph and returned 35 to 40 mpg besides. And with a total length of only 144 inches, the tiny HRG was as nimble as they come.

Amazingly enough, even with a deliber-

Undistilled vintage Britishness, this upright 1952 HRG w

ately antique, cart-spring suspension, HRGs were exceptional racers. In 1949 Peter Clark and Marcus Chambers won the 1500cc class at Le Mans and were fourteenth overall; Jack Fairman and Eric Thompson won the class in 1950, finishing an astounding eighth *overall.* Peter Clark even built a 2-liter version with which he tried to race Formula II, but that was asking just a bit much, even in 1949. The whole idea was fortunately dropped after a predictably disastrous season.

In the slow-moving saga of HRG, 1955 was a momentous year. They put together a double-overhead-cam head for the Singer and dropped it into an all-independent chassis with four-wheel discs, alloy wheels, and an aerodynamic body. But after a couple of prototypes and a few unsuccessful racing attempts, the idea was dropped in 1956, along with production of the old cart-spring vintage replicar, too. From 1935 through 1956, total HRG production was a mind-boggling 231 cars. HRG, the company, stayed in business until 1966, however, as an engineering subcontractor to the British automobile industry.

already a collector's item twenty-five years ago.

Probably three-quarters of all the HRGs built are still around. Because they were designed as collector items right from the very beginning, they've all been purchased and tended by sympathetic collectors since the time they were new. Quite a few were even imported to America in the early fifties, by Max Hoffman. HRGs were never particularly expensive, and $6,000 will get you one today. Most Singer mechanical parts are available in England through the clubs, though of course anything else—like body or frame parts—is pretty hard to come by. On the other hand, the HRG is a prime example of the wisdom of buying a simple, hand-built car. If it was hand-built in a back garden shed to begin with, chances are it can be repaired the same way without too much trouble.

MG-TCs and Morgan flat-rads are the only postwar cars that even approach the vintage Britishness of an HRG, and they're comparatively abundant. The HRG is a truly unique piece among traditional Anglican sports cars, somewhere between the mass-production thousands and the failed specials that num-

bered one of each. Among Anglophile collectors, HRGs are also approached with something very nearly touching reverence. Just as there will always be an England and masochistic Englishmen, so, I suppose, there'll always be a market for that most spartanly British of cars, HRG. Incredible.

Bristol

In 1945 companies all over the world started looking around for something else to do besides build military equipment. Especially high-flying aircraft companies with no civilian market. Cars seemed like a good substitute to quite a few airplane makers, since the materials and construction techniques were at least similar. Convair in San Diego spawned a whole flock of prototype cars, Beechcraft presented the Plainsman automobile, Messerschmidt built bubblecars, and the huge Willow Run, Michigan, bomber plant became Kaiser-Frazer. Bristol Aeroplane was one of the biggest aircraft manufacturers in England, and they, too, felt the postwar squeeze. But they were smarter than most. Bristol started out slowly in the automobile business, and probably for that reason is still in it, unlike all the others who unsuccessfully tried to switch from planes to cars on a grand scale.

Bristol didn't so much go into the car business as start making cars. In other words, they just picked up an existing design and started cranking out cars . . . in small numbers, for a high price, through a very few upper-class dealers. Wouldn't you know it, the guiding force was Aldy Aldington—excuse me, *Colonel* H. J. Aldington—the iconoclastic head of Frazer Nash and a member of the Bristol board of directors. And the prewar BMW importer. Aldy suggested that since (1) BMW's prewar 327 was a smashing car, and since (2) there weren't two bricks standing together in the Eisenach factory, and since (3) Eisenach was now in *East* Germany, and since (4) BMW had the bad taste to be on the wrong side when it came time to say who'd won the war, why, (5) Bristol could just go over there and pretty much *take* BMW and consider it war reparations. And not only that; Dr. Fritz Fiedler—who had been the head engineering honcho at BMW and a personal friend of Aldington's—was languishing in an Allied jail because he couldn't prove that designing Nazi tanks and jeeps and things for a decade didn't ipso facto make him a postwar undesirable.

And so it came to pass that the good Dr. Ing. Fiedler of Munich, with a little help from his friends, came to Filton, Bristol, in the far west of England, with the BMW 327 design drawings rolled securely underneath his arm and the promise of a bright new future before him. The first production Bristol appeared in 1946. It was called the 400, but really it was nothing more than a prewar BMW 327 coupe with a hotted-up engine. This was no bad thing for a car to be. The BMW chassis dated back to the early thirties, but it was one of the first to use two big steel tubes for the longitudinal frame rails—the prototype for all those Tojeiro, A. C., Lister, Frazer Nash, and Cobra cars to follow, in other words. It was strong, light, and easy to make. For the Bristol version, Fiedler updated it with torsion bars all around, though the rear axle was still rigid. But no matter. His BMW 327/328 was the Gullwing Mercedes of the thirties, far superior to anything anybody had ever seen on the street. And the Bristol was just as good, of course . . . and still better than anything else in England, even ten years later.

The old BMW 1971cc six, which went back to 1933, was also better than just about any engine in postwar Britain. It didn't have an overhead cam, but it did have horizontal, overhead pushrods that went across the head to operate the exhaust valves. It was really pretty similar to the engines Opel uses nowadays, which is no surprise since Fiedler went back to Germany in the early fifties as head of Opel Engineering. Anyway, in street trim for the Bristol 400, Fiedler's old six produced 80 hp with three SUs. Of course, Aldy Aldington still had stacks of hop-up equipment at AFN, Ltd., that would extract up to 155 hp out of the versatile engine. More normal was 130 hp from the Mark II engine, which was supplied to everyone from A. C. to Wacky Arnolt later on.

The Bristol 400 née BMW 327 stayed in production from 1946 until 1951, by which time they'd managed to sell over 700. This was pretty good, considering the cars cost well over £2,300 in the late forties when you could get a new Jaguar XK-120 for only £1,300. The Bristol was more of a luxury car, though, surpassingly comfortable, adequately fast, and even pretty economical on gas. It was extremely well built, of the finest materials—something no Jaguar could ever claim—and even with an all-steel body weighed only 2,300 pounds. Like the DB-2 Aston and Jensen Interceptor, it appealed to well-off, middle-aged sports who were tired of having whatever it was doing outside all over them, even when they were sitting inside.

Once the 400 was launched, Fiedler started splitting his time between Bristol and Frazer Nash. So Sir Roy Fedden, head of engineering at Bristol Aeroplane, started working on a new, aerodynamic body for the same chassis. He faired the fenders in and gave it a nice fastback, a bobbed tail, and an impossibly long hood. Then he ran it through Bristol's wind tunnel and faired in the bumpers, too. Fedden even eliminated the door handles. All around, he made it as lovely and aerodynamic as possible. Touring in Milan got the contract to build a few in aluminum over steel tubing. This was Touring's patented, famous "Superleggera" *super* ultralightweight body, which, embarrassingly enough, turned out to weigh 100 pounds *more* than the original all-steel body on the 400.

But no matter; it was a lot prettier. Bristol kept the twin nostrils that were BMW's trademark, since that was what they had on the earlier car. And they called it, logically enough, the 401. The 401 stayed in production until 1953 and Touring even made two dozen convertibles, too. Bristol called them 402s. A revamped version of the 401 coupe, dubbed the 403, appeared in 1953 and stayed in *very* limited production till 1955. Horsepower was now up to 100 in stock trim, but otherwise it was still an aerodynamic BMW with a very high price tag and exquisite workmanship. And it still had that distinctive BMW grille.

Which got to be a problem. Because after they'd supplied Germany with as many motorcycles as the market could bear, BMW got back into the car business in 1951, with, of course, their own aerodynamic version of the BMW 327 with distinctive twin nostrils. BMW called theirs the *501,* which was an obvious dig at Bristol's blatant rip-off. So in 1953 an all-new Bristol appeared, the two-seater 404, built on a short-wheelbase chassis—96 inches instead of 114—with Al-Fin brakes, 105 hp, and a top speed over 110. It was quick and responsive, weighed only 2,100 pounds and even got 25 miles per gallon. Of course, it was horrendously expensive—$9,946 in England in 1953—but it was also put together Bristol fashion. And best of all, where most cars had a distinctive grille, the 404 had . . . nothing at all. A big square *hole* was all it had, which usually got filled with a huge Lucas Flame-thrower driving light, right in the center. Nobody could mistake *that* for a BMW grille.

The 404 was so nice that soon there was a four-door 405 . . . same thing, but on the long-wheelbase chassis. A long time ago now, Ralph Stein wrote down his recipe for a sports car, carefully pointing out that though superlative brakes, handling, steering, acceleration, and top speed were all part of it, open two-seater bodywork was not. "It should have a practical top and windshield," he said, "and although I hate to say so, maybe even sedan bodywork." He must have been thinking of the Bristol 405, which is a sedan, certainly, but also a sports car right enough . . . a wonderful, thoroughbred, high-performance vehicle, rare as dragon's teeth. And unless you looked carefully, you'd never notice there are two doors to a side, it's that pretty. The 404 and 405 are the definitive early Bristols, with their own distinctive styling, good usable performance, and incredible quality control. *Fine* cars, no doubt about it.

In late 1957, Beutler—a small, conservative Swiss coachbuilder—got the contract to restyle the 405 into the 406. They came up with a very pretty two-door notchback, very simple, with the same unadorned air intake that was now Bristol's trademark but squared-up fenders and an angular roof. Bristol bored and stroked the old six to 2216cc and put on four-wheel discs. But otherwise the chassis stayed the same, though the price went up from £3,195 to an astronomical £4,493. And from '57 until today, actually, Beutler's staid body has stayed the same, too. There have been minimal styling changes over the years,

Bristol's lovely, aerodynamic 405 sedan of 1954.

A true businessman's express, the 1957 406.

Beutler-bodied Bristol 406 E, rare and fine.

but the only big switch came in 1961. Bristol finally gave up on the Fiedler six, mostly because A. C. was the only other company still using it, but also because it was expensive to build and, even with Beutler's version of aluminum Superleggera coachwork, the cars had gotten up into the 3,000-pound range . . . much too much for 2-liters. So like their rivals at Jensen—which Bristol closely resembles as both a car and a company—for the old/new 407 they bought big, wedge-head V-8s from Chrysler. And continue to do so, even now.

Despite their big American engines, you can't buy Bristols in America anymore, haven't been able to for years, in fact. But there are a few Bristols—a very few; annual production hovers around two dozen—in the States. *Any* Bristol is worth having. They are probably the best built of all British cars, the Silver Shadow included, and certainly more fun than anything that's come out of Crewe since the Continental Flying Spur. For a *lot* less money. The Chrysler V-8s are no problem to own in America, of course, and the Bristol six is robust as hell. You can still get parts pretty easily from England, and since Fiedler's six was used in so many other cars in so many states of tune, you can fit a Bristol with anything from 80 to 155 hp and still be authentic.

Myself, I'd like to own a 404 coupe, for the simple reason that it's the most sporting of all, except, of course, for the forgotten Bristol 450S. In the autumn of 1952 Bristol Aeroplane bought ERA, who used the Bristol engine in their single-seater Formula II car. Bristol took three ERA chassis, with DeDion back axles and the 155-hp version of the six, and wrapped them up in the ugliest coupe bodies anyone had ever seen. They were smooth and efficient, though a fastback that swooped down between two huge tail fins was the least of their many peculiarities. But they worked. The three 450Ss broke at Le Mans in '53 but won their class at Rheims. And in 1954 they finished 7–8–9 at Le Mans and 10–11–12 at Rheims, winning their 2-liter GT class both times. They did the same thing in 1955, too.

Amazingly enough, even the standard Bristols were pretty fair rally cars. Dobry and Treybal—a pair of crazy Czechs who opened a Bristol dealership in postwar Prague, of all

places—finished third overall in the Monte Carlo Rally in 1949. In the next three years, Bristols took some class wins in the RAC rally and the Tulip, in international competition. Even more amazing, Count Johnny Lurani and Aldy Aldington brought one to Brescia in '49 and got a third in class in the Mille Miglia, running against all those 2-liter Ferraris and Maseratis, which isn't bad for a couple of middle-aged Englishmen very far from home.

The Bristol—any Bristol—has credentials, a pedigree that's not very long on the face of it but that goes all the way back to Fritz Fiedler's BMW 327s of the early thirties and the Mille Miglia–winning BMW 328s of 1940. Bristols were god-awful expensive when they were new—still are in England, for that matter. The Bristol 406, for example, went for £4,300 in the mid-fifties, back when the pound was still a pound. And Bristols are also god-awful expensive, even when they're old. That same Bristol 406 is still worth well over $10,000. But it's worth it, if any car is. The workmanship is exquisite—aircraft tolerances, after all—and the materials are aviation quality, too. Bristol owners tend to be well-off sorts who take great pride in keeping their car in exceptional condition, have the money to keep it to the manner born, and won't part with their pet for less than a king's ransom. But the cars *are* wonderful. And of course, from a collector's point of view, Bristols are *very* rare. So all things considered, they ought to be expensive. And they are.

Frazer Nash

You have to go back to the early thirties—to the twenties, even—to talk about Frazer Nash in the forties. In 1924 Captain Archie Frazer Nash—formerly the N in G. N. cycle cars—started building what amounted to a very sophisticated cycle car. This was the legendary Chain Gang Frazer Nash, which stayed in production virtually unchanged until 1939. Chain Gang FNs were strictly short-course nickel rockets. While they lasted, they went *very* fast indeed, but Captain Archie's famous dictum unfortunately summed up his cars completely: "A half-mile is one thing," he said, "but a kilometer is a very long way indeed."

At least partly because of this cavalier attitude, Frazer Nash sold only some 348 chain-drive cars in fifteen years of production. Early on, in 1928, the captain himself bowed out, leaving H. J. "Aldy" Aldington and his brothers William and David owning A.F.N. Ltd., Makers of Frazer Nash Cars. The Aldingtons, and Aldy in particular, were at least as crazy as Archie Frazer Nash. H. J. was well known for expounding his version of an old theory that "the faster you drive through intersections, the safer you are, because you get across before The Accident has time to happen." So the Frazer Nash of the thirties—even without its namesake to keep things on the boil—retained all the outlandish brio it had been given in 1924. Understandably, even in England, Land of the Stiff Upper Lip, there just weren't *that* many sports willing to sacrifice nearly every creature comfort for the dubious honor of broad-sliding around corners seated on a steamer trunk full of madly whirling chains.

The Aldingtons branched out. They were the exclusive distributors for Aston Martin for a while, then picked up the British distributorship for BMW in 1933, after the new 1.5-liter BMW 315 had beaten the similar-size Frazer Nashes for a class win in the Alpine Rally. Throughout the thirties, the sales of BMWs—particularly the exceptionally advanced 328—gave the Aldingtons enough extra lucre to keep Frazer Nash in limited production. Eventually they got to be such successful BMW agents that the Munich factory started putting Frazer Nash emblems on its cars for Britain.

After the war, Aldy built himself a prototype that looked embarrassingly like the special BMW 328 that won the shortened Mille Miglia in 1940. It also looked a lot like a Jaguar XK-120 with a Frazer Nash grille. But because the FN came out in November 1947, almost exactly a year to the day before the XK prototype appeared at the London Motor Show, there's a persistent rumor that Bill Lyons took his inspiration for the XK-120 from the FN

crew out of Isleworth, Middlesex. In any case, this *very* Bayerische Motoren Werke prototype went no further. Aldy did keep the chassis, though, a sturdy ladder frame welded up from large-diameter steel tubing, fitted with a rigid rear axle suspended on torsion bars, and a simple independent front end with a single transverse leaf spring used as the upper control arm. It was basically a line-for-line copy of the prewar BMW 328 . . . and the 1933 Type 315, for that matter.

Of course, Aldy kept the excellent BMW motor, too. And he had Dr. Fritz Fiedler, the prewar head of BMW's engineering department, to help him. Col. Aldington was a director of Bristol Aeroplane, and through some well-placed connections in the War Office he managed to get Fiedler sprung from a German lockup and assigned to help Bristol Aeroplane start making a copy of the prewar BMW 327 coupe. After he'd straightened out Bristol production, Fiedler refined the similar FN chassis. And Aldy took advantage of his Bristol directorship to ensure Bristol/BMW engines for Frazer Nash in perpetuity. Aldington also bought most of his other chassis bits from Bristol, from big things like transmissions and rear axles to such minutiae as shock absorbers. And Fiedler strapped them all onto a nicely compact 96-inch wheelbase—the same as his BMW 315 from fifteen years earlier.

Aldy opted for a super-simple aluminum body instead of the complex BMW sort. It looked pretty much like Donald Healey's Silverstone or a two-seater Formula car with cycle fenders. But it was light at 1,500 pounds, and aerodynamically clean, which made it fast. Fiedler's engine would produce around 120 hp in Frazer Nash tune, though the real racers were getting 155 hp and more. The first postwar Frazer Nash—aside from that ill-fated Jaguarish prototype—appeared in 1948 as the High Speed. Later that year the line expanded to include the Competition Model . . . which was also the High Speed. Which brings up a characteristically Aldington approach that dated from the early thirties: whenever he needed some new floor traffic in the showroom, he'd create a new model . . . simply by changing the name. There are a dozen different Chain Gang models, for example, most of which are exactly the same car

Jim Haynes's famous brass-trimmed Frazer Nash.

with a different name. Alfred P. Sloan of GM may have invented Badge Engineering, but Aldy took it to the furthest extreme.

In 1949 former motorcycle racer Norman Culpan bought a High Speed/Competition Model FN to race at the first postwar Le Mans. Aldy made it a factory effort by volunteering to co-drive, and amazingly enough, after 24 hours, the two finished *third overall,* behind Luigi Chinetti's Ferrari and a French-chauffeured Delage. It was certainly the longest continuous running any Frazer Nash had ever done, considerably farther than a kilometer. True to form, by the time he got back to Middlesex, Aldy had transformed the High Speed/Competition Model into the Le Mans Replica. Thus, as they say, is immortality born.

The Le Mans Replica was not only *the* postwar Frazer Nash, but one of the most delightful cars ever built. Unlike Allards that were all engine or Jaguars that were mostly good looks, the Replica was a supremely balanced car. No one part was subservient, no one part dominant. For some mysterious reason, perhaps Fiedler's delicate touch, the Le Mans Replica was a real and total masterpiece throughout. It was simple. Lord knows it was simple: no high-winding overhead cams, no shrieking V-12, no independent rear, no streamlined bodywork, no disc brakes. But it worked. It was hefty where it needed to be hefty, in the drivetrain, brakes, and frame, and it was light where it could be light, in the bodywork and cockpit. So the weight—what little there was—rested in the right places. The bare chassis weighed 1,176 pounds, the bodywork another 300. And nothing projected beyond the wheels, so it had a wonderfully low polar moment of inertia.

On smooth airport courses—which was mostly what they had in postwar England—the simple chassis worked superbly, and even on the bumpy roads at the Dundrod Tourist Trophy, Le Mans, or the Manx TT, the long-travel suspension kept the tires pretty much in contact with the road. And it was fast. Zero to 60 took about 8 seconds, quarter-miles came up in under 17 seconds, top speed was over 120 mph. These were pretty impressive numbers for a pushrod, long-stroke 1971cc six in the late forties (or even the mid-seventies, for that matter). The Cad-Allard had just too much horsepower to overcome, but a good 2-liter Frazer Nash would out-accelerate an Allard J2 with its 4-liter Ardun-Mercury. This made the Le Mans Replica just about the quickest little production car you could buy in England.

But it was expensive. The introductory price was £2,250 plus double postwar tax, for a whopping £3,500 tag in England. Aldy later got it down to £1,750 plus tax for a total of £2,723, which still translates to nearly $10,000 for a 2-liter sports car . . . in an era when $10,000 would buy you a small *house,* for Chrissake. But like the Bristol, with which it shared so much, the FN was put together out of just about the best materials one could buy, and the finished product was as nicely finished as any car ever built. It wasn't fancy, certainly, but it was well screwed together. But $10,000 in 1950? *Aargh.*

The Le Mans Replica stayed in production through 1953, at which point it'd simply become outclassed as a racing car. And *much* too expensive for most people to afford for road use. Only sixty were built in five years, and many of those were lightweight, full-race Mark IIs with fiberglass body panels, stripped interiors, and tweaked-to-the-limit engines. Aldy doggedly kept on with FN production until 1960, using the basic Le Mans Replica chassis with full-envelope bodywork to create the Sebring, Mille Miglia, Targa, and Le Mans coupe, among others. Most of these models were built in batches of two or three. Of some models, only one was ever built. Later on, beginning in 1956, FN built a few Continentals powered by the postwar BMW 3-liter V-8. Aldington, still the BMW importer, added Porsche to his dealership in the fifties. So logically enough, in Aldy's mind, I suppose, the very last Frazer Nash Continentals consisted of the old Le Mans Replica frame with coil-spring suspension and disc brakes, the new BMW V-8 for power, and the contemporary rear-engined Porsche 356 Coupe body structure cut to accept an add-on trunk and a long, front-engined hood with Frazer Nash grille. It wasn't the best thing Aldington ever did.

The best Frazer Nash was the Le Mans Replica, no doubt about it. For the well-off amateur racer who had to arrange his own maintenance and tuning, the straightforward FN was a much smarter choice than the intimidating Ferrari that was its main competition. And amazingly enough, in the hands of professional drivers, the unassuming Le Mans Replica was capable of international-level performance. Aside from Aldy and Culpan's famous Le Mans third, Stirling Moss won the British Empire Trophy at the Isle of Man in 1951, and British luminaries such as Tony Brooks, Ken Wharton, Tony Crook, Roy Salvadori, and Bob Gerard all had successful FN rides. Americans Harry Grey and Larry Lulock won outright the first Sebring 12 Hours in 1952, and Tony Crook even broke the FIA Class E 200-mile record at Montlhéry in 1951, at an average of over 120 mph.

But the most successful postwar FN racer was, curiously enough, Italian driver Franco Cortese. Driving with Anglo-Italian Count Johnny Lurani's famous Scuderia Ambrosiana, Cortese had a long string of remarkable placings with his Le Mans Replica. In 1950 he finished sixth overall in the Mille Miglia and in 1951 won both the Enna Grand Prix and the Targa Florio *outright.* Cortese's Targa win is the only time a British car has ever won at the Sicilian classic, in all sixty years it's been held. Another impressive double was accomplished the same year by Eric Winterbottom, who finished 14th at Le Mans and

Third overall at Le Mans in 1949 was enough excuse to name the model Le Mans Replica.

then took the same car, without much more than a wash and change of plugs, and won the 2-liter class and a Coupe des Alpes in the Alpine Rally.

The best-known Le Mans Replica in America belongs to Jim Haynes, doyen of Lime Rock Park. His familiar British racing green FN—with its distinctive brass grille—is a frequent competitor with the VSSC. Jim bought the car nearly two decades ago and swears to keep it forever. From talking around, I guess that's a fairly common reaction, typical of Frazer Nash owners. It is literally impossible to take a Chain Gang FN out of England, because all the surviving cars are owned by club members who sign a covenant never to let their national treasure leave Fair Britannia's shore. Le Mans Replicas aren't quite as well protected, at least not yet, and it *is* still possible to find and buy one. Most of them, understandably, are in England, and the prices are up in the $20,000 range.

Deservedly so. The old Le Mans Replica Frazer Nash has a better pedigree than almost any British sports car you can think of and, happily enough, it's also quite a machine. Which is more than you can say for many other highly regarded sports/racers. Everything about it is so right, so perfect, there's not much more to say other than that if you ever get a chance to drive one—hell, even to ride in it—jump into that seat as quick as you can, before the owner changes his mind. And if you ever get the chance to buy one, sell the old homestead if you have to, or mortgage the kids. There are millions of other houses, but only a few dozen Le Mans Replicas. I promise you, you won't be sorry. Not even a little.

Allard J2-X

In 1930, right in the heart of the Crash, Sydney Herbert Allard came into his majority. His father was a prosperous building contractor, and while his brothers went into construction, Sydney determined to do something with au-

tomobiles. So when a bankrupt London Ford dealership came on the market for a pittance, Allard, Sr., bought it for Allard, Jr. Strangely enough, it was named Adlards, with a *d*, leading to innumerable bits of confusion in which Allard with an *l* characteristically delighted. Within eight years he had a second dealership; soon there were four. He started racing with a Morgan Trike, graduated to a British Ford, then built his first special in 1935.

The very first Allard was two wrecks welded together. In separate incidents, a customer's flathead Ford V-8 and an ex–Earl Howe Bugatti had been totaled and brought to Adlards. Allard took what was left of the Bugatti body and attached it to the Ford frame, making a hideously ugly one-off custom with a flat, heart-shaped grille made from coarse screen. The best part of the Allard Special—aside from the torquey American V-8—was a wonderfully sturdy independent front suspension conceived by Leslie Bellamy. Allard simply cut the rigid Ford axle in half and pivoted the two ends from a bracket welded at the center. The stock transverse leaf spring kept it relatively flat, though as soon as Allard crested a hill the front wheels would tuck under alarmingly, because there was nothing to stop them.

Most pictures you see of these early Allard Specials—there were soon a whole raft of them, and even a racing team called the Tail Waggers—have the front ends off the ground and the wheels swung in about 45 degrees. Allards were for Trials, you see, a peculiarly British sport that roughly resembles modern motorcycle Enduros, except done with cars in mud instead of bikes in dirt. The whole trick was to get as much traction to the rear wheels as possible, which meant the passenger shifted her body—wives were quite popular as ballast—out over the madly spinning, mud-churning tires to get the maximum weight transfer. Needless to say, the V-8 Ford in a lightweight chassis was superb, and later V-12 Lincoln Zephyr–powered Allards were even better.

From 1937 until 1939, Allard built a true "customer" model, merely an 85-hp V-8 Ford with light weight and pleasantly aggressive two-seater body and idiosyncratic split front axle. In Trials, Sprints, and clubmen's road

Sydney Allard's J2-X was the sports/racer of the early fifties—strong, fast, and brutal.

races, these Allards were disproportionately successful, though not more than a handful were actually sold. In 1945, as soon as the war ended, Allard came back with a whole range of similar aluminum-bodied cars, including a two-seater roadster, a two-seater tourer, a four-seater tourer, a convertible, and a sedan. They were all built on the same revived prewar V-8 chassis from Ford's Dagenham, England, factory, with the engine remounted way back in the frame and the front axle split down the middle.

Unsophisticated in the extreme, Allard's cars were still amazingly fast brutes. As England sorted herself out after the war, Allard was able to bring in a few Mercury flatheads, which gave nearly 4000cc instead of the 3622cc of the Ford. The hot setup was the Allard J1, an extremely stark two-seater that weighed 2,000 pounds. With a modified Mercury, you could go *well* over 100 mph, though the standard rear end was a stump puller 4.11. Allard was an acceleration nut, so his cars were geared for fantastic low-speed performance and no top end.

In 1949 the definitive Allard appeared. The legendary J2 was much more than merely a flathead Ford V-8 with a cobbled-up lightweight body. Now the split front axle was car-

ried on coil springs (with radius rods on the similar J2-X), the frame was a special steel tubing ladder, and the rear had a rudimentary—but very effective—DeDion axle with chassis-mounted differential and in-board Al-Fin brakes. Because of his Ford connections, Allard was able to get the new 4375cc Mercury V-8, which he fitted with Zora Arkus-Duntov's overhead-valve Ardun conversion. This produced around 150 hp, which in an 1,800-pound J2 was good for a top speed of 120, quarter-miles under 17 seconds, and 0 to 60 in about 9.5 seconds.

The J2 made Allard's name, particularly in the States. And that name meant big, brutal racing car. Most of the Allards sold were J models, and most of those were raced. Sydney Herbert Allard himself was among the best of his drivers. In his Steyr-Puch V-8 sprint car, he was third in the British Hillclimb Championship in both 1947 and '48, and won it in '49. He also partnered American Allard enthusiast Tom Cole to a third at Le Mans in 1950, behind the two controversial 4.5 Talbot Grand Prix cars. And in 1952 Sydney Allard won the Monte Carlo Rally outright in a P1 sedan, after a fourth and eighth in previous years.

Unlike fellow racer/constructor Briggs

Cunningham, Allard was no larger-than-life macho sportsman but a rather unassuming, bespectacled middle-aged businessman with sight in only one eye. He was an absolute terror on the race track, though, and stories abound of his sheer courage behind the wheel. A typical one is Le Mans, 1953. Allard had built himself a streamlined, Cadillac-engined, 300-hp J2-R as his ultimate weapon against the factory Mercedes and Jaguars. A differential "clunk" developed in practice, and none of the mechanics could determine what was wrong. Allard knew before the race began that something was about to break. So characteristically he decided to go as fast as possible and *cause* it to break, so it could then be found and fixed. At the running Le Mans start, forty-three-year-old Sydney Herbert Allard loped across the tarmac and blasted off to lead the entire field for the first lap. In the midst of lap two, the final drive mounting tabs cracked off and sliced through the brake lines. After a truly heart-stopping slide, brakeless, with no rear suspension, Allard triumphantly returned to the pits to crow empirically, *"There's* your trouble."

In America, the J2 and J2-X were *the* racers to have from 1949, when the first ones started coming over, until 1954 or so, when the competition got to be just too much for the Allard's rather unique roadholding. They were sold uniquely, too. In the early fifties, Britain was desperate for outside funds. Steel was in incredibly short supply, so the only way a manufacturer could obtain it was by proving that his product would be sold overseas. Coming the other way, British manufacturers weren't allowed to import items for which they could substitute home-grown products—like big V-8 engines from America. So a vast majority of J2 Allards were shipped to America engineless, where they would take almost any popular V-8 and transmission. Hemi Dodges and Ardun-Mercs were pretty much the bottom line in the States. Most Allards got overhead-valve Cadillacs or Chrysler hemis, which were good for roughly 180 hp in stock form and 300 hp in race trim.

A good Cad-Allard like Erwin Goldschmidt's, for example, which won the first Watkins Glen race in 1950, would do 0 to 100 in under 12 seconds and top 140 mph with 3.20 gears. At top speed, Goldschmidt—who,

like Allard, was possessed of a surfeit of sheer guts—could be seen bounding from corner to corner, with most of the wheels off the ground at unbelievable angles most of the time. The J2 was the original blood-and-thunder sports car, and there wasn't a refined bone in its body. Allards in general were affectionately known as the Blacksmith's Revenge, and until the Cobras came along were just about the scariest cars to drive at high speed yet invented.

Aside from Sydney himself, the average Allard driver was a real card-carrying speed-hungry crazy, a man's man who couldn't be bothered with technique and all that pansy sporty car stuff. The Allard was a Point and Pray racer, and it was a brave man indeed whose nerves could survive one for much more than a season. And 24 hours at someplace like Le Mans—where Sydney was *pulling* the Mercedes SLRs down Mulsanne at night, in the rain, lap after lap—is unimaginable. Just trying to keep the damn thing in a reasonably straight line would have been a full-time job for most people, even with normal vision. In broad daylight.

In all, Allard made about 2,500 cars, the majority of them J1s and J2s. For almost the entire period they were in production, the big, rock-sturdy Allards were just about the cheapest things you could buy for big-bore racing and had the inestimable side benefit of being not only more than competitive but easily tweaked and repaired. A J2 cost around $8,000 for a rolling chassis in the States, at a time when competitive Ferraris and Masers were up over $12,000. But unlike the superexotics, the Allard could be repowered at any Cadillac agency, for comparatively peanuts. The aluminum bodywork was simple enough to fix, likewise the frame and running gear (which rarely broke, in any case).

Allards never did go down much in price. They were honest legends in their own time, and as soon as they were left behind as competitive racers, the collectors grabbed them. There's not an Allard left in the country whose owner doesn't know precisely what he has, and though you could get a decent J2 for under $5,000 only a few years ago, the going rate today is around $20,000 for a decent one and over $25,000 for a concours car.

There aren't many Allards left. The ones

that didn't get terminally bent on the track were more often than not written off against a parked car or a tractor trailer on the interstate. Of all the cars in the world, the J2 has to be just about the most visceral, the loudest, the most vicious. Dennis May has written that the J-types "looked about as tidy as an unmade bed," but that's unfair. There's not a subtle line on an Allard, true enough, but the spare wheel glued on the side, the huge hood scoop, the multiplicity of louvers and vents, the cramped cockpit, the curiously extended cycle fenders, the huge near-set steering wheel with four spring spokes, the perfectly flat, polished aluminum dash all say *go* very loudly.

It was a man's car, for a man's kind of man. And for a brief—too brief—period, Sydney Allard—who was a man's kind of man, too—kept the lines of supply filled with good red-blooded cars. Around 1956 the market for macho machines dried up and Allard switched to building effete, envelope-bodied little sports cars with prissy names like Safari, Allardette, and Palm Beach. But his heart wasn't in it, and Allard dropped out of the car business in 1960 to concentrate on his own Chrysler hemi dragster and his Adlards garages. Sydney Allard died of cancer in 1966, but his son maintains the family business, having cut short his own rally career to take over. Ironically, just about the time Allard gave up on big, chuffing monsters, Carroll Shelby—who'd cut his racing teeth on a series of Allards—had the same idea all over again. Maybe we're only allowed one brutal, balls-out machine per decade. In its day, the Allard J2-X was *the* one.

Healey Silverstone

Every generation has its small crop of constructor/competitors, men who race the cars they themselves have built. In the immediate postwar era, there was H. J. Aldington with his ultraexpensive Frazer Nash, Sydney Allard with his maniacal Allard, and Briggs

Elliot at 104 mph, Milan autostrada, 1946.

Cunningham with his sophisticated Cunningham. And then there was Donald Healey. Healey was more of a designer than Aldington, Allard, or Cunningham, all of whom were primarily enthusiastic businessmen. Businessmen who coincidentally went considerably faster in a racing car than The Guv'nor is supposed to go. Healey, on the other hand, was an internationally known rally driver long before he ever thought about building cars. His most famous early wins were a 1931 outright victory in the Monte Carlo Rally in an Invicta and a class win in 1934 in a Triumph Gloria. He spent the thirties with Triumph, designing the rare and desirable Glorias and Dolomites from 1934 through '39.

After the war, Healey set up a small, independent factory in Warwick and designed an all-new car. In October 1946 when it first appeared, the new Healey received considerable attention, mostly because it was one of the first all-new British cars to go into production, as opposed to the prewar holdovers of everyone else. The first Healey was an abominably styled, slab-sided convertible, but early in 1947 Donald showed a very pleasant two-door sedan called the Elliot. It looked pretty much like a shrunken Mark VI Bentley, with razor-edge styling, a peculiar kite-shaped grille, and headlamps set into the body.

But it could go. In the late forties, the Elliot was *the* fastest British "saloon" in production, with a timed top speed of 104. It also handled extremely well. The chassis was a super-sturdy affair with six-inch-deep side rails, a stressed driveshaft tunnel, and numerous fabricated crossmembers. Everything on it was double duty, and just the bare frame rails, stretching out to a 102-inch wheelbase, weighed 160 pounds. At the back, Healey used a stock Riley rigid axle, with torque-tube drive, coil springs, and Panhard rod. At the front, the Healey had a really beautiful and unique suspension system. Each side got a gigantic aluminum trailing arm carrying the wheel at the back end and pivoting in a huge needle bearing inside an alloy box bolted to the frame at the other end. With coil springs, tubular shocks, and an antiroll bar, it was light, precise, and not prohibitively expensive. It completely eliminated camber change during cornering . . . admittedly at the expense of minor caster variations. There were also big Lockheed drum brakes and a very quick steering box. The engine was Riley's 2443cc four, which with two SUs and a little manifold tuning was good for 104 hp. Riley supplied the 4-speed, too.

The Elliot sedan weighed only 2,200 pounds, which was mostly the reason it went so fast. But of course it wasn't practical. The Elliot in reality was a lightly disguised racing car with stodgy coachwork. It cost nearly £1,600 in the late forties, and though it was damn fast, it wasn't the sort of car a young sport would pick. Nor were many wealthy executives going to pick it for a family car. It was a superb racer, though. Healey won his class in the Alpine Rally in 1947 and '48, and the Touring class in the '49 Mille Miglia.

But the Elliot chassis was better than that. In July 1949 Healey presented the Silverstone. This had the Elliot sedan chassis but was fitted with a super-light aluminum two-seater body that featured cycle fenders, excellent air penetration, cutaway doors, and a clever flat windshield that, instead of folding, slid down into a slot in the bodywork for less wind resistance. The traditional Brooklands screens that were de rigueur on British roadsters were thus eliminated in favor of a horizontal slot in the cowl that let in lots of rain water along with the glass.

The Healey looked, in toto, pretty much like a cross between the J2 Allard and the Le Mans Replica Frazer Nash, particularly with Allard-à-la-Buick portholes in the hood and

a vertical FN-like grille wider at the top than the bottom. The Silverstone's most curious feature, though, wasn't shared with anybody. This was a slot in the tail into which the spare tire fit like a teething ring into a toddler's mouth. It was supposed to act as the rear bumper. Uh huh. Right.

Silverstone owners didn't care. Healey's funny-looking roadster cost only £1,246 including tax, just a third of what the Aldingtons were getting for the similar Frazer Nash. And the 1,850-pound, 104-hp Healey was beautifully competitive with Aldy's fancy Le Mans Replica. Top speed was around 110, and 0 to 60 took 10 seconds in stock trim. But any good tuner could come up with a few more horsepower and another five miles per hour. The Silverstone's big advantage over the Frazer Nash—aside from price—was that it was a remarkably easy car to drive fast. It became a favorite car to start out in, and Tony Brooks, among many others, ran his very first season at the wheel of a Silverstone his father bought him. It was also sturdy as hell. Donald Healey and Ian Appleyard were second overall in the 1949 Alpine Rally, but the Silverstone just wasn't fast enough for international competition, and that's a fact. This Healey's competition record is all real spear-carrier stuff, with

Healey's legendary 1949 Silverstone was a clubman's favor

the high point being Tony Rolt's fourth overall in the 1949 production car race, appropriately enough at Silverstone.

The Silverstone was the definitive clubman's racer, though, precisely because it was so easy to drive. Just about anybody with both eyes pointing in the same direction could go pottering around in a Healey, thrill family and friends, and pick up some silverware. Like the J2 Allard, it was indestructible if you did even a minimum amount of maintenance, it was pretty hard to bend seriously, and, if you were in a shunt, it was easily repaired. Unfortunately, Donald Healey was in a hurry. He was getting a little too old to be playing around with low-volume, low-profit sports/ racers. So first he made the deal with George Mason that led to the Nash-Healey—a big Nash six in the Silverstone chassis—and eventually Healey made a separate deal with BMC for the Austin-powered Healey Hundred that became the high-volume, high-profit Austin-Healey.

Only 105 Silverstones were built, split just about equally between the Series D and the mildly modified Series E that had a long scoop on the hood. They were only in production for fourteen months, and most of the amateur race wins came after Healey had already gone

on to bigger and more lucrative deals. A surprising number of Silverstones survived the clubman's wars, and many of them are still used in Vintage racing in England. I've only seen one on the street ever, years ago, and that was parked in the corner of a pub parking lot in Dorchester, outside Oxford. The driver was off somewhere and not to be found, but I did get to sit in it and saw at the wheel, pretending I was Tony Brooks. It was bright red, looked perfect, and would probably be worth at least $15,000 if you could find it now. Right across from the old Abbey, next to the half-timbered cottage with the huge purple hollyhocks, ask at the White Horse pub. Tell 'em Dr. Anthony Brooks sent you.

Aston Martin

My father always says that when he gets old enough, he'll take up golf and buy an Aston Martin. The first he scathingly considers an old man's sport; the second, equally much, he considers an old man's car. Well, he'll be seventy in July and I have yet to go home to find a garaged DBS with a golf bag hidden in the boot. What this mostly points out, aside from the fact that Pop is an opinionated old curmudgeon, is that auto executives tend to build the kind of car they'd like to drive themselves. If you're a real wild-eyed piss cutter like Carroll Shelby or Rudi Uhlenhaut, this is great. But an embarrassing number of youthful hell raisers—Colin Chapman comes immediately to mind—have aged less than gracefully. And their cars have gotten pretty stodgy, too. Just compare the first Lotus Elite—a marvelous young-man's car—with the current Elite—a plush-lined box in which to watch your arteries harden.

The same sad thing happened to David Brown of Aston. Back in 1947, when he bought Aston Martin, he had more *cojones* than the whole damn Celtic United rugby team put together. Here was one gutsy Englishman. And he started right in to make Aston Martin a

he perfect "beginner's" racer.

The nicest British road car of the fifties, Sir David Brown's superb DB-2 cabriolet.

real winner. Now Aston Martin—as a name—goes way back to 1914, Lionel Martin, Robert Bamford, and the Aston Clinton hillclimb. The original owners went bankrupt in 1925, and A. C. Bertelli, Count Louis Zborowski, and later Gordon Sutherland tried each in his own way to keep the whole thing afloat. But by the time DB bought it—his money came from David Brown & Sons (hardened steel gears) and the immensely successful David Brown Tractors company—Aston had gone completely under again.

Brown got things stirred up in a fine flurry. There was a leftover 1970cc four and a prewar chassis in the old Feltham factory, so DB had engine and chassis brought together, clothed in aluminum, and sent to Belgium in 1948. Sir John Horsfall and Leslie Johnson won the Spa 24 Hours *outright,* which shook up a few people. Once he'd gotten their attention, Sir David started to revitalize Aston. Hell, what he did was throw out everything but the name and start from scratch, practically.

In 1939, Claude Hill had built up a prototype chassis for a car Aston excruciatingly

called the Atom. Surprisingly enough, the car itself was superb. Hill's chassis had a true space frame, pretty much like contemporary airplanes and a good fifteen years ahead of any other automobile frame. The whole thing was welded up from triangulated square tubing with a boxed sheet-steel area around the cowl. The front suspension was independent, with coil springs and massive trailing arms—not unlike Donald Healey's later Elliot/Silverstone. The rigid rear axle had coil springs, too, radius arms, and a transverse Panhard rod. Even in 1948, when David Brown resurrected it, the old Atom frame was easily the most advanced production-car chassis in the world.

Hill's 2-liter engine wasn't in the same league, so after only fifteen DB-1s had been built, Brown scrapped it. And he bought Lagonda Cars, Ltd., from Alan Good. Now in the thirties, W. O. Bentley had done some superb Lagonda engines, a big racing V-12 and a little 2.6-liter six with double overhead cams. Bentley's Lagonda six was just what Aston Martin needed. In 2580cc size, the Vantage engine made 120 hp. H. J. Mulliner whipped up a

The DB-2/4 Mark III coupe, one of MOMA's "ten best" postwar cars . . . and even better than that.

lovely Pininfarina-ish aluminum coupe and a nice little roadster, and the DB-2 was born.

The Aston Martin DB-2 was some plain and fancy car. It was prettier than any British car has a right to be, as tight and lithe as the best Pininfarina Ferraris. Even the curious grille—an inverted T cut into the front at a slope—was clean and modern, far superior to the traditional radiator shell that Pininfarina preserved on the similar Lancia B.20. The DB-2 coupe was so good, in fact, that Arthur Drexler chose it for the landmark Museum of Modern Art "Ten Automobiles" show in September 1953. Significantly, it was the only British car in the show, and with Raymond Loewy's Studebaker Starliner and a Porsche Super, one of only three not designed by either Pininfarina, Vignale, or Bertone.

You can make a case, actually, for the DB-2's being just about the best British car of the early fifties, all things considered. It weighed only 2,200 pounds, so it was quick, even on only 2.5 liters. Top speed was about 120 mph with a 3.77 rear end, and the quarter-mile came up in just about 18 seconds, which was not slow in 1950, believe me. A V-8 Olds-mobile Rocket 88—which was the quickest American car—was hard pressed to get under 20 seconds in the quarter. And the DB-2 handled superbly, better maybe than anything else, anywhere. It also had great hulking Girling drum brakes that were better than most, too. But most important, while it would perform right up there with a Jaguar XK-120 or a Frazer Nash, the interior was trimmed by Mulliner to their usual standards. This meant it was coachbuilt with Connoly hide and all those other nice amenities that expensive British custom-made bodies have always hidden away from prying eyes.

David Brown went the inevitable direction. The DB-2 evolved into the DB-2/4 in 1953, the DB-2/4 Mark II in 1955—which had a bored-out, 2922cc version of the old six—and then the similar Mark III. By this time power was up to 195 hp in Vantage tune, though an increase in weight to 2,500 pounds kept the performance right around the same. The grille changed shape slightly and the rear window grew, but otherwise the 1959 Aston Martin Mark III was nothing more than the ten-year-old DB-2 with a $10,000 price tag. It

As thoroughly English as you can get. Roy Salvadori with David Brown's new Aston Martin DBR1/300 in th[

wasn't getting long in the tooth, really, so much as . . . familiar. The equally pricy Mercedes 300SL was about the only other street machine with a tubular space frame, and the Aston was still quicker and better than anything *but* the 300SL. But still, it was only a *little* car. Not a real ego-crushing prestige GT, superlative in every way like Ferrari's Superfast or Maserati's 3500.

Well. Not only was the DB-2 getting on, but Sir David Brown himself was no spring chicken. And development chief John Wyer—who later built GT-40s for Ford and raced them as Mirages for Gulf—had been around quite a while, too. Wyer was put in charge of designing a successor to the DB-2, way back in 1955. Young Tom Marek was brought in to design a whole new engine, something larger than the old Bentley design. But even given a clean slate and a wide-open invitation to design something startlingly new, Marek

copped out. The new engine wasn't much different from the old. It was still a six, with double overhead cams, though it was planned at 3670cc and grew to 3995cc in 1962. Even in its day it was pretty old-fashioned. And though it made a fair amount of power, it was just barely competitive with the much cheaper Jaguars and Corvettes, not to mention the real high roller GTs like Ferrari and Mercedes.

Eventually, Marek's engine was rated at 282 hp "cooking" and 325 hp in Vantage tune. Wyer later admitted that these numbers were inflated by 15 percent or so, because Sir David felt he had to compete with the 300+ hp reading that American V-8s commonly recorded. But honestly, the Aston really didn't need any of those lies. It was fine, inflated numbers or no. Harold Beach designed a conventional platform frame, and Gaetano Ponzoni of Carrozzeria Touring designed the body in alumi-

'57 British Empire Trophy Race at Oulton Park.

num over steel tubing. Sir David bought Tickfords Coachbuilders in Newport Pagnell, and because it was easier to move Mohammed than the mountain, brought Aston to Northhamptonshire, leaving the old Middlesex Aston factory—where they'd been since 1926—to Roy and Reg Parnell, the father-son team who ran the Aston service and racing departments.

And finally, after what seems much too long, the all-new—new chassis, new engine, new body—DB-4 finally appeared in September 1958. It was pretty, no mistake, in the same lean vein as the Ferrari 250 GTE. Proud old Tickfords hammered and leaded, stitched and buttoned until the Aston was a veritable tour de force. And the uninspired engine worked. Top speed with a 3.54 rear end was roughly 140, the DB-4 would zap to 60 in less than 8 seconds, and go through the quarter in under 17 seconds. It weighed only 2,800 pounds full

up, so it really didn't need much horsepower. And the four-wheel Dunlop discs were incredible. Until Ken Miles came along with his Cobra, the DB-4 was famous far and wide for accelerating from 0 to 100 and braking back down again to 0 in just 27 seconds. Total. The Cobra halved that, of course, but for years Aston ads challenged any car to match it.

In 1959 the DB-4 GT—the DB-4 was technically a four-seater—appeared. A genuine two-seater—2 + 2, really—the GT weighed 100 pounds less and came standard with 310 hp. Top speed was claimed to be over 150. Still, the DB-4s and derivative DB-5 and DB-6 Mark II that stayed in production right up until 1970 were edging toward the white-shoes-and-double-knit-suit end of the market. The DB-6 weighed over 3,000 pounds, a hefty 500 more than the externally identical DB-4. The performance was still impressive, but it certainly wasn't effortless. And the conventional chassis was starting to show its age. In its day, the DB-2 was considered the most sophisticated thing imaginable. In its day, the DB-6 was called the last vintage sports car. Enough said. These late Astons were rugged cars, with frightfully heavy steering, a tough clutch pedal, and a shifter that was only marginally better than Jaguar's old Moss box. Irony of ironies, the balky gears of course came from David Brown & Sons, Gearmakers.

Sir David started his Astons racing from the very beginning. And the DB-2 series, at least, was a beautiful dual-purpose sort of car that could be raced on the international level—5-6 at Le Mans in 1950, 1-2 in class at the Mille Miglia in '52—and still used as a marvelously mean street car day to day. But by 1952, when the new Eberan von Eberhorst–designed DB-3 appeared strictly for racing, there was no such thing as a dual-purpose sports car, at least not for overall race wins. And overall wins were what Sir David was after. It took him years of mediocre finishes with evolving teams of DB-3, DB-3/S, and DBR1/300 models before Carroll Shelby/Roy Salvadori, Stirling Moss/Jack Fairman, and Paul Frere/Maurice Trintignant finally managed to win the Sports Car Manufacturers Championship in 1959. It took a win at the Nurburgring, 1–2 at Le Mans, and 1–4 at Dundrod to secure the championship.

The DB-3 series roadsters were basically

factory racers, though a few—very few—passed into private hands in Britain. The Salvadori/Shelby Le Mans winner is still being traded around from collection to collection for $50,000 or so, and occasionally a DBR will turn up in a vintage race. But as far as I know, there's only one real DB-3 in the States, and one DBR. A couple may have sneaked by me, but I didn't notice. There are, on the other hand, a handful of DB-4 GT Zagatos in this country, and they're something else entirely, maybe the nicest cars Aston Martin ever built.

In 1960 a few short-wheelbase DB-4 GT chassis were sent to Via Giorgini 16, in Milano, which was Carrozzeria Zagato. For forty years Zagato specialized in taking weight out of cars that were already considered lightweights. Usually it was Fiats or Lancias or Abarths or Alfas. But DB had him do the job on the Aston Martin DB-4. On the 93-inch-wheelbase, 325-hp chassis, Zagato erected a bumperless, aerodynamic coupe that was easily the cleanest machine from Aston since the DB-2. It was all aluminum, of course, and the interior was done like most of the GT Ferraris—adequately, but certainly not luxuriously. The weight came down to nearly 2,000 pounds, and the Zagato was confidently expected to be a real "production" racer, one that could be trundled off to Le Mans or Sebring and run with the leaders.

Which is just what happened. For about the first half hour. Unfortunately, David Brown's DB-4 mechanicals—particularly his gearbox—just weren't sturdy enough for long-distance racing. The Zagato coupe was an Aston Martin that did the quarter in 14 seconds, and 0 to 100 to 0 in 20 seconds. This once again gave them something to advertise. A race win or two would have been the frosting, but they simply weren't quite sturdy enough. In all, twenty-five were built between 1960 and '63, and most of them survive. Genuine 160-mph Grand Tourers, the GT Zagatos are easily the most exciting Aston Martins that you can actually hope to get your hands on, since the *real* racers are pretty much locked up in England and not about to leave the country—national treasures, you know, and all that.

Ne plus ultra . . . 1960 Aston DB-4 GT Zagato.

Astons are expensive, always were. Probably, if things go right, always will be. And yet they sold surprisingly well in the old days. For a while, in the early sixties, Sir David was cranking out almost four a day, counting all the different models. This is virtually mass production in the $15,000-a-copy sports car business. There aren't many DB-2s or Zagatos, of course, but from DB-4 to DB-6 you can find cars pretty easily. And for not that much money—$4,000 to $6,000, maybe. Zagatos, of course, are worth four or five times that. The only trouble is, all Astons are frighteningly costly to repair and not all that reliable. On the other hand, they're as well made as comparable Ferraris, Maseratis, and Lamborghinis, and though they don't have the absolute performance of a GTB/4, they're a lot more comfortable and fancily decorated.

It's a trade-off is what it is. The early Astons were starker but also prettier, sturdier, and (for their size) a lot better performers. The late Astons—and that includes the cur-

The DB-4 GT Zagato: Italian style, British power.

rent DBS V-8—are very near to being personal luxury cars, a British-built Mark V Continental. They are decently quick, very expensively furnished . . . and very expensive, too. But unlike the DB-2—which was a real driver's car—or the Zagato—which was a Mille Miglia Ferrari, only made in England—the later cars don't have much, well . . . character. *Brio.* They're nice and all, but kind of quiet. Not dull, exactly, more, uhhh . . . refined. Understated. To the point that only a very mature enthusiast can appreciate their fine qualities. Which is a nice way of saying the Aston is an old man's car.

Jaguar XK-120/ 140/150

My friend Peter's father, a well-off publishing executive, has owned Jaguars since the early fifties. All of them have been bought new, all meticulously maintained, and all powered by the famous double-overhead-cam XK engine. "This one I have now is the best ever," he says ruefully. "Hasn't cost me a nickel in the last week and a half." The ironic thing is that after twenty-five years of Jaguars, he'll probably still buy another, much as he knows he shouldn't. Like that last nightcap, it seems like a good idea at the time, though you're always sorry in the morning.

For the level of mechanical design and styling finesse you get, Jaguar could charge twice the price and still have a market. But then the cars would have to be well built, instead of thrown together. It's a matter of basic philosophy. Volkswagen, for example, took a really dumb design and made it work spectacularly through the use of excellent materials and superior workmanship. Jaguar has always taken a wonderful design and made it less than it should be through extreme cost cutting and shoddy production. But at the price, they're simply irresistible.

Between trips to the shop, Jaguars *are* grand. Beautiful, comfortable, fast, stable carriages for blasting cross-country at insanely high speeds and impressing the peasants with the glory of your going. Fortunately, they don't know about your garage bills. Listen, this isn't nitpicking—Jaguars are *very* hard to keep running right. For example, a few years ago Jaguar introduced a new model to the press at a posh resort in Switzerland. Selected journalists from all over the world were there, representing the major automobile magazines. Everybody got to drive one of the new models for two full days, so he could evaluate it properly. It was made clear that our blessing was very important to the success of this new model.

The entire Jaguar development team was there, the men who'd designed the car. They had a whole battalion of factory mechanics to watch over the six specially prepared cars they'd shipped in from Coventry. Sir William Lyons himself spent two days there, along with Lofty England and literally everybody important from Jaguar. I was there for four days. And never once were more than two of the six new Jaguars running at any one time. The factory mechanics were literally rebuilding each one overnight, every night, so the press would have something to drive in the morning. By the end of the week, they looked like they'd just done Le Mans race week, and the half of the Jaguar contingent that was in hysterics wasn't talking to the half that should have been. I had the distinct feeling this was SOP at Jaguar.

Things were better back in the old days, I think, when young Bill Lyons and Bill Walmsley got together in Blackpool in 1922 to build motorcycle sidecars. Up until 1935, when Walmsley left to start his own travel trailer company and S. S. Cars Ltd. went public, everything was small enough that the two partners could personally keep track of quality control, design, and all the other bits that went into their incredibly beautiful, inexpensive cars. S. S. cars were said to have "that £1,000 look," even though they cost less than £320. They were good value for money indeed, with lusciously swoopy bodywork and adequate performance from engines supplied by Standard.

Right up until World War II and for a couple of years afterward, Lyons continued to build these classic S.S. cars, though when the works opened in 1945 he had to drop the twin lightning streak initials to avoid confusion with those of the hated Nazi *Schutz Staffel.* The cars and the company were now called simply Jaguar, and they bought Standard's engine department. For the first time, William Lyons built his own engines, starting with mildly modified versions of the 2.5- and 3.5-liter sixes that Standard had previously supplied.

In 1945 Lyons put together his postwar design team. He himself had a marvelous sense of style and was chiefly responsible for the beautiful bodies that graced everything from the very first Swallow Sidecar up until the current XJ 12. Claude Baily was his chief designer and all-rounder, a stolid engineer who'd been with S.S. early on. William Heynes was primarily concerned with the chassis, though he did do some engine work. But the man who pretty much designed the aesthetically superb XK engine was Walter Hassan, who'd started out with Bentley in the early twenties and later did everything from land speed record cars for Thomas and Taylor and Reid Railton in the thirties to the Coventry Climax Formula One engines in the fifties and early sixties.

Wally Hassan was at Bristol designing aircraft engines during the war and came to Jaguar in '45. After a number of false starts with pushrod designs, he came up with a double-overhead-cam four code-named the XF,

Jaguar at the Glen; Ray Mason's XK-120 M, 1954.

which displaced 1360cc. Soon he had a similar, long-stroke six with hemispherical combustion chambers, seven main bearings, and chain-driven overhead cams. Harry Weslake, the acknowledged dean of British engine designers, created the super-efficient XK head, an alloy casting with excellent breathing and combustion, that weighed only 50 pounds. With twin SU carburetors the six in its final 3422cc form was rated at 160 hp, as much as the contemporary Cadillac V-8 that displaced a whopping 5.5 liters. In 1949—it actually debuted at the 1948 Earl's Court Show in November—Jaguar's new XK six was the most powerful production engine you could buy. It would wind to 5,000 rpm and, if you took extremely good care of it, would survive pretty much intact.

The rest of the chassis wasn't as interesting, or reliable. Two deep frame rails connected by fabricated crossmembers mounted the archaic Moss 4-speed, already an anachronism but the only transmission in England at the time capable of handling 160 hp. At the rear there was a dead conventional solid axle on semielliptics. At the front were fabricated upper and lower A-arms with torsion bars and tubular shocks, and Lockheed drum brakes. Aside from the gearbox, the biggest headaches on the new car were these brakes. Even though they were 12 inches in diameter, the drums just weren't up to the speed the Jaguar could reach, which was roughly 120 mph, hence the XK-120 name.

If the brakes were the worst feature, the body was the best. The voluptuous, slab-sided XK-120 looked like a Bonneville streamliner compared to anything else on the road in the late forties. It borrowed a little from Ralph Roberts's prewar Chrysler Newport, a little from the Mille Miglia BMW, a little from the prototype postwar Frazer Nash. But it was an original throughout, from the curiously bulbous front end with its slim, oval grille to the skirted, long pointy tail. The endless hood promised performance, and the tiny cockpit, with its subtle cutaway sides, hinted at the race course. All in all, there wasn't a line, a curve, a point that you could change without upsetting the perfect flowing euphony of the XK shape. It wasn't anything at all like the "Italian look" that Pininfarina was proselytizing, nor was it traditionally British. It was

Introduced in 1955, the XK-140 was far and away the best value for money in the world.

lithe, modern, international, and somehow just right.

The XK-120 was the first modern boulevard sports car in England. At almost 2,600 pounds it was a heavyweight. The suspension was much softer than anything previously built with pretensions to good handling. The bench seat was butter-soft and leathery, and though it was kind of tight getting in, the cockpit was relatively comfortable once you were inside. Even the top and windows worked to keep the outside out, when that's what you wanted. The transmission was awkward, but it did have synchromesh, and even if the engine was powerful, you didn't have to keep it on the cam all the time, nor constantly baby it either. In short, the XK-120 was a real *car,* in the modern sense of the term, not an overgrown toy for masochistic adolescents.

Best of all, like all William Lyons's cars it was cheap. In 1949, when a Frazer Nash cost £3,300, you could get an XK-120 in Britain for £1,250, tax included. In the States that came out at slightly under $4,000, when Ferraris with similar performance started at $12,000 and up, Allards were nearly $10,000, and even a gutless anachronism like the MG-TC cost $2,000. In short, the Jaguar XK was the buy of the century, and enthusiasts stormed the Coventry works thrusting fistfuls of money at Lyons and his crew. And got nothing in return.

In their unbelievable naiveté, Jaguar had tooled up for a production run of 200 roadsters, which they hammered out in aluminum over ash frames. It took months for Pressed Steel to carve dies for mass production. Not until late 1949/early 1950 were there any XK-120s to sell, and most of those went to America to help the critical British balance of payments. By the time the evolutionary XK-140 was introduced in 1954, Lyons's original 200 estimate had grown to over 12,000 XK-120s, with a good majority of them in the States.

The XK-140 was really nothing more than an improved XK-120. You could get overdrive, which was nice, and the cramped coupe cockpit—which was impossible for anybody much over five feet six—was opened up in all directions. The body got a few inches wider as a result, but nobody noticed. And most Jaguars now came with wire wheels instead of steel discs. Originally, the XK-120 had been designed with fender skirts, but knock-off hubs wouldn't fit under them, so Jaguar deleted the skirts if you got wire wheels. The racing head from the Le Mans C-type gave 190 hp in factory trim, though you could also get 210 hp as an option. Right near the end of production, a Borg-Warner automatic became optional. This disgusting travesty was a sure sign of terminal dry rot in Jaguar sports cars, and the XK-150 depressed the old wind-in-the-face types even more.

Even with disc brakes, 265 hp, and a smooth—if bulbous—body, the XK-150 was passé by 1957.

The XK-150 was Jaguar's equivalent of the MG-TF. It was rounded, pudgy, and funny looking. The exquisite lines of the XK-120 had been artificially pumped up to make a freakishly bulbous car out of what had once been the best-styled machine in Britain. The only saving grace of the XK-150 was the S-type, a 265-hp engine option that brought the old six out to 3781cc but made it about as reliable as the Penn Central's old Harlem Division. Ready-to-run weight for the 150 was nearly 3,300 pounds, and even the roadster had wind-up windows. None ever got near a race course, though you used to see lots of them around suburban shopping centers driven by aging ingénues with teased hair and fake eyelashes, even at ten in the morning.

For all its faults, the XK-150 was the fastest Jaguar in a straight line, solely because of that bunged-out engine. A good 150 S would consistently better 130 mph, do the quarter in just about 16 seconds, and get to 100 in a little over 20 seconds, which was pretty quick in 1957. It wasn't as spectacularly fast as the XK-120 had seemed a decade earlier, but then again everybody else had grown up and Sir William was standing still. Or maybe even slipping backward a little.

The 150 did have one superb advance, and that was four-wheel Dunlop disc brakes borrowed from the racing D-types. These were the first discs available on a mass-production machine, and finally cured the Jaguar XK curse. But that was about all you could say good about the XK-150, except that it was still relatively cheap, relatively pretty if you didn't look too close, and very fast for its size. Of course, even a ratty Corvette would eat Jaguars for breakfast seven days till Sunday, and cost less besides.

The biggest problem with early postwar Jaguars—with *any* Jaguar—is simple deterioration. The front end falls apart, the Lucas electrics fall apart, the engine falls apart, the gearbox goes, likewise the interior, the paint, and the bodywork—hell, *everything*. In the hands of the average American klutz brought up in our disposable kar kulture, Jaguars will unfailingly disintegrate within six months. Life expectancy of an XK in New York City is maybe two days, just slightly longer than the best Fiats. Jaguars are flimsy. There's no getting around it. That's why they can sell them so cheaply. On the other hand, they're also fiendishly complex and horrendously expensive to repair.

Par exemple. My local exotic car wizard is restoring an XK-140 drophead for a customer to decent but not concours condition. The poor guy has over $2,000 in the car to start with, the engine just cost him $3,000, the interior is priced at $2,000 for new leather, another $2,000 for paint. And catch this. To get an expert to fit a new padded convertible top—which is a bitch of a job on this particular model—is going to run a cool grand. Just to install the top, for Chrissake. There is no way on earth this poor sap can get out from under that car for less than $10,000, and I'm not going to be the one to tell him that fully restored XK-120/140/150s are going for $5,000 right now.

Postwar Jaguar prices have gone through a curious cycle. In the mid-sixties, everybody and his brother was collecting early Jaguars, maybe because the aura of the XK-E rubbed off on the early cars and restored some of their glory. A really good XK-120 was worth $2,500 to $3,000 ten years ago, maybe more. But though the Ferrari Barchetta you bought then for $3,000 is worth $25,000 today, that Jaguar is still worth less than $10,000 for sure. Somewhere between 1970 and '73, XK Jaguar prices leveled off and then dropped alarmingly, just about the time old-car prices in general started to skyrocket.

I don't know why. They're certainly not cars to buy for everyday use, but then again you wouldn't want to try and maintain that Ferrari Barchetta at today's prices, either. Somewhere in there, Jaguar XKs got lost in some sort of time warp and never came out the other side. But Jaguars have always been collector cars, so personally I don't think the lull is going to last. Which means that XKs of any series are super bargains right now. The very best cars, from a collector's point of view, are the limited-production XK-120 M and XK-140 MC. These were aluminum-bodied lightweight production racers that came with a whole passel of high-performance engine and chassis mods. They were built stronger for racing, so they're stronger today. The aluminum body won't rot away as fast as the cheap steel of the production cars, and of course they're much rarer. And many of the aluminum cars have been owned by either racers or collectors, so they've been well cared for, too.

Most 120s and 140s you find will have been modified at some point. They almost certainly have the later 3.8 or 4.2 engines, three carburetors, perhaps disc brakes, and quite possibly overdrive. Which isn't all that bad, I promise you. Jaguar has made some real improvements since the early days, and everything is a bolt-on swap. In fact, if you're not a Purist-Purist, Jag mechanics universally prefer the 3.8 to any other version. Myself, I'd like a nice

XK-120 coupe, with a 3.8 engine tuned up to D-type specs, overdrive, and disc brakes. With fanatical maintenance, it would be a car you could occasionally drive, perhaps race, and have a lot of fun with. And one you could get into for not very much right now, which is a pleasant bonus not to be sneezed at.

In a very real sense, the XK-120 Jaguars changed the shape of all postwar sports cars . . . made them softer, less demanding, more useful for everyday driving. They were fantastically popular in their day, and will be again. They're not very well made, and that's a fact. But they are excellent designs, and it's possible to intelligently overrestore one so thoroughly that all the bad comes out and the good stays in. All most Jaguars lack is some careful workmanship, the kind any good restorer—amateur or professional—is going to apply as a matter of course. And at that point, they become a viable collector car. Come to think of it, that's probably the mistake Peter's father has been making all these years. He keeps buying *new* Jaguars from the factory instead of *old* Jaguars from a conscientious restorer. I'll have to try that on him next time he starts whimpering about socialized labor.

Jaguar C-type

The Jaguar XK-120 was much too heavy for real international competition. But the chassis could be stiffened up, and of course the Hassan/Weslake six, with its double overhead cams and excellent flow characteristics, was already more of a pure race engine than anything except the Ferrari V-12. And the Jaguar was cheap. For a clubman's racer, it was half the price of an Allard and a third the price of a Frazer Nash, though the performance was nearly the same. And there were racing mods available right from the factory. For less than $500 you could get a lightened flywheel, high-compression pistons, full-race cams, a heavy-duty clutch, dual exhausts, and a chassis kit with heavier springs, shocks, torsion bars, brake linings, and an oversized gas tank, metal cockpit cover, and Brooklands screen for the body.

Because of its weight, even in race tune the XK-120 didn't accelerate very quickly, so it was a dud at sprints or hillclimbs. But its top speed was impressive—test driver Ron Sutton clocked 126.4 mph at Jabbeke in 1949 and 132.5 with a partial streamliner. In 1953 Sutton's successor, Norman Dewis, got a carefully streamlined XK-120 up to 172 mph on the same Belgian autoroute. The average club racer could count on 120 or a little less, which was pretty quick thirty years ago. So the XK-120 was a pretty good car for high-speed courses. And the engine could be made to last. XK-120s simply dominated things like the Dundrod TT and Goodwood Nine Hours, and before the clutch fried, Leslie Johnson actually had one running in third after 21 hours at Le Mans in '49. And he finished an incredible fifth in the Mille Miglia. But that was really about the only big international race finish for the XK-120.

It *was* superb at rallies, though. Ian Appleyard won Coupes des Alpes in '50, '51, and '52, and the first of only two Alpine Gold Cups ever awarded. (Stirling Moss got the other in '52, '53, and '54.) In '51, Jaguars won six international rallies outright and got class wins in the other four. But nice as it was, rallying wasn't the big time, even in the early fifties. And at places like Le Mans, Rheims, the Nurburgring, and Silverstone, the XK-120s were simply outclassed. They were pretty, thoroughbred street cars trying to compete with vicious, single-purpose racing machines designed from the ground up for going fast. Jaguar quickly learned that hoary old truism: the only way to win races is with a race car.

So they built one, from scratch—a real racing car, with no extras. Chief engineer Bill Heynes took William Lyons to Le Mans in June 1950. They decided it was the only race worth winning. Just as Ford realized a decade and a half later, there are races and then there is Le Mans. The only contest that got more publicity was Indianapolis, but that only helped sell cars for Frank Kurtis. For a factory that wanted to promote its everyday cars with a race win, Le Mans was—and is—the only choice.

Starting in September 1950, Heynes built

a Le Mans winner. The stock six was a perfect beginning. With some work on the heads and twin SU carbs, he got 210 hp at 5,800 rpm. Heynes kept the stock transmission, front suspension, and rear axle. The semielliptic springs were cleverly replaced at the rear by a single transverse torsion bar fixed at the center and allowed to twist with the wheels at each end, and the brakes—the big weakness of the XK-120—were modified by Lockheed. The knock-off wire wheels got alloy rims and there were some other bits of trickery. But the running gear was surprisingly stock XK-120.

To tie this all together, Heynes built one of the first-ever space frames out of steel tubing. The wheelbase was 6 inches shorter than the XK-120 at 96, but the rear-set engine gave perfect 50/50 weight distribution. Stressed steel sheets at the cowl, behind the seats, and under the floor tied the whole structure together into a supremely stable triangulated girder. And over it went another Lyons masterpiece, a gorgeous aerodynamic aluminum body with just a touch of the XK-120 about it. A widened, shortened version of the XK grille was the only break on the nose, and the headlights were carefully faired into the fenders. For easy access the entire nose hinged forward in one piece, eliminating a major annoyance of the street machine that had only a narrow, rear-hinged hood.

The new Jaguar was about as low as possible, with the hood brought right down over the cam covers and the fenders right down over the tires. Everything about it was streamlined as much as possible. Even the exhaust was recessed into the body side. A full underpan, passenger-seat tonneau, and minimal Brooklands screen were used, too. In final form, it looked a little like the 1937 Le Mans Bugatti "Tank" and a little like Sid Enever's MGA Le Mans prototype. But mostly, like the XK-120, it was unique.

The new car barely made it to Le Mans practice in '51. Called logically enough the XK-120 C (for Competition), it immediately became famous as the Jaguar C-type. Three were finished by Le Mans time, driven by Stirling Moss/Jack Fairman, Peter Whitehead/Peter Walker, and Leslie Johnson/Clemente Biondetti. In the tradition of Le Mans teams, Moss was the "rabbit" who would go as quickly as possible till something broke; the

Peter Whitehead, Peter Walker, and their C-type Jaguar, minutes after winning at Le Mans, 1951.

others would go more slowly and hope for the best. And it worked. Moss broke the lap record and an oil line. Biondetti broke just the oil line, and Whitehead and Walker soldiered home to win Jaguar's first Le Mans . . . and their first race with a real racing car. Not a bad beginning.

The C-type was a one-race machine, designed for nothing more than winning at Le Mans. That it could be competitive on other circuits never really mattered to Jaguar. But the car was so completely superior that they figured, why not? So at the end of the summer they took three cars to the Irish TT and finished 1–2–4. Moss took one to Goodwood in September and won again. The '52 season was really a continuation of '51 for the C-type. For the Mille Miglia, Stirling Moss and Norman Dewis did have the first Jaguar disc brakes, developed by Dunlop. Moss crashed there, and also at the Monte Carlo GP, run for sports cars that year. And at Le Mans he managed to ruin the whole Jaguar team, through no fault of his own.

Stirling Moss was a fiddler. Always looking for that last tenth, he'd experiment with anything he thought would give him a little more speed. He was a worrier, too, and in 1952, still pretty inexperienced in international racing. Anyway, Moss drove a factory C-type in practice for Le Mans, 1952. And he came in all upset because the brand-new Mercedes 300 SLR coupe was pulling him down Mulsanne, 10–15 mph faster than the Jaguar. "Do something," cried Moss. Jaguar panicked. The team rushed back to Coventry and fitted long, streamlined tails and low, swoopy noses to all the team C-types. But to do it, they had to use smaller radiators. And of course, when they got back to Le Mans for the race, the cars immediately overheated. Within three hours, all three Jaguars were sitting in the pits with cooked engines. Ironically, the Mercedes that panicked Moss in practice had a super-tuned engine that was never intended to last for 24 hours. The Germans switched it for a milder one on race day and never did go as fast as the C-types had gone the year before in stock form. So it goes.

In August 1952 Jaguar started shipping out production models of the C-type, with only a few minor revisions over the factory Le Mans cars. John Fitch won the Watkins Glen

Seneca Cup with his, and *The Motor* got one for a road test. They timed 0 to 60 in 8.1 seconds, 0 to 100 in 20.1, and a top speed of 143 mph with 3.31 gears. Including tax, the C-type cost only £2,327 ready to race, which was astoundingly cheap for a proven Le Mans winner. And of course, since most of the mechanicals were based on the XK-120, it was remarkably easy to keep in spares. Until the middle of 1953, the competition department turned out about one C-type a week, for a total production of 54, including the factory team cars.

At Sebring in '53, Sherwood Johnson/Bob Wilder and Harry Gray/Bob Gegen finished third and fourth behind a Cunningham and an Aston. At Le Mans, the factory cars were in 1951 configuration, except that triple Weber carbs gave them 220 hp, they all had disc brakes, and the bodywork was even lighter than before. After 24 hours, the team cars were first, second, and fourth, with John Fitch and Phil Walters in third in their Cunningham. The big difference was the disc brakes on the Jaguars, which were simply miles and away better than the Al-Fin drums on the heavy American challenger. The new Scottish team Ecurie Ecosse, run by David Murray, traded in their XK-120s and bought C-types with which they finished second at Spa and the Nurburgring to Ferraris. The works team went to the TT, but Moss was the only finisher, in fourth. Moss and Whitehead won at Rheims and there was a veritable slew

C-types were competitive anywhere, any time; this car

of other good C-type finishes all over the world. The factory built D-types for '54, but Ecurie Ecosse bought the "lightweight" factory C-types and won at Spa. They also got a number of other good international finishes within the top half-dozen.

By 1954, the C-types were already obsolete. The 300 SLRs were so much more sophisticated it was shameful, and Jaguar had no choice but to match the Germans or get out of racing. So the C-types trickled down to minor international, then club racing. Jaguar kept the same basic pieces in production for nearly thirty years, though, so it was no problem to update the C-types. Probably the most famous holdout of all was Scottish-American Gordon MacKensie, who simply owned big-bore modified at Lime Rock Park right up until the mid-sixties. By then he had a 3.8 engine, late-model disc brakes, and an entire E-type independent rear end. And he was only a second or two off the lap record, held by a mid-engine Can-Am car with double the horsepower and a lot more tire on the road.

I remember even in the late fifties, when I was a kid hanging around Lime Rock, that MacKensie was already sort of a legend and the crowd favorite, hands down. The local SCCA regional magazine was always putting out some sort of article on him, and it inevitably turned out that when some reporter tried it, Gordon was the only one who could even *drive* his car, the thing was so tweaked around and unpredictable. He sure did go fast,

though, I remember that distinctly. One of my friends, an IBM engineer named Brandt Griffing, had a horrendous-looking but super-sophisticated modified with a Buick V-8 in it, and MacKensie was forever blowing his doors off. We never did figure out how he did it.

All those nice things you can say about early sports/racers as collector cars are true of the C-type, in spades. Like a Devin SS or XK-120 M or something, a C-type is perfectly usable on the street—hell, the *factory* team used to drive their cars to and from *Le Mans* every year—it's robust as Tower Bridge, and you can get almost every breakable part new from the factory, except for body bits. A good C-type—and most of those still around have been pretty carefully restored—is worth way over $30,000 these days, and it's worth it. The C-types established the racing performance image that Jaguar is still cashing in on, and they are awfully nice cars, too, even discounting the race wins and Stirling Moss, Ecurie Ecosse, and early morning mist rising over Mulsanne. The C-types picked up where the Bentleys left off two decades earlier, and a little British racing green was a gladsome sight at Le Mans to a lot of people in the early fifties.

The C-types are pretty, among the best-looking sports/racers ever. And that they are a lot better built than the stock XKs goes without saying, since each one was hand-made by the race shop. But more than any other car from that time, the C-types are pure, unadulterated nostalgia. It's been a long time since British cars figured even a little in international endurance racing—unless you want to call John Wyer's blue and orange Ford/Mirages British—but back when Britons were kings, C-types were their chariots. And damn nice ones, too.

oc" Wyllie at Watkins Glen in 1954.

Jaguar D-type

Even before Le Mans in '53, where the Jaguar factory raced three-year-old C-types, Bill

Heynes was testing a new car for '54. The C-type was a racing sports car, not a Formula car with fenders like the Mercedes and Ferrari Le Mans machines. But the new D-type had everything a racer's racer could want except independent rear suspension. The old six was given a dry-sump oil system to make it shorter, which allowed Heynes to lower the hood. And with 3781cc, he eventually got a solid 300 hp in Le Mans tune. The four-wheel discs now hid behind pressed-steel wheels that were much stronger than the old wire spokes, and though the suspension front and rear was pretty much the same as the C-type's, it was bolted up to a monocoque tub that was six inches shorter between the wheels and seven inches shorter overall. It was a lot lighter, too. But the big difference in the D-type was aerodynamics, for though the earlier cars had been remarkably clean for their day, the Jaguar Ds had just about the best air penetration of any cars in the world, ever. With the same horsepower, a D-type was nearly 20 mph faster than a C-type—almost entirely because of the smoother body. With 250 hp, a D Jag was timed at 169 mph down Mulsanne, with Le Mans gears, and went nearly 200 mph with 2.53 gearing. Not bad for 230 cubic inches in 1954.

At Le Mans, which Mercedes skipped in '54, Froilan Gonzalez/Maurice Trintignant in a Ferrari beat Duncan Hamilton/Tony Rolt in the only surviving D-type by a little over a minute after 24 hours, even though the Jaguar was 10 mph faster down the straights and had better brakes, too. The factory team did win at Rheims 1-2-3. The only other international race they entered was the Dundrod TT, which was scored on a displacement handicap system. Jaguar figured they'd beat the system with a 2.4-liter version of the six, but all they did was outsmart themselves. All the little engines blew spectacularly, early on.

Most people like to forget about 1955 when it comes to racing. That was the year that Pierre Levegh bounced his Mercedes SLR off Lance Macklin's Healey, after Mike Hawthorn cut Macklin off right in front of the unprotected pits at Le Mans. The exploding Mercedes went off the road and through the closely packed French crowd like grapeshot at Trafalgar, killing eighty people and maiming over a hundred. The German team natu-

No sports/racer has ever had quite the impact of Jaguar

rally withdrew, but the organizers were afraid of a riot if they stopped the race, so the benumbed drivers continued around for another night and day. Ironically, Hawthorn's D Jag—shared with Ivor Bueb—went on to win. Blame for the massacre raged back and forth in the papers for months and months—*"Hawthorn es coupable"*—and Hawthorn, who had a reputation for putting his foot in his mouth anyway, inflamed it all by saying in so many words, "If you can't drive it, park it," and refusing to take any blame at all.

Hawthorn and Phil Walters won Sebring in a D-type and Desmond Titterington won the TT in a D-type, but most other races were canceled in 1955. The Swiss, among others, banned racing permanently. English racing wasn't much affected, somehow, and despite Hawthorn and Jaguar being in the eye of the hurricane, Jaguar continued development work on the D-type for '56. For Rheims they had fuel injection and 300 hp and finished

disc-braked D-type, an aerodynamic missile that would go almost 200 mph in 1954.

1-2-3-4. Le Mans was postponed until late summer in 1956 because the entire pit area where Levegh had crashed was being totally rebuilt. After the factory cars broke, an Ecurie Ecosse D-type won, which prompted Jaguar to give its whole team over to David Murray and retire from racing in October.

Ecurie Ecosse was run as a private team of five cars for Le Mans in 1957, and D-types finished 1-2-3-4-6, in perhaps their finest hour. That summer, though, the Commission Sportive International voted to restrict engines for international races to 3000cc. Jaguar made some short-stroke versions of the six, but they didn't work too well. The D-type was officially obsolete.

On February 12, 1957, Jaguar itself was almost officially obsolete. A horrendous fire destroyed the entire production facility to the tune of $10 million, including the race shop and all the D-type jigs and spares. Jaguar had started selling production D-types for about $10,000 in 1955, and forty-two had been built before the shop burned. There was also a plan to make the D-type eligible for SCCA C-production by homologating 100 cars with windshields and tops and other tacked-on street equipment, but only sixteen were built before the fire destroyed everything. Called the XK-SS, the rare street-legal D-type has to be the most curious car ever. Most of them were immediately turned into real racing D-types by throwing away the top and interior. Because they needed to sell 100, Jaguar was selling the SS for under $7,000, when an identical D-type cost $10,000. So a handful of people picked up bargain race cars, all but one of them in the States.

Incredible as it may seem, a D-type Jaguar is now the easiest classic racing car to own. They are so revered in Britain—only a 4.5 Bentley confers more status—that at least two companies are building replica D-types with exact suspensions and monocoques and body

John Fitch leading SCCA C-modified in Briggs Cunningham's blue-striped D-Jag at Thompson, 1956.

panels. So not only is it possible to get engine parts new, but you can now buy body and chassis parts, too. Hell, you can get a whole new *car* if you want to, for about $30,000. Everything is original, right down to the DeDion rear end and fuel injection that appeared on late-model D-types, and unless you're an expert on racing Jaguar serial numbers, you'd never tell the copy from the original. In a few years, there will be *more* D-types than there were in 1957.

Which is not a bad thing, I promise you. The D-type Jaguar is the most exciting racing car you could even consider owning for occasional street use. And even though you'd have to be out of your mind to actually drive one very often except with the VSSC, it can be done. And as I say, now that there's a new supply of parts, it's as painless to own as any Jaguar, or even better. Because like the C-types, the D-types—and the replicars, too, for that matter—were built in the race shop, one

at a time, carefully, by hand. And most of them have been lovingly restored the same way. So the workmanship is guaranteed to be a helluva lot better than on some clapped-out XK-150 you pick up off a suburban car lot.

The D-type—and the C-type, too—are also the most famous of all British sports/racers, legends even when new. There'll *always* be a demand for them, and it's one of the few cars I will absolutely guarantee will *never* be worth less than it is right now. Of all the blue-blooded, pedigreed sports cars you can pick from—and there really aren't all that many— the big Jags with their production-based running gear are among the most practical. Also the most beautiful, fastest, most evocative, most nostalgic, and the best. When it comes to postwar English cars, the D-types are *it,* followed closely by the C-types. Nothing else is even close, and if you're an Anglophile with $30,000 to spend, don't screw around. Do it now before it's too late.

Bentley Continental

After years of indecision, I've finally figured out what I'm going to drive in Heaven. Silly; of *course* they have cars in Heaven. And willing girls, Mums Cordon Rouge, Coors, and Pinch by the gallon. And lots of good coarse country paté and well-aged steaks. Heaven, the way I figure it, is going to be a reward for all these years we've spent denying ourselves, sort of like an Easter feast at the end of Lent. And since it's Heaven, we all get to pick our own pleasures. Right? I mean, how else could it be Heaven if we had to enjoy ourselves with somebody else's idea of a good time?

Anyway, to go with Candy Bergen, I figure I'll have a 427 Cobra. That's for weekdays. Weekends, I'm ordering a nice 275 GTB/4 Ferrari, bright red, of course, and maybe sort of a rotating . . . uhhhhm . . . harem, I think is the word, all smoldering Mediterranean brunettes. And for evenings out and Sunday afternoons, I'm reserving Karen Graham, who is that absolutely *perfect* little girl—ain't but this tall, but the most beautiful girl I have *ever* seen—who does the Estée Lauder ads.

And to go with perfect, sophisticated Karen Graham, why, the perfect, sophisticated automobile—a Bentley Continental, of course. I haven't decided whether I want an R-type, or one of those S-type two-door versions of the Mulliner Flying Spur. Maybe one of each, so I can let Karen choose which color will go with her outfit best. Of course, it being Heaven and all, we could probably get 'em to change the color whenever we wanted, but that might be asking a bit much.

You're asking, why a Bentley Continental? Well, son, Ah'm glad you asked me that there question. Because normal Bentley sedans—though very nice—are about as exciting as having Julie Eisenhower all to yourself. I mean, whatever turns you on, but *still*. And why not another flat-out, foot-to-the-floor, macho sports car like the Cobra and Ferrari? Simple. Because number one, who wants to go out to a fancy-dress evening in Heaven with all those saints and everybody in a Cobra, and number two, petite Karen Graham is much too much of a lady to ride in a Cobra, fancy-dress ball or not. For which you might say, to hell with her. But then, love *will* find a way.

Ralph Stein wrote years ago that he wanted a machine that was perfect neither for lugging kids around nor for winning races. He wanted something in the middle, that wouldn't really be good for either extreme but perfect for in between. And that's the Bentley Continental. It's a lot more sporting than a standard Rolls/Bentley, but on the other hand it's easily the most luxurious and flexible high-performance automobile ever built. And pretty, too. Sophisticated, expensive, and, for most people . . . well, just the perfect combination. Here, let me show you, and see if you don't agree.

Obviously, the R-type Bentley Continental has credentials, a pedigree above reproach. But it's a lot more than just another Bentley. The idea for the Continental was to take the standard Mark VI, which was really a Rolls-Royce Silver Dawn, and make it into a 120-mph motorcar with brakes and handling to match, without, of course, losing any of the traditional Rolls/Bentley virtues like silence, comfort, and exquisite workmanship. In other words, to make a car that would really live up to the "Silent Sports Car" tag some wit at RR advertising had given the Bentleys of the thirties.

In 1950, when Rolls-Royce decided to build the new Silent Sports Car, the project was given to Harry Evernden and John Blatchley, the chief development engineer and chief stylist at Crewe. Evernden took the standard chassis—120-inch wheelbase, independent coil spring front suspension, rigid rear axle—and gave it harder shocks, stiffer

1952 Bentley Continental R-type by H. J. Mulliner.

springs, and quicker steering: not enough to be obtrusive, but a lot better than the standard cars. He fiddled a bit with the standard brakes, too. The engine was the same 4566cc six they'd been using for an embarrassingly long time in various displacements—since 1933, in fact, when Rolls-Royce bought the Bentley name. And before that, it had been in the famous 20/25 Baby Rolls that went all the way back to 1922. But it was solid, reliable, almost inaudible, very torquey—with a 4.5-inch stroke it should have been—and about as well debugged as anything made by human hands can possibly be. Evernden raised the compression ratio a smidgen, but that was all he could do without losing all those wonderful things—silence, reliability, longevity—that Bentley stood for.

Blatchley designed an all-new aerodynamic body that was adopted for the Rolls-Royce Silver Cloud and Bentley S-type later on in 1955. He shortened the classic grille, faired the razor-edge fenders into the body, and stuck the headlamps into—rather than onto—the fenders. For all intents and purposes, it *was* the familiar Silver Cloud shape, at least as far back as the B-pillar. But instead of that superb notchback of the later sedans, the Continental had a dramatically sloping fastback captured between gentle tail fins. Blatchley spent a lot of time in the Rolls-Royce aircraft wind tunnel, and the body—given that he had to retain the upright Bentley grille—was just about as smooth as he could make it. Unfortunately, it came out looking very much like the '49–'52 General Motors fastbacks, particularly—*Oh, the shame*—the low-buck Chevrolet Fleetline. Blatchley always insisted the similarity was just coincidental, and you have to admit it's pretty hard to imagine the head of styling at Rolls-Royce sitting down and copying a *Chevy*. But on the other hand, the GM Fleetline body went out of production before the R-type Continental even began, so it's equally hard to imagine that the folks at Crewe didn't know about the Blue Flame Special. Probably just didn't give a good goddamn.

H. J. Mulliner—Royce's captive coachbuilder—whipped up the prototype, the famous OLG490, known as Olga. Her body was all-aluminum, and even with burled walnut trim, heavily padded Connoly hide seats for four, and typical Rolls-Royce sound deadening, the whole body weighed only 750 pounds. The total car came in at 3,600, a startling 500 pounds less than the Mark VI. About the only differences between Olga and the production cars were a split windshield and overdrive on the prototype and a one-piece curved window and direct-drive fourth on the later cars. Oh, and the roof was made an inch lower. Otherwise, Evernden and Blatchley had done pretty well. The Continental was 20 mph faster than the Mark VI—an honest 120 mph on the nose—and 2 seconds quicker up to 60—only 13.5 seconds, according to *The Motor.*

When the Continental finally went into production in 1952, the Mark VI had already become the almost identical R-type, and in '54 it became the 4887cc "big bore/big boot" version. The Continental got the bigger engine, too, so the series was changed to series D and later series E. For that reason series D and E cars are the most desirable. Of course, you paid a bit more for the Continental. In '53, for example, the standard R-type cost only £3,170, or roughly $9,000. The Continental was a whopping £4,890, or nearly $14,000, just about seven times the price of a nice Chevy Fleetline. No matter. There were only 193 Mulliner Continental R-types, and 208 chassis, so Crewe could have charged virtually anything they felt like. And when you realize that Bristol was selling their 2-liter 404 for £4,000, it doesn't seem that steep.

There are no racing successes to chronicle with the Continental; no anecdotes, no tall stories. The nearest one ever got to a race track was Le Mans in 1953 when Briggs Cunningham—obviously no piker—had Bentley Continentals for team transportation during race week. But everybody knows what a Bentley is and why they're held in such esteem. It's just that the Continentals are even better than that. They really are. I've honestly driven no other car that's given me such pure, sweet pleasure as an early Continental. It's not exciting the way a Cobra is exciting, but getting deafened, pummeled, and rained on can get to be a bit tiresome after a while. The Continental is diametrically opposed. It doesn't ever get its feathers ruffled, it never seems like it's working, it never loses its poise. Just every once in a while you'll look down and there'll be triple figures on the clock when you thought you were under the speed limit. Just like that. The thing is geared so high—50, 80, and 100 in the indirect gears—everything just effortlessly happens at a little faster speed than you expected. All in absolute silence, of course, in perfect comfort and with matchless grace.

Style is expensive. A nice, well-cared-for Continental R-type is worth $25,000 these days. On the other hand, that's half the price of a new Silver Shadow/T-series. And I promise you, the R-type is a better car than a new Bentley. Not a better car considering it's twenty-five years old, but a better car head to head. It's faster, quicker, quieter—yes, *quieter*—much better built and also much, *much* prettier. And just as inexpensive—or expensive, depending on how you look at it— to service and repair. Don Vorderman, writing in *Automobile Quarterly,* said of the T-series: "Again old engine in new chassis. Infernally complicated and not terribly effective. One can only hope that better days are coming." But Vorderman on the R-type Continental: "One of the postwar era's great cars, with remarkable performance, handling and stamina. The fastest sedan in the world in 1953." There you have it. And only one correction to be made. The better days aren't yet to come; they've already been and gone.

If you can't find an R-type, there's still hope for you. Now I'm not going to have this problem, because I don't expect to be able to afford either one in this life, and Karen Graham and I will just order up anything we want to, where we're going. But for the rest of you sinners with a spare $15,000 burning a hole in your pocket, run, don't walk to the nearest used-Bentley store and ask the man there for an S-type Continental by Mulliner. Doesn't matter which series, whether two-door or four-door, and if you have to, settle for a Park Ward or James Young version. Then hold onto it for the rest of this life and on into the next, too. If you're good, maybe they'll let you take it with you.

S-type Continentals appeared in 1955 and continued in production right along with the regular Silver Cloud/S-series until 1965, when the abominable Silver Shadows came out. The S-types have a 123-inch wheelbase, but otherwise the S-I Continentals are virtually identical to the R-types. Mulliner even kept the same fastback shape for a few early cars, though most of the S-types have a similar notchback body that's even prettier. This came as a two-door coupe and later as a much more popular four-door, with the scrumptious appellation Bentley Continental Mulliner Flying Spur.

Timeless style and grace under pressure, the 120-mph Bentley Continental S-type by Mulliner.

"Delectable, high-geared motorcar," the 1958 Bentley Continental Mulliner Flying Spur.

"A delectable high-geared motorcar" is what old Ralph Stein called the Flying Spur, and it's even better than that. The best of all is the S-II, because even though it weighs only 3,700 pounds or so, the S-I always seems a little short of breath with just that little six. With the S-II in 1959, the new Rolls-Royce V-8 appeared. Utterly conventional—pretty much a small-block Chevy in an expensive wrapper—the 6230cc V-8 came with only a GM automatic, not the lovely 4-speed of the early cars. It chopped a couple of seconds off the 0-to-60 times, kept the 120 mph top speed, but added a lot of *Sturm und Drang,* vibration, and unnecessary drama to an otherwise gracefully gentle motorcar. But it *is* a better proposition than the S-I, though not as desirable as the R-types. The S-III has those ugly quad headlights, of course, so it's not as nice as the S-II, either, but still better than 99 percent of the cars you might consider buying.

The S-type Continentals were built by the hundreds—431 S-I Continentals, to be exact, and similar numbers of the two later series—so they're not as rare nor consequently as desirable as the R-types. This is great if you want to buy one, obviously, as the price is a lot less.

Personally, I think the most desirable of all Bentley S-II Continentals is the Mulliner coupe, the two-door version of the Flying Spur. It has everything: reasonable initial price, impeccable styling, slightly lighter weight than the four-door, and best of all, it's the rarest model, with only fifty built and less than that surviving.

I've driven a number of S-type Continentals over the years—quite a few car collector friends have them as everyday cars—and they are easier to live with than any exotic car I know. There's just nothing wrong with the Continental, and that's a fact. For a dignified gentleman's carriage—that will blow the doors off a lot of surprised wind-in-the-face sports cars, not to mention super cars—it's the only answer. The S-IIs cost an incredible ten thousand new—that's pounds, not dollars—which equated to about $25,000+ as the pound devalued in the sixties. And now, incredible as it may seem, the price is hovering at the $15,000 level—that's dollars, not pounds—mostly because I think a large percentage of contemporary Rolls/Bentley shoppers are nouveau riche enough that they're moving up from Eldorados or something. The understated, elegant, quiet perfection of the Flying Spur is lost on them. They all want wide whites and a Rolls-Royce Flying Lady mascot so their jerky friends will know it's not a Jaguar. My advice: get new friends.

Me, I'm just gonna sit back here and watch till my time comes. The fix is already in, see, and along with that GTB/4 and Cobra roadster Candy Bergen has waiting for me, there's a lovely shell gray Mulliner Continental two-door saloon floating around in the clouds of my future. And little Karen Graham, in matching gray Ultrasuede from Halston, is floating up there, too. Don't worry, Lord, Ah'm a-coming. Wouldn't miss it for the world.

Jensen 541

Richard and Alan Jensen were primarily body makers. Not coachbuilders, in the sense of one-off customs, but mass-production makers of steel bodies for standard cars. Their equivalents in the States are Murray or Briggs Body; in France, Facel S.A. They started out in the early thirties making lightweight bodies for Standards—along the same lines as William Lyons's S.S.—and expanded into limited production of their own Jensen tourers with V-8 Ford, Lincoln, and Nash engines starting in 1936. After the war their main business was stamping out bodies for Austins, for whom they made a particularly ugly, slab-sided brick called the A-40 Sports.

Wouldn't you know it, but in 1950, right alongside the homely little Austin, the Jensens brought out their own sports car. It looked exactly like the Austin A-40 inflated to maybe double life-size, a great hulking lump of a car and the very picture of the indecision that paralyzed postwar British designers when they were asked to create something more imaginative than a razor-edge copy of a Bentley Mk VI. Everything about it was naive, right down to its Battle of Britain-ish name—Interceptor—and the 4-liter six out of

the Austin/BMC Princess. Jensen claimed 130 hp and over 100 mph, though. And they continued a prewar tradition of supplying everything they figured anyone could possibly ever need as standard . . . overdrive, a radio, and all sorts of nice touches, from Connoly leather interior to lots of walnut trim. Obviously, all this luxury weighed something—about 2,800 pounds for the hardtop, 3,100 pounds for the convertible—but the Interceptors could still get through the quarter in under 19 seconds, which was faster than almost any big American V-8 in the early fifties. The Jensen Interceptor cost a bundle, however, and though it was what the British like to call a businessman's express, it wasn't suited for anything more rigorous than high-speed running on the motorway. Some fool did bring one to the Monte Carlo Rally around 1953 or so, but then there used to be Rolls-Royces entered there, too. Which doesn't mean it was right. Or prudent, even. In four and a half years of production, Jensen Motors Ltd. managed to roll exactly eighty-seven—count 'em, eighty-seven—goddamn cars out the West Bromich factory doors. This makes Morgan look like the Lordstown Vega plant.

Anyway. In 1953 Richard and Alan finally got into it. The all-new—well, mostly new—Jensen 541 appeared. This was some nice car. For starters, it had a really attractive body; not pretty, exactly, more uhhhh . . . rugged, maybe. It looked kind of like a DB-2 Aston Martin—which was their high-priced competition, after all—and kind of like a Cunningham. And it had those eyebrows over the wheelwells like the Mercedes 300SL. And one of the damndest gizmos ever seen. The oval grille, Ferrari-ish almost, wasn't filled with anything as mundane as egg-crate chrome or grille bars. Oh no. There was this big horizontal crosspiece shaped like an airfoil. And it was deep. At slow speeds, when the engine needed air, the crossbar was maybe an inch thick and lots of air got in. But at high speeds, when the engine was running cooler, the airfoil swiveled up by a little electric motor hooked to a thermocouple, and the entire grille opening blanked itself off. The theory was that this made the car more streamlined. Crazy Englishmen.

This nice coupe body was fiberglass, which in 1953 in England was a revelation.

The handsomest of Jensens, the 1960 541 S, with 4-liter six, disc brakes, and fiberglass body.

Jensen's 541 actually beat the Corvette into production with Glass Reinforced Plastic, though of course even the Corvette's stop-and-start production—minuscule by American standards—was stupendous compared to Jensen's. The British were able to do hand layups with no problem at all—hell, they built only 225 cars in three years—while Bob Morrison at Molded Fiber Glass was building a whole new *factory* just to mold Corvette parts. However, the Jensen was not only the first production fiberglass car but was also the first *quality* production fiberglass car. The perfect finish on the Jensen 541 made the 'Vette look like it'd been carved from Play-Doh.

Underneath this lovely creation, Jensen used a long 112-inch wheelbase with a conventional independent front suspension and rigid rear axle borrowed from Austin's Princess limousine. The frame was basically two large-diameter tubes, like A. C.'s and Lister's, and the engine was the 3993cc six from the biggest Austin. In the 2,600-pound Jensen, it was good for a timed 115 mph and 0 to 60 in

under 10 seconds. And that's with a long-legged 2.93 rear end and overdrive. True to form, Alan and Richard put in all sorts of little extras, from fire extinguisher to integral jacks, from first-aid kit to Positraction.

The 541 got four-wheel disc brakes in 1956—long before the production Jaguars—and in 1957 turned into the lighter, 150-hp R model, with a top speed over 120 mph. From '60 to '63, Jensen built the 541 S, with a standard-equipment Hydramatic. This absolutely ate horsepower. Top speed dropped to 110 and another second was added to the quarter-mile times. But the 541 S did have a nicer-looking grille—with conventional chrome mesh instead of that trick trap door—and a new little hood scoop. The 541 was still handsome, quick, and very expensive. Jensen sold another 308 between 1956 and '63, not bad for what was originally a 1953 design. Considering you could get more performance, better looks, and better handling in an XK-E for about half the price, Jensen sensed it was time for a change. Richard spent most of his time playing gentleman farmer and Alan retired to his country home in 1963, so Brian Owen took over.

Owen revamped the nice-looking 541 body by excruciatingly splicing four headlamps into the front, thereby reducing the grille to an embarrassed little grin. He also chopped off the fastback in favor of an awkward turret top and ditched the optional wire wheels. Austin stopped production of the Princess in 1959 and stopped making engines, too. Jensen's production was so slow, they simply bought engines from Austin spare parts, but by '63, BMC just wasn't supplying big sixes anymore. So Owen straightforwardly solved the power problem by dropping in a huge, American Chrysler 361-cubic-inch V-8 and 3-speed automatic. From '63 to '66, Jensen used the 383, in 330-hp tune, which was a lot of power to be channeling into those arthritic old frame rails designed for 130 hp way back in the forties. The old Austin six was the original boat anchor, so the weight didn't change much. Top speed went up to over 130 mph, though, and the quarter-miles got down into the 14s and over 90 mph. This was pretty much super car country in the sixties. And really, that's what the Jensen had become— an overpowered, overpriced, horrifyingly ugly super car, with typical British myopia to compound the problem.

The earlier 541 R is the Jensen to have. Balanced, pleasant, good-looking, and fast enough for mortal man. There aren't many around, but the clientele seems to have been well-off executives buying one last high-performance car before the onslaught of social security, so they're well kept and often low mileage. Very few came to this country, though Jensen did have a regular distributor here. Even if 20 percent got here, which is a generous number, that's still only 100 cars, out of all the 541 models. The Chrysler-powered ones would be a lot easier to own when it comes time to pay the repair bills, but they're just so sinfully ugly it would be tragic to preserve one longer than necessary. Better to let it die a well-deserved death and spend your dollars on a high-class, pretty lady: the Jensen 541R.

Triumph TR-2/TR-3

Look. I know you're not gonna believe this, but you remember those funny-lookin' little TR-2s and 3s? Well, in just about two minutes here, or maybe three, those little turkeys are gonna turn into the investment of the decade, right behind Pet Rocks and clean Ford Mustangs. Listen. Not even a year ago, you could pick up a nice little TR-3 for maybe $800. A grand. Today that same car is bringing two, twenty-five, even three. And the sky's the limit. I won't be surprised to see the day when those charming uglies with the tractor engines are going for ten thousand dollars. Don't say I didn't warn ya.

Among other things, the Triumph TR-2/ TR-3 is probably the simplest sports car ever built, except for maybe the MG-TD, which means that every mechanic who ever turned a wrench in anger is a Triumph expert. And the things are *sturdy* . . . robust . . . indestructible, even. Which means they last, are super-easy to restore, and were dynamite race cars in their day. This in turn means there are tons of good hop-up parts and spares and experts all waiting to help you out. And there's a huge club. So a TR-2/TR-3 has to be about the easiest British sports car you can think of to own.

Now a lot of people, me included, don't think much of their looks. But then again, a lot of pretty cars are sort of, well . . . effemi-

A true British bulldog, the 1957 Triumph TR-3.

One hundred hp and "dollar grin," the 1958

nate. Like Karmann Ghias. Or MGAs. But the TRs are undeniably masculine; about as tough as a 2-liter sports car can be. It's something indefinable, a combination of the bluff front end, light hindquarters, cutaway doors, boxy hood, and frog-eye headlamps. But the TR— though uglier than any car has a right to be— is *lovably* ugly, like English bulldogs, Winston Churchill, and Ernest Borgnine. And it's tough, too. The first TR-2, totally stock except for an undershield and Brooklands screen, went 124.89 mph at Jabbeke in 1953, which was just a tad less than the first XK-120 had gone on the same road five years before, blessed with nearly twice as much horse-power from nearly twice as much engine displacement.

So the TR-2 was tough, and it was logically arrived at. The Standard/Triumph distributor in the States was Fergus Motors, run by the brother of Harry Ferguson of Ferguson Tractor. Ferguson, using the 2.2-liter Standard four in his best-selling tractor, had nothing but praise for it. He and his brother suggested to Sir John Black in 1951 that Standard ought to take their nice, sturdy tractor engine—originally designed by Continental in the States—hot-rod the hell out of it, stuff it in a chassis they already had lying around, cover it with a roadster body, and ship a bunch to America. Fergus Motors figured it would be like a license to print money.

Sir John took them up on it. The Vanguard engine was sleeved down to 1991cc to fit under the 2-liter class limit and stuck into the 90-inch wheelbase frame from the sorry little Standard Nine. The thankfully forgotten Tri-

umph Mayflower sedan (they were going to "pilgrimize" America . . . get it?) contributed its independent front suspension and rear axle. Engineer Harry Webster managed to fit a fourth gear into the Vanguard 3-speed gearbox . . . and there, in essence, they had it. Walter Belgrove—who'd styled the prewar Triumphs—came back and drew up the funny roadster body. Sir John's prime requirement was that it be cheap to build—which is why the TR-2 is totally welded up from shallow, single-draw stampings.

The prototype 20TS—there never was a TR-1—appeared at Earl's Court in 1952. Right after the show, BRM racer Ken Richardson was asked to evaluate the prototype. "Frankly," said Richardson, "I think it's the most bloody awful car I've ever driven." Sir John hired him on the spot. Richardson spent the rest of the winter redesigning the frame, brakes, suspension, and body. He also got them to boost the Fergie sodbuster up from 75 hp to 90 hp at 4,800. In May he took it to Jabbeke. The rest, as they say in the pulp books, is history.

According to *Road & Track,* "The TR-2 will out-drag any stock American car [this in 1954] from a standstill. Aside from the rare and expensive cars, the Ferrari or Frazer

A TR-3 factory rally car in the 1958 Liège–Rome–Liège;

Nash, the TR-2 should have a field day in Class E. It should have a field day as well at the corner stoplights." Well. Maybe in 1954. A good TR-2 would do the quarter-mile in about 19 seconds, 0 to 60 in under 10 seconds, and go about 110 mph. The TR-3—which was the same car with an egg-crate grille, disc brakes, and 100 hp—took a full second off both times.

And the TR could handle. It wasn't the best by far, but on smooth roads—or a race course—a well-prepped TR-3 was quicker than it had any right to be. The steering was tight, the gearbox notchy but precise, and the funny little bucket seats—they really are buckets, look like a nail keg split down the middle and upholstered—were not only reasonably comfortable but very good at holding you in place. The windshield was too low for me—my head always pooched out the top like a tobacco chaw in an old man's cheek—and most of the minor controls like windshield wipers, turn signals, horn, and such were pretty flimsy. But otherwise I liked the car.

By 1958, there was a TR-3A, the one with the wide, toothy grin instead of the little rosebud mouth. And there were a few virtually identical TR-3Bs in 1961 and '62, after which Leyland bought Triumph, brought out the Mi-

chelotti-styled TR-4, and became an international automobile company doing commerce in faraway places and trading on the high seas instead of a nice down-home British sports-car maker in little ol' Coventry. A total of 75,000 TR-2/TR-3s were built, a majority of which ended up in this country.

By 1960 or so, the TR-3 was going for $2,675 . . . only a hundred more than the anemic Sunbeam Alpine, *eight dollars* more than the much less potent MGA, and hundreds of dollars less than the Elva Courier, Healey 3000, and Morgan Plus Four (which used the TR-3 engine). *Road & Track* said, "The TR-3 is not the fastest sports car in the world, nor is it the best handling or the most beautiful. It is, however, just about the best *buy* on the sports car market."

As John Christy bubbled years ago in *Motor Trend,* much to his subsequent chagrin, "It was a great car then and it's still a great car today." True enough, actually, particularly at that price. As I said before, TRs are just getting up to being worth what they sold for new, which is not a particularly fast rate of inflation for cars that have been around for well over two decades at this point. The hot items from the fifties are already worth double or triple their price new, and still

TRs also won the GT class in the Monte Carlo Rally and a Coupe des Alpes in the Alpine the same year.

climbing. So TR-3s are bargains right now. And they're fun, easy—enjoyable, even—to work on, sturdy, cheap to repair, and surprisingly nice to drive, in an elbows-out, wind-in-the-face, roar-of-the-exhaust sort of way.

Personally, I'd like precisely the car my college scutmaster drove . . . and that I got to polish every Saturday morning for a semester. It was British Racing Green, had a full-race suspension and some mild engine work, headers and a megaphone exhaust, competition belts, a rollbar, and driving lights on an AMCO bumper bar. John always drove it with the tonneau cover buttoned over the passenger seat, rain or shine, winter and summer, and expected me to do the same on my weekly trip to the local car wash. What I never let him suspect was that if I polished at double time, I could leave myself an hour on the way back to the campus to cruise along the river through the park, looking for a date for Saturday night. Usually got one, too.

Sunbeam Alpine Mark II

Way back in the teens and twenties, Sunbeam was just about the most glorious name in Britain. Under the stewardship of brilliant Louis Coatalen, they built Grand Prix cars, land speed record cars, huge limousines, and tourers. But Sunbeam was never very glorious financially, and they ended up in an Anglo-French co-operative called Sunbeam-Talbot-Darracq. Unfortunately, STD's Depression-era models were all expensive luxury cars, and the firm went down the tubes in 1935. The Sunbeam name was bought by the Rootes Brothers, who stuck it on a badge-engineered Hillman in the late thirties and forties.

In 1948 Rootes came out with their first postwar new car. They took the prewar 1944cc Hillman four, converted it to overhead valves, and plopped it into a dead-conventional chassis complete with straight front axle on semi-elliptics. They wrapped this whole affair in a typical British small saloon body that bore

an unmistakable similarity to the competition from Standard and Triumph, all trying to look like miniature Mark VI Bentleys. In 1950 this Sunbeam-Talbot 90 got considerably better. The cart-spring front end was junked in favor of unequal-length A-arms on coil springs, and the old four was bored out to 2267cc and 70 hp. There was also a surprisingly pretty two-door convertible. It weighed too much, 2,600 pounds, but would still go 90 mph and run forever.

Rootes started running factory teams of rally cars . . . and got incredible results—much better than they deserved, considering the plebeian sedans they used. Murray Frame got a Coupe des Alpes in '49, George Hartwell finished fifth overall in the '50 Alpine, and in 1952 young Stirling Moss got a Coupe and the four Rootes cars took the team prize with three Coupes des Alpes, and of course won their class. And Moss came in second *overall* in the Monte. They did so well over the season, in fact, that the RAC awarded them the Dewar Trophy for the year. Through some stroke of luck or planning, the Sunbeam-Talbot 90s were perfectly balanced and had good, strong, usable power and neutral handling. This wasn't enough to go racing but was perfect for rallies. And at 2,600 pounds, they were overbuilt. While the faster, lighter competition was beating itself to death on the frost-heaved back roads of central Europe, the solid Sunbeam-Talbots just kept motoring along.

Rootes also did something very clever. Now most rally teams are made up of second- or third-rank racing drivers, and the cars are probably quicker than the drivers. Sunbeam didn't have very fast cars, but they got every last second it was possible to get out of them. Stirling Moss, Mike Hawthorn, John Fitch, and Leslie Johnson were nothing if not first-rate racing drivers, and the rest of the Sunbeam factory drivers were nearly as quick, particularly Sheila Van Damm.

George Hartwell did all right by them, too. He not only rallied Sunbeam-Talbots but had a Sunbeam dealership in Bournemouth, and wanted something a little more distinctive for himself. So he took a new Sunbeam-Talbot convertible, cut the back off, pulled the rear seats out, and had a smooth deck lid welded on all the way from the bumper to behind the front seats. He trimmed the door sills down a bit too, punched the hood full of louvers, and built a lightweight windshield and roadster top. Presto: a sleek, streamlined two-seater that weighed a good hundredweight less than the convertible. Hartwell also made a high-performance head that he sold to boy racers. Hartwell's head drew 80 hp out of the Rootes four.

As these things have a way of happening, Hartwell showed his sleek roadster to somebody at Rootes, and in early 1953 the first production copies appeared. By now it was a mandatory tradition for each new British sports car to make the trek to Jabbeke in Belgium for a top-speed run on the motorway. Sheila Van Damm took one of the first cars, streamlined with a tonneau, undershield, and Brooklands screen, and went exactly 120 mph, which was very competitive with the similar-sized but much lighter TR-2. The only hitch was, her Sunbeam was pretty heavily reworked. Production cars were good for only 100 mph and trundled through the quarter-mile in about 21 seconds.

Like the later Alpines and Tigers of the sixties, though, the new Alpine roadster—they named it after their biggest rally success, logically enough—was much more luxurious than the competition. TR-2s and MG-TDs were still using build-it-yourself tops and side curtains, but the Alpines had roll-up windows, one-hand tops, column shifters for the 4-speed, a decent heater, a comfortable ride, and fewer pretensions to high performance. In truth, the Alpine was strictly a boulevard sports car, the perfect sort of thing for your wife to drive to a country-club golf date or the hairdresser's.

On the other hand, it was also a *demon* rally car. Stirling Moss won Coupes des Alpes in '53 and '54, to get an Alpine Gold Cup when added to his '52 Coupe in a sedan. Ian Appleyard's triple-header in a potent Jaguar XK-120 earned the only other Alpine Gold Cup ever. The rest of the team also got Coupes in '53—four in all—plus Sheila's Coupe des Dames and the team prize at Monte Carlo. In 1954 they did even better, with a team award in the Monte and a Coupe des Dames in almost every international rally. In '55 Malling and Fadum won the Monte *outright*. And Peter Harper got a third overall in '56.

By then, however, the Alpine was obsolete. Production stopped in the autumn of

Leslie Johnson winning a Coupe des Alpes, 1953.

1955, by which time they'd built nearly 10,000. You'd never know it by the number left today. For a mass-market sports car with a list of famous competition successes, the Sunbeam Alpine is rarer than the proverbial hen's teeth. For some reason nobody took care of them, and they just fell apart or got cut up. Mike Stouffeur, one of my friends at school, built a white '55 Alpine roadster, very nicely redone with a red interior . . . and a Chrysler hemi and Torqueflite automatic. He just would *not* listen to reason, insisted on swapping in that boat anchor, and then always had to carry a passenger to help turn the wheel. Flat ruined that car, as well you might imagine. He was typical, I'm afraid.

When Jean and I were first married, I bought her a Sunbeam-Talbot convertible, which was what she wanted. I told her she could have *any* car. Because it was small, good-looking, comfortable, and economical, that's what she picked. She said it was the cutest car she'd ever seen. Remember what I said about a car for your wife to go shopping?

1954 Alpine, George Hartwell's bright idea.

It turned out to be a perfectly useful and pleasant car to drive; certainly no ball of fire, but fun just the same. Unfortunately, we left it with her parents one summer while we were in Europe and my father-in-law sold it in a fit of pique. So it goes.

Sunbeam Alpines—and Talbot convertibles, too, for that matter—are worth twice what they cost twenty years ago. A good one will cost you $5,000. And they're getting a following. No club yet, for some reason, but a devoted following, nonetheless. I'll tell you just how devoted. True story: Just last week, a guy called me to offer his car for a magazine story. What he has is Stirling Moss's 1954 Alpine Rally car—or so he claims—with a factory hotted-up engine, floor shift, and Brooklands screens. He swears it has been documented by Rootes's competition department. And who am I to call him a liar? Anyway, the point of the story is that this poor sucker . . . uhhhh, gentleman . . . has just had the car restored by a large and well-known East Coast restoration shop, which shall remain nameless for obvious reasons. In three years, at a cost of $30,000—thirty *thousand* dollars—they've given him back what I sincerely hope to God is the world's best Sunbeam, bar none. Thirty thousand dollars into a $5,000 car. Astounding. But that's not the end of the story. He was calling me because he wanted to get pictures of it immediately. It was going away in less than two weeks. The sucker, see, had already sold his $30,000 Sunbeam. For $50,000.

A. C. Ace

Nowadays, it's pretty common to think of A. C. Cars Ltd. as those nice but slightly backward Englishmen from Thames Ditton who meekly provided the raw material from which dynamic Texan Carroll Shelby fashioned the Cobra. True enough. But that disregards over sixty-some years when A. C. *didn't* build Cobras, had never heard of entrepreneurial chicken farmers from Texas, and moreover didn't much care. They were doing perfectly well on their own, thankyewverymuch. In fact, A. C. can trace its parentage in a straight line all the way back to 1903, to the very dawn of motoring, which is more than Carroll Shelby can do. And if that doesn't count for much in today's marketplace, it does at least give them the authority of a bloodline longer than virtually anybody except Mercedes and Oldsmobile.

Thames Ditton, where A. C.s have been made since before the Great War, is invariably described in travel folders as "a sleepy little Thames-side town." Except for Malvern Link, where Morgans are made, or Henley, which housed the short-lived Squire garage of the thirties, there's no more charming place in which cars have been built. Except, well . . . the sleepiness has rubbed off a little. For example, in 1963 when they switched over

The most famous racing car in England in 1953, Cliff

into full-time Cobra production, A. C. was still using a 2-liter six designed by the company's founding genius, John Weller, for 1919. This forty-four years of continuous production is a rather dubious world's record but one that perfectly illustrates the somnolent pace at A. C.'s engineering department.

Happily enough, Weller's engine was one of the classics of all time. In 1919 when it appeared it was years ahead (not forty years ahead, but *still*). From six long-stroke (65 × 100mm) cylinders, Weller got 1991cc. His engine had a single chain-driven overhead camshaft with a patented "Weller" spring plate chain tensioner that's still a common item today. Except for the cast-iron head, the engine was aluminum, with shrunk-in wet liners in an alloy block. Even with a steel flywheel, the entire engine weighed only a little over 350 pounds. This was remarkable for its day, and led to A. C. advertisements heralding the new "Light Six."

The Light Six was rated at 40 hp in the beginning. Over the years it got a fifth main bearing, three carburetors, progressively higher compression ratios as the quality of gasoline improved, and a sprinkling of minor modifications. By the mid-fifties, this surprisingly spry old-timer was rated at 102 hp from the factory, and a good tuner could give you a few more in race trim. Even A. C. realized

Davis's LOY 500 Tojeiro-Bristol at Goodwood.

it was pretty long in the tooth, however. They kept building pleasantly upright sedans, roughly out of the same mold as Donald Healey's early postwar Elliot, but they were also looking around for something with a little more élan.

Significantly enough, the brilliant roadster that saved A. C. from postwar extinction came to them totally conceived and tested from outside the company. Way back in 1949, Charles and John Cooper—who were then nothing more than hot-rodders working out of a two-car garage in Surbiton—built a front-engine MG special. This thing was ugly as all get out, but it did have a tubular space frame, all-independent suspension on transverse leaf springs, and a ready-to-race weight of under 1,000 pounds. Now one of the six Cooper-MG buyers was an amateur racer named Cliff Davis. And being something of an aesthete, he junked the horrid Cooper body—"give an Englishman a piece of aluminum and he'll do something stupid with it"— in favor of a totally different body from his local panelbeater.

Davis was clever. Instead of slapping some awkward, homebuilt body on his Cooper, he looked around. And *the* most beautiful roadster around in 1949 was the Carrozzeria Touring Barchetta 166 Ferrari. It was the prettiest car anyone had *ever* seen. It was also streamlined, compact, and lightweight, but mostly . . . gorgeous. So Davis had his Cooper rebodied with a line-for-line copy of Touring's Barchetta. It wasn't very original, but it sure was beautiful. He happily raced this Cooper—which had the distinctive license plate JOY 500—until 1953.

When Davis went back to Cooper for a replacement racer, they were too busy. So he went to John Tojeiro in Cambridge, a Portuguese who'd been building blatant rip-offs of the Cooper chassis. Davis had Tojeiro weld up one of his Cooperesque tubing frames, with all-independent suspension, leaf springs, and alloy Turner wheels. Into this they put a 2-liter Bristol/BMW six—which was what simply *everyone* was using in 1953. When it came time for a body, Davis allowed as how he was perfectly happy with the one he already had. So Tojeiro hammered out a second copy of Touring's Ferrari Barchetta, this time for LOY 500. And LOY 500 was even better than

A simply delightful 2-liter GT, the '54 Aceca.

Ken Rudd's 2.6-liter, 170-hp A. C. club racer.

JOY 500. Cliff Davis absolutely cleaned house in British club racing in 1953. LOY 500 was easily the best-known amateur racing car in England.

Between races, Tojeiro took LOY 500 over to Thames Ditton and convinced general manager Charles Hurlock—who'd bought A. C. in 1930 with his brother William—that an A. C.-Bristol was just what he needed to get the company moving again. Hurlock agreed, and at the autumn 1953 Earl's Court Motor Show A. C. displayed their version of Tojeiro's special. At first it could be had only with the ancient Weller Light Six. But after 1956, for nearly $1,000 more, you could get the Bristol/BMW proprietary engine, supplied by Bristol Aeroplane and installed by A. C.

In 1954 Hurlock extended the rear fenders into nascent tail fins and stuck a pretty fastback top onto the A. C. Ace, to form the lovely A. C. Aceca coupe. And later on, in 1959, he stretched the wheelbase out an extra 10 inches and made the four-passenger A. C. Greyhound. All of them, no matter which body style, were basically Tojeiro's special with the rough edges smoothed out for production. And they were *good*. A. C.-Bristols, in particular, simply cleaned up the 2-liter production classes in both America and England. And at Le Mans, Peter Bolton and Ken Rudd—who ran his own A. C. speed shop in Worthing, called Ruddspeed—came second in class and tenth overall in '57. Bolton and Dickie Stoop were eighth in '58 and seventh the following year. In '57 Jack Fernandez and Ramon Droulers won the 2-liter class at Sebring, and A. C.-Bristols virtually owned SCCA E-production—except for occasional wins by the similar Arnolt-Bristols—right up until the early sixties.

In 1961 Bristol decided to stop building their venerable six and A. C. went looking for another engine. Eventually they ended up with Shelby's Ford, of course, or more correctly, Shelby ended up with A. C. But for a brief period Ken Rudd convinced the factory to stuff the 2553cc six from the English Ford Zephyr into the Ace. This was a lot cheaper than the Bristol, and gave up to 170 hp in Ruddspeed tune. Top speed was over 120 mph—faster than the Bristol-engined car—and 0 to 100 dropped to less than 19 seconds, compared with the 28 seconds of the A. C.-Bristol. Shelby's Cobra made that performance look sick, of course, and in '63 A. C. dropped not only the A. C.-Zephyr but their own Weller engine as well. From then on, everything that came from Thames Ditton, right up to the A. C. 428, had a big Ford V-8.

The Cobra was incredibly cheap for what it could do. The A. C.-Bristol was correspondingly expensive. For most of the time it was in production, the A. C.-powered version of the Ace hovered around $4,500. The Bristol engine added between $700 and $1,000 more. By comparison, you could get an XK Jaguar or Corvette for less than $4,000. So the Ace was no bargain, on an absolute scale. But it was just about the most refined, delightful British sports car you could buy at any price, with quality control that must have made William Lyons weep. The A. C. was a truly fine piece throughout, and though $5,000 for an 1,800-pound car wasn't much of a bargain

The car that started it all, MG's little TC was a revelation to Americans in the late forties.

Sydney Allard's aggressive Cadillac-powered J2-X, commonly known as the Blacksmith's Revenge.

Designed for the thirties in the style of the twenties, the timeless HRG was still selling in 1955.

Triumph's quirky 1800 had windows in the trunk lid and the expression of a hyperthyroid chipmunk.

Vertical grille, flaring fenders, fold-down windshield, wire wheels, and cutaway doors, the 1955 MG-TF was

the last mass-production British roadster in the classic style, a delightful throwback to a charming era.

Jaguar's XK-120 was the one car everybody wanted. . . 120 mph, aerodynamic body, reasonable price.

Triumph's indomitable bulldog, the TR-3A gained a grille but lost none of the TR-2's appeal.

Colin Chapman's Lotus Elite—fiberglass chassis, 1216cc, 113 mph—was decades ahead in 1957.

Peter Morgan's +4—ash framing, 2088cc, 85 mph—was either decades ahead or decades behind in 1953.

Donald Healey's brightest idea, the versatile, tough, and pretty 1956 Austin-Healey 100-6.

judged by weight, every pound was good red meat.

Believe it or not, a concours A. C.-Bristol is worth almost as much as a 289 Cobra today. Upwards of $10,000 is not unusual. Being pretty simple and robust, they're easy to work on, easy to repair, and not above learned amateur restoration, one-piece aluminum body notwithstanding. Personally, I'd rather have the Cobra if I were planning either for a car to drive or for an investment, since not only does the 289 have a lot more guts without upsetting the lovely balance of the A. C. chassis, but I think ultimately the Cobra is going to be worth considerably more. On the other hand, small-displacement cars are going to be the only kind we'll have in a few years. But none of them will have the sort of effortless performance that's so characteristic of the A. C.-Bristol. So maybe future generations will be more in tune with the old 2-liter six than Shelby's overkill V-8. Me, I'm just old-fashioned American enough to vote for cubic inches.

Austin-Healey

Donald Healey's Elliot was nice enough for a sedan; his Silverstone roadster was a demon on the track. But they were dead-end streets. And the hybrid Nash-Healey was a cul-de-sac of monumental proportions. Late in 1951 George Mason at Nash decided that rather than have Healey put bodies on the Nashes in Warwick, he'd ship Pininfarina coachwork direct from Italy. This meant that for the second series Nash-Healeys, Donald Healey really didn't have much work to do, and of course he had a whole little factory set up. Even worse, Healey's cars for the British market used the 2443cc four from the Riley 2.5 saloon. And Riley—part of William Morris's Nuffield Group along with Morris and MG— merged with Austin in 1952. So there was a pretty fair chance that Riley—and Healey's supply of engines—would be cut off in its prime. As it turned out, the 2.5 did die in 1953 just as Healey feared, but the engine stayed around in the Riley Pathfinder until 1957.

A. C.'s somnolent Thames-Ditton factory in 1956, clogged with left-hand-drive Aces for America.

But now for the good news. Healey's long-time contacts at Nuffield—particularly managing director Sir Leonard Lord—had jurisdiction over Austin's line. And Austin had a funny old aerodynamic sedan with *three* headlights called the A-90 Atlantic, powered by a long-stroke four that had started out in a delivery van. And it was even funnier than that sometimes. The Austin engine was heavy as Big Ben Tower, but at 2660cc it had more potential than the old Riley, even though it was only rated at 90 hp. So Healey borrowed a stack of parts from Austin. Along with the engine, he got the 3-speed transmission plus overdrive. The rigid rear axle on semielliptics, brakes, the complete independent front suspension—A-arms and coil springs—and some necessary smaller bits and pieces came from the little 1200cc A-40.

To tie it all together, Healey built a simple box-section frame with a wheelbase even shorter than the A-40's, at only 90 inches. Over this he built a combination steel and aluminum body that—along with the Aston Martin DB-2, the MGA, and the C-type Jaguar—is one of the handful of really superb designs to come out of England in the fifties. They're all pretty similar, actually, smoothly slab-sided, low-slung two-seaters with impossibly long hoods, tiny cockpits tucked between the rear tires, and virtually no chrome decoration. They borrowed from Pininfarina's new "Italian style," certainly. Britishers may have been backward, but they didn't live in a vacuum. The cars weren't Italianate at all, however. They borrowed a little but they copied from nothing, European or American. For a short space there, the British—and not just one designer, either—styled some really superb machines.

Healey's car was one of them. He abstracted his Elliot grille shape into a broad kite and mimicked the hideaway windshield of his Silverstone with a low, flat pane that could be folded back to be almost horizontal. The taillights were little buttons, the headlamps faired into the fenders, and—ballsy touch—he even left off the door handles.

The 1953 Austin-Healey 100–4, the smoothly slab-sided and low-slung epitome of British style.

The all-aluminum Austin-Healey 100 S of 1955—132 hp, 1,700 pounds, and disc brakes.

Designed around a too-tall engine, Arnolt-Bristol fashion, the Healey was just about as low and aerodynamic as it could possibly be (at the expense of ground clearance, even). But Lordy, was it ever pretty.

By 1952 top-speed runs on the Belgian Jabbeke autostrada were just about mandatory for new British sports cars. So the week before the Earl's Court Show, Healey took his prototype to the Continent and ran a kilo at 117 mph, which wasn't as fast as they'd hoped, but all they had time for. By the same process that made the new Jaguar the XK-120, the Healey became the Healey 100. It was propped up on a pedestal for Earl's Court with a sign to that effect. Almost every year, the Earl's Court Show saw a new star born overnight—XK-120 in '48, MG-TD in '49, DB-2 Aston in '50, Healey 100 in '52, A. C. Ace in '53—but the Healey was probably the most spectacular success of all.

When they make the movie, Peter Sellers can play Healey. And we'll need a kindly old Sir Leonard Lord: Rex Harrison, maybe. And Laurence Olivier to play the Devil. As Sellers walks through the big doorway into Earl's Court, with the hustling mob all around, Satan will grab Healey by the lapels and pull him over conspiratorially. "You're going in there a bloody has-been rally driver, mate," Olivier will say. "But you're coming back a star." And shaken, white as a sheet, Sellers will stagger into the coliseum, with scorched lapels still trailing off little puffs of steam. And Rex Harrison will come sauntering up, with that backward-leaning gait of his, and grab him around the shoulders and lead him off, both their eyes shining like beacons and the flush of fortune abloom on their cheeks.

What Healey did at Earl's Court was sell Sir Leonard Lord a fantastic, unprecedented *twenty-year* contract to use his name. And to make a car—called Austin-Healey—on a royalty basis. Healey would keep his Warwick garage, to build and maintain the Austin racing and rally team cars. Austin built the cars at their Longbridge factory until 1957, after which all the BMC sports cars—MG and Healey—were put together in the Abingdon works. Austin-Healey production started in May 1953, with surprisingly few changes.

It was an immediate hit. For not much more than an MG, you could buy a lot more performance. And despite its plebeian origins—the Austin Atlantic was a flat *terrible* car—the Healey was somehow more of a, well . . . *middle-class* sports car than the TR-2 and MG-TF. It was a cheap Jaguar, not an expensive MG, and it rapidly got even better than that. Soon there was an all-aluminum production racer—the 100 S—that was nothing at all like the stock roadsters. Fifty came from Warwick in 1955, with 132 hp, a 4-speed, and disc brakes. The 100 S weighed under 1,700 pounds, and it arrived in the States with only a plastic Brooklands screen and no top. The 100 S was, as you might surmise, strictly for racing. Top speed was 125 mph, with a price still less than a stock XK-140. There was also a steel-bodied 100 M, with the hot engine, that stayed through 1956. The extra weight didn't seem to make much difference in performance, and either model was a holy terror in amateur racing. Even though it was stuck in D-production, the Austin-Healey 100/100 M/ 100 S won the SCCA national championship in 1954 and '57–'59 inclusive.

Best of all, these early Healeys were built like trucks. The bodywork was pretty flimsy and the rocker panels rotted before Hambro got them off the boat. And the electrics were typical Lucas. But otherwise, the Austin-Healeys were pure joy. Mechanically they were indestructible, except of course for the Laycock de Normanville overdrive, which usually blew its servos within a week or two. But every British car had the same overdrive, and they *all* did that. It wasn't welcome, but it *was* expected. About the only other thing that drove Healey racers—and hard-driving streetsters—crazy was that even on skinny tires, the car had too much cornering power for its wire wheels. It's almost impossible to find a Healey that doesn't have at least a half-dozen broken spokes rattling around in each rear wheel. But it happened right away, hell, like maybe a thousand miles from the docks those spokes were gone, so you can almost think of it as an authentic period modification, like Abarth exhausts or Raydot mirrors.

One of the first corporate projects after the merger at BMC was a new six-cylinder engine for the middle-size Austin, Morris, Wolseley, and Riley lines. It first appeared in the 1954 Austin Westminster and Wolseley 6/ 90, then spread to the Morris Isis and the Riley 2.6 two years later. In 1956 the contagion also hit the Austin-Healey, which became the 100-6 as a result. Not much else was changed, and the long-stroke 2639cc, pushrod six slipped into the Healey with the addition of only two extra inches to the wheelbase and another hundredweight.

Starting with 102 hp and 2639cc, the six grew to 2912cc in 1959 and up to 148 hp in 1964. From a spartan roadster with side curtains and minimal top, it blossomed into a relatively luxurious convertible with front disc brakes, roll-up windows, a proper roof, and even . . . wait for it . . . outside door handles. It also got progressively porkier, up around 2,400 pounds near the end. But with 148 hp, acceleration was much quicker than even the early S models—0 to 60 in 9 seconds, quartermiles in 17 seconds. And the top speed went up over 120 mph in touring trim. In race

Healey borrowed BMC's 2639cc six to create the definitive middle-class sports car, the 100-6.

trim—like Ronnie Bucknum's famous West Coast Healey from Hollywood Sports Cars that catapulted him into a Formula One ride—the Healey six would give around 200 hp.

Understandably enough, Donald Healey's interest was in rallying. So even though Austin-Healeys appeared in jillions of races—from Le Mans to Willow Springs, which is further than you think, I promise you—their real forte was the international rally. Particularly for the rather overweight late Healeys—which took just an unconscionable amount of time and money to turn into competitive road racers—rallying was about the only thing they *could* do. Curiously enough, Donald Healey—a world-famous rally star—didn't build his own rally cars. All Healey factory rally cars after 1958 were built by Marcus Chambers at Abingdon in BMC Competitions, which had opened in 1955.

Right from the start, though, the factory teams were superb, getting a Coupe des Alpes in '58 and winning almost everything given out at the Liège rally. And in the sixties when BMC ran full teams of Sprites, Minis, and "Big Healeys," they were literally unbeatable. Historian Martyn Watkins figured out that from 1960 to 1968, when the Healey 3000 went out of production, it had some forty class wins just in international rallies, with two outright wins in the Liège–Rome–Liège and three overall wins in the Alpine. And Pat Moss had gotten more than a dozen Coupes des Dames.

The big Healey was dropped in 1968, for a variety of reasons. U.S. safety and emissions standards would have required quite a few changes in the old-fashioned Healey, which in truth was already pretty long in the tooth. And unlike the early days when the engine came out of the standard sedans and was used for free, so to speak, by the mid-sixties all the BMC cars were much smaller Mini derivatives. The Healey alone used the old six. Even more, though, Donald Healey's contract expired in 1972, and there was really no reason for a huge conglomerate like BMC to keep him on the payroll.

So after just about 150,000 Austin-Healeys had been built, BMC went its way into British-Leyland and perdition and Donald Healey went his way into Jensen and bankruptcy. For both Austin and Healey, their composite car was the high point of an otherwise mundane

Austin-Healey 3000, a lovable grand tourer.

existence. If you include all the rally wins, the Austin-Healey was just about the winningest British sports car ever in FIA international competition. And, of course, one of the most beloved old brutes ever built. Pat Moss aside, it was a real man's car, heavy to steer, cramped, uncomfortable, and harsh. But they loved it out there. Still do.

Austin-Healeys—all Donald Healey's cars, in fact—are fantastic collector cars, though it's pretty hard to find a good 3000 at any price. A good original is worth over·$3,000, a restored car near $5,000 (they cost only $3,000 new). The early 100-4 and 100-6—and especially the S and M models—are worth much more, particularly the S, which is as hairy a car as you'd want to have . . . strong, quick, and a real brute for its size. Unlike the petite MGA, the unreliable Jaguars, and the ugly Triumphs, the Healey has it all. It's not superlative in any one aspect, but it's a grand all-rounder that can accomplish almost anything with the right man behind the wheel. Plus, it'll stand up to all sorts of unnatural punishment with nary a whimper. Indeed, Healeys are positively Churchillian in their steadfastness, in the utter remorselessness of their going. "They are a tough and hardy lot. They have not journeyed all this way across the centuries, across the oceans, across the mountains, across the prairies, because they are made of sugar candy."

MGA

George Phillips was an amateur racer and personal friend of MG general manager John Thornley. He took a rebodied MG-TC to Le Mans in 1949 and '50 and astonished everyone—including himself—by finishing second in class. So for the next year, he talked to Thornley about a factory version. Sid Enever was enthusiastic and came up with a very pretty, very streamlined envelope body remarkably similar to the contemporary C-Jaguar, though on a much smaller scale. This was fitted to a new TD chassis and Phillips trucked off to France, where the car attracted lots of attention but failed to finish.

Enever liked the shape of Phillips's car so much that he built another, lower version in 1952 for himself. The Austin-Morris merger set things back a bit and the Austin-Healey project even more. So it was the summer of 1954 before Enever got back on the

Sid Enever's EX182, Le Mans racer prototype.

One of the best-looking British sports cars of the fifties,

stick with his streamliner. By now he had the nice 1489cc "B" engine and gearbox that BMC had brought to the Magnette sedan, for which he got Harry Weslake to design a cross-flow head. Three cars were eventually built in aluminum, dubbed EX182 in the BMC development department, and sent to Le Mans and the Tourist Trophy. Unfortunately, '55 was the year there were horrendous disasters at both races, so that kind of took the shine off the first factory MG racers in twenty years. The best performances were twelfth, seventeenth, and a crash at Le Mans. Which wasn't much to write home about.

The EX182 trio were line-for-line prototypes for the MGA, which debuted in late '55. Much better received than the betwixt and between MG-TF, the MGA stayed in production until 1962, by which time they'd sold 100,000 of the little dears. Underneath, it wasn't much more than a repowered TF, so the handling stayed classically neutral, with quick and light steering, decent roadholding, and a beautifully forgiving nature. The B engine gave it lots more punch than the T-series, though, and with its perfectly streamlined

carefully controlled MGA coupe.

body, even a raggedy MGA would go nearly 100 mph. Race-tuned cars were good for about 115, and BMC supplied a cornucopia of hop-up parts to supplement the huge aftermarket catalog.

Because of its carefully controlled body shape, there isn't half as much room in the cockpit or under the hood of the MGA as in the Ts. The tiny top-opening bonnet in particular makes engine work back-breaking at best. The bodywork is all big pieces—not little ones—so it's more difficult to repair. And because of the water-trapping propensity of envelope body designs, it's considerably more prone to rust than the early cars. On the other hand, as a car to *drive,* the MGA is spectacularly better, though admittedly not as much fun. At $2,444, it was a bargain in its day, and fully restored cars are just inching up to that level now. You can still find a perfectly good MGA in usable shape for under $1,000, and last week I passed up a local enthusiast's MGA coupe with two spare engines, spare rear ends, transmissions, and another whole parts car for $300 *total.*

Twin-Cams are another story. When MG

went racing in 1955, both the MG group and the Austin division came up with 1500cc, double-overhead-cam fours. For the Tourist Trophy, both engines were tried in the team cars. The MG version was selected for production, appearing in 1958. This was nothing more than the standard B block cleverly converted to take a pair of chain-driven camshafts topside in place of the pushrods. Power went from 68 hp at 5,500 rpm to 108 hp at 6,800, from a capacity of 1589cc. This was good enough in stock form for 110 mph, and the production Twin-Cams got excellent Dunlop four-wheel disc brakes with real knock-off steel wheels.

Unfortunately, not only did the Twin-Cams drink a lot of oil but the cam timing was fanatically critical. Most of them spent a majority of their days in the garage with the head off. Back in my MG days, I frequented a shop whose mechanic had spent two years of his life as a full-time tuner for a team of Twin-Cam racers. He'd finally quit when his nerves went—a malady he blamed solely and bitterly on the vagaries of Sid Enever's double overhead cams—and he could not be induced to look under the hood of a Twin-Cam for love nor money. The only thing that kept me from trading my TD straight across for a race-prepped double-knocker coupe was his dire threat of a relapse, with consequent medical bills sent straight to me.

While I was considering that Twin-Cam coupe, though, I spent as much time as I could driving it around—which was a lot, since it belonged to a fraternity brother. With racing Blue Dots and a stiffer suspension, it wasn't comfortable, but *very* solid. Compared to my T-series, it was also surprisingly quiet. Instead of flapping fenders and creaking wood, the only sounds were a slight whir from the cam chain and a healthy roar from the Abarth exhaust. By way of comparison, I distinctly remember coming down Benefit Street in Providence one night, in my accustomed third gear, with what seemed like the normal *Sturm und Drang.* In the TD that I usually drove, this was a slightly illegal 45 in a 25 zone. Only when my passenger pointed out that I was doing a highly noticeable 80 did I realize just how far MG had come between the T-series and the Twin-Cam.

Unfortunately, there was more wrong

with the Twin-Cam than right, not the least of which was a $4,000 price tag. Between 1958 and 1960, they built less than 2,000, making the Twin-Cam not only the most expensive of fifties MGs but just about the rarest, too. For both reasons, the market for Twin-Cams is surprisingly strong, and concours cars are up in the $5,000 range. Parts cars start at $0, so it's still an affordable car to get into. Normal MGA parts fit, of course, and except for the valve gear there's not too much to go wrong. I personally wouldn't buy a Twin-Cam to drive, because the reliability problems that plagued it new are still there today. As a collector's car, however, it'd be lots of fun to have, and though not a big-bucks blue chip, Twin-Cams have held their value surprisingly well for a model with an admittedly lousy reputation.

Somehow, when MG went to the pretty, streamlined, efficient, practical, economical, inexpensive MGA, they lost most of the charm that made the T-series cars so desirable. The TC was a unique, special, wonderful device, a Jordan Playboy for the masses. It was a car to give your mistress if you couldn't afford an XK-120. The MGA was a car to give your wife if she didn't need something as big as a Country Squire with fake wood trim. Being British, the MGA was still quirky—the heater didn't work, the instruments burned out even faster than the valves, the transmission synchronizer rings were worn before they left the factory, the interior started to fall apart on the boat coming over. But the MGA *was* a good sports car, and that you were required to fiddle with it a little was just part of the appeal. Still is. There just isn't a cheaper, more enjoyable collector car you can buy to use on a day-to-day basis, nor one that will be less of a headache to own. Given, of course, that you *enjoy* fiddling with cars.

Lotus Seven

I don't care who you are, Colin Chapman should be one of your heroes. Honest. Chap-

man is a classic example of lifting oneself up by one's bootstraps, and even if you don't always agree with everything he does, you can't help but admire the man. He is, among other things, the only smashing success the British automobile industry has had in the last twenty years. And a pound sterling millionaire many times over. Which is a lot more of an accomplishment than you might expect in England these days. Unlike so many of his wealthy compatriots in the harried world of the British well-to-do, Chapman has also manfully resisted—as far as I know—the impulse to hide behind a Swiss address when the tax man comes around. He's stood right there and taken it on the chin, for which they ought to make him a viscount, at least.

Not to mention *five* world championships in Formula One in less than two decades, innumerable F/1 race wins, a string of successes in USAC and Indy, absolute domination in Formulas Two, Three, and Ford, sports/racers of all descriptions, Le Mans class winners, and probably more racing triumphs per number of cars built than any other manufacturer. And those are just the highlights I can remember off the top of my head. In other words, Chapman is far and away the most successful manufacturer of pure racing cars in the history of the sport, and the greatest British owner/racer/manufacturer since, oh God, I suppose Woolf Barnato or somebody. Second only to the Beatles, Chapman did more to boost British prestige during the sixties than anyone had been able to do since they showed Kaiser Bill what for. In a socialistic system absolutely stacked to the goddamn rafters against the independent businessman, Chapman not only made it all work but came out smelling like a rose besides, for which they ought to give him a dukedom. Hell. What they *really* oughta do is just sign the whole sumbitch *island* over to Colin Chapman, and let him run it as an empire or something.

Chapman really did start from less than nothing, building Austin Seven Trials specials in his girl friend's father's garage. He had an engineering degree from London University, a prospective wife with the patience of the young and innocent, and a depth of boyish charm that makes Paul McCartney look like a stick. On top of all of this he managed to coerce his friends into some outlandish donations of time and money for little or no recompense. . . a characteristic that soon wore thin. But there were always new supplies of friends waiting cheerfully to be used.

And Chapman made it all fun; at least in the beginning. Lotus racers—he and Hazel never *have* satisfactorily explained just where the name comes from—were built in a madcap whirlwind that usually saw them loaning the factory demonstrator to a prospective customer for a weekend of racing, because his own car was weeks overdue and he had nothing else to race. But the customers were as charmed as the friends—often the two were interchangeable—and the happy Lotus crew have come down in legend and song as an enviable blend of Robin Hood's band as depicted by Sir Walter Scott, the public bar at Ye Olde White Horse Inne, and the Sons of Britannia Social Club and Racing Society.

The Mark 1 Lotus was a simple Austin Seven Trials car, a schoolboy's spare-time project built in 1948. So were Marks 2, 3, and 4, on an increasingly sophisticated basis. On January 1, 1952, Lotus Engineering Co. was formed between Colin and Hazel, operating out of some old stables Chapman's father owned in Hornsey. The couple incorporated just a year later. The Mark 5 project was shelved, and the Mark 6 was an all-new car—as opposed to modified Austin—with a tubular space frame that also supported the angular aluminum body. It was meant as an inexpensive kit for British club racing, which the buyer could help build himself in the converted stables and power with the engine of his choice. It weighed only 1,000 pounds and with a 1500cc Ford Consul engine would go very fast indeed. The Mark 6 looked pretty much like a front-engined Formula Two car with cycle fenders, though the rear fenders faired into the body and had full fender skirts besides. It was all-aluminum, and most owners simply polished them up instead of bothering with paint. Chapman and Co. managed to sell one hundred between 1953 and '55.

The classic early Lotus is the Seven. It's nothing more than a revamped version of the Mark 6, really, though it was the fall of 1957 before it appeared. During the years in between, Chapman had turned himself into the brightest little star in British road racing, with superlative, aerodynamic sports/racers . . .

the Mark 8/10 and 9 and the legendary Lotus Eleven. And already there was a successful front-engine Formula Two single-seater and the brilliant all-fiberglass Elite, which debuted alongside the Seven at Earl's Court. The Seven arrived late, mostly because there was just too much else going on. On the other hand, it was a *much* better car than the early Mark 6, because all the technology Chapman and aerodynamicist Frank Costin had absorbed while doing their sports/racers was stuck into the Seven for free.

The Lotus Seven consisted of a Lotus Eleven chassis, stripped of its streamlined body, with stressed aluminum panels attached right to the space frame. The independent front suspension—simple A-arms on coil springs—came straight off the Formula Two racer; the rigid rear axle was from a British Ford. It rode on coil springs with twin trailing arms and a transverse Panhard rod. The early Sevens had drum brakes and the 1172cc flathead that Ford of England called the 100E. This little four had its own 1172 racing class, so it was a natural. Ready to race, the whole thing weighed only 725 pounds. The wheelbase was 88 inches, and the overall length (there was virtually no overhang, front or rear) was an incredible 125 inches, almost a foot and a half shorter than Healey's Bugeye Sprite.

Chapman was pretty much the first to apply extremely lightweight aircraft construction to street machines (to racing machines, too, for that matter). And the results were spectacular. The Lotus Seven was—hell, still is—the closest thing ever built to a Formula car that can actually be driven on the street like a real car. It came with a windshield, top, side curtains, all the electrics, and even a small hole behind the seats into which you could stuff some luggage. There were no *doors,* of course, nor other candy-ass superfluous bits like that. And the seats—which were only thin foam-rubber pillows glued to the stressed-aluminum floor—were adjustable by the somewhat imperfect system of squinching yourself around until you got comfortable.

But it was grand. There is nothing—*no thing*—that will outcorner a well-driven Lotus Seven except a full-blown sports/racer or Formula car, and even then it'll be close. And nothing else with a rigid rear axle can come

Knee-high to an SCCA racer, Colin Chapman's brilliant Lotus Seven at Bridgehampton, 1964.

even near. The Lotus is perfectly balanced and has perfect suspension geometry and a frame that's built like a jet-fighter fuselage. So the suspension works the way it's supposed to, not the way some Flexible Flyer of a frame lets it. All of which means the cornering is indescribable—you kind of just *wish* it around without moving your hands. It's more like a racing motorcycle than something as mundane as a car.

Because it weighs almost nothing—the Seven's power-to-weight ratio is pretty much dependent on your own—it's also amazingly quick in a straight line. With almost no frontal area—except for the windshield, the highest point is only 27 inches off the ground—it has an equally amazing top speed. And unlike most other production sports cars, when you get up around 130 mph or so, the handling doesn't go all to hell. Remember, the Lotus Seven is really the sports/racing Lotus Eleven with a cheapie body. So it's as predictable as the eleven o'clock news and as stable as the *Times* editorial page.

And cheap. In 1961 you could get a complete Series 2 car—with improved chassis, better steering, and a handsome fiberglass nose plug that looked like they'd pulled it from the Lotus 18 Formula One car—complete with overhead-valve Ford 105E four, for less than £500. Or in those halcyon days of the sturdy pound, just a blink under $2,000, which, when you consider it would beat a Healey 3000 all hollow and was miles and away better than the similarly priced Sprite, was a bargain that makes the Louisiana Purchase seem like flagrant misuse of funds.

One indication: The $3,000 Healey 3000—with the addition of a few thousand dollars more for modifications—made a reasonable D-production SCCA racer. A competitive Healey Sprite for H-production cost at least $4,000, by the time you went through it completely. Now you have to remember that SCCA classes are set up by performance. The fastest cars race in A-production, the slowest in H. Lotus sold an optional Super Seven—which was the standard car with an 1100cc Coventry Climax and later a 1500cc Ford-based Lotus Twin-Cam—that ran in *B-production* against Jaguars and Corvettes in the mid-sixties. And won. And cost less than half as much. Phenomenal. And not only that, Lotus Sevens are *still* competitive for SCCA racing. Not overwhelming winners, to be sure, but what the hell do you expect from a twenty-year-old design? And they cost less to run than anything else on the track. Their race-car suspensions and light weight mean they don't use up tires or shocks, and the production-based Twin-Cam engines—shared with other Lotus models—aren't all that expensive, either.

Even better, the Lotus Seven is *still* in production. In *three* different forms. Chapman's original design was softened and modified over the years and, as these things have a way of doing, even got restyled with a silly and awkward fiberglass body for the Series 4. This made it look pretty much like a cheap California dune buggy, so nobody bought it. And in 1973—probably fifteen years later than he originally expected—Chapman took the Seven out of production. But he sold the rights and the dies to Caterham Cars, a London Lotus dealer that still does a brisk trade in brand-new Lotus Seven Series 4s. But since most people prefer the better-looking Series 3, Caterham makes those, too. And there's a new U.S. firm selling rebuilt Sevens imported from England.

The thing about Sevens for Americans, at least, is that anything newer than a '72 is illegal in this country because of emissions and safety laws. I mean, how do you pass a bumper requirement when you don't have bumpers, or side-guard door beams when you don't have doors? You understand the problem. On the other hand, the Lotus Seven has always been available as a kit, a big box of parts to which one adds gas, oil, water, and 25 man-hours. Mix well; serves two wind-in-the-face enthusiasts. So there are diehards shipping kits through Canada, or one piece at a time through friends in England or God knows how. All I know is that if you know the right American garage in which to look, poof—a brand-new Lotus Seven.

Like everything else, the price of Lotus Sevens keeps going up and up. From under £500 it's zapped up to over £2,000 in Britain, which actually isn't too bad, the rate of ex-change being what it is today. Over here, $4,000 is about right to pay for a decent one. But since the cars were designed as U-build-it kits, they're incredibly simple to work on—a characteristic of Lotus cars in general. So you can save a few dollars if you can do it yourself . . . and it's an easy restoration. Virtually all the parts are available from Lotus in this country or Caterham as a last resort. And there's no law against importing parts, as far as I know.

In its way, the Lotus Seven is among the cleverest cars ever designed. It was meant to be a young man's car, certainly, with the discomfort, inconvenience, and unreliability that implies. But more, as a young *racer's* car, with the joyful precision, balance, and sturdy simplicity *that* implies. In sum, it's the perfect car for an impecunious club racer to drive to work during the week and race on weekends, someone who does his own repairs, never worries about a thing, and lives life to the absolute fullest: a car for the original "work hard, play hard" enthusiast; a car, in other words, for young Anthony Colin Bruce Chapman, B.Sc. (Eng.), to drive and race circa 1957. And for others like him, too.

Lotus 11/15/17

Colin Chapman made his reputation with a series of similar sports/racers in 1954, '55, and '56. Before that he was merely one of the multitude of enthusiastic young engineers who perpetually hung around British Trials and club racing, selling stripped-down cars when he could, parts and tuning when he had to. But when he joined forces with Mike and Frank Costin in early 1954, Lotus suddenly became known for slippery aerodynamic bodies that were beautiful and, even better, extremely efficient. Frank Costin, a designer for DeHavilland Aircraft, merely applied what he knew to Chapman's comparatively mundane automotive problems. He was just about the first to do it, though, and between Chapman's innate understanding of suspensions and Costin's superior aerodynamics, the pair were able to get mind-boggling performance out of tiny engines with no horsepower.

The first of the Chapman/Costin cars was the Mark 8, which was basically the Mark 6 with a very unusual two-seater body. The fenders protruded into sharp points at the front, flanking a wide and grilleless mouth. The hood pooched up to make a slim eyebrow hood scoop at the front. There were tall, thin tail fins at the back and full fender skirts. It was planned as a 1500cc car, weighed under 1,000 pounds, and would run 125 mph on 85 hp. Like most sports/racers of the fifties—including the C-type and D-type Jaguars—the Mark 8 was not only street-legal but driven to most races. To be honest, however, there were no headlamps, windshield, or top, to mention just a few oversights for street use. But the Mark 8 was so far advanced over the Mark 6 (and most of the competition, too) that it was an instant winner in British club racing.

The Mark 9 was a shorter version of the 8—less overhang, but on the same 87.5-inch wheelbase—powered by the new 1100cc FWA Coventry Climax portable fire-pump engine. The Mark 10 was merely the Mark 8 with a 2-liter BMW/Bristol six. The big changes were disc brakes to handle the extra speed—150 hp in only 1,100 pounds—and a pop-top hood to clear the tall old Bristol mill. All three versions were equally successful, though of course since they were hand-built sports/racers, usually finished up by the new owner, there weren't very many built. Nor are there very many left, since a good number were either crashed or discarded as they became obsolete. In their day, however, the Mark 8/10 and the 9 pretty much dominated the 1100, 1500, and 2000cc classes in England, and a small handful—maybe six at the most—found their way to America. Curiously, they were never as successful over here as when driven by Chapman and crew.

A word about Chapman. Not only is he a real charmer, probably the best suspension designer in the world, and a crackerjack businessman, but until he got a bit too old and a bit too valuable, "Chunky" Chapman—oh yes, and a bit too overweight—was very nearly the best small-bore road racer in England. Partic-

Coventry-Climax Formula One four: 2495cc, 239 hp; pl

ularly at the wheel of his own cars, he was perfectly capable of beating Stirling Moss, Tony Brooks, Mike Hawthorn, and just about anybody else on a given day, using identical equipment. He also drove class winners at Sebring and Le Mans, won some big sedan races in a borrowed Jaguar, and was even invited to race for Vanwall in Formula One until he crashed seriously on his trial run (through mechanical breakage, I might add, not any fault of Chapman's). He was a tidy, careful, and impressively quick chauffeur. One of the proudest moments in Chapman history was a Goodwood race in 1956 in which Colin beat Mike Hawthorn fair and square, both driving identical Lotus Elevens.

Ah yes. The Lotus Eleven. If there is such a thing as the perfect front-engine sports/racer, the Lotus Eleven is it. In one of those happy accidents, everything about it came out just right, from the mechanicals to the marvelous aluminum body. It was another Chapman/Costin collaboration, of course, and by far the best. It was also the first model designed after Chapman and Mike Costin (Frank the aerodynamicist's brother) had decided to become full-time car builders. Up un-

50 pounds, superb aerodynamics, and Chapman strut suspension equals Lotus Fifteen, at Cumberland, 1960.

til January 1955, Chapman ran Lotus as a part-time thing, though Nobby Clark and Hazel were there all day every day. But after that, they had a real company going.

Chapman himself raced a full season in 1955, and it was November or so before the Eleven got started. Typically, it was pretty much a Mark 9 chassis with necessary modifications they'd discovered through racing. The tubular space frame got a stressed cockpit floor, but otherwise it was the same right down to the independent front suspension with single leading arms. But the Eleven was different in several ways. First, Chapman started a one-model policy. Instead of dithering around with modifications for various owners, they'd make just the one model, in three states of tune. The cheapie version, which cost £872, was homologated as a "production" sports car. It had a rigid rear axle, drum brakes, and the old Ford flathead 1172cc 100E. Stock horsepower was only 36, but in a 900-pound car with unexcelled aerodynamics this was good for nearly 100 mph. It also delivered a spectacular 65 mpg at a steady 40 mph.

The middle version of the Eleven was the Club model, which was nothing more than the "production" version fitted with the expensive 1100cc Coventry Climax FWA. This gave 75 or 85 hp, depending on carburetion, and cost £1,083 in England. Finally, there was the Le Mans Eleven, which could be had with either the FWA or 1500cc FWB Climax. It also had the DeDion rear axle from the Mark 9, with inboard disc brakes, and outboard Girling discs on the front. It came with a metal tonneau cover and head fairing, and cost £1,337 to £1,650, depending on engine and options.

All the Elevens had full electrics, with headlamps faired into the fenders, thinly padded seats sort of like those in the Seven, the fuel tank in the front fender, and a full undershield. They still had knock-off wire wheels, too, and a superb aluminum body that started very low at the front with a tiny rectangular opening for the ducted radiator, only to sweep back into completely faired—there are no wheel openings as such—fenders with a very low rise. Tiny flop-down doors on piano hinges were meant to prove it was a real sports car, I think, as everything else about it said "thinly disguised Formula car."

After the Eleven, there came the very similar Fifteen and Seventeen, which stayed in production until 1960. They were the last front-engine Lotus racers. The 2.5-liter Fifteen was replaced by the Formula One–based Lotus 19, and the 1100cc Seventeen was replaced by the famous Lotus 23, a Formula Junior with full-width bodywork. Nobody would ever consider a Lotus 19 or 23 as anything more than a full-blown race car, and there was no top, windshield, and side curtain kit for the later cars as there was for the Eleven. So the last legitimate dual-purpose Lotus sports/racer—and even that's bending over backward till your ears touch—is the Lotus Eleven/Fifteen/Seventeen series. And I still wouldn't count on driving one of them regularly unless you happen to live in Lime Rock, Connecticut, or Flowery Branch, Georgia, or Daytona, Florida.

As collector cars, they are superb. And if you just want something to race with the VSCC, there's nothing finer. The Lotus Elevens are among the nicest, most satisfying, most vicefree cars ever built, and an absolute ball to drive. They have some idiosyncrasies—don't we all—but for fun per dollar they can't be beat. Only a few years ago you could get a competitive Lotus Eleven—you wouldn't win very often, but you could place every once in a while in C-sports/racing—for under $3,000. The price today is four times that for a competitive VSCC mount; they're relatively easy to work on, and they're not impossible for spares. At least there are quite a few Climax engines around, and they have lasted surprisingly well with regular rebuilds.

Curiously enough, the Lotus Eleven is one of the few sports/racers I know that racing drivers seem to keep. Lots of people raced an Allard or Corvette for a while, then converted it back to a street car. But most racers aren't too sentimental. They use a car up and either sell it for another or get out of racing. But the Elevens hit some deep chord somewhere and a racer who would *never* keep what is to him a useless, noncompetitive old racing car will still be found with a dusty Lotus Eleven tucked in the garage behind a bunch of spares. He's the one to find. He'll not only have three complete engines, a spare gearbox, and twelve wheels but will know how it all goes together and probably want to help work

on it. You can even let him once in a while, if you're feeling magnanimous.

Lola 1100

Most of the British enthusiasts who tried to make it big as car manufacturers in the fifties had been around for a while as drivers or me-

Eric Broadley's impossibly sleek answer to Lotus's

chanics or businessmen, had survived the war, and were looking to put something away before settling into their dotage. Healey, Allard, Jaguar, Aston Martin were the result. But there was a younger generation, totally postwar, who were concerned only with getting on, and right now, too. Colin Chapman was the pushiest, best known, and most successful of these youngsters . . . and certainly the most brilliant. John Tojeiro had his one bright

idea—the A. C. Ace. Brian Lister simply copied his friend Tojeiro's car and pushed that concept as far as it would go, ultimately into the formidable Lister-Jag.

Eric Broadley fit the pattern too, at least at first. He's from that generation—he was still in swaddling clothes when Donald Healey won the Monte in '31—and in the way Brian Lister copied John Tojeiro, Eric Broadley copied Colin Chapman. Broadley, in fact,

Eleven, the 1959 Lola 1100 Sport absolutely decimated European small-bore racing for two seasons.

had a regular Chapman fixation going for over a decade; sad to say, usually one jump behind the maestro. When Broadley decided to contest the 1172 class with a line-for-line copy of the Lotus Mark 6, Chapman was already on to the 1100 Climax. When Broadley went to that, Chapman was into Formula Junior and Formula Two. About the time Broadley's racers could finally whip Chapman's in F/J, Colin was already doing Formula One.

Luckily for Broadley, just when he and John Surtees decided to make a big expenditure in F/1, Ford Motor Company came along and gave him the GT-40 to do instead, based on his own Lola GT coupe. This was really the first time he stepped out from Chapman's shadow. The big-bore experience he got with Ford set Broadley up perfectly for the Can-Am, and the Lola T70 made his name in '66 and '67. So these days, when Lotus builds expensive personal cars for aging executives and recently revived F/1 cars, Lola is still the name for extremely successful Formula cars of all sorts, with a big percentage sold in the States by Carl Haas.

Chapman had a choice. "Two roads diverged," etc. And he took the one most traveled by, the one that led to passenger cars, mass production, and lots of money. Broadley took the one less traveled and indeed, that *has* made all the difference. Every Lola has been strictly a racing machine, except for the Climax-engined Mark 1 of 1958/'59, which was just about the last dual-purpose sports/racer in England. Now dual-purpose, understand, in the sense that yes, once a month you could drive it to the race circuit under its own power if you had to, though you'd have to be slightly bonkers to *want* to. It was the same sort of car as the C-type, D-type, and Lister-Jag, but what it was, undeniably, was a virtually line-for-line copy of the Lotus Eleven.

It had the same 85-inch wheelbase, with a multitube space frame. At the front were unequal-length A-arms; at the rear, a Chapman Strut independent setup complete with inboard Al-Fin brakes and the half-shafts used as the upper control arms. In suspension design, it took after the Lotus Formula Two and Fifteen, which shows that Broadley was at least clever enough to copy a better Chapman system when he saw it. The engine was the tried and true single-overhead-cam 1098cc

FWA Coventry Climax with twin SUs. The wheels were Dunlop mags. The smooth aluminum body was not only embarrassingly similar to the Lotus Eleven—though it was fully 2 inches shorter, at 132 inches overall—but even hinged open the same way with panels that split along the same lines. It weighed roughly 850 pounds. And that was within a chit of the Lotus Eleven, too. The prototype appeared in 1958, but Broadley—no match for Colin on the track, either—wrecked it. So it was 1959 before the Lola 1100 really appeared.

As a footnote, Broadley first started thinking about building his own car in '56, when a hit single was "Whatever Lola wants, Lola gets." Eric, a young architectural student, thought this pretty appropriate. And presto, Lola. Despite the name, they didn't always get what they wanted, but surprisingly enough, Broadley's copy of the Lotus was just marginally faster around a corner, probably because the Lola's Chapman Strut suspension was better than the DeDion rear end on the Lotus Eleven. Ironically, then, Chapman was being, as they say in Tom Swift adventures, hoist by his own petard.

Broadley's copy was *so* good, in fact, that Chapman was forced to come up with his own Lotus Eleven copy—the even smaller Lotus Seventeen—which had a lightweight Chapman Strut suspension, too. Fortunately for Broadley, Chapman was so busy trying to sort out his new Formula One cars—easily the *least* successful Lotuses ever built—moving into a new Lotus factory, and getting the Elite into production, that the Seventeen was never really debugged. Broadley's cars dominated small-bore club racing both in England and on the Continent, and a fair number came to the States.

Between 1958 and '61, Broadley turned out thirty-five Lola 1100s, some in aluminum and some in fiberglass. They sold for £1,540, about the same as the Lotus Seventeen with an identical engine but with disc brakes. They were quite popular in their day, and *Motorsport* or *Autoweek* would be a good place to track down someone who's held onto his. I suppose you'll have to spend $10,000 for a decent one, but for a 130-mph sports/racer you can race, play with, or put in your den—hell, it's small enough—that's not a bad price to pay. The cars were well built, sturdy, pretty, and easy to work on. And it's not every day you'll have a chance to buy something that's been proven time after time to outhandle even the magnificent Lotus Eleven.

Lister-Jaguar

There's a Colin Chapman anecdote that pretty well sums up motor-racing entrepreneurs. As the story goes, Chapman is standing on the pit wall at Indy, looking at two brand-new Lotuses, each with a $30,000 engine blown higher than the grandstand roof. And then some dumb-ass Hoosier official starts threatening to disqualify them both because of weak lug nuts, or something. And Chapman turns to his major-domo, Andrew Ferguson, and says, "You know, Andrew, we're bloody mad. We've got 150,000 pounds in capital investment here for a return of 2 percent. It's bloody stoopid. Point is, we couldn't have as much fun doing anything else."

· Well. Point really is, Chapman, Carroll Shelby, and Roger Penske are about the only entrants who've ever made even that slim 2 percent. For most manufacturers of racing cars, it's an overwhelming and ultimately disastrous progression from new ideas, bright hopes, and lots of money to worn-out equipment, dejection, and, inevitably, bankruptcy. And that's the truth. There isn't anybody who's made a living out of racing . . . ever. The money either comes from outside of cars and racing completely, or from production cars or ancillary sponsorship deals and related publicity. But *nobody* makes a living purely out of motor racing, no matter what they tell you.

Lord knows, enough have tried. England was, is, and probably always will be filled with pale imitations of Colin Chapman, all slaving away in borrowed stables and back garden garages, trying to build a Lotus-beater. Eric Broadley did it for a while with Lola, Frank Nichols with his Elvas, and Mo Nunn looks to be on his way to an Ensign empire. But

that's about all. Oh yes. And then there's Brian Lister. Lister tried to build just sports/racers and consequently never got that broad financial base you need and can build with mass-market street machines. And so, even though he had a superior product, he still went down the drain within six years. The only reason he managed to stay around even that long was backing from a benevolent family and some wealthyish patrons.

Lister was from Cambridge; his father was an engineer. The family business was wrought iron, which meant they had a shop set up for working with metals. Brian started racing with a Cooper-MG and a Tojeiro-J.A.P. 500cc Formula car. Early in 1954 he decided to become a manufacturer himself, just like Cooper and Tojeiro—who was also from Cambridge—building racers in borrowed quarters. So he roped off part of his father's wrought-iron shop and started welding. The first car was pretty similar to Tojeiro's Bristol-engined special for Cliff Davis, the one that became the A. C. Ace.

Lister used two big 3-inch tubes for the chassis, just like Tojeiro, with unequal-length A-arms at the front and a DeDion rear axle. He had Al-Fin drum brakes, an MG-TD engine . . . and a boxy aluminum body that looked like a homebuilt copy of the A. C. About the time he got done, he decided he'd rather be a builder than a driver. So Archie Scott-Brown, an irrepressible tobacco salesman born with only one hand, became the paid "factory" chauffeur for meals and expenses.

But the Lister-MG wasn't very good; mostly, it was too slow. So they built another just like it, but with the time-honored Bristol/BMW six. The Lister-Bristol was a whole nother smoke completely, and Scott-Brown became a contender overnight. The team went so well, in fact, that people started asking for copies. Lister went into limited production in the corner of his father's shop in 1955. The chassis was still the same Tojeiro-like tubular ladder, but in talking with Bristol about engines they linked up with Tom Lucas, who did for Bristol Aeroplane what Frank Costin did for DeHavilland.

Aerodynamicist Tom Lucas did for Lister what Frank Costin did for Lotus. The new car was super-low, with a long, pointed nose and chopped-off tail with funny fins. It wasn't

Monstrous creation of Brian Lister and Carroll Shelby, a 400-hp Lister-Chevy at Cumberland, 1960.

pretty, but it was fast. The 2-liter Bristol was good for 130 mph, and until Chapman got his Mark 8/10 sorted out, the Lister-Bristol was the hot setup in small-bore club racing. In '56 Lucas came up with a smaller, neater body. By this time the customer cars had Bristols, but the factory racer for Scott-Brown had a Maserati Formula Two six. Unfortunately, the lighter, cleaner, more sophisticated Lotuses were less than a third the price . . . Lister-Bristols went for a stupendous £4,000.

Lister did the only thing he could. He abandoned the small-bore field to Chapman and moved into the big-bore ranks, where you could get by on sheer horsepower instead of sophistication. What he did was simple and logical. Jaguar had dropped out of racing, so Lister proposed to take their place. He modified the Lister-Bristol to take the Jaguar XK engine and transmission. He gave it big disc brakes with Dunlop mag wheels. Over all went a wonderfully brawny body, the most forceful ever fitted to a British sports/racer. It looked like a cross between a Reventlow Scarab and a Ferrari Testa Rossa, with just a hint of Maserati 450S. It wasn't pretty like the D-Jag, but it looked like 5000 hp just sitting there . . . and it went like the wind.

The Lister-Jags were virtually unbeatable from the moment they appeared, in the spring of '57. Archie Scott-Brown fought Roy Salvadori's Aston Martin DBR all over England throughout the season, and usually won. The car weighed only 1,450 pounds and with 300 hp from the D-type engine was a real goer. So the next year Lister went into production. He built fifty cars, for major teams like Ecurie Ecosse, Equipe Nationale Belge, and Briggs Cunningham. John Bolster tested one for *Autosport* and got 0 to 60 in 4.6 seconds, 0 to 100 in 11.2, and a top speed of 155 mph. (With Le Mans gears, the 3.8-liter cars would run 180 mph, but, unfortunately, with Le Mans gears you had to run the short-stroke 2986cc XK engine, because the FIA had decreed a maximum limit of 3 liters. And the 3-liter Jaguar engine was a dog.) The Lister-Jag was a grand, competitive car, a real handful to be sure, but an invincible weapon in the hands of someone who knew what he was doing.

It was even a bargain. With the 3.8-liter D-type engine for unlimited class racing outside the FIA, a Lister-Jag cost only £2,750. And in the States there was an even better deal. Carroll Shelby—already working toward the Cobra—wangled himself the American distributorship for Listers. He had the Jaguar engines left at home and instead stuffed in Chevy small-block V-8s. You could get any size you wanted, in any state of tune, though the hot setup in those days was a bored and stroked 324 cubic inches with six Stromberg 97s. This added at least another 50 hp over the D-type, and Weber carbs could get you up near 400 hp in full-race trim. So the Lister-Chevy was ungodly fast.

In 1958 and '59, Listers with either engine stormed around everywhere from Laguna Seca to Rheims. Scott-Brown was killed at Spa in May of '58, but people like Stirling Moss, Walt Hansgen, and Masten Gregory were major international stars with Lister-Jags. By 1959, though, the new Cooper Monaco and Lotus Fifteen—even with half the horsepower—were just as fast. The last gasp was '59, when Frank Costin left Lotus after a fight with Chapman and redesigned the Lister body. But it was too little too late, and Brian retired to the family wrought-iron works. For one brief, shining moment, though, in 1957 and '58, he really had a shot at it all. The cars were big and strong, and he had the backing of enough important people to really put it over. But he made a crucial mistake: in concentrating on producing big front-engine cars, he failed to notice all the little mid-engine cars working their way up the grids. And, unlike Chapman, who had a new idea every minute and a new car every month, Brian Lister copied John Tojeiro's concept and refined it for six years until it was just played out.

The total of Listers was less than a hundred. Most of them were Lister-Jags, which is good, because they were the best. The Lister-Chevys are cheaper and more reliable, but a bit rarer still. Shelby got quite a few over here before the music stopped, and though most of them got cut up and swapped around and repowered and rebodied and all the other terrible things that happen as a matter of course to old racing cars, there are some good ones left. If you can get a decent uncut, complete Lister-Jaguar or Lister-Chevrolet for less than $20,000, take it. You never know when

Two approaches to aerodynamics, Dr. Dick Thompson's Sting Ray with body by Bill Mitchell, Lister

you might see another, and if you want a unique and hairy big old sports/racer, it's about as big and hairy and unique as you can get.

Lotus Elite

Some things are collectible because they're now obsolete, and they evoke the past more strongly because of it: Duesenberg SJs, Flash Gordon decoder rings, and detachable collars, for example. Some things are collectible because though old, they fill modern needs more gracefully than contemporary counterparts— like Trumpy houseboats, Waterford crystal, and Tiffany lamps. Or Lotus Elites. Really. I have the distinct feeling that ten or twenty years from now, when we're all driving lightweight monocoque coupes with minuscule engines, Colin Chapman's brilliant Elite will still be right in style. If you think back to 1957 when the prototype was shown, it was easily

at least a whole generation ahead of everything else. So right from the beginning, everyone knew the Elite was special. A classic in its own time, as they say. And they were right.

Mostly, the Elite was a technical tour de force. All Lotuses are light, even to the point of being dangerous sometimes. And most of them have a very high aluminum and fiberglass content. The Elite was Chapman's attempt to cut the expensive, hand-hammered aluminum down to zero, replacing it with mass-produced fiberglass untouched by human hands. Fenders, body, *frame . . .* everything. And he did it. The Lotus Elite was the first production car in the world with a totally plastic unit body/frame. And all things considered, it worked. Now admittedly many Elites haven't lasted too well. The stressed fiberglass chassis simply decomposes. On the other hand, fiberglass is pretty easy to restore. And otherwise, overlooking the surface crazing and aging of the plastic, the all-plastic *idea* has survived intact.

Chapman himself was responsible for the chassis design, and it took him the better part of a year to do the research and draw up a rigid structure that would also be light and capable of being cast in sections, which were

...aguar with body by Frank Costin, at Meadowdale, '59.

then pasted together by hand. The exceptionally clean body was drawn by Peter Kirwan-Taylor, a personal friend of Chapman's, and revised by the aerodynamicist Frank Costin. Among other things, it featured a full streamlined underpan and exceptionally good air penetration. On 75 hp, for example, a stock Elite was timed by *The Motor* at 113 mph.

It was two years before Chapman was able to get enough money together to start production, in 1959, by which time he'd refined the Elite concept into three big pieces of fiberglass. The entire body was one piece, except for doors, hood, and trunk lid. Then came an inner liner, with the transmission tunnel, floor, trunk floor, and door frames. A steel hoop went up in front of each door and over the windshield, a second went over the cowl. This projected slightly below the rocker panels as a jacking point and gave Chapman someplace to hinge the doors and suspend the steering wheel and dash. Finally, a full-length belly pan with fender liners and bonded-in steel engine mounts snugged up underneath.

The running gear was basically from the new front-engine Lotus Formula Two car, the Mark 12, which of course means it was pretty much identical to the Seven/Eleven. Except

that the Elite got disc brakes at the front and a modified Chapman Strut independent rear suspension with inboard discs, which made it easily the most sophisticated production sports car in England at that time. Wally Hassan helped Chapman come up with a short-stroke version of the all-aluminum Coventry Climax four. They took the stroke from the 1098cc FWA and the bore from the 1460cc FWB, ending up with the all-new 1216cc FWE. With a single SU they got 75 hp, though two carbs brought 85 hp and full-race tuning was well over 100 hp.

Ready to run, the Elite weighed just over 1,300 pounds, which, while astonishingly low, was high for a Lotus. The Elite had the same tiny wheelbase as the 1,000-pound Seven—88 inches—but it stretched out to a great, whopping 144 inches overall, the same as the MG Midget. And since it was meant as Chapman's first "grand" tourer, it was trimmed a lot more luxuriously. And expensively. The Elite cost over $5,000 in the States. Curiously enough, it was almost identical in every way to the Alfa Giulietta Sprint Veloce in size, displacement, performance, and price. As an indication, however, the all-steel Alfa Giulietta—on an identical 88-inch wheelbase with 153-inch length—weighed 2,100 pounds, some 700 more than the Lotus.

The Lotus Elite is probably the most efficient production sports car ever. In tests of two different Elites in 1959 and 1963, *The Motor* averaged 54 mpg at a steady 40 mph and a fantastic 29.5 mpg at a steady 100 mph, the obvious point being that no car built before or since has been able to return that kind of economy at that kind of speed. Logically enough, Elites finished one-two in the Indice au Rendement Energique at Le Mans in 1960 and '62. They also won their class at Le Mans from 1959 through 1964, along, of course, with many, many other races, large and small.

The most famous Lotus Elites were Les Leston's DADIO and Graham Warner's LOV 1, which battled each other for years in British club racing championships. Someone even had the foresight to get some acceleration numbers off Warner's race-tuned Elite. With an extremely tall 4.90 gear for Brands Hatch, top speed was still 130 mph, 0 to 60 took 6.6 seconds, and 0 to 100 only 17. The quarter-mile time was a mere 15.1, which as Chap-

"Chunky" Chapman with his all-fiberglass 1957 masterpiece, the first of 988 Lotus Elites.

The most efficient high-performance GT ever, the Elite returned 29 mpg at 100 mph.

man's biographer, Ian Smith, points out, was even better than the performance returned by the full-race Lotus Eleven. Fantastic.

Between the Earl's Court Show in '57 and the beginning of true production in 1959, Lotus built a handful of racing Elites. Limited mass production went on at the Cheshunt, Hertfordshire, factory until mid-1963, when the Elite was phased out in favor of the cheaper-to-build Elan. Only 988 Elites were built, total, and I would guess less than half of those are left. Most seem to be either in the throes of restoration or already restored, and prices range from $5,000 up. Curiously enough, one of the best views of the Elite is during restoration. With everything stripped off the fiberglass monocoque, you can really appreciate the wonderfully right shape, among the best from the fifties. Even better, fiberglass is translucent. So with the body up on horses, stripped of paint and lighted from below, the whole thing takes on an almost ethereal glow. It is a small and beautifully controlled piece of sculpture, with all the organic, rounded smoothness of a pebble-inspired work by Henry Moore.

The Elite is, to be honest, not the most pleasant car to ride in. The one-piece fiberglass cocoon is extremely tight fitting and transmits a lot of road and engine noise. It's like riding inside a snare drum while a particularly inept amateur beats out poor imitations of Buddy Rich. As a car to drive, on the other hand, the Elite is absolutely superb, particularly the Series II, which has a ZF all-synchro 4-speed in place of the stiff BMC transmission in the earlier cars. In either case, the wonderful handling, acceleration, top speed, and mileage are simply unexcelled, and the over-the-road averages you can put up in an Elite are limitless.

Only one thing has puzzled me about Elites from the very beginning, and that's the knock-off wire wheels. I've never heard a good explanation. The Formula Two car from which Chapman took the suspension already had those wonderful "wobbly web" cast-magnesium wheels that look like Ripple potato chips. They are pretty, much lighter than knock-off wires, and as technologically advanced as the rest of the sophisticated Elite. Wire wheels, on the other hand, are a throwback to the twenties and always seemed completely out of character on the Elite. They're hard to keep round, fragile and heavy; all in all just not in keeping with the adventuresome spirit of Chapman's tour de force. But of course, if you buy one, you could always remedy that situation with a NOS set of hubs and wobbly web wheels. Seems like it should work to me. And then the Elite would be . . . why, just about perfect. Yes. That's the word. Perfect.

Austin-Healey Sprite

It's the summer of 1963: Bridgehampton, maybe, or Lime Rock, or Thompson. An unnamed Eastern road-racing track, gritty and impossibly dry in the airless heat. You're crammed into this tiny roller skate of a car with big popeyed lights on the hood. Manacled right in beneath your roll bar, helmeted, gauntleted, nerveless, and cool. Flat-top haircut and gunfighter's eyes, you wait flinty-browed for the damn starter to drop the flag and get this over so you can grab a beer. Around you are twenty guys just like you, in identical cars. Just about the only one-design class in racing. The cars are all identical. So the winner'll be the one who *drives* best. Period. Lays your old manhood right on the line, it does.

Red, white, blue, yellow—racers tend toward simple primary colors—the bright shining stones finally skip through the summer sun, heat waves flowing off them like fog from the highlands. Noise like a trillion locusts in full cry. And you've got these humpties licked. Round and round, in a dizzying procession, you effortlessly lead the multicolored horde, old Sam Stud, the coolest racer on the track. And then the last turn . . . Diving Turn at Lime Rock, Arents at the Bridge, Grandstand at Thompson. And *braaap . . . brraammmp*. Before you can react, out of the bright primary pack zips this goddamn hot-flaming-pink Sprite and *whooose*. She's gone. God*damn*. You had it all sewed up there for maybe the trillionth time this year, and that freaking blonde just did it to you again. Shee-ut. You're second best. You humpty.

Understand. There is nothing, just flat *nothing* that is calculated to puncture a hero racer's bubble like getting his doors blown off by a leggy blonde in a hot pink Sprite. And not some he-woman like Pat Moss, who makes Stirling look like a weenie twit. Oh no. By petite little Donna Mae Mims—dumb name, even—the Pink Lady of Racing.

Fact. In 1963, there were probably 400 H-production macho seekers absolutely *pouring* money into their racing cars trying to beat a kooky blonde in a pink Sprite. Hell. Pink everything. Donna Mae had pink driving suits, pink helmets, pink boots, pink gloves, pink scarves. Even pink underwear, from all reports. But it worked so good, the rest of you ought to try it. Donna Mae Mims was SCCA H-production champion of the world in 1963. Honest. You can look it up somewhere.

Now what this proves, except that Donna Mae Mims is some dynamite lady and that H-production is full of humpties, I'm not sure. Except that, well . . . H-production really is— or *was,* at least—just about the only "amateur" racing class in which you couldn't *buy* yourself a championship. Almost any other class, there's a bunch of guys staggering around with clapped-out cars they built up themselves, and they're getting beat into the ground by one or two hotshots with factory money who really do have the old unfair advantage.

But that's not as true in H and G production, for the simple reason that—like small-boat one-design classes—there is only one car that works. And that is the Austin-Healey Sprite/MG Midget. It's been this way since 1958, believe it or not, which in the history of racing cars slots right in between the Sermon on the Mount and the first sacking of Rome. I mean, Austin Sprites are about as sophisticated as a punch in the mouth and as powerful as raspberry Kool-Aid. And they look silly. Well, not silly, really. Ummmm. Kooky. Kinda like Donna Mae. Funny. Warm. Earthy. Kinky, though. But lovable, in a weird sort of way.

The first Austin-Healey Sprite appeared in May 1958. In the combined world of BMC

at that time, the only sports cars were the MGA—which had moved up into the lower-middle $2,500 market—and the Healey 100-6 —which was really pushing upper-middle at $3,000. The under-$2,000 "beginner's sports car" cupboard that the old T-series MGs had spectacularly filled was completely bare. But Austin/Morris had more cheap little boxy sedans than you can shake a stick at, so the basic parts were there. It was a matter simply of designing a roadster to fit them, kind of like redoing the Austin-Healey, only in HO scale. And of course, BMC was already paying the Healeys, father and son, for the use of their name. So it was no problem for a combined BMC team from Abingdon and the Healeys from Warwick to clap together something suitable.

The prime consideration was expense, so the Sprite turned out so cheap the stitches fell apart the first time you wore it in the rain. You were forever having to baste the cuffs back in. But if you didn't care much what you looked like, the Sprite was more unadulterated fun than anything since the MG-TC. And if you broke something—which you usually did—you just threw the whole outfit away and got another. Big deal.

Back in 1951—even before Longbridge and Abingdon got together—Austin had come up with their first postwar engine. This became the famous A-series BMC, which—embarrassingly enough—is *still* in production. A dead-conventional, long-stroke four, it started out at a measly 803cc but grew to 948cc in 1956. In the Austin/Morris sedans it made a booming 34 hp, but two carbs and a little hotting up gave them 43 hp for the rip-snorting sports version. This had a perfectly nice little 4-speed with it. And of course Healey used the conventional chassis that was under the A35/A40 Austin all snugged up to a simple steel body. With *quarter*-elliptic leaf springs in the rear.

To save money, there was no exterior chrome except for a simple oval grille, and trim rings around the lights, of course. And bumpers . . . which were really just two eensy bumperettes at the back. The hood and fenders were one piece like the C-type Jaguar, which gave marvelous access to the engine. There were doors but no door handles, and no trunk. The spare tire rode behind the seats

Donald Healey's magic car, the 43 hp, 1,400-pound, $1,800 Austin-Healey Sprite of 1958.

over the axle, and you got at it from inside. Side curtains, a nonfolding windshield, a laughable top that wanted to fold too much, two bucket seats, a lot of pressed cardboard trim, and presto . . . instant excitement.

The Sprite *was* a magic car in one respect. The MG-TC cost $1,895 in New York in 1948. A decade of inflation later, the Sprite cost $1,798. And its performance was better, incredibly enough. The Sprite weighed only about 1,400 pounds, so even 43 hp was enough to get it over 80 mph, and up to 60 in about 16 seconds, which *felt* faster than it sounds, I promise you. The 80-inch wheelbase—the same as a Meyers Manx, if that means anything—super-tight steering, tiny cockpit, and instant handling made it the closest thing to a go-kart with big wheels it's possible to find, kind of like a slow Formula V with fenders. It wasn't much for freeways, understandably enough, but for back-road horsing around it was dynamite. Slow, predictable, safe as houses, but terribly exciting. All the sensations were magnified a hundredfold because of the Sprite's miniature size, and on a tiny road you could really scare yourself without being in any more danger than you'd be falling out of a pram.

My senior year in high school, I drove a brand-new Morris Minor 1000—which was nothing more than a Sprite sedan with torsion bars—and one of my buddies had a Bugeye Sprite. Nearly every afternoon, we'd split after school and spend hours racing each other over the tree-lined back roads of rural Dutchess County. Every so often we'd switch cars. Alec Issigonis's brilliant Morris 1000 design would handily outcorner the less sophisticated Sprite, but my car not only spotted Jeff's a hundredweight but had to get by on six less horsepower, too. We both shared that big gap between third and fourth, though, which gave you lots of time to contemplate the scenery whilst awaiting the return of torque. So on our back roads—hell, there's not a road in Dutchess County you can average more than 50 on, Lord knows I've tried—we were just about even, all things considered.

Mechanically, everything pretty much evened out, too. Our distributor caps cracked with depressing regularity, so I habitually carried two spares. Those little carbon throwout bearings got eaten like malted milk balls. And minor annoyances like loose plug leads, hubcaps whistling off into the weeds in the midst of a corner, never to be found, bum odometers, splitting seats—mine were real leather, too—and carpets that went from bright red to a kind of desert rose within weeks were pretty much the norm. My poor long-suffering father got to finance an engine rebuild at 17,000 miles, which we fig-

Happy Face at play, the charming Bugeye Sprite.

ured was a bit sudden. I mean, I always double-clutched down *and* up, and shifted when the valves started to float . . . just like *Road & Track* said you should for maximum performance.

In 1961 Austin revamped the Sprite with a new nosepiece and tail, disc brakes, roll-up windows, a true convertible top, outside door handles, and a real trunk lid. And ruined it, for all intents and purposes. It was later badge-engineered into the MG Midget, as well, and though it wasn't nearly as noticeable or as much fun, it was a better car. But instead of a lovable imp, a sparkling gamin that endeared itself to a legion of young owners, the Mark II Spridget was simply a conventional sports car shrunk down so far it wasn't practical for much of anything. The Bugeye had its faults, but somehow it didn't matter. You never expected it to be a real car. But the Spridget was close enough to being real that you expected more from it, I guess, and were consequently disappointed.

The later Sprites *still* dominate H-production—and G-production with larger en-gines—a virtually unbroken string of success for nearly two decades. This is a miracle of sorts. But with big rubber snoots, desmogged engines—and lately, travesty of all, the 1500 mill from the unfortunate Triumph Spitfire—the modern Spridget is a rolling anachronism, a brutal indictment of everything that's wrong with the British motor industry. And of course, since 1972, it's been merely an MG Midget, not an Austin-Healey Sprite. Donald Healey's contract expired after twenty years and British-Leyland failed to renew their option. So the Austin-Healey name—which had really meant a lot to hundreds of thousands of happy enthusiasts—dropped from production.

Significantly, every car Healey built is a collector's item: Silverstones, 100-4s, 3000s, and Bugeye Sprites. The later Spridgets were BMC cars with Donald's name on them and, for that reason or another, aren't being collected by *anybody*. But Bugeyes are holding their own. An original or poorly restored—there are *lots* of those—Mark I Sprite can be had for under $1,000 these days, and of course junky ones go down from there. Concours Sprites are bringing over $3,000 and climbing. And the BMC Specials are worth even more. Specials, you say? Indeed. BMC was very heavily into racing in the fifties and sixties, and built a variety of specials for Le Mans and Sebring. John Sprinzel did, too. And Graham Hill's Speedwell Performance Conversions was also involved in making Sprites into real racers, and would sell you anything from a $200 aerodynamic hardtop to a complete car.

For $2,600 in 1960, for example, Speedwell sold a genuine 110-mph racer that broke a bunch of lap records. They put on a fiberglass front end with headlights in the fenders. This hinged from the bow, by the way, so you didn't have to lift what seemed like the whole front of the car as you do on the stock Bugeyes. And they put a nice fastback hardtop on and lots of gauges all over the dash, and a fancy steering wheel and boy-racer bits like that; as well as disc brakes on the front, a sway bar, and heavy shocks. Speedwell got 70 hp at 6,800 rpm out of the little A-series engine. This was basically Formula Junior tune, for which class the BMC engine was reasonably competitive with Fiat's 1100 and Ford's Anglia. The crowning touch was a pair of Amal GP motorcycle carburetors off Norton's Domiracer Twin, complete with cables.

The factory Sprites were out of the same mold. They had hardtops, knock-off wire wheels, disc brakes, and anywhere from 55 hp in "Stage 5" tune to 80 hp and over. Virtually all the things needed to make a standard old Bugeye into a Sebring Sprite were for sale from BMC, so not only are there dozens of *genuine* Sebring and Le Mans racers—homologated as FIA GT cars—but lots of homebuilt replicas, too. An authentic Le Mans Sprite—where the later ones were hitting 130 mph down Mulsanne—is worth at least $5,000 in good condition. In 1967 a factory car—an aluminum-bodied coupe—finished fifteenth at Le Mans at an average of 100.9 mph . . . which would have won outright in 1952 and gotten them a fourth as late as '58. Not bad for an archaic, 1-liter pushrod four designed in the forties.

These later road racers look and act much more like Mark I Bugeyes than the Spridgets from which they were actually built. So they are eminently collectible, actually quite sophisticated, famous in their own small way . . . and consequently expensive. But they're more fun than anything even remotely near that size except for a Fiat Abarth, and Abarths cost about twice as much to buy and a zillion times more to maintain. A Sprite—anything with the BMC A-series, really—is reliable enough, cheap to fix, and tweakable within an inch of its life. And, nice to know these days, will return 30 mpg besides. Sprites are also about the winningest cars ever to run SCCA. In fact, if you're *really* lucky, maybe you can find a hot-flaming-pink roadster sitting forgotten in some Pennsylvania garage. And if you're really, *really* lucky, maybe Donna Mae will condescend to show you how to drive it the way it's supposed to be driven.

Lotus Elan

The thing about mid-engine sports cars is that though they are demonstrably quicker around a racetrack, they're not half as logical a layout for cars that actually have to carry full-sized people and luggage in reasonable comfort at less than racing speeds. Which means this: in the fifties, Lotus could sell variants of the same car for street use and racing, but by 1960, when the last of the front-engine Lotus sports/racers went away, the only vehicles Chapman had for road use were the spartan Seven and the overexpensive and muddlesome Elite. Both of which, to be honest, were more racing cars than serious everyday transportation anyway.

Besides, both the Seven and the Elite required too much hand work to be really profitable. And Lotus was having a really big year if they sold 300 Sevens and Elites. Chapman had a nice new factory, though, and the obvious inclination to go big time, for which he needed a conventional sports car that could be truly mass-produced and powered by something a little less exotic than that gold-plated Coventry Climax. And the car had to be a proper roadster.

The stressed fiberglass top on the Elite coupe was a main structural member, so it was impossible to slice it off. What Chapman came up with instead was almost as ingenious as a fiberglass frame. He drew up a fabricated steel box section, shaped roughly like a tuning fork. The front engine went between the tongs, the handle formed a backbone around the drive shaft, and the differential bolted to a little triangular subframe at the rear. Typical Lotus unequal-length control arms were used at the front. The rear had a simple Chapman Strut independent suspension with lower A-arms only. There were outboard disc brakes all around and high-mounted coil spring/shock absorbers. It didn't weigh but a few pounds, was strong as a bridge—it even looked like a bridge, in fact—and it left lots of room for feet and fannies and luggage.

For an engine, Lotus wanted something that was clearly their own but that could be based on proprietary engine bits. So Steve Sanville and Harry Mundy—who'd developed the Coventry Climax FWE—designed a double-overhead-cam aluminum head for the standard Ford 105E four. By the time Lotus got it done, Ford had the larger 109E. And when they got the head for that one done, Ford already had the 116E ready—with five main

The nearest thing to race-track handling in a street car, the 1,250-pound Lotus Elan of 1964.

bearings and 1558cc. So that was the engine Lotus ended up with not only for the Elan but in the Super Seven, the Lotus Cortina sedan, and the Europa Twin Cam, too. It was a good little engine—great, even—strong, oversquare, light, and relatively unburstable. By 1971 a big-valve version of the Twin Cam—modified by Tony Rudd—was rated at 126 hp in street trim. Cosworth's race versions scaled nearer 170 hp.

The Elan got a nonstructural fiberglass body with hideaway headlights that looked like the slimline Elite gone to seed. It was pudgier and stubby, and not very well made. The bumpers were only painted fiberglass, and though the door handles were the only exterior chrome and the shape was undeniably slippery, it just didn't have the exquisite lines of the Elite. No way. More like a slab-sided brick with a pointed nose. On the other hand, it was much cheaper to build—Chapman claimed he lost £100 on every Elite—and things like stamped-steel wheels and cut-rate upholstery kept the price way down. Base

price for the 1,250-pound Elan was a little over £1,300 in 1963, rising to nearly $7,000 in the States by the end of production in 1973. Prices today go down from that to under $1,000.

The Elan started out as a kit car, a U-build-it project that came in a huge shipping carton on Christmas morn. Unfortunately, it never lost that flavor. The detailing was abominable no matter who assembled it, the electrics were worse, there was no heater worthy of the name, engine work was almost impossible because the damn block was tucked away so tightly into the tuning fork frame, and the tiny hood didn't open far enough to get at anything anyway. The retracting headlights promptly contracted Lazy Eye and, most embarrassing of all, little bits and pieces would literally fall off as you drove along. You could track an Elan by its trail of glittering hardware. Pat Bedard once said, "Lotuses shed parts like Alsatians shed hair," but that's catty.

It also clouds the issue. The Seven and Elite are so rarefied that even most Lotus enthusiasts have never seen one. But the Elan came over here in comparative droves. So what if they all ripped their exhaust systems out trying to drive away from the docks? It's a Lotus. Designed and built by the very same Colin Chapman and his merry band of World Champion Constructors who gave us the Lotus 25, 49, 72, and 78. And honestly, for what it does, the Elan is very good. Being a Lotus, it will outhandle virtually anything you can name. And it is very quick. The late Elan Sprints are 125-mph cars and will get through the quarter-mile in the 14s—which is uncanny for 1600cc. For comparison, Elans ran in C-production for most of their tenure in SCCA racing, against cars with up to three times the displacement.

The light weight makes for good acceleration and marvelous brakes, but the raison d'être for an Elan is back-road handling, pure and simple. The Elan was as good as any Lotus, and better than mere cars, on any back road. Commuting in one would be a crushing bore, what with bits and pieces falling off all the time and pedestrians making rude remarks and your knees bent under your chin. But for those two Sunday mornings a year— one in May and one in October—when you *have* to have a sports car with the top down, tonneau drumming, to go chasing your youth down some winding blacktop road, patchy in the early dawn light, the Elan is the perfect car to have. It's useless for anything else, but then there are lots worse cars you could keep around just to use two days a year.

Jaguar E-type

A lot of English businessmen consider Sir William Lyons some sort of wizard. In a nation famous for overpriced, curious cars, labor problems, and declining production standards, Lyons has always built beautiful cars, had relatively happy assemblers, and sold better and better cars at better and better prices. A wizard indeed. For example, in 1959 BMC virtually owned the U.S. foreign car market.

They sold 68,000 cars over here. In 1967 they sold 33,000. Not exactly a supah showing. Lyons's Jaguar division, on the other hand, sold 6,000 cars in each year, and in all those in between. You can't judge that seemingly poor standstill by American standards. In Britain during the sixties, to have held even was spectacular enough for a peerage. The only one who actually *gained* ground was Colin Chapman, but Lotus was so far down they had nowhere to go but up. And of course, Chapman is a regular magician, too.

The Jaguar that made Lyons's stand was the XK-E. The E-type was an absolute bombshell in 1961, as marvelously advanced as the XK-120 had been a dozen years before. The E-type was more sophisticated than the DB-4 Aston Martin—or Ferrari's GT Berlinetta, for that matter—just as fast, more reliable, and less than half the price. A good Corvette was cheaper and quicker—and more dependable—but in 1961, at least, preposterously funny looking. But the Jaguar E-type had it all. It was a consummate crumpet collector, a truly elegant carriage that had "come hither" written all over it. It wasn't inconspicuous, Lord knows, but Jezus, was it pretty. And it had the long hood proportions of the twenties. The tiny cockpit was tucked in the back and the hood made up nearly half the total length. It was extravagant, streamlined, sensual, and flamboyant. It looked like every schoolboy's doodle of what a modern sports car should be . . . long and low and mostly smooth, a big oval bullet with no afterthoughts tacked on.

It was also the first Jaguar—and really, just about the first mass-production sports car—to come directly from the race track. For the E-type was really nothing more than the D-type made habitable. And not only that, in some ways it was a *better* racer than the D-type. In the late fifties, after the mess of the famous factory fire had been cleaned up, Bill Heynes started adapting the D-type to a production line. The old jigs had been destroyed, so there was no need to try to use up leftover bits, which was a distinct advantage. Heynes brought the wheelbase out to an even 8 feet, the same as the C-type and 6 inches more than the D-type, which made the E-type a lot more stable at speed.

The late D-types had DeDion rear axles,

which were much too expensive and complex to bother with for production. Heynes gave the new car a fully independent rear suspension . . . easier to build, cheaper, and better besides. He used two shocks with coil springs on each side; four in all, and big tubular wishbones, trailing arms, and an antiroll bar. And inboard rear disc brakes, of course, just like the best racing cars. The entire XK-E front suspension was straight off the D-type and bolted to a subframe welded out of square tubing. The rear end had a similar space frame that likewise bolted to the central monocoque tub. The monocoque itself was essentially the D-type too, with bigger cutouts for the doors and a place for a dashboard . . . and passengers' feet. It was immensely strong (as it needed to be with the independent rear), and it was light. The XK-E, ready to roll, weighed only about 2,500 pounds, just 800 more than the stripped D-type that was a full two feet shorter. More importantly, the new E-type weighed nearly 800 pounds *less* than the production XK-150 S it replaced.

The E-type got the three-carb, 3.8-liter, 265-hp engine from the 150 S, unfortunately complete with Moss 4-speed. Just about the *only* thing early road testers found to complain about was this archaic gearbox, nonsynchro on first and synchro in name only on the top three. Balky and slow, it added a second or two to the quarter-mile acceleration through sheer obstinacy. It took until 1964 for

Better than a schoolboy's dream, the 1961 XK-E.

Peter Lindner in his rare aluminum-bodied, fuel-injected

Jaguar finally to replace it. Even with the slow-shifting Moss box, however, a decent XK-E would get through the quarter-mile in less than 16 seconds at over 90 mph and from 0 to 60 in roughly 6.5. Which was—hell, still is—*very* quick for a fully equipped luxury street car with a long-legged 3.31 differential and a top speed over 150 mph.

When it came out in '61, the E-type cost $5,670 in New York. A comparable fuel-injected, 360-hp 'Vette was $5,000. But though the 'Vette was a shade quicker all the way up to a virtually identical top speed, it looked like a truck by comparison. Malcolm Sayer, an aerodynamicist Jaguar inherited from Bristol Aeroplane, had done a lot of work in the Farnborough wind tunnel. It showed. The XK-E weighed only about 200 pounds less than the Corvette, but with 100 hp less it had identical performance. Most of that speed, certainly in the high ranges, came from the svelte body that made the Chevrolet's look sick and overworked. With tall gearing, the Jag would run over 170, something a '61 Corvette couldn't do with a million horsepower.

The XK-E prototype was taken to Le Mans in 1960 by Briggs Cunningham, the U.S. distributor. A finned headrest was about the only noticeable variation from the eventual pro-

ightweight E-type, at Nurburgring in 1963.

duction car, since even the plexiglassed headlights were kept for production. But the federal safety laws pretty much wrecked the XK-E. The headlight covers had to go and then the bumpers got heftier, the wheelbase grew nine inches on the 2 + 2 and stayed for all models, and pretty soon you had a big, overweight boulevard "personal car" with not a hint left of Le Mans in '57, D-Jags in line-ahead formation, and the glory of the Empire.

On the other hand, the E-type V-12 that appeared in 1971 is a damn nice car. Widening the body, opening up the grille, and curling the lip on the wheel openings made the XK-E body if not pretty at least uhh . . . brawny; virile. And the new 5343cc, single-overhead-cam V-12—designed under Harry Mundy, Jaguar's executive director—made about 325 hp gross, 250 hp net. So the V-12 was quick, quicker than any E-type except the very first ones, even though the weight went up to 3,300 pounds, the price went up to $9,000 and the top speed went down to 135 or so. But still, the V-12 E-type is one of the last of the really nice British cars. It went out of production three years ago now, but quite a few dealers and enthusiasts purchased them new and just plain put them away. They *knew* that the V-12 Jag would be a gold-plated invest-

ment. And all things considered, the V-12 is just about the best E-type.

Series I XK-Es—that is, anything from '61 through '67—are worth upward of $3,000 right now and climbing steeply. I predict that'll double in the next few years. Of course, being Jaguars, even the best of them are already undergoing restoration, and you'd be hard put to find any six-cylinder E-type that hasn't had—or doesn't need—a complete engine rebuild, suspension work, a new interior, and repainting. I once asked an E-type owner how come his car looked so new and if it was much trouble to keep it up that way. "Hell, no," he said. "I just get the sumbitch repainted and rechromed every three years whether it needs it or not."

By the time the XK-E came along, the old Jaguar six was pretty much outclassed as a race engine. Briggs Cunningham and Roy Salvadori got an XK-E into fourth at Le Mans in 1962 and ninth in '63, but that was it. A few XK-Es tried to run B-production SCCA, but the Corvettes were not only a lot cheaper to race but quicker, too. About the only really significant E-type win was Bob Tullius's USRRC title at Atlanta in 1975 with the last V-12, and that was the product of a factory racing program that probably would have been cheaper if they'd just bought the other two dozen cars and told them to stay home.

Very rare, but very nice, are the few lightweight E-types running around. These were

Gold-plated investment, the 1971 E-type 2 + 2.

built in the early sixties and have features like aluminum bodies, alloy engine blocks, and fuel injection. Each one was different, and not even Jaguar knows how many were made or where they might be. Most of them were roadsters with the optional hardtop. The giveaway would be the body. If your E-Z Pocket Magnet doesn't stick—and the whole thing's not Bondo—buy it quick. An aluminum E-type is the single rarest Jaguar, scarcer than the XK-SS, even . . . and even more desirable.

Personally, I'd settle for a 1965 roadster in steel, with the good Jaguar close-ratio 4-speed, 3.8 engine, triple Webers, racing oil coolers, and the factory hardtop. And the alloy knock-offs—drilled for lightness—that were used on Cunningham's prototype and the factory lightweights. I'd paint it white with blue stripes, Cunningham's colors. I'd also do sort of a stripped-for-racing but still livable interior . . . roll bar, Recaro buckets, and wide-belt racing harness. The engine I'd have in pretty much stock tune, with only the racing bits that add strength, not horsepower. What a helluva Jaguar. I'm not sure what I'd do with it. Go looking for Corvettes and crumpets, I guess. Even if I didn't find any, it sure would be fun.

MGC/V-8

How the MGC came about is easy to tell. British Motor Corp. had the nice little MGB and the even nicer fastback MGB-GT. But compared with all the competition, they were pretty old-fashioned, and *very* underpowered. BMC also had the Austin-Healey 3000, which was a perfectly nice, even longer-in-the-tooth roadster. It wasn't underpowered, but it *had* been designed along lines laid down by Herbert Austin himself. So in 1968, when the U.S. federal safety laws came along, BMC decided to rationalize their lineup and save themselves the trouble of revamping the Austin-Healey all in one fell swoop. They discontinued the Healey 3000, which left them with

only the little 1798cc MGB to defend Queen and Honour.

Instant inspiration: out came the nice little 2-liter MG four. In went the nice big 3-liter Healey six—a former truck engine and ungodly heavy—and presto! Instant disaster. In order to fit the Healey into the MG, they had to redesign the gearbox, the clutch, the front suspension, and ultimately the engine itself. In other words, for the amount of effort expended, they could practically have designed a whole new car from scratch. The big Healey 2912cc six gave 150 hp versus 95 hp from the MG four. So the car went fast in a straight line and had a top speed of over 120 mph. Unfortunately, the Healey millstone added 250 pounds to the MG, right over the front wheels. Two men and a boy could get it around a corner, but nobody could parallel-park an MGC, not even Popeye the Sailor Man.

After less than two years and 9,000 cars, the MGC was quietly dropped from the Abingdon lineup. Along with many other lemons, the C is curiously popular in retrospect and has a dedicated following. The crucial point, I guess, is that cars bought new—e.g., an MGC in 1968—are expected to perform under relatively demanding conditions. They have to be able to rush around corners, zoom down straights, carry a few laundry bags and some groceries, and do all sorts of things that collector cars don't have to do. Nobody in his right mind would parallel-park a concours MGC in the Pathmark lot, mostly because he'd find his delicate pre-DoT bumper embedded in some suburban Pontiac wagon when he got back. Likewise, a collector's MGC is never going to be hurled around corners at ten-tenths, for the simple reason that collectors don't drive at even eight-tenths. So as a pseudo mantelpiece racer, an MGC is a pretty good investment right now. Which just goes to show, I guess, that quality and collectibility are two *very* different things.

The abominable MGC was followed by an even bigger disaster called the MGB V-8. This is a whole different story and one with a sad ending. The MGC deserved to fail. The V-8 deserved to succeed, and that makes all the difference. Since the mid-sixties, Rover had been making the old 215-cubic-inch Buick aluminum V-8 under license. It isn't a bad engine, though the twin SUs the British stick

The hood bulge is hiding 150 hp worth of Austin six, which turned the MGB into an MGC in 1968.

on it make it a lot worse than when a simple Rochester four-barrel lives on the manifold. In any case, Morgan was stuffing Rover V-8s into the Morgan Plus 8, and Rover had made the Rover 2000 into a 3500 through the same simple swap.

It was a natural for the MGB. A British garage owner named Ken Costello started dropping Rover V-8s into his customers' MGB-GTs, creating the Costello V-8. British-Leyland was so impressed by the 130-mph Costello—which, unlike the MGC, had less weight on the front wheels than the stock MGB four-cylinder—that in 1973 they started making factory replica Costello V-8s. U.S. emissions requirements pretty much emasculated the two or three that came over here, but it honestly was a damn nice car. No funny hood

bulge like the MGC and no funny handling, either. If it had come out five years earlier, the MG V-8 could have been British-Leyland's Sunbeam Tiger and a really sweet performance bargain. As it was, with only 137 hp from 215 cubic inches, the desmogged Rover V-8 didn't really offer that much of an improvement over the old four. And when B-L management decided to drop Rover from the American market, there went any impetus to keep the engine certified with the EPA. So the MG V-8 died stillborn.

It's a shame. *Very* few V-8s got into this country. I drove the first one off the boat for a magazine test—the photographer and I literally picked it up off a New Jersey dock—and it was lovely. Reasonably quiet, with only a rorty exhaust note to hint at the unusual. The

Morgan

Imagine you're writing a humorous novel about England, full of charming eccentrics with funny names and even funnier habits, tiny picturesque out-of-the-way villages unchanged since the Invasion, quaint country customs and costumes reminiscent of another, grander era, and spindly, old-fashioned machines left over from the nineteenth century. It will bristle with Guardsman mustaches, unpronounceable place names, sympathetic "Mums," pampered pets, cheery old pubs, twisty little roads that lead nowhere, windswept moors, elderly brick buildings on ·the verge of collapse, poverty, tragedy, a sense of destiny, and the overpowering aroma of cheap soap. It will be Edwardian England, as it still exists in more places than the English like to admit.

If you wish, perhaps you can set your novel around a motorcar factory, a homey, family-owned place where they make an antiquated out-of-date semblance of an automobile now and again, in no particular hurry, for no other reason than to keep the blokes busy. Grandpa can be immensely wealthy and rather brusque, but kindly to the children and his golden-hearted housekeeper. Papa is a country gentleman who drives an Italian Ferrari and wouldn't be caught dead in one of his own cars. Mumsy is a tweeds-and-sherry type whose major accomplishment is to get young Lady Jane married off to a genuine lord of the realm. The "works"—next door to their country estate—is a cute little brick factory built before James Watt, operated by crochety old machines and kindly old men, all of them working out of love for The Guv'nor rather than the pittance he pays them. They live in spick-and-span little cottages rimmed with hollyhocks and overlooking a vast range of rolling West Country hills.

Your plot might revolve around The Guv'nor's attempt to meet emissions and safety laws so he can export cars to America, and how he fails—but saves the company by opening new markets in Europe and the Far East. Your major subplot can be an affair between a lovely young tourist from the local health spa and the works parts manager, who is also the mainstay of the informal factory racing team. The climax comes when Papa

Ken Costello and his Rover-powered MGB V-8.

carburetion was a bit off, nothing strange on the Rover V-8, and if it had been mine to keep, I think a nice pair of headers, a Rochester carb, a little suspension work by Group 44, and perhaps a fat set of mags would have made that V-8 MGB-GT into the long-legged grand tourer it so nearly was. Even at $5,000, an MG that would do quarter-miles in 16 seconds, 0 to 60 in 8 seconds, and still handle was the best thing since Brooklands screens. I don't think even British-Leyland knows how many V-8s came over here—certainly less than a dozen—but if you find one, grab on tight and don't let go. Short of an XK-E, it's the most exciting car Leyland's made since the Healey 100-4. Someday it'll be a sleeper of a collector car. And think of the fun you'll have in the meantime.

sells the entire next year's production to a Japanese consortium, and the wealthy tourist chooses to go off to the mysterious East with the new distributor rather than cheer for our mud-bespattered hero at the Land's End Trial. His disenchantment opens his eyes to The Guv'nor's gorgeous secretary, who has loved him from afar since the first chapter and catches him on the rebound. They take their honeymoon at Le Mans, where the factory team does not do well but better than expected. The Guv'nor is so pleased that he promotes our hero to be chief—and only—road tester, at fifty quid a week, replacing Old Charlie, who's been chief tester for forty years and finally retires to a houseboat in Devon.

One advantage you'll have as a budding novelist is that you'll be able to go off to England and live your story. I mean, you really *can* go to the picturesque little town of Malvern Link, to the storybook factory, and watch the old blokes hand-carve vintage motorcars out of ash and aluminum, under the purple shadow of the famous spa-lined Malvern Hills. Peter Morgan really will show you around and take you for a ride in his Ferrari, and point out the musty photos of his daughter, Lady Jane Colwyn, and Grandpa— H. F. S. Morgan—and Great Grandpa—the Reverend Prebendary H. George Morgan— that hang in his cluttered old office. And if you're *really* good, after the factory tour— which is simply not to be missed, I promise you, if you want a real feel for what light industry was like in Queen Victoria's day—the Guv'nor will hand you over to one of the pleas-

ant young factory racer/parts manager types for a demonstration drive through the hills in the latest works model.

Driving a Morgan is like motoring around inside an invisible atmospheric bubble of pure, undistilled 1935. A Morgan, after all, is not a replicar of anything. It's a genuine midthirties British sports car, more olde English than anyone since Gracie Fields. You even drive it differently from modern cars. Oh, it has a steering wheel and pedals and a shifter, but they do different things from what you're used to. The steering wheel is like the big knob on a good stereo. It takes a lot of muscle to turn, it sits right up under your nose, and it's for *approximate* turning only. You steer the car roughly where you want it to go and then get on the throttle. More than most classic sports cars even, a Morgan is steered with the gas. The throttle is like the little knob on your stereo that says "fine tuning." To drive a Morgan correctly, you have to get the tail hung out and sliding. This is easy, since the antiquated suspension is so stiff it's as good as not there at all, and any little piece of gravel will send you off into the air, sliding sideways.

The idea is not to fight this natural sliding but to make it work *for* you. The rear end wants to slide out around a corner? Let it. *Make* it, even. Cock the wheel roughly to the outside, get on the gas, and swoop that rascal around in a full-floating, two- and/or four-wheel drift, fine tuning with the throttle. On modern cars, with sloppy suspensions, slow throttle response, five turns of the wheel lock to lock, and low-pressure tires, this is an open

The 1961 Morgan 4/4 Mark III: 43 hp, 1,900 pounds, a top speed of 80 mph, and bags of class.

invitation to a lightning trip into the bushes, probably upside down. A Morgan, on the other hand, has wish-quick steering, incredible torque, and a zero-travel suspension that insists on being tossed into a controlled—or uncontrolled, that depends on you—slide around every corner. For someone brought up with modern motorcars, it's scary. But only at first. Then you get into the spirit of the thing, start throwing that Morgan around with gay abandon, and pretty soon you're wearing your cloth cap backward and pretending you're Henry Segrave. And the archaic Morgan, carved from ash in a storybook factory in the west of England, claims another zealot.

Morgans—any Morgan—are probably more good fun than anything else you can think of spelled with more than three letters. They're quirky, demanding, idiosyncratic, eccentric, outlandish, and delightful, which is to say, thoroughly *British*. Many people—technocrats who like Mercedes-Benzes and BMWs, pragmatists who lust after Impalas and Dodge Darts, connoisseurs who worship at the altars of Ferraris and Maseratis—think Morgans are downright silly, old-fashioned, hard-riding, slow, unreliable, drafty, and not very pretty. These people, like most modern men, have no souls and cannot appreciate machines that do. Insensitive as these folks are, they habitually underestimate anything they can't understand. It's the same mistake Louis XIV and Bonaparte and Adolf Hitler all made—ignorantly underestimating the sheer doggedness of the English race. And a Morgan, as I say, is English in every fiber and sinew of its being.

Morgans really *have* been made since 1911 in the tiny town of Malvern Link, in the pastoral western county of Worcestershire—where the sauce comes from—just down the slope from the nineteenth century spa of Malvern, nestled in the ruggedly green Malvern Hills. Wales isn't too far away in either distance or attitude. The sons and grandsons of the original blokes are still Morgan makers. And they still work in the same ways—often with the same tools—that were used seventy years ago.

I mean, there's not a machine tool in the place newer than 1940, when His Majesty's Government gave them a bunch of new equipment so they could make airplane parts for the war. The Morgan factory is in a time warp, pure and simple. In one corner there'll be an old codger with an antique table saw making the frames for the bodies out of ash. *Wood* frames. Another *glues* them together. Other old-timers take large sheets of steel and battered plywood patterns and, using little scribes, draw out fenders and body panels, ready to be cut out by hand with tinsnips—honest—and fastened to the wood frames with *tacks*. The entire upholstery shop consists of two old Mums, a big homemade table, and a pair of sewing machines that must have been amortized around 1938. The treadles are run, like the equipment in the little machine shop, by a system of overhead shafts and big leather pulleys such as Dickens deplored in the Lancaster mills. I mean, it's downright archaic. Until a few years ago, one man painted every car with a *brush*. Nowadays he has a well-used spray gun.

The first Morgan was a two-passenger three-wheeler. The engine was a motorcycle V-twin that hung out the front; the single rear wheel was chain driven. The unique front suspension was one of the earliest independent front suspensions in England. It was designed by John Black—later head of Standard-Triumph—and consisted of a little vertical tube near each front wheel with a coil-sprung shaft to slide up and down inside it. H. F. S. Morgan patented it and called it a sliding pillar. Peter Morgan *still* uses it. Every Morgan for the last sixty-odd years has had the same wacked-out front end, with built-in shimmy that would be inexcusable on a shopping cart, suspension travel that's so limited you'd swear there was none at all, and a guaranteed propensity to crack the fenders right in half from the pounding.

Unbelievably, in essence that's the design history of the Morgan. In 1909 H. F. S. laid out the basic configuration, a few years later he included a body . . . and in 1935 he added a fourth wheel to the Model F. This first Morgan "4/4" (four wheels/four cylinders) looked pretty much like your standard-issue small British sports car from the mid-thirties, with a flat radiator, swooping wings, and very few compound curves. It was the same size and shape as the MG-TA/TB, with a little 1122cc overhead-valve four built by Coventry Climax and a super-low price of only 185 guineas,

Edwardian upright in the modern era, a 1959 Morgan +4 nestled in the Malvern Hills.

about half the tab for the cheapest S.S. In 1939 H. F. S. Morgan even started using engines supplied by his old friend Sir John Black at Standard, but Morgan, unlike William Lyons, who got his big engines at the same store, bought only the baby 1267cc four from the little Standard 10.

After World War II, H. F. S. kept on with the 1939 4/4. But in 1948 Standard introduced the new Vanguard, with a 2088cc Continental-designed four, and in 1950 Morgan dropped it into the prewar chassis to make *the* classic Morgan, the 68 hp, 85 mph +4. After that, all Morgan engineering followed Standard-Triumph's TR-series engine for engine, beginning with the 1991cc, 90-hp version of the Vanguard that came out with the TR-2. Morgan characteristically hooked it up to an archaic Moss 4-speed, eccentrically located between the seats, with a short drive shaft from the clutch to the transmission, and another from transmission to differential. The latter, by the way, was part of a rigid axle hung on semielliptic springs above the underslung, Z-shaped frame rails.

The thing is, for all its quirks—including surprisingly comfortable "air-cushion" seats, which were nothing more than a pair of big, inflatable rubber pillows you could blow up like an air mattress to the desired firmness—the Morgan +4 was a *very* competitive car. It shared an engine with the TR-2/TR-3. So

what if it wasn't so aerodynamic? It weighed nearly 300 pounds less—only 1,900 pounds or so—the weight distribution was almost perfectly 50/50, and on a smooth road or a race track the stiff Morgan suspension wasn't much stiffer than a race-tuned Triumph suspension. And it cost less than $200 more than the TR, which wasn't bad, you know? I mean, one Morgan has more charm than a thousand TR-3s, the steering and front disc brakes were a lot better, and it was just as sturdy, just as fast, and a lot more distinctive.

And unlike the spartan TR, the spartan Morgan +4 could be had in four stages of comfort. For your wife there was a drophead coupe with high doors, real windows, and a convenient convertible top. For the family there was a four-seater that had a top like a Conestoga wagon and more blind spots than a Sherman tank, but that you *could* get 2 + 2 adults in, at least for short rides. The standard car was a strict two-seater, with cutaway doors and a U-build-it top. And finally, there's the ultimate Morgan of all, called the Super Sports, which appeared in 1960.

You see, there was a garage owner/tuner/racer/Morgan fanatic named Christopher Lawrence. Lawrence built a few super-fast Morgan racers that were simply unbeatable. Peter Morgan got him to put together a steady supply of blueprinted TR engines, with headers, two Weber carbs, lots of interior mods, and 120 hp. Back in Malvern, Morgan taught his blokes how to hammer aluminum instead of steel, and they started making lightweight cars—identical to the normal roadsters except they weighed only about 1,600 pounds—with standard knock-off wire wheels and a subtle little hood scoop over the Webers. This scoop is really the only way to tell the Super Sports from a steel car short of a magnet or a ride around the block. The top speed went up to 120 mph, and acceleration got under 10 seconds for 0 to 60 and into the 17s for the quarter-mile, which was pretty good for a car with all the subtle aerodynamics of Winchester Cathedral.

The Super Sports cost a little more, of course, but it was worth it. With the little old-fashioned Triumph engine, Morgan Super Sports ran in SCCA C-production in the sixties and, particularly in the hands of Californian Lew Spencer, were perfectly capable of beating Corvettes and Jaguars head to head. The late Peter Revson got his start in a Morgan too, racing the Elvas of Jay Signore and Mark Donohue for a national championship back in '63 or so. The thing is, the racing Morgans weren't all *that* different from the street Mor-

gans. It wasn't like racing a Healey 3000 or something, where you had to rebuild the car from the ground up to be competitive. You could take a Super Sports, pull off the windshield, and, on a short track like Lime Rock or Tucson or Bryar, go out and whip ass among the big-bore pigeons with no trouble at all.

In 1961 Chris Lawrence and Richard Shepherd-Barron even took a Super Sports to Le Mans. And were sent home. The Morgan was deemed "outside the spirit of the regulations," which was a nice way of saying the French thought it was old-fashioned and funny looking. In '62 Lawrence and Shepherd-Barron doggedly trooped back again and pointed out that their "obsolete" Morgan had just broken the 2-liter lap record at the Nurburgring by over 7 seconds. And so, storybook fashion, after *Les Vingt-quatres heures du Mans,* Shepherd-Barron trundled by to win the 2-liter class, finish thirteenth overall, and average 94 mph in a car that had been obsolete the year before. Needless to say, that's the favorite Morgan racing story of all, combining as it does victory over Continental foes under grueling conditions, an ironic twist, and

Genteel vintage motoring, the Morgan +4 Super Drophead at Goodwood Test Day, 1964.

The ultimate cult object of the frenetic sixties, an aluminum-bodied, 120-mph Morgan +4 Super Sports.

a stubborn persistence proven right in the end. A perfect Morgan victory. A perfect *British* victory.

In the mid-sixties, Peter Morgan's son got the company to start offering colors like Day-glo Green, McLaren Racing Orange, and Hot Sin Yellow. For the first time, Morgan broke out of the die-hard enthusiast niche and into the swinging and swirling mass-market youth culture. Production bounced up over two per day—500 a year, most years—and there was at least a nine-month waiting line. So of course, prices for used Morgans started sky-rocketing. For example, way back in 1964 or '65, an English club racer named Adrian Dence was selling the Shepherd-Barron/Lawrence Le Mans winner—that he'd bought in '62—for £700. I missed it by a week, and it was bought by a Britisher who was "not an enthusiast." I tracked that car for a few years, then gave it up. The point is, ten years ago you could have purchased the most famous Morgan in history—fully restored and con-

cours—for less than $2,500. Nowadays, just run-of-the-mill +4s are going for three times that much.

And the +8s are even more expensive. Plus 8, you say? Indeed. In 1967, Triumph replaced the old four in the TR-4 with a new six, to make the TR-6. The six was just long enough not to fit in a Morgan without a lot of butchery, and it wasn't all that much more powerful. So like A. C., Sunbeam, TVR, Jensen, and a lot of others, Peter Morgan got himself a nice thumping American V-8 and stuck it in. Instant excitement. The top speed went up to 125 mph in the cooking version, and quarter-mile times dropped into the 14-second bracket at over 90 mph, which was super car performance. And all this on only 3529cc. You see, Morgan didn't do anything as rash as installing a Chrysler hemi. He just started buying the Buick 215-cubic-inch V-8 that Rover was building under license. It wasn't a bad engine as these things go—light, sturdy, and powerful. Repco made a 3-liter Formula One

After scrutineering, Chris Lawrence's 1961 Super Sports broke the 2-liter lap record at Nurburgring.

engine out of it that was good enough to give Brabham two world championships, so the basic design was obviously sound.

Fitting it into the +4 was a matter of a moment. The air cleaner housing for the twin SUs had to be bashed in with a rubber hammer, literally. They used an electric fan. And eventually, former racing-car designer Maurice Owen, who was in charge of the conversion, added 2 inches to the chassis, both width and wheelbase. And Peter Morgan had some fancy mag wheels cast up. But for all intents and purposes, the +8 was nothing more than a repowered +4, which was only a 1939 4/4 with a Triumph engine. And the 4/4 was nothing more than the Model F three-wheeler with an extra tire in the back. And the 1933 Model F was only a four-cylinder version of the V-twin Morgan trike, not all *that* different from the original 1909 prototype. In other words, you can make a pretty good argument that the current Morgan +8 is nothing more than a jazzed-up Edwardian cycle car with one more wheel and a smoother grille.

About that grille. By 1953, with the demise of the MG-TD, Morgan was the only manufacturer in Britain still using separate headlamps (HRG doesn't count; they weren't really manufacturers). Anyway, Lucas refused to make little headlamp bullets just for Morgan, so Peter redesigned the grille. The famous "flat rad" was replaced by an even more distinctive curved prow, and the headlights were recessed into the fenders, MG-TF fashion. At the time, Morgan people groused and moaned, but the front end turned out to be much cleaner, more aerodynamic, and possessed of considerably stronger visual identity. But of course, the fender welds still broke over the sliding pillars. No matter. The "new" Morgans were as nice as you could want.

Still, the Vanguard-engined flat rads are the most desirable Morgans of all, followed closely by the aluminum Super Sports, +8s, and four-seater +4s. They're all worth about the same—a low of $2,500, a high of $10,000—depending upon condition and how badly you want that particular car. There's a veritable cult surrounding Morgans, of course, which has helped to drive prices up and which will keep them high. On the other hand, there are Morgan experts scattered everywhere from here to Malvern, spares are easy to come by—they're all the same as the current cars, after all—and the factory even runs a restoration shop if you're willing to schedule the work well in advance (like a year or two) and go to England to pick the car up.

This is not such a bad idea. You could get your publisher to pick up the tab—you're doing research for your novel, after all—and any incidentals you can at least write off on your tax return as a legitimate business expense. And besides, if you're even the tiniest bit of an Anglophile, a visit to the Morgan works on Pickersleigh Road just down a bit from the nineteenth-century country club in Malvern Link will be one of the highlights of your life. Honest. You haven't lived until you've watched a Morgan grow haphazardly right in front of your eyes, put together in a combination blacksmith's shed and lumberyard. And there's charming Peter Morgan himself, and all the wonderful blokes in the works, and . . . you get the idea. More ingratiating atmosphere than you'll use up in a dozen novels.

And if by some slim chance you get bored with Malvern Link, there're still all those rich, fading ingénues up at the rich, fading spas, and miles and miles of smooth, twisty back-country blacktop roads, damp, shimmering, and empty in the late afternoon light, just begging for you to Morgan up them, top down and fenders flapping, to some forgotten Jacobean half-timbered tea house with big bay windows made up of lots of little panes, burning-hot tea with weak blue milk, and buttered scones and little jellied cakes. Quaint country customs and old-fashioned machines left over from another, grander era. God, I hope there'll always be an England. And a Morgan in which to savor it.

Europea

CHAPTER 3

Sports Cars

The great European cars can be legitimately grouped together. They all share a basic understanding, an underlying conception of just what constitutes a good car. This ideal is based largely on the car that best suits the type of driving that the European elite can do. First are the autostradas, autobahns, and autoroutes, which until recently were unfettered by speed limits. So foremost, a car's worth is judged by its cruising speed. Often enough, this is its top speed, an antisocial heresy unthinkable in England and America. Germans and Italians who drive Mercedes and Maseratis actually expect to be able to *use* that 150-mph top speed on a daily basis, and they still think nothing of averaging 140 mph down the length of the Autostrada del Sol, dodging half-hearted efforts at law enforcement.

Then there's back-road handling. European secondary roads are, in a word, secondary. So not only do great European cars have to be able to blatt down the autostrada, they also have to be able to blatt down Tobacco Road without loss of poise. And of course, since they have to deal with situations that Americans and Britons never see—a 140-mph Ferrari rounding a hairpin corner only to run afoul of a 30-mph Fiat passing a 15-mph Motobecane—they need exceptional brakes and transient handling. And then there's the toughest test of all, crossing the Alps, through the twisty Saint Bernard pass, for example, driving for a long day on elaborately winding mountain roads always on the very edge of disaster.

The Alps. There are cars built all over Europe, in Eindhoven, in Poissy, in Lindkoping, in Havre-Sandouville. But with the exception of the Spanish Pegaso, which was designed by an engineer trained in Italy at Alfa Romeo's racing department, *every* great European sports car has been built within a two-hundred-mile radius of the center of the Alps. And seemingly, the closer to the mountains—like Lancia and Monteverdi—the better the roadholding. High-speed mountain driving is what these cars are designed for, and the precise steering, excellent braking, and quick acceleration that characterize all the European thoroughbreds are merely logical responses to a given set of conditions. All, of course, paired with that high-speed cruising capability demanded by the autoroutes.

Among other things, all this means that the best European sports cars are more versatile machines than most from England or America and are at home on a variety of road surfaces and types. Also, since gasoline has been prohibitively expensive on the Continent since well before World War II and the cars have always been taxed on displacement, there has been a constant impetus to get the most possible out of small engines. The prime Alpine area classics—the Gullwing Mercedes, the GTB/4 Ferrari, the Turbo Porsche, the Maserati Ghibli, the Lamborghini Miura—are all comparatively small-engined by American standards, and three are under 3 liters. Americans have traditionally considered this engine size too small even for Falcons and Valiants.

If Americans have the big, blustery cars (the Cobras and 'Vettes) and the British have the little, precise cars (the Lotuses and MGs), then the Germans and Italians have the perfect in-between cars, the performance of a big V-8 with the nimbleness of a little sports/ racer. And, in addition, there are basic tenets of excellence and pride at work in Europe. Socialism and inflation are changing all this now, but until the past decade the best styling, inarguably, came from the small carrozzeria around Turin, the best engineering from Maranello or Stuttgart, the best workmanship from Zuffenhausen and Unterturkheim.

Conversely, in most—not all, but most— of the exotic Alpine cars, that intense interest in handling, performance, and style has make the cars inbred to the point where they're virtually unusable elsewhere. The heaters are laughable because it never gets that cold, even in the Alps. The fresh-air vents are laughable because it never gets hot. The seating positions are planned for race drivers because at the speeds you're expected to go on terrible roads, you cannot break concentration for a second. You don't motor along, one arm out the window, head resting on the seat back. The cars are meant to be *driven,* hard, and at anything less than full chat they'll foul plugs, overheat, spurt gasoline into the oil, and generally behave miserably.

Unfortunately, most of us live life at less than ten-tenths. The intensity required to drive one's Ferrari, or oneself, constantly on the limit is something few of us are equipped for. In Evelyn Waugh's *Decline and Fall,* Professor Silenus describes life itself as an amusement-park whirling disc. The center is virtually motionless. Few people reach it. Most people won't even get on the disc, they just sit outside and watch. But others get on the edge where the speed is greatest, and hang on like hell, enjoying the ride. Others are staggering toward the motionless center, where everthing becomes clear and controlled.

Buick owners never get on the disc. Rolls-Royce owners are in the center, surrounded by staggering groups of MGs and Healeys and Triumphs. On the edge, going like hell and very near to falling over the rim, are the owners of Ferraris and Gullwing Mercedes and Maseratis, racing along at ten-tenths, madcap maniacs enjoying the ride of their lives. Significantly, nearly all the cars on the rapidly whirling edge of the disc are built near the Alps. The disc is a mountain in two dimensions. And the cars that keep you on the wild-riding, nervous edge are from the Alpine area: mountain cars.

Cisitalia

Lord knows, the car business has had more than its share of flamboyant crazies. From

Barney Oldfield and Ned Jordan to Fon Portago and Colin Chapman is really not such a long way to come. And then there was Piero Dusio, who makes the rest look like a squad of Boy Scouts. In the late thirties, Dusio was the nearest thing auto racing had to a Harry Schell or Pops Turner. He was a caricature Italian playboy who couldn't resist swinging from the heels, and from all reports he never did settle the question of which he liked better, cars or girls. Cars did have the added advantage that you could build them and sell them and make money, so logically enough, all things considered, Piero Dusio got into the car business.

One thing you have to say for him, Dusio *always* went first class. His money came from a textile company, and in 1939 he put together a loosely knit conglomerate of friends called Consorzio Industriale Sportivo Italia. Predictably, they concentrated on what today's entrepreneurs would call the leisure-activities market. They made tennis rackets and bicycles, sports clothes and swim suits. And when the war came, they made uniforms for Mussolini's Black Shirts. But this was all preamble. What Dusio really wanted to do was build racing cars. His personal high point was a fourth overall in the '38 Mille Miglia driving an Alfa, and he also sponsored Piero Taruffi in the late thirties. Building his own car was just the next logical step.

Dusio took some of his incredible wartime earnings (Cisitalia supplied all the uniforms for the entire Italian army) and, as early as 1944, while Allied bombers were still plastering northern Italy, he installed Dante Giacosa in a spare room in his suburban Turin country house. Giacosa was an acknowledged genius moonlighting from Fiat, one of the best engineers Dusio could have chosen. Their idea was to build an inexpensive 1100cc single-seater to fit the prewar—and presumably postwar—Formula Two regulations. They would build so many that soon Cisitalias would form a class of their own. It was the same concept that motivated the postwar Norton-based Formula 500, Formula Junior, and Formulas Ford, V, and Super V. As far as I know, Dusio was the first to try seriously to build up an inexpensive one-design class.

Giacosa, who still worked for Fiat, after all, was nothing if not practical. He took the

front and rear suspension from the Fiat 500 Topolino and used the Fiat 1100 engine and gearbox. Best of all, in the back of Cisitalia's bicycle factory he discovered a huge stock of chrome-moly tubing that had made Dusio's prewar Beltrame bicycles famous for their lightweight strength. By a fortunate coincidence, Giacosa had designed airplanes before he designed Fiats. And here were the makings of a first-rate tubular space frame, just like those used by most aircraft. So the Cisitalia monoposto, through sheer luck, got one of the first true automotive space frames anywhere.

By the spring of 1945, when it was obvious the war was nearly over, Giacosa started construction on the prototype. Then he went back full time to Fiat, eventually becoming head of the engineering division. Dusio replaced him with Giovanni Savonuzzi, whom he hired away from the same company by the simple expedient of offering him ten times his Fiat salary plus a company car. Even though he had to order and install all his own machine tools, Savonuzzi had a prototype running by the spring of '46. Piero Taruffi—one of the best development drivers in Italy as well as a superb engineer—debugged the Cisitalia, and by August there were enough cars to dominate the Coppa Brezzi, with Dusio himself taking the win. The only rivals, French Gordinis, were far behind.

All sorts of well-known European drivers ordered Cisitalias, including Harry and Phillipe Schell, Robert Manzon, and Franco Cortese. In the immediate postwar years the Cisitalia monoposto was just about the only new racing car to be had in Europe, and eventually Dusio was able to sell something like 42 of the little dears at $5,000 each before the newly formed Commission Sportive Internationale increased the Formula Two limit to 2000cc as of January 1948. Purely one-design Cisitalia racing never caught on, despite Dusio's sponsorship of an all-Cisitalia race in Cairo in 1947, and after the CSI changed the rules, the suddenly noncompetitive Model D.46 just sort of dried up and blew away overnight.

Long before, however, Dusio and Savonuzzi had widened Giacosa's tube frame chassis into a two-seater and started running in sports car events. Savonuzzi designed the first body himself, an aerodynamic berlinetta with

The most important postwar body design of all, Pininfarina's seminal 1947 Cisitalia 1100 coupe.

tail fins and fender portholes that stylist Ned Nickles later copied for Buicks. Alfredo Vignale left Stabilimenti Farina to open his own shop where early Cisitalia bodies were built, and Farina also built a few. The cars were exceptionally light, of course, and with nearly 70 hp from their dry-sump, hot-rodded Fiat engines—as opposed to 32 hp in Fiat trim— amazingly fast. The 1100cc Cisitalia coupes would go nearly 110 mph, in years when the 3400cc Jaguar XK-120 was considered very near to being something out of Flash Gordon, since it would go 120.

For example, in the 1947 Mille Miglia— which Nuvolari's Cisitalia roadster barely lost to Biondetti's huge Alfa through a dumb mechanic's goof—the clapped-out prototype Cisitalia aerodynamic coupe *averaged* 96 mph for the final hour and a half. Nuvolari's roadster was even faster. That's on 1089cc, thirty years ago. Two other Cisitalias were right behind Nuvolari in third and fourth. The Cisitalia sports cars were the sensation of 1947, and orders started pouring in. In addition, Taruffi won the Italian championship, was second in the 1948 Targa Florio, and came close to winning the '48 Mille Miglia before breaking.

Incredibly enough, the fantastic racing record of the Cisitalia 1100 is purely incidental to the value of the cars. In the fall of 1946 Dusio sent the sixth two-seater chassis over

to a comparatively small but well-respected carrozzeria down the street from Stabilimenti Farina. This was run by his brother, Pinin Farina, and Dusio pretty much forgot about the chassis in the excitement of the 1947 race season. After nearly a year, he finally got the chassis back, with a coupe body attached. This was shown at the Coppa d'Oro show in September 1947, held in Como. And it won the *grand* prize. *Mama mia.* Dusio knew he had something special. In October he sent the new Pininfarina coupe to the Paris Auto Show, where it was the undisputed star. Racing wins made the Cisitalia name well known in Europe, but Pininfarina's little coupe became, literally overnight, an international design cult object.

In 1951 Arthur Drexler organized the first exhibition of automobiles ever held in an art museum at the Museum of Modern Art in New York. Eight cars were shown, among them a Pininfarina Cisitalia coupe. Said Drexler in the show catalog, "The Cisitalia's body is slipped over its chassis like a dust jacket over a book . . . the openings Farina cuts into the jacket provide some of the most skillfully contrived details of automobile design . . . to maintain the sculptural unity of the entire shape, its surfaces are never joined with sharp edges, but are instead wrapped around and blunted. The door is minimized.

The back of the car, particularly the fender, is lifted at an angle rising from the strict horizontal base line which gives stability to the design. Thus both ends of the car gain an extraordinary tension, as though its metal skin did not quite fit over the framework and had to be stretched into place. This accounts, in part, for that quality of animation which makes the Cisitalia seem larger than it is."

Arthur Drexler *still* likes the Cisitalia. In fact, the Museum of Modern Art owns and displays only one automobile. Two years ago, Drexler persuaded Pininfarina to restore a Cisitalia coupe that had been discovered in a Turin chicken coop and donate it to the museum. As far as Drexler is concerned, this is the most important example of automobile styling *ever* produced, the one that truly explained what "envelope styling" was all about. In addition, of course, it not only started Pininfarina on his postwar way, but revitalized the entire Italian coachbuilding industry and started the "Italian style." It's a textbook example of what art historians call a seminal design.

To Piero Dusio, of course, it was a gold mine. Pininfarina couldn't build bodies fast enough, particularly when he introduced a roadster version. Brother Farina was enlisted to take up the slack, and the two shops clothed chassis as quickly as Dusio could weld them together. The exquisite little cars continued in production until the summer of 1949, with perhaps 200 being built in all. Today, a restored Pininfarina Cisitalia will set you back anything from thirty to forty grand. It was never just an automobile, you understand, but became an art object almost as soon as it appeared. The Turin auto museum has one, and Greenfield Village in Detroit, and MOMA, and a very few others. There are surprisingly few left. According to Drexler, it took Pininfarina himself nearly two years to find even a restorable car to donate to MOMA.

At $6,800 in 1948—XK-120s were only $3,600—Max Hoffman had a hard time selling them on Park Avenue, even if he was right in the middle of Art Gallery Row. Fergus also brought in a few, but I don't think there're a dozen in the whole United States at this point. Pete Petersen of Petersen Publishing bought one new and had a mold for a fiberglass body pulled from it. These were actually produced

in limited quantities in 1953. Just a few months ago a fellow in New Jersey was trying to sell one of these plastic copies, set up to fit an MG-TD chassis, for $300. I must say I had to think twice, maybe thrice, before I told him no. I don't think I would have mounted it on a chassis, actually—just painted it flawless red, polished the hell out of it, and set it at one end of the living room on a dais with a pair of spotlights on it.

Almost unbelievably, the Cisitalia story has a tragic ending. In 1947 Dusio had the world by the tail. The monopostos were so good they were uncanny. The racing two-seaters were winning everything in sight. His accessory business was flourishing. He couldn't keep up with orders for the Pininfarina coupes. For Piero Dusio, who'd never had anything go wrong in his whole life, I mean never, this was *it*. There was no place to go but up. But Dusio, typically, had to swing by the heels. So he paid a cool million francs to the French government to ransom the legendary Ferdinand Porsche from his Nazi war crimes cell. And Dusio set up Dr. Porsche, his son Ferry, Carlo Abarth, and Eberan von Eberhorst as a design team to build a radically new Formula One world-beater.

I don't have to tell you the rest. Against an ample budget of 20 million lire, Porsche's crew spent over 100 million lire without ever getting a single car within ten miles of a race

Pininfarina's organic, truly timeless style.

track. They built one mid-engine 1492cc flat-12 with a four-wheel drive unit and 5-speed transaxle that never came within 50 percent of its projected horsepower. The whole plan was a white elephant of monumental stupidity, and you'd think Porsche would have chopped the whole thing up in little bits instead of exhibiting it in the lobby of their museum. Anyway. Dusio had even naively cleared out his lucrative accessory department to make room for the expected GP car production, so by the middle of 1949 there was almost no money coming in at all, while the Porsche group was spending like drunken sailors. Cisitalia went bankrupt at the end of the summer.

The Porsche family went back to their new Gmund factory and became VW-based car builders under their own name—a project that was already well under way while they worked for Cisitalia—and poor Piero Dusio sold what was left of his company to an Argentine truck maker called Autoar. And beaten into the ground, he even followed what was left of his dream to Argentina, where he had the exquisite embarrassment of helping convert the machinery that had built works of art for the museums of the world into something for making diesel trucks for banana republics. On the other hand, he had the four swingingest years in automotive history, when Nuvolari was his driver, Taruffi his race chief, Porsche his engineer, and Pininfarina his stylist. It's not every Italian playboy who gets to lord it over four legends all at once and finance the creation of a fifth. Next time you're in the Museum of Modern Art, say a small prayer for Piero Dusio, builder of legends . . . who just couldn't resist swinging from the heels.

Delahaye

Let's assume just for a moment that your constant companion has been inordinately good to you lately and her Silver Cloud has been acting like it wants a new set of $3,000 valves. She likes cars, even old cars—which is rare, as you *must* realize—but she's definitely *not* into clapped-out racing cars, anything made in Italy or that has to be driven at ten-tenths before its sterling qualities manifest themselves. In other words, she wants a car for a *lady,* a hard-driving, accomplished lady, but a defiantly feminine person nonetheless. And like any pretty lady, she doesn't mind a bit of attention.

Buddy, have I got just the car for you. Not a masculine bolt in its body, but one of the great, all-time classics nonetheless . . . with an extravagant, voluptuous femininity that makes men blush to be seen in one but that women, certain women to be sure, absolutely crave. It's the automotive equivalent of the classic Parisian boudoir—not a place for mundanities but for profound explorations of all that is best in life. Not a mere bedroom but a salon, a public place in which to entertain friends, trade bons mots, and in general enjoy *la vie joyeuse.*

As you might expect, this deliciously feminine carriage is thoroughly and completely French, from its curving fenders to its magnificent top. Indeed, not just French, but that most wonderful sort of aristocratic French, as far removed from a Renault 5 as Versailles is from an Amiens farmer's *boue-*covered cottage. It is not a car for shrinking violets or for people who drive around in old Impalas because they don't want the maids to feel deprived. If you can carry it off, though, a Delahaye, even a postwar Delahaye, has more class in its lug nuts than most people have in their whole lives.

Delahaye. Weiffenbach. These two go together. There's always one strong personality behind every classic, no matter what the field. Monsieur Charles Weiffenbach *was* Delahaye. Ah, Monsieur Charles. He came to Delahaye before the turn of the century and was still running it in 1954, when they finally went under. Understandably, the cars never became Weiffenbachs, but there was no question who built them. Monsieur Charles was the consummate French autocrat—he might have taken lessons from Bugatti—and he outlasted them all.

Delahaye, Emile Delahaye, started in the car business in 1894, but by 1901 he had already retired. Monsieur Charles was put in charge, and he never looked back. For most of the years, Delahaye tried to be the Buick of France, making big cars, little cars, expensive cars, cheap cars, anything M. Charles thought he could sell. This means that for much of the time, they were dealing in pretty pedestrian stuff. It was a career remarkably similar to that of Talbot, right down to the boring cars.

In 1935, though, Delahaye bought Delage. They were making enough money to be actively acquiring, and already in 1933 they'd come out with a rakish sports model built around a 3.5-liter six. These Delahaye Type 135s had independent front suspensions, Cotal semiautomatic transmissions, and aerodynamic coachbuilt bodies. They weren't on the same level with Bugatti and Talbot by any means, but the Type 135s got the company started in the right direction.

This even included racing. Old M. Charles got sucked into defending La Belle France from the Aryan hordes, and like Bugatti and Tony Lago, put up light blue spear carriers to follow the Mercedes and Auto-Unions home at a safe distance. It was mad, of course, and totally futile. But out of the nervous years of the False War, both Talbot and Delahaye learned enough about making high-performance engines that they could seriously enter the ultra-high-performance sports-car market after the war.

Right away, in 1946, Delahaye built a whole fleet of 3.5-liter cars with envelope bodies but the old prewar chassis. In 1948, however, M. Charles unveiled a new 4455cc six, with independent front suspension, DeDion rear, and a Cotal gearbox. The box-section frame was as sturdy as can be, and with 185 hp in a 115-inch wheelbase, the Type 175 was good for over 120 mph. More popular, and obviously less expensive, the prewar 135 had its name changed to become the 235, with 152 hp and performance equal to the heavier Type 175s. Both models were in production from

This Delahaye Type 235 by Figoni and Falaschi was a lascivious anachronism even in 1949.

1948 till 1950, then the Type 235 was left by itself again to go it alone until the end in 1954. Delahaye became part of Hotchkiss, then Brandt, and then the name quickly disappeared.

But there are still those Type 175s and 235s. Most of them got lightweight aluminum bodies by Franay, Figoni and Falaschi, and Henri Chapron. They were expensive—$10,000 to $20,000 in the early fifties—and a bit temperamental. And the bodywork, still reminiscent of the wild, overchromed Delahayes of the thirties, is often excruciating. On the other hand, the best postwar Delahayes are gorgeous . . . big, elaborate cars with oval grilles, fleet lines, and huge drum brakes behind wire wheels. And the racers—a Type 135 got fifth at Le Mans in '49, a Type 175 finished twelfth overall in the first Carrera PanAmericana, another pair were first and fifth at Monte Carlo. The prewar V-12 GP cars were even competitive for a short while in the first 4.5-liter postwar Formula One. But it was all just so much finger exercises. Delahaye—like Lago-Talbot—was going nowhere. In 1950 M. Charles sold 483 cars; in 1951, only 77.

Really, Delahaye, Delage—which was just a badge-engineered Delahaye—and Lago-Talbot were all victims of the same set of circumstances. The boss was getting old without selecting an heir apparent, the tax situation was bitterly set up against them, the market was rapidly changing, the prices for custom coachwork were astoundingly higher than they had been before the war, fine materials were in short supply, and finally, sadly, the old standards just didn't mean that much to the postwar generation. The Delahaye died, finally, simply because it had outlived its time, and no one was sure how to change it to fit the new demands.

The Delahaye was a very special car, an extraordinarily expensive car for ladies with lovers to whom cost was no object. It wasn't a car a man would buy himself nor that he would buy his wife. Nor that a woman would buy herself, for that matter. It was a car so ostentatious you could only get one as a gift, and then only from the most intimate of friends. It was always a trifle, a bauble for the super-rich. And after the war, there weren't too many of the ostentatious super-rich left in Europe. Nor were there many De-lahayes, of course, so it all kind of evened out. Even today, the Delahaye name is still worth a stupendous amount. Upwards of $50,000 is not too much for a fine one. No matter who you are, that's still a helluva gift for a lady of the night.

Lago-Talbot

Tony Lago's cars, for all intents and purposes, are really prewar cars that stayed in production into the mid-fifties. And they were tremendous coachbuilt anachronisms. Companies like Bentley and Jaguar and all the Americans were able successfully to sell prewar cars long enough to come up with new designs, but France was so devastated there was no room left for prewar Grand Marques. Ironically, though, at almost the very moment Delahaye/Delage and Lago-Talbot went under, Jean Daninos appeared with his Facel Vega to capitalize on the booming economy of Europe in the late fifties. If Lago had just been able to hold on a little longer, perhaps skipping the racing that seems to be the kiss

Pierre Levegh's 52 Lago-Talbot sports/racer next to a GP

of death for so many small manufacturers, perhaps, just perhaps, France might have had a Grand Marque to compete with Aston and Ferrari and Mercedes. Alas. *C'est la vie.*

Still, Tony Lago was *un vrai original,* another of those crazy characters, those larger-than-life movers and shakers who get things done. He bought Talbot in 1936, after Sunbeam-Talbot-Darracq had gone down the drain. STD was a transchannel company headquartered in England with factories in Wolverhampton and Suresnes, France. And Major Antony Lago was one of STD's few assets in the thirties. He'd worked on the Wilson preselector gearbox, went to Armstrong-Siddeley, then to Sunbeam, all after a successful career in the Italian army during World War I. In 1933 he was sent to France to save the STD holdings in Suresnes. When Sunbeam decided to abandon all hope, Lago bought the French factory for peanuts.

Really, the Lago-Talbot saga is a hopeless one. Talbot was already gone when Lago got it, and there just wasn't much he could do to get it started up again, not that he didn't try. There were golden years in the late thirties when French Blue Lago-Talbot Grand Prix cars tried futilely to challenge the Auto-Unions and Mercedes. He had a big 4.5-liter six of 250 hp, and though the blue Talbots were laughably slow, they could sometimes

Saoutchik-bodied Lago-Talbot 4.5 of 1949.

Lago on the same chassis.

outlast the gas-guzzling Aryan Wunderkars. And they were reliable. So someplace in the middle of the pack, you'd find the Talbot team following the Germans home at a respectful distance.

The war killed Talbot for good. Lago was just getting things turned around and really, some of his Pourtout coupes and Figoni and Falaschi convertibles of the late thirties are among the most delightfully hedonistic sporting machines of all time. Not the sort of cars for masculine ego massages, but lovely, voluptuous bolides of definitely feminine character. Not soft, particularly, but undeniably feminine. Unlike most French manufacturers (Bugatti, for example), Lago was lucky enough to escape the Occupation with his factory intact. Bugatti wasn't a French national either, but Molsheim was in the wrong place at the wrong time. Italian Tony Lago kept a low profile under the Occupation, and got to keep Talbot.

So in 1946, Lago dusted off the old GP cars and returned to racing. He also resumed selling street machines on the same chassis to anyone who'd buy one. The big twin-cam sixes were set in a conventional ladder frame, with independent front suspension on a transverse leaf spring. Lago's Wilson preselector gearbox was still used, too, just about the last car anywhere to stick with that curious gimmick. Of course, all the bodies were coachbuilt—by

Saoutchik, Figoni and Falaschi, even little-known carriage builders like Pennock of Den Hague. Lago claimed a top speed of 125 mph for the street two-seaters, on 160 hp from the slow-turning six, which was really impressive in the late-forties, right up there with the XK-120 and suchlike.

But the Lago-Talbots were understandably ultraexpensive. And the French style, particularly as practiced by Phony and Flashy, never really did catch on in America, which is where all the postwar money had settled. If you weren't in the American market you didn't exist. Nobody cared that the old 4.5-liter GP cars were able to win lots of European races and that scarcely disguised Talbot GP cars dominated Le Mans. The Rosier family's win in 1950 was a record breaker, for example. And crazy Pierre Levegh came within half an hour of single-handedly winning Le Mans in a Lago-Talbot in 1952, tragically wrecking the car after he fell asleep at the wheel after 23½ hours, 25 miles ahead of the nearest Mercedes 300SL.

Talbot was like that. Almost but not quite. Lago was selling old-time style in an era that didn't give a good goddamn but was only con-

Levegh's Lago-Talbot 4.5, a rebodied Formula One car, was

cerned with getting on with it, and the sooner the better, too. Americans didn't care about Le Mans victories in 1950, and most of them had never heard of Louis Chiron and Phi-Phi Etancelin. In other words, the Talbot racing program was draining off big chunks of cash for dubious returns. When Lago started talking about a 1.5-liter V-16 to rival BRM, the handwriting was on the wall.

The 1957 Lago-Talbot Sport, with 2.5-liter four, was later sold with a flathead Ford V-8.

clocked at 150 mph at Le Mans in 1952.

French taxes didn't help, and that's always given as the reason Lago failed to make a go of it. Balderdash. Tony Lago was spending all his money running a team of outclassed GP cars that probably did more harm than good to the Talbot reputation. And the cars he offered for the street were huge, ungainly, curiously styled machines, nightmarishly expensive and totally out of step with the fifties. He sold an amazing 433 cars in 1950, a more realistic 80 cars in 1951. For a while, he stemmed the inevitable with smaller cars patterned after the big ones, and even in 1959 you could still buy a car from Tony Lago. The factory was now owned by Simca, though, and the Talbot came with the ancient Ford V-8 60 flathead that had been sent to Ford-France/Simca after it bombed in U.S. Fords. Tony Lago died in 1960, of a broken heart as much as anything.

Lago-Talbots went through a long period when nobody, anywhere, cared one whit. But then sometime in the last half-dozen years a few classic-car types began realizing that postwar Talbots were just as good as prewar Talbots and cost a lot less. And really, once they started to investigate, it was clear that Tony Lago's cars were right up there among the best cars from the fifties, no matter that they were hopelessly old-fashioned. Quality and style like that just aren't to be found anymore. And though the overdone, overchromed masterpieces of Phony and Flashy are almost caricatures today, virtually all of the Talbot competition berlinettas are at least as neat as

comparable DB-2 Astons or 212 Ferraris. And of course the Lago-Talbots have a booming 4500cc to tow them around in style. The best of these Talbots are really delightful cars, achingly fast, precise, and sporting, with a masculine style completely different from run-of-the-mill cars.

They were costly beyond belief in the early fifties, and $50,000 would not be too much to pay for the right one, even today. If you can find one, a genuine Le Mans car would be the thing to have, but that's the sort of machine you're already too late to find. Lago-Talbots are the kind of automobiles that become family heirlooms, passed down from generation to generation, always perfectly tended and groomed. And, of course, always within the right families, the sort who had $20,000 to spend on a coachbuilt motorcar in 1950 and were tasteful enough to grace Tony Lago with their patronage. If you're fortunate enough to have inherited one, keep it in the manner to which it's accustomed. Major Antony Lago would have liked that. And it's only right.

Ferrari [1946-1964]

Little Phil Hill comes diving into White House Corner in the dark, in the rain, wispy French clouds drifting across the smooth, puddled, ominous asphalt at eye level. He is knowingly, willingly, going in harm's way, to that place where there is a question whether or not he will return unscarred. Ken Purdy used to say, to that place where when you wake up, perhaps all you'll be able to move is your eyeballs, and all you'll *ever* be able to move is your eyeballs. Phil Hill is too intelligent to be a racing driver, and eventually it will be his undoing. He will lose his nerve. But this is 1958 and he is about to win *Les Vingt-quatres heures du Mans* by over 100 miles.

Oblivious to the solid sheets of rain, to the incessant trickle of icy water down his neck, to the slick, black puddles, to the scattered wrecks of others who have gone where he is going and who have failed, to the possibility of pointless death or worse, Hill submerges the sensations that his mind tells him are all wrong for a fragile human being to endure. And he catches fourth as he drifts, ever so slightly sidewise, through the right-hander, right up to the lethal, rainy grass verge and across the narrow road into the oblique left. And all the while, with the blinding spray of a hundred previous passers hanging heavy in the air, bouncing back off the light from his headlamps, adding an incongruous note of Watteau romanticism to this otherwise insanely otherworldly, mystical scene, the banshee shriek of the racing V-12 wails on unhindered. *Raappp!* This is what is meant when you hear the word Ferrari.

Enzo Ferrari has been winning races for nearly sixty years at this point, thirty of them with cars of his own manufacture. And for all that time his cars have been indisputably the best that there is. Ferrari is, I suspect, the reincarnation of Ettore Bugatti. Il Commendatore and Le Patron. Like Bugatti, Ferrari is a self-taught engineer. He is an artist of exquisite taste. He was a first-rank racing driver in his youth, graduating to the running of teams, of factories, and ultimately to building cars with his own name. The prancing horse of Maranello is as well respected as the horseshoe-wrapped radiator of Molsheim. Both men lost beloved, brilliant sons—Jean Bugatti and Dino Ferrari were both consummate stylists—both men were notorious for impenetrable blind spots when it came to certain aspects of performance—braking, for instance—and both were unpardonable martinets. Bugatti and Ferrari used men the way you and I use hand tools, and both were feared and hated more than loved. But for all their monumental faults, their quirky, idiosyncratic cars were never accused of the sin of dullness.

At Bridgehampton in 1950, a Ferrari was already the car to own; Charles Moran's Touring-bodied 166 Barche

Even more than the sometimes foppish and foolish Bugatti, Ferrari has consistently built cars that are considered the absolutely ultimate conveyances of their era. There are bad Ferraris, of course, and when the Italians build a dog, you can smell it for miles. But overall, Ferrari has been the most consistently well-respected name in automobiles since World War II, rivaled only by Rolls-Royce. Which is remarkable, when you think about it, for the Ferrari tradition goes back only to 1946, disregarding the Fiat-based 815 of 1940. And yet it's hard to imagine a world without Ferraris. What did rich people drive before?

We tend to forget that Ferrari the man had already been through two successful careers before there was ever Ferrari the car. Enzo Ferrari started racing for CMN in 1919 at the age of twenty-one, after invaliding out of World War I. He went to Alfa Romeo the following year, and through the early twenties built up a respectable career as a driver. But his real forte was organization, and before long Ferrari was Alfa's team manager, director of the racing department, and finally, in 1929, head of his own factory-backed but independent Scuderia Ferrari, racing Alfas and Rudge motorcycles. In 1938 Alfa took its racing cars back and Ferrari was on his own. There was an abortive project for the shortened 1940 Mille Miglia, consisting of two Model 815s powered by paired Fiat fours to make a straight-eight. But the war put Ferrari into a machine tool shop and the two unsuccessful cars into oblivion.

So Ferrari Automobili, as such, dates from only 1946. Now a thing to be kept in mind is that Enzo Ferrari is autocratic. Always has been. And the eras of Ferrari cars—rather than by models or formulas—are marked by the hiring and firing of engineers and designers. Which is convenient for us if not for them.

leads George Rand in Briggs Cunningham's 166 Spyder Corsa and Jim Kimberly's Berlinetta 195 by Touring.

Otherwise, the incredible proliferation of Ferrari models would be literally impossible to sort out. Even the acknowledged experts, Warren Fitzgerald and Dick Merritt, got themselves a bit confused sometimes.

The problem is this. Ferrari introduced new models the way other factories changed paint colors. And for many models, only a handful, maybe five or three, or even one, examples were built. Total Ferrari production for the first decade was only something like 600 cars, and that includes all the Formula racers and such. Nowadays, Ferrari production averages around 1,000 a year, primarily of only one or two models. But in the early days they were literally building specific cars for each race or each wealthy customer. To add to the confusion, all Ferrari bodies are coachbuilt.

But happily enough, there are lots of shared components among all those models, particularly engines. Which is in fact how Ferraris are grouped—by engine/designer. Now you have to realize that the heart of any Ferrari is the engine. It's really all there is and all the factory really cares about. The chassis is merely something to hold the engine off the ground, and the bodywork is done outside and worried about by other specialists like Touring, Bertone, Scaglietti, and Pininfarina. So the factory is left in the happy position of being able to concentrate almost totally on the refinement of its power plant.

For 24 hours at Le Mans, or something, Ferrari engines work fine. But over five or ten or fifteen years of daily driving, you'd be better off in a Dodge Dart. Leonard Setright touched on this in *Ferrari.* "The early cars," he said, "have a reputation for being noisy, rough-riding, heavy to handle, temperamental, vibratory and often deficient in braking ability . . . with such idiosyncrasies as a fragile clutch, a dubious final drive, recalcitrant electrics, water pumps that leak into the sump, etc."

Anyway. Ferrari engines are grouped by designer. From 1937 till 1949, Gioacchino Colombo was Ferrari's chief engineer. And his first engine, a 1497cc, single-overhead-cam, 60-degree V-12 that appeared in 1946, set the pattern for all that followed. The Colombo engine eventually went out to 2.0, 2.3, 2.6, 2.7, 2.9, 3.3, and 4.0 liters, becoming remarkably sophisticated, all things considered, in the process. But in 1950 Ferrari was mostly interested in Formula One racing. Sports cars were just a sideline to support the monopostos. The early postwar Grand Prix formula was 1.5 liters supercharged, 4.5 liters unsupercharged. Colombo argued fervently in favor of supercharging his little 1.5-liter V-12. But his assistant, Aurelio Lampredi, who had Ferrari's ear, argued for a great hulking 4.5-liter V-12.

Lampredi won, Colombo went to Maserati to design the brilliant 250F, and Ferrari introduced the Lampredi-designed long block in 1950. Colombo's engine, called the short block, had shrunk-in wet liners with conventional detachable cylinder heads. Lampredi eliminated the head gasket, cast the cylinder heads and block in one piece, and used screwed-in liners. This made the block taller, which led to this long-block designation. Curiously enough, even though it was designed to fit the 4.5-liter formula, Lampredi's engine—still a 60-degree V-12 derived, admittedly, from Colombo's—appeared as a 3.3 in 1950. It then grew over the years to 4.0, 4.5, and 4.9 liters, but also shrank to become a 3.0.

During the winter of 1951 Lampredi also designed a new 2.0-liter four for Formula Two, to replace the little Colombo V-12. This was a double-overhead-cam unit with dual ignition, that almost immediately appeared in 2.5- and 3.0-liter versions. By simply adding two more cylinders, Lampredi got two new sixes, one at 3.7 liters, the other at 4.4. This went on until the fall of 1955, when Il Commendatore tired of Lampredi and he went over to Fiat. Eventually, Lampredi became chief of Fiat engineering, and that old fox of Alfa Romeo's golden years, Vittorio Jano, came to Ferrari and redesigned the Lampredi four to be both stronger and lighter. With the cam covers painted red, in 2.0-liter form, it appeared in 1956 as the marvelous Testa Rossa, literally "red head."

After the Le Mans debacle of 1955, the FIA sports/racing formula was reduced to 3 liters. And simultaneously Lancia handed its GP team over to Ferrari, which was how Jano, who had designed the Lancia Formula One car, happened to come to Maranello in the first place. Jano and Franco Rocchi, in typical Ferrari fashion, pretty much erased Lampredi's image. They brought back the Colombo V-12 for Le Mans and suchlike and

Touring's Barchetta stayed in production from 1949 till '53 and inspired the A. C. Ace/Cobra.

The Barchetta came with a V-12 of 1992cc, 2341cc, 2562cc, or 4101cc, Type 166/195/212/340, depending.

designed a new V-6, called the Dino after Ferrari's son, for Formula Two. There was a similar V-8 for Formula One that unfortunately had to run against the Vanwalls in '57 and against the rear-engine Coopers later on. It soon disappeared.

The history of Ferrari divides very neatly at 1964, the last year for the front-engine sports/racers. After that date Ferrari engine development becomes confusingly specialized. But between 1946 and 1964 there were just four major series of Ferrari engines—the Colombo V-12, the Lampredi V-12, the Lampredi four/six, and the Jano/Rocchi V-6. They were used virtually interchangeably in street machines, sports/racers, and GP cars. Obviously, the race engines were more highly stressed, but they did use the same blocks as the comparatively docile street machines, right down to having a place to mount a starter. In other words, despite the incredible proliferation of early Ferrari models and types, it was all done, as they say, with mirrors. A V-12 popped into what was formerly a four of similar displacement, and . . . presto! A whole new car.

Another problem for early Ferrari historians is that the model names and numbers follow no logical sequence until the late fifties. Not only were new models created simply by splicing a new engine into an old chassis, but just as often the same model name would stay, even though the car underneath was totally different. And since, externally, it's impossible to tell the difference between a 4.1 and 4.9 V-12, many of the cars—particularly the sports/racers—were unknown quantities even when new. Somewhere, somebody in the factory knew which engine a particular car used, but at the track it was just rumor. And with Ferrari's penchant for cloak-and-dagger secrecy—Enzo Ferrari puts Howard Hughes to shame—nobody ever really knew what the hell was going on, which is the way Ferrari liked it.

Out of this frustrating Italian maze, certain verities do present themselves. Given: *any* early Ferrari is a blueblood classic, the ultimate in collector cars. But certain Ferraris, as the saying goes, are more equal than others. Logically enough, the best Ferraris are ones that were built in relatively large quantities, for the simple reason that if a design was successful, it stood a better chance of being reproduced than if it was a dog. So you have the contradictory situation where a super-rare one-off Ferrari can be less interesting—and worth much less—than a relatively common production model.

There's also no real logic that says the early cars are dogs, the later ones better, or vice versa. Ferrari development staggered along, with failures just as apt to follow triumphs as the other way around. For example, one of the best of all Ferraris was also one of the first. In 1948, Ferrari started building a production version of the Colombo GP chassis, which he called the 166 Inter. With only a single Weber carb, the little V-12 made 110 hp at 6,000 rpm. The 2-liter Type 166 grew into the 2341cc Type 195 in 1950 and later that year into the 2562cc Type 212. In the hotter Sport versions you could get up to 180 hp for a top speed of nearly 120 mph.

What really made the 166/212, though, was the body. A high-revving V-12 was neat, of course, and the cars were faster than you had any right to expect—dynamite race cars, they were—but mostly the Inters were judged by their looks. This took a while to happen. The earliest cars were bodied pretty unimaginatively by Farina, Ghia, and Vignale. But in 1949 Carrozzeria Touring introduced the famous Bianchi-designed Superleggera Barchetta, or Little Boat. At the time, it was a complete revelation. Maybe the best way to place it is to trace its influence. The Tojeiro-designed Bristol special that became the A. C. Ace had a body copied line for line from the Barchetta, and that, of course (with a few detail modifications) became the Cobra. And the Shelby Cobra, even in 1967, looked perfectly contemporary. By this point the body design was really twenty years old, though nobody talked much about that.

The Barchettas have a wonderfully curvaceous look, with rocker panels that tuck way under. The fender line swoops up and over the wheels and down around the cockpit. The short, smooth tail wraps around into a bulbous deck, and the hood rises gracefully up and over the tall air cleaners from a simple, oval, convex egg-crate grille. With knock-off wire wheels, in blood red, the Barchetta is a sight to behold. Oh. About that name. Probably the most distinctive feature of all is the cockpit

Jim Kimberly's 195 Inter at Buenos Aires, 1951, forerunner of a long line of Ferrari GT coupes.

shape, a smoothly rounded hole cut into the top of the body just ahead of the rear wheels. The sill is trimmed with a leather roll literally stitched to the body with leather thongs. It looks for all the world like one of those gorgeous mahogany Chris-Craft inboard runabouts from the early fifties, the ones with the big chrome guard down the bow and brightwork hull. Anyway, the Italian press thought Touring's Inter looked just like a powerboat, and the name stuck. Barchetta, indeed.

Barchettas were made until 1953. There was a coupe version—a berlinetta—that looked like nothing so much as an A. C. Aceca. Some of the later cars got a 4.1-liter version of the big Lampredi V-12 and became 340 Americas. With 220 hp and an all-up weight less than 2,000 pounds, they were good for nearly 140 mph and, as the name implied, most of them went to the States. Wealthy sportsmen like Bill Spear and Jim Kimberly (Kimberly-Clark), big guns in American racing in the fifties, were the only sorts who could afford to race them. Which was as it should be, all things considered.

Barchettas have stayed pretty much in the same high-class league. John Bond of *Road & Track* has both a roadster and berlinetta, for example, and the rest are owned by similarly wealthy if lesser-known enthusiasts. The going rate is up well over $30,000. On the other

hand, the Barchettas were the cars that really made Ferrari's name—winning Le Mans in 1949, among other things—which helps to make them expensive. In addition, of course, they're delightful to drive fast—not much fun to drive slow—and among the most beautiful cars ever built.

Nobody in his right mind would buy a Barchetta to actually use, but as a superb mantelpiece decoration nothing could be finer. Like most Ferraris, they're a little rich and unreliable for my blood, but I'm perfectly willing to admit that there're damn few cars that come anywhere near exciting my visual interest the way the Barchetta does. They take skill, time, and money to own, and I hate to think what spares cost. On the other hand, there is no car like a Ferrari and no Ferrari like a Barchetta.

In the early fifties, the Lampredi V-12 ended up in a bunch of lovely cars, most of which unfortunately were built in model runs of three or four and nearly all of which are long gone. There were some delectable berlinettas built for the Carrera PanAmericana—called, logically enough, 340 Mexicos—and some similar coupes known as 375 Mille Miglias. Most of them were styled by Michelotti and bodied by Vignale, and they are *exquisite.* A very few are still around, and you'll know one the minute you see it: tall, spidery wire

The most beautiful GT coupe of the early fifties, Pininfarina's Type 250 Mille Miglia.

wheels, recessed oval grille, vestigial little tail fins, sliding plexiglass side windows, and the leanest, starkest, slab-sided styling you can imagine. They all have the same look, of overgrown, sun-reddened grasshoppers ready to spring.

There was even a true production version of the Michelotti/Vignale berlinetta, the Type 250 Mille Miglia, with a 2.9-liter version of the short-block V-12. The "production" cars, built by Pininfarina, are identical to the Vignale racers, except for trim changes around the windows. For my money, the 250MMs are just about the most beautiful mid-fifties sports cars of all. They're surprisingly small and low and have a tightness in the surface development that makes the body merely a skein of aluminum struggling to contain the exotic Ferrari viscera. These berlinettas really look like nothing else before or since, cleaner and sharper than you can imagine a car could be.

In retrospect, I'm amazed the 250MM didn't have more influence than it did. There was no popular-priced equivalent of the 250MM, the equivalent of the Barchetta-inspired A. C. Ace, and frankly I'm surprised. California fiberglass wizards pulled a mold off everything that rolled by, from Cisitalias to MG-TDs. You'd think Pete Petersen or somebody would have put up the money. Lack of influence notwithstanding, the Vignale ber-

linettas of the mid-fifties are at least as good as the early Barchettas, considerably rarer, and not quite as expensive, all good things for a car to be if it wants to be collected.

The Ferrari of the fifties is the Testa Rossa. The first 2-liter four appeared in April 1956, after Lampredi had already left for Fiat and Jano/Rocchi were hard at it to replace the four/six line with the V-6. The Testa Rossa still had a live rear axle like all early Ferraris, though now it was carried on coil springs in place of the transverse leaf springs of the early cars. Indeed, the TR was something of a stopgap measure as far as the factory was concerned, but it still went like stink. Soon there was a 2.5-liter version, and in late 1957 a 3-liter made by fitting the old Colombo V-12 into the same chassis. Scaglietti and Fantuzzi built a series of lovely sports/racer bodies for the 92.5-inch wheelbase, V-12 TRs, and with 300 hp hauling 2,000 pounds, they were simply dynamite. The TRs eventually got De-Dion rear ends, disc brakes, dry-sump engines, and heavier frames. Incredibly enough, the basic TR remained in production and competition up until 1962 as a factory racer, by which time it had 4000cc and more horsepower than the chassis could handle. The TRs were just about the last valid front-engine sports/racers, at least on an international level, and when you consider that the hardware was mostly a decade old, that's going some.

Of all the Testa Rossas, probably the best are the first V-12s, the TR250s of 1957/'58. Scaglietti used weird styling—sometimes the fenders were separate from the body at the front, zooming back to the cowl as headlight-carrying pontoons—and the body sides were drastically cut away for cooling. There was always a tall headrest concealing the gas filler, and the tail was surprisingly square to take the mandatory FIA suitcase. A capacious oil reservoir sat in the left front fender, and of course there was a huge hood scoop that became a Ferrari trademark. All in all, a most remarkable car; one that defined the mid-fifties style.

Testa Rossas were remarkably successful, too. When Phil Hill and Olivier Gendebien won Le Mans in '58—and Ferrari won Sebring and the Targa and the Manufacturers' Championship—it was with the TR250. Revised 5-speed versions won the championship again in 1960 and '61, including Le Mans both years and Sebring in '61. Again in '62, the ultimate Testa Rossa, the TR61, won Sebring, Le Mans, and the championship. Of all Ferraris, the Testa Rossas probably won more races than any others, and certainly with four Manufac-

turers' Championships in a row (with time out for Aston Martin in 1959, won mostly on the strength of having Moss, Shelby and Salvadori as drivers) they were the absolute rulers of international sports-car racing.

Over the years, a fair number of Testa Rossas were built for a long line of wealthy amateur racers who wanted the latest and best. So surprisingly there are quite a few TRs still available for sale. The going rate is up around $35,000 for an average one, more if it's a famous race winner. Any Testa Rossa is a ball to drive, and since they all date from that halcyon period when sports/racers—even international championship models—were still street-legal, it is possible to take one out and drive it around without wearing Nomex. Of course it's also going to be a racing car, which means the ride is jouncy, the noise overwhelming, and the body built with all the careful skill of a toddler modeling mud. You can stick your finger through the door seams, you can look through the floor at the ground, and water, grit, dust, and anything else that's on the road inevitably ends up on you, too. On the other hand, a Testa Rossa is more fun than anything else you can think of, a magnificent slice of compressed Le Mans history, and if you're really good perhaps you can talk Phil

The grid at Nassau in 1957: John Fitch in the Maserati 2-liter behind Fon Portago's 2-liter Ferrari 500 Testa Rossa.

Ernie McAfee's 121 LM, a 4.4-liter six, in 1955.

Tony Parravano's 375 Plus, rebodied by Sutton.

Von Neumann's 250 Testa Rossa at Nassau, 1959.

Hill into showing you the right way to drift it around Laguna Seca next year at the old-car races.

The Testa Rossa spawned another model that if anything is even more of a collector car. That's the 250GT, which started out as a street/racer berlinetta for the Geneva Auto Show in March 1956. The engine was a 220-hp version of the 2.9-liter Colombo V-12, tucked into a 102-inch wheelbase. The first ones were Pininfarina coupes built by Boano that weighed nearly 2,700 pounds and were useless for competition. To race with the 300SL Gullwings and Aston Martins, Ferrari had Scaglietti build some Superleggera berlinettas patterned after the Pininfarina cars but with plastic windows instead of glass, no bumpers, etc. Scaglietti saved a couple of hundred pounds this way, which made the competition 250GTs more than a match for the Mercedes coupes.

Scaglietti and Ferrari kept at the 250GT without a major change until October 1959, when the ultimate Ferrari berlinetta from the fifties was introduced at the Paris auto show. Simply enough, it was the 250GT with 8 inches chopped from the wheelbase, disc brakes from the Testa Rossa, a super-slick Superleggera body that gave an overall weight of only 2,500 pounds, and a six-carburetor engine rated at 280 hp. Amazingly enough, the Short Wheelbase Berlinetta—the beloved SWB—even had a mostly steel body with aluminum doors and a heater that sometimes worked. The SWB was the ultimate development of the competition berlinetta concept, and an incredibly nice dual-purpose sports car, besides.

Some people bought them to race, and they were virtually unbeatable. Some people bought them to drive, and as street machines they're delightful. Some people bought them to do both, and incredibly enough, that was okay, too. Even better, quite a few were built over the years, so they're around. And a lot of mechanics worked on them, so there's a fair fund of knowledge stored up, too. The SWBs in their heyday were considered pretty well appointed for racing cars, with handy little touches like roll-up windows, vent windows, radios, and lots of things you normally don't expect to find on international class machinery. On the other hand, they absolutely go like scat, with a top speed up around 150 mph and quarter-mile times in the 15s at nearly 100 mph . . . which is going some for any relatively luxurious 3-liter steel-bodied coupe.

At Sebring in 1962 Phil Hill and Olivier Gendebien finished second *overall* in a re-vamped, lightweight SWB with aluminum body, aerodynamic nose, wide wheels, and plastic windows. This was the prototype for a series of 100 identical cars, meaning they could be homologated with the FIA as Grand Touring machines. So this Ferrari became Grand Touring Omologato, or GTO. Now of course you know and I know and the FIA knows that when any Italian factory counts up production for homologation purposes, they stick a model number on everything from the secretary's Fiat to the concession truck that brings *caffè latte* at ten thirty every morning. Except that with the GTO, somebody complained. The CSI started counting, and lo and behold, there actually were somewhere near 100+ GTOs. Incredible. At least half of them or more are still around, and combined with the dozens of SWBs from the previous era, there's really a pretty good pool of delectable cars to choose from.

The GTOs are distinguished mostly by a tiny oval radiator opening, something like a Sebring Sprite, embarrassingly enough, with three semielliptical NACA ducts in the nose. These ducts were a tricky little feature, and I don't know why nobody else ever used them. Each individual hole had its own cover that clipped in with Dzuz fasteners. On a cold day you left them all on; on a warm day, took out the center one, and on a hot day opened the whole nose up for more cooling. A brilliant idea; simple and workable. The later GTOs came right at the beginning of the aerodynamic era, actually. In addition to the nose slots, they had two or three cooling slots in echelon behind each front wheel for brake cooling and a single slot behind the rear wheels. And the GTOs were among the first cars anywhere to use a rear spoiler bolted on the deck lid. They are slippery brutes and, except for wire wheels, still look extremely advanced today.

The GTOs were all-conquering in 1963, though by 1964 Carroll Shelby's Cobras were pretty much in full cry, Ford was already working on the GT-40, and Ferrari was starting its roughest years since Mercedes retired at the end of '55. There was a lot of thrashing

Two of the incredibly successful 1957 Scaglietti-bodied 250GTs, being guarded by Phil Hill.

Beautiful, fast, and something of a legend—the 1960 Ferrari 250GT Short Wheelbase Berlinetta.

The SWB: 3 liters, 280 hp, 2,400 pounds, styled by Pininfarina and bodied by Scaglietti. Cumberland, 1960.

on the Formula One team (Ing. Chiti took most of them away to found ATS) and both Phil Hill and John Surtees gave up on Il Commendatore around that time. The mid-sixties were not the best years for Italian racing red. And until the mid-engined 250LMs got sorted out, the GTOs and derivative GTO 64s—the last front-engine Ferrari racers—were left to defend things as best they could, which was none too well, as things turned out.

Nonetheless, it had been a good fight. For nearly twenty years, Enzo Ferrari had *owned* international racing. He made a stupendous number of striking cars, each one better than the last. But for my money, the Barchetta and the V-12 Testa Rossa are the only roadsters to own; the 250 Mille Miglia, 250GT, Short Wheelbase Berlinetta, and GTO are the only coupes to consider. Some of the others are brilliant, but some are horrendous, too, and it sometimes takes a real expert to tell the difference at first. But Barchettas and SWBs and the rest are *guaranteed* Ferraris.

This brings up an interesting point. Of all the Ferraris built, with four major series of engines and uncounted minor variants, the best Ferraris have all been built on derivatives of the same chassis, with Colombo's single-overhead-cam, short-block V-12. And that always in 2.9-liter size. In other words, of all the varieties of Ferrari, there is only one combination that consistently *works*. Curiously, since there was really only this one definitive Ferrari chassis that succeeded year in and year out, it doesn't seem to have mattered who did the body. Touring, Vignale, Scaglietti, Pininfarina are represented in my short list of most desirable Ferraris. And the factory was obviously able to get the consistency of design and the quality of construction they needed, no matter who was the builder.

Ferrari is maybe the hardest of all marques to assimilate. Most car factories either diddled along for years, had one good idea that they built for a short time and then went back to diddling, or else had one good idea early on and built it without change till it was so old nobody would buy it. But Ferrari's not like that. True enough, they used the same engine for nearly twenty years—hell, they're *still* using it—but at the end, it was just as competitive as at the beginning. True, their chassis were almost always half a step behind

Phil Hill's GTO, second overall at Sebring in 1962.

the times. But the chassis always worked, empirically, with no apologies needed. And the bodywork was usually right at the absolute forefront of styling trends. There's a lot of Short Wheelbase Berlinetta in Bill Mitchell's current Camaro, for example, and though the Camaro is the best-styled American car being made, it's significant that it's patterned after a car that went out of production over fifteen years ago. Pontiac is *still* using the twin-nostrils sort of grille that characterized Ferraris in the Chiti era. And Chiti left in 1962.

Enzo Ferrari has been the dominant personality in international racing for decades, and in the fifties, particularly, everything that was done by others had to take into account the reaction from Maranello. When Ford and Shelby went racing in '64, they didn't go racing to win, they went to beat Ferrari. Tony Vandervell built his Vanwall Formula Ones to "beat the bloody red cars," and after he'd done that he quit, as did Ford, after only a few years.

In the end, that is the difference. Tony Vandervell went racing to defend British prestige from the onslaught of papist hordes, Ford went racing to sell cars, but Ferrari went racing because, well, racing was all there was to life. And when all the dilettantes had packed up and gone home, Ferraris were still there, winning. Consistently. Not for a race, or a season, but year after year for a lifetime. As Stirling Moss told Ken Purdy a long time ago, "One's either a racer, or one's not." Enzo Ferrari was a racer.

Maserati

Maserati is the Dodge Brothers of exotic cars. They've been in business for over fifty years, which is a long time. They've built some grand automobiles, truly grand. They've won a lot of races. But no matter what they do, Maserati has always been well . . . invisible. If you're listing one exotic GT, you list Ferrari. A list of three adds Lamborghini and Aston Martin. Only when you get down to including middle-class stuff like Jaguars and Corvettes do you include Maseratis, too. Jaguar was always the cheap car that could be legitimately compared to the high-priced competition; Maserati is always the expensive car to compare unfavorably with Jaguars. Not *bad*, necessarily, just kind of lacking somehow, deficient in some certain élan, some requisite thoroughbred bloodline that lifts Ferrari from the realm of mere automobilia into something more.

In a reverse kind of snobbism, of course, there are Maserati fanatics who wouldn't give you two cents for *any* Ferrari. They're the ones who drive Bentleys instead of Royces, wear Sebagos instead of Top-Siders, and live on big estates in Utah—*outré* types. At least *some* Maseratis *are* really good, kind of secret cars that nobody quite appreciates and that are priced at maybe half what a comparable Ferrari would cost for the same level of luxury, performance, and exclusivity.

Obviously, though, Maseratis aren't blue-chip investments. For all I know, or Bob Grossman knows, Maserati may ultimately turn out to be the Edsel of exotic cars, the sort of thing the wrong class of people buy because they're cheap and red. On the other hand, when future enthusiasts come to appreciate just what a brilliant stylist Giorgetto Giugiaro is—and realize that his best bodies have been done on Maserati chassis—there could be an absolute run on Maserati Ghiblis that will make Ferrari Daytonas look like DeSoto Adventurers with three-tone paint and push-button shifters.

Ironically, the Maserati name goes back to 1926, two full decades earlier than Ferrari. The five Maserati brothers who liked cars— Mario was a painter—were building cars for other people before the turn of the century. And they were good. In European road racing,

Gioacchino Colombo's 1953 Maserati A6GCS 2000, the pr

The A6GCS 2000: 2 liters, 170 hp, 1,800 pounds, and the

tiest sports/racer of its day.

wonderfully low and efficient body.

Maserati-built cars were always significant factors—if not always winners—in the under-2-liter voiturette classes. By 1937, however, they were in trouble, and the three Maseratis still connected with the firm—Ernesto, Bindo, and Ettore (Carlo and Alfieri died in races)—sold out to the huge Orsi conglomerate. They signed a ten-year contract to run the company, though, and flush with new funds, in a new and bigger factory, they built some of their nicest cars. Probably the best was the 8CTF single-seater, with which Wilbur Shaw won the Indy 500 in 1939 and '40.

The Maseratis served as part of the Orsi war matériel combine for the duration of World War II and in '46 merely resumed production of their limited prewar line of racing cars. Incredibly enough, in twenty years the Maserati works had never built a street machine. As did Eric Broadley at Lola, they depended solely on customer sales of Formula cars to pay the bills. After the war, however, owner Adolfo Orsi let his son Omer make most of the Maserati decisions. Omer decided to put Maserati on a businesslike basis for the first time. He wanted to expand into sports cars and luxury GTs; the Fratelli Maserati wanted to stick with monoposto racers. In 1947, by mutual consent, their ten-year contract was not renewed. The Maseratis went back to their pre-Orsi factory in Bologna and started OSCA to build only racing cars. Orsi and Guerrino Bertocchi—who had been the works chief since 1926—started a campaign to bring Maserati onto the street.

The first Orsi/Bertocchi car was actually put together while the Maserati brothers were still in Modena. Called the A6GCS, it was a spidery sports/racer, sort of an Italian Frazer Nash Le Mans Replica, with a cigar-shaped body and four cycle fenders. The lights and fenders were quick-detach, so the thing could also be run as a Formula car. The engine was a 1978cc six of 130 hp that was all-new and designed by the Maseratis before they left. This engine sat in a simple tubular ladder frame, with a modern independent front end but a rigid rear axle with archaic half-elliptic springs. Despite their shortcomings, A6GCSs made super-competitive 2-liter sports/racers as well as adequate Formula Two mounts for low-budget racers who couldn't afford a real monoposto A6GCM.

Maserati factory driver Luigi Musso virtually owned the 2-liter class in European endurance racing in 1953

with his A6GCS 2000; this is the Dolomite Cup in July.

The A6GCS stayed in production into the mid-fifties, though the entire car was redesigned in 1953. Gioacchino Colombo, the brilliant Ferrari designer who lost the 1950 power struggle with Aurelio Lampredi, went to Maserati in the fall of '52. He naturally started revamping everything in sight. Among other projects, Colombo had his assistant, Ing. Massimino, fit the old Maserati six with double overhead cams. This was primarily for Formula Two, but the engine also ended up in the sports/racers at either 165 or 170 hp, depending on the compression ratio. The chassis was revised, and since nobody in his right mind would try to race a de-fendered sports car against true Formula machines by 1953, the stripper A6GCS contraption was dumped in favor of a lovely two-seater, envelope body.

The A6GCS 2000, as this was called, is honestly one of the prettiest sports/racers from the fifties, aesthetically right up there with D-Jags, Testa Rossas, and Lotus Elevens. The whole car was a consistent series of flattened ovals. The body section was an oval through the cowl; the mildly cutaway doors had a nicely rounded oval edge. All four fenders were subtle ovals, too, the wheel cutouts weren't quite round, and the grille was a perfectly proportioned ovoid with delicate concave vertical bars. Lovely. The Maserati body was smooth and efficient, with none of the add-on fins and ducts and louvers that spoiled the basically good shape of so many Ferraris from the same era. The A6GCS 2000 was the furthest thing possible from a "hairy" sports car. It was delicate, effete even, with a softly delineated line that was natural and right without looking at all contrived.

Happily enough, the A6GCS 2000 not only looked good but went well, too. The factory at that point had Moss, Fangio, Behra, Musso, and Salvadori in the sports cars at various times, depending upon who had a better ride for Mercedes that week, and they got a fair stack of class wins in the Mille Miglia and Targa Florio. Musso even captured a third overall in the 1954 Thousand Miles. This wasn't quite in the same league with Nuvolari's 1947 Cisitalia second on 1100cc but was still pretty impressive for 2 liters. Musso was dynamite on a good day, but even he had to have something under him that would go. The little Maserati was definitely head and shoulders above the British Bristol-powered 2-liter cars, and on a given day quicker than the class-dominating Ferraris, too.

Obviously, there aren't very many of these little Maseratis around, and you might have to look for years until you find one. Some *did* come to the States, however, and though they didn't do anything spectacularly memorable in this country, they were well respected and, consequently, well cared for. England is just full of Maseratis, has been since the twenties for some strange reason, and of course they often show up in the paddock if not actually on the track at vintage sports-car meets. Prices are only so-so, like all Maserati prices, and a competitive A6GCS shouldn't require more than $15,000 to put into your stable. And of course there's an active club.

To replace the old-fashioned A6, now *retardataire*, Maserati built one of the all-time great sports/racers beginning in 1955. Actually, the only reason Maserati could introduce such a neat sports car was that Gioacchino Colombo had designed the classic 250F Formula One machine for 1954. Colombo was riding high at that point. His prewar Alfa 158/159 totally dominated Formula One from 1947 till '51, and when the postwar Ferraris finally drove the Alfas off the tracks, it quite literally meant the end of Formula One. For two years, the *Grande Epreuve* was tried in 2-liter Formula Two cars, thanks to Colombo and Lampredi. After Colombo left Ferrari and joined Maserati, the old devil delivered yet another spectacular success for the all-new 2.5-liter Formula One.

Colombo's 250F was a safe, sure bet, a straightforward, uncomplicated, viceless new monoposto built strong like the Golden Gate Bridge. Nearly three dozen 250Fs were sold to privateers—an unheard-of number for Formula One machines—and they were simple enough that the private cars—Stirling Moss's Alf Francis–maintained machine, for example—could easily be made as quick and reliable as the factory team cars. The 250F had a heavyweight space frame, wire wheels, drum brakes, a sturdy DeDion rear end with 5-speed transaxle, and a 2.5-liter, double-overhead-cam six punched by Ing. Bellantani and Guerrino Bertocchi out of the old 2-liter A6GCS mill. They got 285 hp running on AGIP fuel that was somewhere between White Light-

ning and JATO packs. On top of it all, the 250F also had the prettiest monoposto body ever put on a racer. Only Mike Costin's later Vanwall approaches it for clean aerodynamics, and then in a passionless, scientific way. The 250F was the last good *intuitive* Formula car, the last one that was right because "it looked right."

Obviously, the 250F was too good to waste just on Grand Prix racing. So the six was bored and stroked to 2991cc, to give 245 hp on pump gas. The space frame was widened through the middle to take the FIA-required passenger seat, and the monoposto body was replaced with a pudgier version of the A6GCS 2000 body that looked like hell. All the beautiful proportions were replaced by awkward, ugly slots and vents. No matter. Aesthetically, the 300/S left a lot to be desired, that's true. But on the track it was unequivocally the best Maserati sports/racer *ever,* so nobody cared very much if it was ugly. It was light, tough, and fast, and it handled. This was not as common as you might expect in the mid-fifties, in the age of flexible frames, wobbly wire wheels, narrow tires, weird suspension geometries, and massive forearms.

Typical of Maserati, they managed to botch up the 300/S too—not the cars, but the racing. In 1955 when the 300/S came out, Mercedes was whipping ass with the 300SL, Jaguar had its D-type, and Ferrari was pretty much nowhere. Maserati was somewhere downstream from Ferrari. They got a few good placings just by having crazy-ass drivers on the team, and then the Pierre Levegh debacle at Le Mans wrecked the rest of the season for everyone. The only good thing that came out of the Le Mans tragedy as far as the Italians were concerned was that Mercedes dropped out of racing again. Which meant normal Italian car builders could go racing without getting their teeth shoved down their throats every weekend by a bunch of Teutonic Supermen.

Of course Maserati blew it again. In '56 they raced the 300/S, which was a good piece. But they also got ambitious. So they decided to go head to head with Ferrari, which, as anyone from Tony Vandervell to Henry Ford Deuce can tell you, is flat dumb. First Bellantani popped the old six out to 3495cc and 275 hp, but that wasn't good enough for Maserati.

Nassau, 1957: Masten Gregory and John Fitch with Fitch's Maserati 200/S.

So they designed a whole new engine, a whopping 4.5-liter, double-overhead-cam V-8. This monster they dropped into a beefed-up 300/S chassis, which, as any fool could tell just by looking, wasn't up to the job. Mostly, even with people like Behra and Moss driving, the 450/S crashed a lot. When it could be kept going in a straight line, it was awesome indeed. But mostly it was simply too much engine and not enough car.

Tony Paravano bought a 450/S for Carroll Shelby to race in SCCA Nationals, where he did pretty well, and in '57, with Fangio and Behra driving, another one won at Sebring. Behra crashed his Mille Miglia car in practice, though, and Moss had the exquisitely ridiculous luck—widely publicized by his riding navigator, Denis Jenkinson—to have his brake pedal fall off after *seven miles* in the Mille Miglia itself. Moss and Jenkinson limped back to Brescia before Bertocchi got his first cup of coffee after the start. Maserati, despite Fangio's '57 Formula One championship, was doing itself great bodily harm. And it got *worse*. After the Mille Miglia fiasco, you'd think nothing more could go wrong. And despite their problems, Maserati was actually

tied up with Ferrari for the Manufacturers' Championship with one race left to run in 1957.

It was pure Monty Python's Flying Circus. The deciding race was in Caracas, Venezuela, of all places, and since only the highest-placed car from each marque gained points, it paid to get as many Masers on the grid as possible, just in case something went wrong . . . went wrong . . . went wrong . . . went . . . Maserati took out a bank loan and built four 450/Ss plus a 300/S. Masten Gregory—who went through racing cars the way normal people go through cigarettes—totaled his. Moss, who was leading, T-boned an A. C., cutting it in half and wrecking *his* 450. Behra's 450/S spontaneously burst into flames during a pit stop, and Bonnier, who had the 300/S, crashed into Schell's 450 while in the lead. Both cars burned to the water line. Maserati did not win the Manufacturers' Championship in 1957.

The only good thing you could say about Maserati after Caracas was that they saved money on air fares by not having any cars left to ship home. In fact, old sourpuss Omer Orsi failed to see the humor in the situation at all. In dollars the loss would have been mas-

El Chueco, the old master himself, Juan Manuel Fangio, on his way to winning the 12 Hours of Sebring in 1

sive, but in lire poor Orsi must have needed his whole accounting department to total up his tax loss. It's not every man who can lose the world championship and 50 quadrillion lire in one afternoon and pretend nothing's happened. Orsi didn't even try to pretend. Maserati's race department was disbanded even before they got off the tramp steamer from South America. Which was no more than they deserved, I promise you.

Orsi was vindictive but greedy, so in return for tons of money, Bertocchi was allowed to try one last racing car. Stirling Moss drove the first one at Rouen in 1959 and won, too. That was better than the old days, at least. This new Maser was built to fit the 3-liter sports/racing limit that had gone into effect almost as soon as the 4.5-liter Masers crashed. The new car was actually the logical summation of Maserati development in the fifties and the swan song of the front-engine sports/racer. And it was even better than that.

Back in 1955, along with the successful 300/S, there had been a pair of abortive small-bore racers—abortive even by Maserati standards—created by cutting two cylinders off the 250F six. There was a 1486cc four and also a 1994cc version. In 1959, Bertocchi took the four, bored it out once again to 2888cc, and stuck it in an all-new, ultralightweight space-frame chassis that had so many little tubes running around that it instantly became known as the Birdcage. Ah yes, the famous Birdcage Maserati. Visions of Jim Hall at Riverside, Roger Penske at the Bridge, Lucky Casner at Nurburgring. You see, for some reason, the Birdcage Maserati was one of those happy designs that *worked*. For no apparent reason, it was miles and away better than the competition. The Birdcage was easily the best car Maserati ever built, even better, judged against its peers, than the fabled A6GCS 2000 and the 300/S.

What makes a legend? Well, the Tipo 60—which was the official name of the 2-liter Birdcage—and the Tipo 61—the 3-liter version—were the only lasting results of Lucky Casner's marvelous Camoradi team, one of the few successful race teams ever to make it on public relations alone. Casner was crazy, but it worked. He was a Cadillac dealer from Florida, and in 1958 he decided that what America

with his new and brutal Maserati 300/S.

really needed was its own blue-and-white team to contest the Manufacturers' Championship. And what Maserati needed was a financial angel to get Bertocchi out of Orsi's hair and back in the race shop.

Casner and Omer Orsi made a deal, pretty much the same arrangement Scuderia Ferrari had with Alfa Romeo in the thirties or David Murray's Ecurie Ecosse had with Jaguar in the fifties. Just like that, Casner Motor Racing Division became the Maserati factory race team. Of course, at that point there were no Maserati factory racers, but that was just a minor inconvenience. There was no Casner Motor Racing Division, either. Bertocchi and Ing. Alfieri grabbed up the old fours and a few thousand yards of high-tensile steel tubing and the rest, as they say, is history.

Casner was some talker. Once he had Maserati, he got Goodyear. Camoradi was the official Goodyear road racing team, with factory technicians, kilodollar tractor trailers, and all the accoutrements of success. Before he'd ever entered a race, Casner signed Stirling Moss, Dan Gurney, Carroll Shelby, Jo Bonnier, Masten Gregory, and everybody ex-

cept Mom Unser and Linda Vaughn to grace the seats of Birdcage Maseratis. It was incredible. Back in 1960 you could buy Stirling Moss for two or three grand a race, and Casner bought by the barrelful. Camoradi would enter eight or ten cars in a weekend, and in 1959 at Havana race week, for example, won *every* race and *every* class.

The heart of Camoradi was the Birdcage Maser, though. And a lot of other independent drivers—particularly in the United States—bought them too. In all, Orsi sold twenty-one Tipo 60/61s, which, when you realize that the engines alone cost nearly $6,000 in 1960, is going some. The cars had four-wheel Girling disc brakes, 5-speed transaxles, and DeDion rears. And they were quick. The top speed wasn't as good as the Lotus, Ferrari, Cooper, and Porsche competition, but the Birdcages had superb acceleration and excellent handling. Zero to 100 was claimed in 11 seconds, with a top speed of 170 mph for the 3-liter cars. This was more than competitive. The Birdcage, particularly after Moss's winning debut at Rouen, was the object of great expectations.

Typical Maserati, it all evaporated. The Birdcage Maserati is one of the best Masers ever. It was the acknowledged class of the Manufacturers' Championship in '60 and '61. Casner had the world's best drivers—no bullshit—all under contract and more money than God. And total, over two and a half years,

Moss tries the first Tipo 60 at Modena, 1959.

The most successful Tipo 61, driven by Gaston Andrey, won an SCCA championship in 1960.

there were precisely *two* Birdcage Maserati wins on the international level. Moss/Gurney won the Nurburgring 1000 in 1960; Gregory and Casner won the same race the following year. Briggs Cunningham got a Birdcage into eighth overall at Le Mans, and Gaston Andrey won the '60 SCCA national championship. Roger Penske got the same championship with his Birdcage in '61. And that was it: two international race wins, and two national championships.

Now understand, lots of manufacturers would kill for that record. But somehow, everyone expected more. Despite its legendary reputation, the Birdcage Maserati was a disappointment to all concerned. Camoradi either led or set fastest lap in *every* race they entered in 1960. But with the high-priced talent they had hanging around, well . . . they should have. But the cars inevitably broke, particularly the 5-speed transaxle and De-Dion tubes. Casner's crew was obviously way overextended, the cars were never properly prepared, and the money well ran dry at the end of 1961. The Birdcage died in favor of a series of ill-conceived mid-engine Maserati racers, none of which accomplished anything. Casner was reduced to bumming rides from other people, eventually getting himself killed practicing for Le Mans in '65 in a clapped-out Maserati coupe he borrowed from John Simone.

The Maserati racing department pretty much went away after the Birdcage. Sure, they continued building one car a year for Le Mans, big ugly things that never lasted more than a few hours, when they managed to make the race at all. But that was just death throes. Maserati had long been through as a force on the race tracks. But they had had their moments and built some fabulous cars. Incredibly enough, out of the twenty-one Birdcages built, nineteen survive. They cost over $30,000 now, and the price is climbing rapidly. But despite the high price and dubious race record, the Tipo 60/61s are honestly just about as neat as any Testa Rossa or D-Jag. Sure, Maserati is invisible. Sure, a lot of their cars are bombs. But the A6GCS 2000, the 300/S, and the Tipo 61 Birdcage are so good that they make up for all those other terrible mistakes. Any normal car company would be memorable if they'd built just one of these cars. Except invisible Maserati.

Officine Specializate Construzione Automobili Fratelli Maserati was the menopause plaything of the last three Maserati brothers. In 1937 they'd sold the Maserati name to the Orsi family, moved to Modena, and signed a ten-year contract. But after the war, young Omer Orsi was given his choice of family businesses. Not surprisingly, he chose racing cars over investment banking. Orsi was relatively smart, all things considered. He realized that the only way Maserati could make any money out of racing was to start selling street machines with the same prestigious name, so he started pushing for big GTs. General manager Bertocchi sided with Orsi.

Ernesto, Bindo, and Ettore Maserati, however, were racers. Period. They were not interested in making fancy coupes for the courtesans of Rome and the *maricónes* of Madrid. So they told Orsi to stuff his GT coupes and moved back to Bologna where they'd started out. On December 1, 1947, they incorporated OSCA in the same tiny factory they'd used before Orsi moved them to Modena . . . and went back to their first love, voiturette racing. Maseratis were always more successful in the under-2-liter classes, even when they were called OSCAs.

The Fratelli Maserati built a forgettable sports car for the postwar 1100cc class, but the Cisitalias and Gordinis blew their doors off. So they built a huge 4.5-liter V-12 engine that could be swapped into the old Maserati 4CLT chassis for people who wanted to race in the new Formula One with old cars. Needless to say, that wasn't such a good idea, either. Then they built a whole new car to go with the big V-12, but the CSI changed the Grand Prix formula and that was that. The Maserati brothers were in full flail and rapidly getting nowhere fast.

Happily enough, they still knew how to make little sports/racers. These were overweight and old-fashioned, but then so were the Maserati brothers. But both brothers and cars were dependable. Using the same basic double-overhead-cam engine, in 750, 1100, and 1500cc versions, the Fratelli built a veritable fleet of little racers. They all had simple ladder frames with big tubular side rails, rigid rear axles on leaf springs, wire wheels, and simply styled roadster bodies built by Morelli of Ferrara. Over the years the rear suspension was switched to coils, the wire wheels turned into cast alloy, the engines were reworked in

a minor way, and the bodies were changed to imitate the evolving aerodynamics of Ferraris. But for the most part the OSCAs never changed.

No reason to, actually. In 1954 Stirling Moss and Bill Lloyd won Sebring outright in a 1500cc car, averaging 73.6 mph. And in 1960 John Bentley and Jack Gordon won the Sebring Index of Performance in a 750cc version that averaged 73.46 mph. Those cars, despite the difference in displacement, were nearly as identical as their lap times. Over that period, of course, sports-car racing changed dramatically. It made no difference at OSCA. They knew what they wanted to build and how to build it, and that was that. There was no fooling around with independent rear ends, disc brakes, or other such modern nonsense for Fratelli Maserati.

Of course, with a production area the size of your carport, OSCA couldn't really afford to screw around. They had to get it right the first time, then develop the hell out of it over the years. You can think of the entire OSCA production as merely variations on a theme. It even makes very little difference when any particular car was built—1950 or 1960—or what size engine it has. No matter which engine, the performance is more than enough to bring a smile to your lips and a tingle to your tongue. The 1500s just go a little faster a little quicker, that's all.

Obviously, OSCA never built very many cars. And most of the later ones—some early Formula Juniors, some Fiat-based GTs—were pretty forgettable. As they got older, the Maseratis tapered off, and finally, in 1963, they sold the whole shebang to Count Agusta of Meccanica Verghera, makers of MV-Agusta motorcycles and helicopters. MV diddled around for a couple of years, but in 1967 they closed up shop and killed the OSCA name for good. Just as Omer Orsi had found two decades earlier, a Maserati company with no Maseratis isn't worth the powder to blow it up. You either have to build yourself a whole new empire or let the thing die. Officine Alfieri Maserati SpA met the first fate, OSCA Fratelli Maserati the second. Who can say which was kinder?

In any case, the little OSCAs from the mid-fifties are some of the nicest small-bore sports/racers ever built. They're not as fa-

The classic style of the Fratelli Maserati, this is Phil Stewart's 1452cc OSCA with body by Morelli of Ferrara, a

mous as Colin Chapman's Lotus Elevens and Fifteens, for the simple reason that they weren't as successful, nor were they anywhere near as prolific. Plus, OSCAs were always frightfully expensive. But if you like miniatures, they're really fun. For example, in 1952/ '53, the little OSCA roadster was almost line for line a copy of Touring's Ferrari Barchetta (quarter-scale, of course). And around the same time there was a wonderful 1.5-liter Morelli-bodied coupe that was the spitting image of Vignale's Ferrari 250 Mille Miglia berlinetta.

Examples of both are in the States today, for the simple reason that quite a few American drivers grabbed OSCAs for early SCCA events. Al Garthwaite had one, as did Phil Stewart and a handful of others. In an era when wealthy young amateurs raced with the SCCA—and didn't like to go *too* fast—there was a ready market for expensive cars that didn't go very fast either. In the early fifties, little OSCAs had it made with the stringback glove types. Later on, if you wanted to go slow, you went production racing, and if you wanted a small modified sports/racer, you went to Colin Chapman, not Bologna.

Still, for $7,000 or so—half the price of one new—you can find nice little OSCAs, most of them restored, squatting in heated garages just waiting for you to stop by and rescue them from oblivion. Dollar for dollar, they're outrageously expensive for the performance involved, and I hate to think what it would cost to fix a broken one. On the other hand, OSCA has always had an inviolable cachet in certain circles and they *were* built by the Maserati brothers, after all. That has to be worth something, even if by the time Ettore, Ernesto, and Bindo got around to forming OSCA, the Fratelli Maserati were a lot closer to Harpo, Groucho, and Chico than to Fred and Augie Duesenberg.

Alfa Romeo

God. Alfa Romeo. In the twenties and thirties, in the golden age, Alfa was *it*. Vittorio Jano was there, and Gioacchino Colombo, and Enzo

atkins Glen in 1954.

Ferrari, designing and building the wildest racing cars anyone had *ever* seen. And the street machines—the 1750s and 2900Bs—were winners the day they left the factory. Alfa, right up until 1951 when the factory retired its incendiary 158/159 GP cars, was indisputably one of the Grand Marques. After that, though, there was only one Italian name that meant what Alfa used to mean . . . Ferrari . . . ironically enough, the product of Enzo Ferrari, Gioacchino Colombo, and Vittorio Jano. The state-owned Alfa works contented themselves with little sedans, tiny coupes, and an occasional tentative foray into racing. Sad to see old friends die.

But out of the postwar malaise of Alfa Romeo, there have actually come some pretty good cars. Alfa got into production as soon as the war stopped, with a rebodied version of the old bread-and-butter 2500 six. But the 2500 was a car remarkably out of step with the times, an expensive, sophisticated relic of the opulent thirties. The old 2500 actually remained on the books until 1953, but in 1950 its replacement was already on the dealer's shelves.

The little Alfa 1900 was all-new, with a nice 1884cc, double-overhead-cam four rated at 80 hp. This went into a unit-body sedan that looked like a breadbox, but also into a separate model with a conventional ladder-type frame, independent front suspension, huge drum brakes, and Borrani knock-off wheels. The 1900 Sprint, as it was called, was the last Alfa supplied in bulk to carrozzeria for custom bodies. The 1900, then, is the real transition piece between the big prewar coachbuilt Alfas and the little mass-production postwar cars, having in some ways the best of each. The 1900 stayed in production until 1958, and some 20,000 were built . . . nearly as many as all the prewar Alfas put together.

Only a small percentage of these 1900s were Sprints or Super Sprints, of course, and these are the only two models worth having. The Sprint is the 1884cc version; the Super Sprint had a slightly bored-out 1975cc. Most of them were extremely smooth coupes with bodies by Bertone, Pininfarina, Castagna, and Vignale, and all of them bear an unmistakable similarity to Volkswagen's Karmann Ghia. Remember those stick-on triangular grilles they used to sell for Karmann Ghias? Well, that's what the Alfa 1900s look like, K-Gs with a modernized version of the classic Alfa grille.

Modern as it was in 1950, the 1900 has that pseudo-vintage feel, something like a DB-6 Aston Martin. The outside says 1970, but the inside says 1930. Alfas are like that. The steering is precise but stiff. The handling is quick, but the roadholding limits are actually not very high. And the little four, though it's smooth and peppy, sounds like it's working too much. Unlike some small cars from the early fifties—Porsches, Lancia B.20s, 3-liter Ferraris—which still feel perfectly modern, the Alfa 1900s show their age. That's not bad, necessarily, for these Alfas *look* modern enough, they go acceptably well, and considering their scarcity, the price is right. Around $3,000 would be enough to pay for a decent 1900 Sprint.

From 1958 till '67 there was a much more distinctive Alfa available that didn't look like anything else, not even another Alfa. Built on the Giulietta/Giulia chassis, in either 1290cc or 1570cc form, the Bertone-bodied Sprint Speciale is one of the wildest coupes *ever* put into production. Some people think it's the best-looking Italian car ever: fleet, smooth, and delicate. A lot of others, myself included, think it's pretty effeminate in a derogatory sense. The curvaceous aluminum body is just so . . . well, *precious* doesn't even begin to say it, that it turns people off. On the other hand, the Sprint Speciale *is* exquisitely worked out, thoughtful to the point of cleverness, with a strident surface development that's as sophisticated as that on any car I've ever seen. Like most works of art, it evokes strong feelings. You either love it or hate it; there's not much middle ground. You can think of it as a late-fifties bit of Helen Frankenthaler Abstract Expressionism. If you like that sort of thing, you'll never get enough of it, and if you don't like it, it will positively set your teeth on edge.

Unlike the 1900, the SS is a real car. The chassis isn't all *that* different from the cars Alfa was selling up till last year. And the performance is outstanding. From only 95 cubic inches, pre–smog controls, you get 129 hp, which is going some, even with a big Weber carb and two camshafts. A typical Alfa 5-speed sits behind this four, and though the rear axle is rigid, there's a whole panoply of trailing arms and links to keep it located. Front disc brakes and Pirelli radials gave *Road & Track* better than .8G braking in their road test, and they called these brakes "among the best we have tested." *R & T* also got a top speed of 112, 0 to 60 in 12 seconds, and 20 mpg. And except for a too-low roof, they even liked the interior packaging. At $4,961 in 1966, they thought it was a great bargain.

I hate to admit it, but this same *R & T* road test sums up the Sprint Speciale as well as anyone could. "It is a unique, controversial machine. . . it has beauty, performance, handling, mechanical interest, personality, class . . . it has everything. Our conclusion then, is that the Sprint Speciale will not attract everyman, but that its owners will regard it as an exquisite jewel beyond comparison or price." Well. What more can you say, except that to find one now will cost at least $5,000. But as the man said, if it turns you on, it's a bargain at any price.

Everybody has his albatross, that perfect idea that's so perfect it hangs around and hangs around until finally you *do* something about it, just to get it out of your mind. And it turns out that all those years of hanging around have sucked the life out of your perfect idea . . . and there you are, stuck with a dead bird. Alfa Romeo's albatross was the Giulia TZ, better known as the GTZ. They started thinking about it in 1959 or so, they had prototypes in 1962, but it was the end of 1963 before it appeared. All this seems reasonable enough, except that the GTZ was a racing car meant to challenge Porsche's Carrera coupes. But by the time it finally appeared on a race track, Porsche had the 904. Alfa drivers were struggling to whip the Lotus Elans in the 1600cc production class, when the 904s were going head to head with Cobras and Ferraris. In other words, a classic example of too little, too late.

Alfa had to build 100 in order to get them homologated. And 100 there are—no more, no less—minus the usual percentage for crashes, parts cobbling, and a decade and a half of normal wear and tear. So maybe, worldwide, you might have a pool of, say, fifty clapped-out GTZs to choose from now. They are definitely worth the trouble, because though they didn't beat the 904 Porsches, they did beat just about everything else. They are also the only Alfas between the classic 158/159 Grand Prix cars of the late forties and the Type 33 sports/racers of the early seventies that were built from the ground up as competition machines.

This means mostly that the GTZs are about the nicest cars you will ever find to drive. Of *course* they are noisy and rattly and make you feel like a corn kernel in an E-Z-Pop pan—what do you expect from an all-aluminum stripped coupe that weighs only 1,650 pounds? If it rode like a Thunderbird, you wouldn't like that either. No, the GTZ is a real racing car, as direct and purposeful as anything you'll ever encounter. But like at least a few other cars from that same era—Porsche's 904, for example—the GTZ is a real race car that's still street-legal and acceptably civilized to drive on the street. Of course, you'd better be able to call the local constable Uncle John and have him over for chicken and ribs a lot, which is to say that GTZs are about as marginally street-legal as you can get and still carry license plates. But no matter. Any Alfistte who wouldn't trade his mother plus a good Giulietta for a GTZ just isn't all that serious about cars.

The GTZ is a textbook study on how to

Alfa Romeo's transitional model of the early fifties, the Castagna-bodied 1900 C Sprint.

The basis for Alfa's postwar line was the pleasant little Bertone-bodied Giulietta of 1954.

design a small-bore, front-engine racer, circa
1960. In other words, the very last gasp of the
front-engine design just before it was super-
seded by mid-engine contenders such as the
904. So the GTZ is really a summing up, the
last glorious fireworks display of the front-engine era. Just reading the spec pages, even
fifteen years after the fact, is a technological
treat. You can just imagine how excited all
those Italians were when they presented this
albatross to the world.

It looked so good on paper: a multitubular
space frame, made up of a zillion little small-
diameter tubes just like the Birdcage Maserati
and all those other status sports/racers. A
short 87-inch wheelbase, for great response.
A fabricated independent front suspension—
lightweight tubes welded into upper and
lower A-arms—with coil springs, tubular
shocks, and radius rods. And an antiroll bar,
of course. And disc brakes. At the rear, a total
departure from typical Alfa practice. An
independent rear suspension, built just like
any Lotus with Chapman Struts, lower A-
arms, and coil springs. And inboard disc
brakes tucked next to the differential. All in
all, a wonderfully advanced chassis complete
with knock-off alloy wheels, racing Dunlop
tires, and super-tight steering. A chassis to
make an Italian engineer weep.

Where the GTZs fell down was in the engine compartment. Now nothing serious, you
understand, just that two seconds a lap by
which the Porsches could absolutely devas-
tate them. The standard GTZ engine was the
129-hp version of the tried-and-true 1570cc,
double-overhead-cam four from the Giulietta
that's just about the only engine Alfa has ever
had, seems like. In other words, basically the
same engine as in any street Alfa, right up
until the present day.

That's great if you're restoring a GTZ. All
the parts are just standard stuff, right out of
the box. There was a 175-hp version built by
Conrero the Tuner, and of course that's the
one the factory raced. Being basically conservative myself, I'd opt for the standard mill
or, even better, being no purist, for a late-
model engine from the 1750 or 2000, suitably
desmogged. With the proper bits, you could
get 200 hp and solve all the problems that sent
the GTZs down in flames so long ago.

The gearbox is straight Alfa 5-speed, the

Alfa Romeo 1570cc Giulia Sprint Speciale with custom

An albatross on the track but a superb road car, Alfa's

body by Bertone; a precious, effeminate jewel.

1963 aerodynamic, Zagato-bodied GTZ.

same one they've been using since time began, so that's no problem. And the rest of the car is equally straightforward: a totally stripped interior with a couple of plain bucket seats, a few gauges, and a nice little Nardi wheel. Typical Italian sports/racer. And the body, too. One of *the* most aerodynamic coupe bodies ever built, from the famous house of Zagato—that's why it's GTZ, get it?—looking more than a little like a cross between a shrunken version of Pete Brock's Shelby Cobra Daytona Coupe and one of Zagato's own Fiat-Abarths. A smooth, truncated nose and covered headlights. Only 45 inches high at the top of the rounded roof. A perfect Kamm tail with nearly horizontal roof line. A totally useless rear window and sliver quarter-windows. And that was it. A perfect, aerodynamic coupe, in other words, obviously just out of the wind tunnel. And only 150 inches long.

And it works. Top speed with a stock engine is about 150 mph, 0 to 60 takes 9 seconds, 0 to 100 about 17. This is extremely good for 1600cc, even today. And the Alfa GTZ is extremely good, even today. Compared with almost any other small-bore machine around, it handles better . . . perfect 50/50 weight distribution, a sophisticated suspension, huge disc brakes. And more car in an unassuming package you'll never find. They're rare and consequently expensive, but a lot of people think the GTZ is the neatest Alfa ever. A lot of other people just look at the race record, which was zilch, and dismiss them as Alfa's albatross, the car they'd most like to forget. That's not fair, of course. Granted, the GTZ *is* Alfa Romeo's albatross, a monumental failure, but it wasn't the car's fault. The GTZ was clearly better than the cars it was designed to beat. It's just that by the time Alfa finally drew a bead and fired, the target had shifted.

Easily the best postwar Alfa street machine—and this time everyone agrees—is the Gran Turismo Veloce, the fabulous GTV. Everything about it is just right. Among other experts, Formula One stalwart Rob Walker—who can afford any car he wants—drove a series of GTVs for many years. He may still have one tucked away, for that matter. The GTV chassis was based on the Giulietta, which made it not *that* much different from any previous Alfa. The engine started out as the same 1570cc, 122-hp engine used in the Giulia—and

Everybody's favorite Alfa, the marvelous Gran Turismo Veloce styled by Giorgetto Giugiaro.

Sprint Speciale, too—with the traditional Alfa all-synchro 5-speed. Later, in 1967, it grew up to 1750cc along with the rest of the Alfa line, and later still to a full 2000cc. But from 1965 till 1975 there was no significant change in the car at all, and the increasing engine size was mostly to counteract the effects of additional pollution controls.

The chassis of the GTV was excellent, granted. But the body was even better. The GTV was one of the very first designs by the youthful stylist Giorgetto Giugiaro, then working for Nuccio Bertone. In just about all ways it's a lovely design, easily masking the fact that it's only 161 inches long on a 94-inch wheelbase. There's plenty of headroom, reasonable glass area, a comfortable seating position . . . and some of the tightest, finest styling on any production sports car. Giugiaro kept more than a hint of the old Giulietta/Giulia but rephrased it in a much more modern idiom. The GTV was almost completely free from chrome trim when it appeared, and unlike most other clean-limbed designs, it wasn't gunked up over the decade of production. The last cars are just as nice looking as the first.

GTVs even made dynamite race cars, curiously enough in sedan racing. Back in the mid-sixties, the same interior height measurement that allowed the Porsche 911 coupe to race as a sedan let the Alfas in, too. The factory even catalogued the GTA sedan as a separate model, and this car won the under-2-liter Trans-Am in 1966 and '70. Socialite Harry Theodoracopulos stuck with Alfas longer than almost anybody, but his best season was '69 when he won SCCA C-sedan. In European saloon car racing, the GTAs won the Touring Car Championship in '66 and '67, and also the hillclimb championship for their class in 1967. For most of the time, however, the GTV/GTAs had to run against Porsche 911s, Ford Escorts, and Capris. All things considered, they did remarkably well, making the GTV/GTA one of the last great Italian small-bore all-rounders.

The problem with the GTV—or any Alfa, for that matter—is that they're made by Alfa Romeo. I've an acquaintance who sold his old Ferrari about four years ago and bought a brand-new GTV. This guy is a fanatic, driving gently and maintaining the car perfectly. After about three years, he finally had the nerve to add up what he'd spent. He was floored to find that between the rebuilt engine, new transmission, necessary paint job, etc., etc., he'd spent more than the $4,995 price of the car just in repairs. His cost per mile came out to something incredible, like $1.05. Point is, this kind of expenditure is pretty commonplace if you expect to have a decent-looking Alfa. And despite what they do at the factory, it never seems to get any better. After decades of complaints about Italian electrics, all the important electrical bits in the GTV are Bosch, made in Germany. Doesn't make a bit of difference . . . the spaghetti is still in there.

This can be corrected, of course, admittedly at the cost of a little time and lots of money, and I'm sure for every Alfa horror story there's some guy who hasn't changed the oil in 50,000 miles and never had a bit of trouble. And the GTV really is a delightful car, quick steering and superbly braked, with incredible handling; the sort of car in which you find yourself going thirty miles an hour faster than you intended, just for the sheer joy of it. Up around 80–90 is where the GTV likes to cruise, and it really does feel like you could do it all day. There is an Alfa club of fanatical owners who can't say enough about the cars.

The cars must have something: a certain élan, perhaps, good looks, thoughtful engineering . . . and though Alfa Romeo is no longer a Grand Marque, it has a certain cachet, right up there with Porsche and Jaguar. I don't claim to be a particularly avid Alfa nut. I like driving them a lot; I like looking at them. But I don't trust them for a second, and I don't think I could ever in good faith own one, no matter how much fun they are. I just think about those mountainous repair bills and know I've made the right decision. On the other hand, I sure wouldn't mind having a nice, snug little GTV coupe for rainy mornings, when nothing else would be quite right for going out and playing in the slick, wet leaves. And then, yes, I guess I can understand the Alfa mystique, if only for hours at a time.

Car people are maybe the most impractical schemers in the world. Take Wilfredo Ricart,

for example. He was your basic crazy Spaniard, and though he was already on the other side of middle age after World War II, the Franco government put him in charge of a new truck works (ENASA) quartered in Hispano-Suiza's old factory in Barcelona. Ricart had a particularly undistinguished career in the minuscule Spanish motor industry, but he was one of the few people who'd ever gotten out—to Alfa Romeo in the late thirties and during the war. Enzo Ferrari supposedly hated him on sight, and one of the reasons Scuderia Ferrari dissolved was that Ricart had started designing the race cars. Significantly, none of Ricart's racers ever raced.

Still, he had a pretty good background in trucks. The new ENASA factory was created for the dual purpose of making all-Spanish trucks and also acting as an apprentice school to train craftsmen for a renaissance of Spain's moribund car industry. So Ricart, who'd just been building racing cars, started on trucks. If they wanted trucks, he'd damn well build trucks. In 1946 they built 38; in 1947 and '48, 100; in 1949, a whopping 169.

But there was nothing glamorous about diesel trucks, and if the ENASA school was going to become a government favorite it had to attract attention. Besides which Ricart was just full to the brim with all these great racing ideas he couldn't wait to try. So he convinced the Franco bureaucrats that just what Spain needed was a prestigious, damn-the-costs GT car to shine up her reputation in the world car market. With their new GT successfully attracting attention, they could go looking for investors and engineers and presto! . . . a revitalized Spanish car industry.

Life should be so simple. Anyway, in the summer of 1950 Ricart and his students started drawing up a super-original sports car they named for Pegasus, *caballo volador*. The flying horse was a truly appropriate symbol for a high-performance GT. Because Ricart wanted to design a tour de force—and had basically an unlimited budget—he gave it every trick in the book. The engine was a dry-sump, all-aluminum V-8 with four double overhead cams (*gear-driven* overhead cams, at that). The whole engine weighed less than 400 pounds, complete with four dual-throat Webers. The first engines were only 2.5 liters, but later on there were some that went 4.0, 4.5, and a full 4.7 liters. But ninety-nine out of a hundred Pegaso V-8s were either 2.8 liter, 210 hp, or 3.2 liter, 280 hp, which was plenty. Remember, this was in the early fifties, when 200 hp was a big deal, even for 5.5-liter Cadillacs. To go with this fancy engine there was even an optional supercharger—Roots-type— for going very fast for not very long. Only a couple of speed-record cars got the blower, though it was catalogued for anybody who wanted one. Indeed, you could even order a double supercharger, if you really wanted a nickel rocket.

To handle all this power the Pegaso had an equally fancy chassis. The wheelbase was only 91.5 inches; the chassis was a pressed-steel platform. This was fairly unusual—if not downright weird—among high-performance street machines. At the front, the frame was carried on parallel A-arms, suspended on torsion bars and shock absorbers made by ENASA. At the rear there was a full DeDion axle with radius rods and transverse torsion bars. Even better, the DeDion axle incorporated a 5-speed transaxle, with the gearbox hung off the rear. This was a constant-mesh setup, like most motorcycle transmissions, and featured a separate oil pump and cooler. The brakes were big drums, unfortunately inadequate for the car's incredible performance. Around town they were fine, but Ricart never did get them sorted out enough to bring on a race course without scaring everyone in sight.

Overall the Pegaso Z-102, as it was called, had—and still has, for that matter—just about the most intriguing specifications page ever drawn out for a front-engine, strictly street GT. And remember, this was back in the era when Ferrari was still using transverse leaf springs and rigid rear axles, nobody had more than four speeds forward, and even Jaguar was still years away from a DeDion independent rear suspension. And in 1950, disc brakes were still something that came only on big airplanes.

The crazy Pegaso, then, pride of Barcelona, turned out to be a genuine spit-in-their-eye masterpiece, Ricart's revenge for all those nasty things Ferrari had said about him. And the cars could *go.* The weak brakes kept them away from Le Mans and suchlike, but Celso Fernandez drove one at Jabbeke in 1953, going 151 mph for the flying kilo. And the next year Joaquín Palacio was running second overall in the tough Carrera PanAmericana until he crashed. When they did appear, in other words, the Pegasos went pretty fast. The problems were that, one, the factory had no racing department; two, the cars were too expensive for most private owners to race; and three, cars and spares were both hopelessly rare.

The total production of Pegasos was a whopping 125, and that's over a seven-year period. Understandably, most of them were built to order, usually either for Spanish officials or wealthy Spanish-speaking enthusiasts in Mexico or the Dominican Republic. Since the Barcelona plant had only one work area, the cars were assembled off in the corner next to the trucks and, if the truth be known, were eventually more trouble than they were worth. ENASA surely lost money on each one.

Pegasos were never cheap. Only chassis were built in Barcelona; they cost over $7,500 in the early fifties. By the time they were shipped to coachbuilders in France or Italy to be bodied, the average Pegaso ended up costing around $15,000. Eventually, José Serra started building Pegaso bodies in Spain, which was a lot cheaper, but there was still no way to buy a Pegaso from the factory and get change from a $10,000 bill.

For some reason, most of the bodies that ended up on Pegasos were Saoutchik abominations, some of the worst panelbeating ever to come out of that flamboyant coachbuilder. But there was also a semicatalogued coupe body by Touring that's one of the best postwar designs for any car. It's not as clean as the average Touring Ferrari, but it's a million times better than the Saoutchik junk, and right in line with the best cars of the Italian style. Indeed, the only inharmonious area was the cross-barred grille, and that was cleaned up on the later Touring cars. So by 1955 the Touring-bodied Pegaso Z-102B was one of the best-looking cars in production, available either as a coupe or a roadster, with or without faired headlights. Touring's body, in truth, was equal to Ricart's grand chassis.

Obviously, there aren't many Pegasos left. Out of 125 built, maybe a quarter survive. And most of the best Touring cars are tidily tucked away in Continental collections. There is a weird, Ghia-bodied coupe with a removable

Wilfredo Ricart's tour de force, the Touring-bodied Pegaso Z-102 was rarely raced; Campione, 1955.

plexiglass hardtop called El Dominicano floating around. It was originally built as a show car for Generalissimo Trujillo of the Dominican Republic in 1952, back when his kid owned Ghia. It changed hands in New York last year for $10,000, which I thought was pretty cheap. Of course, the body is nothing to write home about, and it needed a thorough going over. But still, $15,000 ought to be about right for a nice Touring coupe, and you could add a few grand if you find one with a supercharger.

Ricart's Pegaso accomplished some of his goals. It certainly didn't revive the Spanish auto industry, nor make any money. But it must have taught his students something about designing and building to exacting standards, it bolstered the reputation of both Ricart and Spain, it brought a little life back to the old Hispano-Suiza works; and of course it provided one of the few no-holds-barred technological wonders anybody ever earned a chance to build. If you were given a clean sheet of paper today and asked to design the ultimate front-engine sports car, there's a pretty good chance you wouldn't be far off the mark if you laid down Ricart's Pegaso with the addition of disc brakes and a fully inde-

pendent rear suspension, though with today's wider tires even DeDion axles are staging a comeback. So really you can think of the Pegaso as being a dream, easily thirty years ahead of its time. An acknowledged masterpiece, in other words. Don Wilfredo Ricart would have been pleased to know that, though I think he suspected it all along.

Porsche

Of all car enthusiasts, Porsche nuts are generally acknowledged as *the* anal compulsives. There is no such thing as a mere Porsche *owner*. One is either a Porsche fanatic, or . . . invisible. To Porschistte, the whole world is divided into them and us. *No* other car inspires this kind of white gloves blind devotion, not even Bugattis and prewar Alfas, Bentleys, or Ferraris.

The weird thing to me is that standard

Porsches just aren't all *that* good. They're not particularly exciting to drive, all things considered, and though they aren't really *ugly,* they're certainly no more than, well . . . functional—at best. On top of which, for their size they're horrendously overpriced and still lumpen-bourgeois rather than ultraexclusive. On the other hand, Porsches *are* as well made as any machine can be, and for their size the performance *is* remarkable.

Porsches are named, of course, for Dr. Ferdinand Porsche, who, curiously enough, had virtually nothing to do with the Porsche company. Dr. Porsche was one of those late-nineteenth-century self-taught automotive pioneers. At age twenty-five, in 1900, he designed an electric car with drives in the hubs. Then he advanced to a gasoline engine driving a generator to produce electricity for the hub drives—one of the very first hybrid power systems, in other words, the forerunner of a lot of low-pollution concepts being bandied about today. He eventually became the chief designer and managing director of Austro-Daimler. Porsche's first success was the 1910 Prince Henry Trials Austro-Daimler, similar in concept and execution to Pomeroy's great Prince Henry Vauxhall designed for the same speed trials.

In 1923 Porsche went to Daimler in Stuttgart to do the string of Mercedes S, SS, SSK, and SSKL classics, then to Steyr for a few years and into his own independent design firm. As a free lance, Porsche designed the all-conquering Auto-Union GP cars of the thirties and, of course, the Nazi-backed Volkswagen. He also designed the famous Tiger tank and, though he was in his seventies when the war ended, the French arrested him as a major Nazi war criminal. Piero Dusio of Cisitalia ransomed Porsche to design the ill-fated Cisitalia Formula One car, going bankrupt in the process. This left old man Porsche, his son Ferry, daughter Louise Piech, and attendant spouses all at the tiny hamlet of Gmund, Austria, in 1947, rebuilding wrecked VWs and wondering what the hell to do next.

One of these ex-Nazi Volkswagens was reworked into a two-seater roadster with a body like an upended pie pan. This was free-lance project number 356 for Porsche—he started with number 7 so his first client wouldn't realize the long shot he was taking—and so the car was named the Porsche 356. In 1948 das Porschewerk started making VW-based cars in Gmund. In 1950 they moved to Stuttgart and went into limited production . . . with new, not used, VW parts. The early Porsches—hell, *all* 356s, really—are glorified Volkswagens in the same way that Shelby's GT-350s are glorified Mustangs or Abarth's cars are gilded Fiats.

Unlike Shelby and Abarth, however, the Porsche people went to elaborate lengths to camouflage this embarrassing fact. Virtually the entire running gear on 356s is VW . . . with the cast-in Volkswagen emblem and part number ground off and a new Porsche emblem and number stamped on. And of course the price tag bumped up a couple of hundred percent. In the fifties, clandestine mimeographed folders revealing VW equivalents for Porsche part numbers were hot items among Porsche club members. They try not to let on to outsiders, but lots of 356s and Speedsters are running around with $17 Volkswagen steering boxes instead of $80 Porsche boxes. The same goes for Microbus clutches, VW steering arms, half-shafts, and Lord knows what all. Your local Porsche club will still sell you a copy of the equivalency book—only after you pay your dues, of course.

Anyway. Just about the time Porsche started up, Dr. Ferdinand had a heart attack and died in the winter of '52. His son Ferry was a pretty decent engineer-businessman, though, and financed largely by royalties on the Porsche-designed VW Beetle—rumor has it, something like a deutsche mark on each of over 9 million cars—Ferry and Louise Piech started from scratch and built themselves into one of the Grand Marques in less than two decades. Incredible, when you think about it. And not only that, they established one of *the* great free-lance industrial design firms in the world, with clients from all over. And they linked up with VW, logically enough, for distribution and money and sponsorship for new Porsche/VW projects. And not only *that,* but they consistently supported road racing at all levels—SCCA regionals to Formula One—rigorously enough to take up Ferrari's reputation as the unbeatable one.

Really, if Ferry Porsche wasn't such a reclusive, mild-mannered nice guy, he—and Louise's husband Anto, the financial wizard

A 70-hp, 1,800-pound, 90-mph, oversteering bathtub, the beloved 1954 Porsche Speedster.

at Porsche—would be as personally famous as Enzo Ferrari or Henry Ford II. But because the Porsche/Piech family aren't autocrats or socialites, they don't do flamboyant, newsworthy things. There are no good Ferry Porsche anecdotes as far as I know, the way there are Enzo Ferrari tales or Colin Chapman stories. Porsche cars are similarly passionless. Competent, innovative, significant, perhaps, but not soul stirring. Teutonic if you will, though I know that's a terrible cliché. Still, just as Morgans could be only English and Maseratis could only come from Italy, so Porsches are unmistakably Germanic.

Ironically, probably the least Teutonic Porsche ever built is also the most beloved. That could only be the Speedster, because no other Porsche is truly something to *love*. But the Speedster is one of those cars about which it can be said that being a car is secondary to its being a fascinating *personality*. A Speedster is just about the nearest thing to a four-wheeled person since the JAP-engined Morgan Trikes, and those things were missing a wheel anyway. Even more ironical, the lightweight Speedster was built primarily as a price leader to lure impecunious American kids into the closing booths where they could be hooked on a more expensive 356 Coupe instead.

As it turned out, the Speedster was *it* for the rear-engined hordes of the mid-fifties. From late '54 until August of '58, Porsche built 4,825 Speedsters. The early cars were 1498cc flat-fours based on the classic VW design. But from September 1955 on, they used the bored-out 1588cc version from the normal 356 1600. With only a 7.5 : 1 compression ratio and two little Solexes, the Speedster cum VW four puts out a miserly 70 hp at 4,500 rpm, which is more than an MG Midget, but not much. With a 4-speed VW transaxle, a Speedster will go nearly 100 mph downhill, through the quarter-mile at not much more than 70 mph, in not much less than 19 seconds. This isn't even competitive with Sprites, let alone VW Campmobiles.

However. The whole point of a Speedster was to go around corners. The 356 had a unit-body and frame with a relatively tall, albeit very aerodynamic, coupe body. The Speedster has the same chassis, but with the lowest, smoothest, cleanest skin stretched over it. The

whole car weighs only about 1,800 pounds ready to go, and what weight there is, is all down low. And hung behind the rear axle, I will confess. The Speedster has 57 percent of its weight on the rear wheels, which honestly isn't as bad as you might expect. Still, throw one into a tight, third-gear corner and you'll have a concise textbook example for your home-study course in terminal oversteer. If you like oversteering cars—and have the reflexes to keep up with a wagging tail—a Porsche Speedster is one of the all-time great fun cars to drive fast on twisty roads. If you push it, you'll be constantly right on the edge of spinning out backward into the weeds. It's one of the best tune-ups for your nervous system this side of a race track.

As it came from the factory, the Speedster had a few deficiencies. But it was a perfect platform for amateur tuners to experiment with more horsepower, handling aids, and so

Ricardo Rodriguez in his fantastically successful Porsche

on. And for years—I mean, from 1956 till 1978, which is a *very* long time in racing—Speedsters have absolutely ruled SCCA E-production. The engines have gotten hotter and hotter, the wheels have gotten wider and wider, the tires have gotten fatter and fatter, the bodies are now fiberglass replicas. But E-production in this country can still be successfully contested with a curious bathtub of a car with vicious handling developed two decades ago out of a lowly Volkswagen Beetle. Remarkable.

What makes the Speedster work is the same thing that makes the similar Beetle work: simplicity. The Speedster is nothing more than the brilliantly unassuming Volkswagen Beetle with a simple one-piece body, a sad excuse for a top, side curtains, bucket seats, and three rudimentary gauges. About as simple a car as can be imagined, in other words, the very direct forerunner of the VW-based Meyers Manx and all those other simple dune buggies. The Speedster even elicits the same sort of bemused affection dune buggies receive, which suggests that it isn't a *real* car—no heater, no windows, a laughable top, a funny-looking body. But on the other hand, Speedsters cost less than $3,000 new between 1954 and '59; they cost at least $7,000 now. They must be doing something right to somebody.

Of all Porsches, the Speedsters are by far the most revered. Revered, I'd venture, because of that very simplicity that makes them comprehensible to mechanics, racers, and collectors alike. A Turbo Carrera or 917 requires a real Dr. Ing. to get the most out of it; a Speedster merely asks for a basic understanding of high school auto mechanics and a smallish billfold. Happily enough for collectors, though Speedster prices are absurdly high, replacement parts are no farther away than a

50 RSK at Nassau, 1957 . . . mid-engine, aluminum body, 1587cc, double overhead cams.

VW dealer or Bap/Geon store. If the body is rotted you can get one in fiberglass that will look just as good, and there's a simply fantastic amount of Speedster knowledge holed up in the garages of America. Everybody who was anybody in the SCCA owned at least one Speedster at some time in his career. All things considered, it's probably about the cheapest blue-chip collector car around. It may not cost as much as a Ferrari, but the appreciation rate is about the same. And the demand for Speedsters will *always* exceed the supply.

After the Speedster, Porsche got, well . . . serious. And consequently, not so easy to love. No more funny-looking bath-tubby bodies, no more slitlike windshields, no more nonexistent side windows. No more drafty cockpits, even. Well, except for the 550/RS/RSKs. The 550 was Porsche's mid-fifties *real* sports/racer, as opposed to the pseudo-racer Speedster. It was Porsche's equivalent of Ferrari's Testa Rossa and Maserati's A6GCS. And it was, if not better, at least as good. But it was still a Porsche, make no mistake. The body still looked like a flattened pie pan, the engine was still a VW-based flat-four, the wheels were still those funny steel jobs with the big hole in the center to fit over the VW hubs.

But in most other ways, the 550 was different. For starters they threw out the stamped-steel unit body and used a conventional tubular space frame. And while the styling was unabashedly *Porschewerk Funktionell,* it *was* lightweight aluminum. And best of all, like the very first Porsche 356 prototype, the engine/transaxle was turned back to front, which made the 550 a true mid-engined race car at a time when the only other cars with that configuration had 500cc Norton singles and came from Cooper's back garden. The 550s appeared for the Carrera PanAmericana in 1953 and after that, everywhere from Torrey Pines to Nurburgring.

Particularly in the United States, Porsche 550s were the ultimate small-bore giant killers. Ken Miles, Roger Penske, and Bob Holbert were in the habit of almost casually blowing the doors off big Ferraris, Masers, 'Vettes, and V-8-powered Specials. Miles in particular was perfectly capable of winning the under-2-liter preliminary *and* the unlimited main event at Pebble Beach on any given weekend. In the

same car. What was the secret? Only a few hundred pounds separated the 550 from the Speedster and the running gear was much the same. So why was the 550 so much faster?

Engine. Porsche came up with a double-overhead-cam conversion for the 550 that doubled the horsepower, just like that. And putting the engine in the middle of the car gave it just incredible balance without that big weight attached just inside the rear bumper. So the 550 was much faster, like maybe 140 mph, it was much quicker, like maybe 10 pounds per horsepower, and it went around corners a lot better, like maybe a zillion percent. All of which allowed hacks to look good and good drivers to look positively divine.

In 1956 the 550 became the RS, with a 5-speed and a lighter frame. And in 1957, with an all-new suspension, 1587cc, and around 170 hp, it became the RSK. The RSKs were so good that the 1500cc Formula Two/Formula One Porsches of 1959/'60/'61 were really nothing more than single-seater versions of these sports/racers. Fitted out as Formula cars they were less than adequate, so the only time Dan Gurney was able to win with a Porsche was when all the Coopers and Lotuses and BRMs broke. Which was precisely *once* in all the years that Porsche contested F/1. In that league, at least, it takes an incredibly specialized machine to go racing. None of this Cinderella stuff of beating the 4.9 Ferraris with 1500cc and a lot of guts.

But in small-bore sports/racing, the Porsches were virtually unbeatable. Thousands and thousands of races have been won by 550/RS/RSKs, including Maglioli's outright win in the 1956 Targa Florio and fourth at the 'Ring. Porsches were 6–7 at Sebring, and after a slow year in 1957, 3–4–5 overall at Le Mans in '58 and second in the Targa. Barth and Seidel won the Targa Florio in '58, Bonnier-Herrmann repeated in 1960, and Gendebien-Herrmann won Sebring. The list could go on and on, except in 1962 the factory switched from the successful four-cylinder cars to a whole new group of sports/racers designed around the flat-eight Formula One engine that appeared in 1962.

Private owners, of course, continued to race RSKs right up until the mid-sixties. They were virtually unbeatable in the 1.5- and 2.0-

liter classes, mostly because they were comparatively simple, extremely robust, and viceless. These are all not only good qualities for a race car but for a collector car, too. Or for one that you might think about running in vintage car races. And since the race cars—even the F/1 mounts—were based on the production 356, a surprising number of stock Porsche bits either fit or can be made to fit on the 550 series cars, which helps keep the costs and hassles down, too. About the only problem you'll have from a collector's point of view is the same one that plagues Speedster buyers. Because the cars were competitive for so many years, and because they were so easily tweaked, it's almost impossible to find a stock early Porsche racer. Every damn one of them has been updated with later factory parts or aftermarket stuff to prolong its competition life.

Now granted this makes them better cars in many ways. But if you're into the collector car originality bag, there's not much choice but to strip off all these improvements and get back to basics. On the other hand, if you just want to go fast, you can leave all the good stuff on and have a bona fide—if ungenuine—racer. Since changes in the basic specifications were so slow, there's a remarkable degree of parts swapability among Porsche models. I mean, if for some reason you wanted to there's nothing to stop you having a double-overhead-cam RS engine in a Speedster nor, even more far-fetched, anything to stop you running an RSK with 70 hp and pushrods. Mild to wild is all a matter of bolt-on parts, and most of it is easily done, too.

There aren't all that many 550/RS/RSKs around, and that's a fact. Many of them stayed in Europe, which isn't a huge obstacle, but many more were significantly pranged against everything from Sicilian cliffs to Belgian stone walls. Maybe because they were giving away so much horsepower to the big cars, the little Porsches had to be driven right on the limit most of the time. And when you're at the limit, it's only a twitch to cross over it with the greasy side up, off in the bushes. Maybe because of this attrition, maybe because I haven't been looking closely enough, I've seen *very* few early Porsche racers for sale lately. But I know they're out there, hiding. Less than $20,000 ought to be enough to

Jo Bonnier's RS61 at the Targa Florio, 1961.

pay for one, and it really ought to be one of the most exciting small-bore vintage racers you could think about. A definite blueblood, steady as Olivier Gendebien down Mulsanne and guaranteed to be rare and in demand as the years go along. Definitely a reasonable alternative to that clapped-out Testa Rossa or Lotus.

For 1962, the 550/RS/RSK and similar RS60/RS61 prototype Porsches were pretty much eliminated from international racing by a CSI rules change. Porsche's emphasis shifted to GT coupes, particularly a limited production of very pretty little cars designed by Carlo Abarth, similar to his Fiat-Abarths and Simca-Abarths. However, Porsche is nothing if not a company of independent thinkers. And though the Abarth-Porsche ties go all the way back to the Cisitalia GP project, they were never close. So in the fall of 1963, Porsche came out with their *own* GT coupe, built in an edition of 100 to qualify for homologation.

Introducing, Ladeez and Gennelmun, for your driving pleasure, the most exciting Porsche ever built for "street" use. The marvelous, fabulous, stupendous Porsche 904. Indeed. Of course, it was intended as a homologated "production" racing car. The SCCA put it in big-bore A-production, which was purely Cobra country in 1964. Of course, the 904 had only 2 liters to throw up against the 7-liter competition. But it had a lot more besides—more than enough, in fact, to go out and whip ass for *overall* wins at places like the Targa Florio and even—it was a *production* car, remember—to get a second overall in the 1965 Monte Carlo rally. Versatile is hardly the word.

Most amazing, the Porsche 904 is one of the least assuming race cars of the sixties— not particularly complicated, not particularly pretty, not particularly innovative. But like the simple Speedster, the 904 turned out to be much more than the sum of its parts. It was a genuine street/racer classic from the moment it appeared. And so adroitly designed that it eventually took two completely different engine transplants with total sanguinity. Porsche has honestly built nothing before or since as intriguing an all-rounder. Personally, of all Porsches—of *all* Porsches—I like the 904 the best.

Why? Easy. First off, the chassis on the 904 is as straightforward and solid as any ever built. Amazingly, there's no space frame, not even a unit body. Just two great box-section frame rails to tie together front and rear. And at the front, a conventional independent suspension with upper and lower A-arms, anti-roll bar, and disc brakes. At the rear, wide-based wishbones with lower trailing arms, disc brakes, and stubby half-shafts. And of course a midships-mounted engine. The first 904s had the tired old 1966cc, double-overhead-camshaft four rated at 198 hp at 7,200 rpm. Later cars had 1991cc sixes—prototypes of the 911 motor of around 230 hp—or 2200cc versions of the Formula One flat-eight, rated eventually at a heady 270 hp. All three versions bolted up to the same 5-speed transaxle, with the top two gears both overdrives.

Most unusual of all, the 904 was the first Porsche with a fiberglass body. A smooth coupe, it looked a bit like early Ferrari midengine cars, a bit like Ford's contemporary GT-40, a bit like the later Porsche 911. It was designed by Ferry Porsche's son, Ferdinand II, and though it's not one of the grand postwar designs, it *does* have a unique and strikingly individual look. The flying-buttress roof concealing a tiny vertical rear window was a Ferrari trick, and the extravagantly pointed front fenders with plexiglassed headlights were pure Pininfarina, too. Otherwise, it's definitely north-of-the-Alps modern. But one detail on the 904 sums up the whole car. The underbody wraps up from a full belly-pan to end at hub height. And the upper body, cast

At the Targa Florio in 1964, Porsche 904s finished 1-2-6

separately, covers the chassis like a lid. But the edge where the two meet, instead of being smooth, shows a definite lip. The thickness of the fiberglass is allowed to project, to define the utilitarian skin of the car, to show that it does in fact have depth to the body, that the top half really *is* a removable lid. Simple and functional, of course. But also very, very subtle.

Because the chassis bits are basically from the Porsche F/1 car, the 904 would out-handle *anything* in its day. Even now, it's one of the nimblest cars you can buy. And at 161 inches overall, 90-inch wheelbase, one of the smallest. It's only 42 inches high, as well, just a dot taller than Ford's truncated GT-40, the all-time chop-top champ. So, yes, the 904 (given that it's a nearly fifteen-year-old design) handles remarkably well. But not only will it outhandle most newer cars, it will also handily outrun them.

his is the Balzarini/Linge car, helping prove that the 904 is one of the greatest cars of all time.

The unassuming Carrera motor in the 904, with a tall 4.4 : 1 differential, not only recorded an honest 160 mph for *Car and Driver* in 1964 but also got off a blitzen quarter-mile in only 14.2 seconds at a whisker under 109 mph. Which, friends, I don't have to tell you, is faster than almost any street machine of any size. Ever. Right up there in Cobra/ZL-1 Corvette/Lamborghini/Ferrari 365 Daytona country. And that's on just 2 liters, geared for an impossibly high top speed. And with just the cooking, four-cylinder motor, besides. The later eight added another 100 hp, without bouncing the 1,500-pound total weight up one ounce. So the 904/8 will outperform nearly any car ever built, all on 2200cc.

Notice that the standards of comparison for the 904 are ultimate ones. One doesn't compare it with Lotus Europas, Ferrari Dinos, and other small-bore mid-engine street machines. The 904 is just simply miles away, up

in a whole higher performance league. On just 2 liters, the 904 is one of the fastest street cars of all time, certainly faster than the pricy 5-liter Ford GT-40, in a similar streamlined package.

Best of all, the Porsche 904 cost only $7,425 in 1964. Astounding. There was only one car with comparable performance that was cheaper, and it was made by Carroll Shelby. But even a Cobra wasn't as fast around something like the Targa Florio's insanely twisty circuit, nor around Nurburgring either. It was all brute force compared to the Porsche's finesse. The 904 was honestly the only 2-liter production car of its era—hell, of any era—capable of getting around the Ring under the magic eight-minute mark, and at a bargain-basement price, besides.

Dozens of 904 Porsches still exist, many of them in perfect shape. They've always been popular, always well-regarded, and nearly always owned by Porsche fanatics who've taken exceptional care of them. Prices are hovering in the $25,000 range, which, compared with $18,000 for a mild-mannered new 911, isn't bad at all. Of all Porsches, the 904s are the neatest street-legal machines ever, miles and away more exciting than the Speedster, capable of Turbo-Carrera performance on an unblown 2 liters. Really, quite a remarkable car . . . the best Porsche *ever* built.

The Porsche to end all Porsches, of course, is the 917. Exactly forty-six 917s were built. Total. A few of them were immediately reduced to expensive junk, more have been left to deteriorate, a handful still belong to the factory. But most of them are securely in private hands. Vasek Polak has a bunch—four or five as this is written—and John Wyer has a couple. And there are others. I wouldn't expect to see one appear on the open market, even in *Autoweek,* but if you know the right people and have the bucks, you too can have your very own 240-mph Le Mans winner, or turbocharged Can-Am car. Take your choice.

Now for your ninety grand or whatever—more like a hundred thousand, really—you'll have maybe the ultimate racing car built up until this point. What precisely you're going to *do* with it, I've no idea. The 917 is about as far as you can get from the old dual-purpose C-Jag drive-'em-to-Le Mans days. Still, a 917 Porsche has to be the ultimate mantelpiece racer, a totally unusable six-figure extravagance that ranks right up there with that little Monet water lily sketch you've always coveted or that half of an Olin Stephens offshore racer your partner keeps offering you. I mean, really, if you sit down and think about it, there are *lots* of dumber things to spend $90,000 on than an obsolete racing car. I can't really think of one right now, but give me a minute.

The 917 grew, logically enough, out of Porsche's earlier endurance racers. There was the wonderful 904, and the derivative 906, 908, and 910. All these were really just variations on the 1962 Porsche flat-eight Formula One car. Eventually, this engine grew up into a 3-liter eight, so it was no big deal at all to add four more cylinders to get a 4.5-liter flat-12. This finally went out to 4999cc for the 5-liter FIA Group 4 and to 5022cc or 5390cc for the unlimited Can-Am. With fuel injectors, it made 520 hp at 8,000 rpm, 665 hp at 8,300 for

Mark Donohue's all-conquering Porsche 917-30 of 1973, t

the 5.4-liter version, and with the twin turbochargers of the famous Penske-Donohue 917-10s, some 900 hp and 650 lbs./ft. of torque. In other words, more horsepower than any road-racing car *ever*. And that's including the supercharged prewar Mercedes and Auto-Unions, Cobras, Ford Mark IVs, and anything else you can think of.

This incredible engine went into a chassis almost exactly the same size as the 180-hp 904. In fact, the 900-hp 917 is exactly the same length but weighs 300 pounds *less* than the 70-hp Speedster. Makes you stop and think. Yes. The Can-Am 917 is only 155 inches long on a 90-inch wheelbase and weighs all of 1,500 pounds ready to race, which, when you figure the engine alone scales some 600 pounds, is pretty damn unbelievable. Now obviously there is nothing you or I could do with such a beast except *look* at it. But I swan, it *would* be fun to take one of those big monsters to an SCCA A-modified race and play games, wouldn't it, though. Beats Oscar Kovaleski's clapped-out McLaren four ways till Sunday on the old one-upmanship circuit.

The Porsche 917 first appeared as a homologated endurance racing coupe for 1969. Twenty-five identical cars were built, with aluminum frames, long swoopy bodies, and

most powerful road-racing car ever.

aerodynamic pointed tails. And they were *terrible*. Fast, certainly, but crashingly unstable. So for 1970 John Wyer/David Yorke got the contract to run Porsche's endurance racing team. Wyer went to a high-rise tail to make the cars handle, and ended up winning seven out of eight endurance races in '70, including Le Mans. He did just as well in 1971, so of course the CSI reduced the engine limit to 3 liters for '72. Porsche, predictably, told them to stuff it, got hold of Roger Penske/ Mark Donohue, and came over to kill off the Can-Am. The 917s—now short-tailed open cars with boxy bodies—put the Can-Am out of business simply by beating everybody else so badly they all went home and the SCCA dropped the series. Porsche dominated the similar European Interseries, too.

And well they should have. There was nothing dramatic about the success of the 917 and 917-10 Turbo. Virtually the entire Porsche factory, J. W. Engineering, and Penske Racing spent the better part of four years making the cars easily the best-thought-out, best-developed, best-run racing cars in history. They made Ford's $7 million Le Mans effort look like rich-bitch doodling. It was just like the old days when Mercedes was racing. The hand-rubbed mahogany storage boxes for matched sets of sparkplugs weren't in evidence, nor the polished, nickel-plated spanners. But the interminable testing and omnipresent recording notebooks were just like the old Neubauer days at Mercedes.

Obviously, if your bank book would be strained to handle a Speedster, this discussion is all pretty academic. But the Porsche 917, even more than Ford's GT-40/MkII, is the ultimate sports/racing car of the last three decades. And you just plain can't leave it out. What's more, unlike most factory racing efforts that comprise a handful of cars at most— like *six* Cobra Daytona Coupes, which are my own wet-dream favorites—there actually were four dozen 917s built. This is enough to mean that if that's what you really want, there's one with your name on it. Obviously, not everyone can afford the best sports/racing car ever built. Even more obviously, lots of people wouldn't want one, even if they could afford it. But we're not talking about them. We're talking about you. And if you don't run right out and trade the ol' manse in on a 917, you may be a notorious anal compulsive, you may be a fanatic, but you are no true Porsche collector. And that's a fact.

Siata-Fiat

Look, I know you've never heard of Siata. But that's okay; *nobody* has ever heard of Siata. You've heard of Fiat? Well, Siata was to Fiat as Shelby was to Ford. Ing. Ambrosini took stock Fiat cars and parts, modified the hell out of 'em, and built a whole line of teensy hot rods, beginning in 1926 and ending in 1970. For a while he was linked up with Carlo Abarth—who did the same things to Fiats but even better—until eventually Siata managed to go broke all on its own. Curiously enough, two of their biggest sellers were a front-engine replicar patterned after the MG-TD that appeared in 1951 and a rear-engine replicar patterned after the MG-TD that appeared in 1967. Siata wasn't always noted for originality nor good taste.

Rare and weird, Fiat's 1952 8V Coupe.

However. For some definitely weird reason, in 1950 Fiat and Siata got together and collaborated on a pair of cars. It was totally atypical of giant Fiat—I mean, *all* of Siata would fit in Agnelli's pocket—but for some reason that still escapes me, the deal was this: Siata would design the engine and chassis, with help from Fiat, of course. And they'd debug it. Then Fiat would manufacture the running gear and each would design and build bodies to fit. And they'd sell 'em separately. In theory, I suppose it all seemed reasonable enough, but in practice? After an outlay of God knows how many trillion lire, Fiat built a measly 114 cars in two years and Siata maybe half that many.

The weirdest thing of all is that neither car was all that bad. They were horrendously overpriced and not very pretty, but so were lots of other early postwar cars. I guess the real problem was that the Siata/Fiat concept—a luxurious, expensive, strictly street GT coupe—was just a couple of years too early for postwar Italy. Ferraris were still nearly all racing cars in 1952 when the new Siata/Fiats appeared, as were Maseratis and OSCAs. And the brilliant B.20 Lancia coupe cost millions of lire less. It's the old, old story. The Siata-Fiat was just not competitive in its in-

tended market. And when that happens, what can you say after you've said I'm sorry?

The thing is, some cars deserve better. And that's the case here. In 1960 Fiat would have been fighting off buyers for this car. For starters, it had a nice 1996cc V-8 rated at 127 hp. Now this was strictly a cooking engine by Italian standards: 6,000 rpm redline, pushrods, 8.5 : 1 compression ratio, twin carbs, 4-speed gearbox. On the other hand, though it wasn't anywhere near as high-strung as the Italian competition, it *was* a lot more potent than anything else with just 2 liters made in England or on the Continent at the time. This new V-8 went into an equally nice, all-independent-suspension chassis, with doubled shocks on the back, antiroll bars front and rear, and coil springs at each corner. In 1952 this was real pie-in-the-sky stuff, when even Ferraris were still using transverse leaf springs. With knock-off Rudge wheels and big drum brakes, the whole thing stretched out to a 94-inch wheelbase. And it was only a super-short 159 inches overall. Complete with an aerodynamic coupe body, the Siata/Fiat weighed a respectable 2,200 pounds and would reach 120 mph, which was pretty fast in 1952.

About that body. On the Fiat it was a cobbled-up version of an old aerodynamic coupe Fiat's own stylists created in 1950 for a prototype turbine-powered Futuremobile that finally appeared in 1954. As applied to the new V-8 chassis, it looked like a bad copy of the aerodynamic Adlers that came to Le Mans in the late thirties. Man, this car was definitely *weird* (not to mention at least two whole styling cycles behind the rest of Italy). It had the headlights hidden in the grille like Pininfarina's mid-fifties Nashes, full rear-fender skirts with bubbles over the knock-off hubs like Bob Koto's old Briggs Body Company mock-ups from 1935 or something, a grille made up of little bars that crept up over the nose, full-disc covers for the wire wheels—an affectation that died out most places in 1929—a split windshield, and a drooping fender line that wasn't quite an envelope body, but that's all you could call it. The rear was a lot better, very smooth with early-Corvette–like bumperettes and a huge quick-fill cap right in the middle of the fastback. But put it all together and, as old Uncle Tom McCahill would say,

Pininfarina's brilliant Cisitalia 1100 of 1947 had an influence all out of proportion to its size.

One of the small-bore classics of sports/racing, the 1452cc, Morelli-bodied OSCA of 1954.

Alfa Romeo 1963 GTZ, a wonderful, 150-mph, Zagato-bodied coupe of great refinement.

A brilliant design, years ahead of its time, the Pininfarina-bodied 1951 Lancia B.20 Aurelia GT.

Jean Daninos's Gallic Thunderbird, the 390-hp, 3,400-pound, 150-mph, $12,000 Facel II of 1962.

The ultimate "production" sports/racer of all time, Ferrari's V-12 250 Testa Rossa of 1958, complete with

300 hp from 2953cc, tubular space frame, a dry weight under 1,800 pounds, and top speed of 170 mph.

One of the fastest of all street machines, Pininfarina's 174-mph Ferrari 365 GTB/4 Daytona.

"The greatest road car that was ever built," the blue-chip 1954 Mercedes 300SL Gullwing.

Citroën's rare and arcane SM, one of the most enjoyable GT cars, but also the most complex.

The zenith of the Italian style and Giorgetto Giugiaro's masterpiece, the 1972 Maserati Ghibli.

The most desirable of all Ferrari street machines, the Pininfarina-bodied 1967 275 GTB/4.

you had one of the strangest bolides ever to come down the pike like a peanut through an elephant's trunk.

After the '52 Geneva Show where the car was introduced, Fiat revised the front end. The grille became a conventional oval opening not unlike those on the little Ferraris. But the stylists still managed to ruin it. The Fiat 8V was one of the first cars with quadruple headlights, tunneled into the fenders on an angle kind of like the later Jensen V-8 from the early sixties. And there were little rubber Cadillac Dagmar Nipples on the bumpers. Still exceptionally weird, and virtually indefensible when you consider the absolutely feverish aesthetic revolution going on all around them in Turin at the time, the very Renaissance of modern coachbuilding.

On the other hand, Siata was right in step with the times. After the lovely Diane coupe Stabilimenta Farina supplied for the little Siata 1400—which, though it had a gorgeous body was a nothing car—they couldn't very well regress to something less pretty. So the Siata 208 V-8—which was Siata's name for the Fiat 8V chassis—got a really nice, slightly bulbous, slab-sided berlinetta body by Boano.

It had traces of Vignale styling all over it and the basic shape was made in a couple of variations—with headlights in the grille or retractable headlights, with horizontal grille bars or vertical, with fender vents or without. In each case the basic shape was excellent, and though the detailing was slightly heavy—particularly a horizontal chrome strip cutting off the top of the rear wheelwell—the car held together visually as successfully as anything from that era. It was tight, smooth, streamlined, and not in the least fussy—all in all, an exceptional design.

By 1954 both Fiat and Siata had dropped the V-8 from their lines for lack of buyers. Curiously enough, for a rather porky street GT the Fiat 8V actually did fairly well in privateer racing. One won the Pescara 12 Hours in '52, and Capelli got a fifth in the Targa Florio and another fifth at Bari. And in both '56 and '57, a tired 8V won the 2-liter GT class in the Mille Miglia. One of the later cars even went to Le Mans, without accomplishing much. Siata 208s were never raced on an international level that I know of. Most Siata racers bought the 1100 or 1400 Fiat-based cars and left the bigger V-8 strictly for the street.

Fiat's 1952 1996cc V-8 looked like some forgotten aerodynamic Adler from the late thirties.

Bulbous but smooth, Siata's Boano-bodied 208.

Amazingly enough, there are both Fiat 8Vs and Siata 208s available in this country, and aside from their curiosity value they are surprisingly pleasant to drive. I tried a Westchester-based 208 last year, and though the car is absolutely tiny it *seems* larger, both inside and out. The Boano body was tight and rattle-free, the engine—which has curious headers that exit *up* before turning down and connecting to the dual exhausts—sounded just like a small-block Cleveland Ford pitched an octave higher. And the thing could go. There's no place to really open one up in Scarsdale, but the acceleration was terrifically good fun.

And of course the 8V/208 is a secret car. *Nobody* knows what the hell it is. For between $5,000 and $7,000—they cost exactly $6,000 in the States when new—you can buy a crowd-gatherer that puts Barchettas to shame. I mean, everybody *knows* what a Ferrari is. But they've never seen or heard of a Fiat V-8, and Siata might as well be one of the canals on Mars. For my money the 208 Siata is by far the more desirable of the two, just for the body styling alone. There are some mechanical parts still available from Fiat in Italy, believe it or not, and the aluminum bodywork is just run-of-the-mill Italian carrozzeria quality, which any restoration shop worth its $20 per hour ought to be able to fix without even blinking. All of this makes the Siata 208—and yes, the Fiat 8V, too—a fascinating bargain at the exotic, ultra-rare, very *weird* end of the spec-

trum. They're obviously not for everyone, but then I know guys who don't like Goldie Hawn either. Talk about *weird* chicks.

Lancia

Vincenzo Lancia was a big, blustering ex–racing driver, an innovative engineer with a fine technical mind and a hopelessly overbearing personality. He built cars to suit himself, and that there were customers with the same taste was a happy coincidence. Fortunately, Lancia had exquisite taste in cars. They were never flashy, but his unassuming little coupes and sedans could put up over-the-road averages that made big cars look sick. For example, Vincenzo's last design before his death in 1937, the 1352cc Aprilia, used a narrow-angle overhead-cam V-4, rear transaxle, inboard rear brakes, and four-wheel independent suspension on torsion bars. The semi–unit body was a model of lightweight design, and even the tiny Aprilia's 48 hp was enough to post shockingly high averages on back-country roads.

After the war, Vincenzo's son Gianni rebuilt the bombed-out Turin factory and continued Aprilia production, but that was just a stopgap. In 1943 Giuseppe Vaccarino (who had been Vincenzo's technical director) and Vittorio Jano (the most famous engineer in Italy) started work on a 60-degree V-6 with hemispherical combustion chambers. It displaced 1754cc and made 56 hp. For starters it was stuffed into an inflated Aprilia chassis, still with the rear transaxle but also including trailing arms and coil springs. The front had an unusual sliding kingpin independent suspension.

It was 1950 before Gianni felt this new car was good enough to sell. Called the Aurelia, it fit perfectly into the same low-volume, high-price, high-quality small-car niche that Lancia always occupied. And it got better. In 1951 the V-6 was punched out to 1991cc and

70 hp, and Pininfarina designed a 2 + 2 coupe to supplement the sedan. Called the B.20, the Pininfarina coupe had 75 hp and a top speed of 102 mph.

The B.20 was the fastest car Lancia had ever built. The handling, like all Lancias, was unbelievable. Aprilias, for example, pretty much dominated 1500cc international rallying right up through 1950, long after the factory had stopped production. But curiously enough, there were never any factory-backed Lancia racers. Vincenzo was a first-rate driver himself in the Edwardian period, a true international celebrity in the days of iron cars and iron men. But because he had seen close up just how expensive racing can be, he wisely decided to spend his money elsewhere.

Predictably, I suppose, Gianni Lancia thought just the opposite. And with racing wizard Vittorio Jano lurking in the engineering research department, a quick new sports coupe of unlimited potential and a fairly substantial profit coming in, Gianni decided to revive his father's glorious name at the track. After a trial run with four sedans in the Tour of Sicily, Lancia entered four B.20s in the 1951 Mille Miglia. Bracco and Maglioli finished second overall, just two minutes behind Villoresi's 4.1-liter, Vignale-bodied Ferrari 340 berlinetta, with a top speed nearly 60 mph greater than the Lancia. This is probably the greatest testimony ever given for the incredible handling of the B.20 Lancias, for Villoresi was no slouch and the big Lampredi-designed Ferrari was easily the fastest sports/racer in the world at that point.

The B.20 wasn't just good, it was fantastic. Nothing else under 2 liters could touch it, particularly in the long endurance races that still made up a major chunk of the international calendar in the early fifties. Pininfarina coupes fought for overall wins at Le Mans, the Mille Miglia, the Targa Florio, the Carrera PanAmericana. And in the small-bore rally class they were simply unbeatable. Louis Chiron won the '54 Monte Carlo Rally, and there were wins in the '53 Liège–Rome–Liège and '54 Acropolis among dozens of others. Bonetto won the Targa Florio outright in '52, with two other B.20s right behind. Fagioli was third in the Mille Miglia, Maglioli fourth in Mexico. And so it went.

In 1953 the B.20 got even better. The V-6 went up to 2451cc and 118 hp. The next year

Chassis by Vittorio Jano and Giuseppe Vaccarino, body by Pininfarina—the superb Lancia B.20.

Alberto Ascari with his Lancia D.24, 1954.

there was a DeDion rear. And happily enough, that's the way the B.20 stayed until production stopped in 1959. All too many cars have been ruined by that unfortunate human predilection to screw around with a good thing, but the B.20 survived totally intact. Part of this was simple economics. With Jano on the staff, Cisitalia only just gone, and Maserati and Ferrari just down the street, it was pretty hard for young Gianni Lancia to avoid catching the dread Formula One Fever.

In 1953 Jano had built a small group of 2962cc sports/racers designed around B.20 bits on a space-frame chassis. Called D.20s, some were even supercharged. These eventually evolved into the 3.3-liter D.24s, with something like 265 hp. There were some good placings—second in the '54 sports-car championship, with wins in the Targa Florio and Mille Miglia, second at Sebring—but all in all, the big Lancia sports/racers were no match for C-Jags and the big Ferraris. Jano was undeterred, so in August of 1953 he started work on a Formula One monoposto. This was the ill-fated D.50, which, though brilliant, never got itself sorted out. Lancia raced it inconclusively for little more than one season.

And then went bankrupt. From a solid financial position in 1953, Jano and Gianni managed to spend their way into receivership in less than two years. When Ascari was killed at Monza testing a Ferrari—only four days after his spectacular flip into the harbor at Monte Carlo in the Formula One D.50—Gi-

anni withdrew from racing and sold the entire Formula One team (including Vittorio Jano) to Ferrari. Where, wouldn't you know it, within a year the D.50s were massaged into world's championship cars. So it goes.

That was too late to help Gianni Lancia. In late 1955 he went looking for buyers. The Pesenti family—northern Italian cement mixers—bought the whole thing. Gianni left in '56, and though the name remains today, there hasn't been a Lancia at Lancia since. Ironically, Gianni Lancia resigned almost fifty years to the day after Vincenzo Lancia founded the company. On the other hand, the Pesenti were pretty good people, and though they got Antonio Fessia from Fiat to design a new line of cars, they kept the old line—including the B.20—in production without alteration.

The change of ownership, then, meant nothing as far as the cars themselves were concerned. All things considered, the definitive B.20s are the 2.5-liter, DeDion-suspended cars, most of which were built by the Pesentis. No matter. The B.20 is probably the nicest small GT car I've ever driven, regardless of era. I personally happen to like the styling, though it *is* a bit upright and stodgy compared with most of the competition. On the other hand, it's a true four-passenger car, and Pininfarina wanted to keep the traditional Lancia grille shape at the front, which required a vertical sort of design. There's no chrome spear to break up the slab sides, the wheels are tall, the overhang is short. So it does look a bit stumpy.

Arthur Drexler was so pleased with his 1951 MOMA show of eight cars—the one with Pininfarina's Cisitalia—that he organized a similar exhibit in '53, with ten cars. And of course the B.20 was in that one. Said Drexler, "Both body and chassis are formed in a single unit, like a box. An unusually successful part of its design is the relation of the sloping back to the rear fenders: flat and curved planes are here contrasted without irrelevant detail." From a stylist's point of view, the important thing about the B.20 was that it was a real 2 + 2. Which made it the first practical car in the new Italian style that didn't cost $10,000 or barely squeeze 1.78 passengers into a tiny compartment. Because of its sedan ancestry, the B.20 was someplace between a sports car and a sedan. A true GT car, in other words, and one of the best.

There is a very active Lancia club both here and in England, and prices are surprisingly low. You can buy a good B.20 for less than $4,000, and concours cars go for $6,000, which is just about what they cost new, twenty years ago (that's in America, of course). Lancia has a bigger following in Europe, and consequently the cars are more expensive. But for some reason, Lancia never caught on in the States. There are *some* over here, and now that Fiat has decided to push the Lancia name—which they acquired from the Pesenti in 1969—there's a pretty fair chance that *all* Lancias will start to appreciate in value if the new cars turn out to be a popular success.

By extension, this means that a good time to be buying a B.20—or even better, a D.20 or D.24 sports/racer if you can find one—is right now. They aren't big-bucks classics, that's for sure. And very few of them that I've seen are in concours condition. On the other hand, they *are* lovely cars to drive, they will cruise all day at 80 mph without a whimper, and they can be had for relatively nothing. You'll never make a lot of money dealing in old Lancias, but maybe you don't want to. Maybe all you want is a light, responsive, fantastic handler, with more than adequate performance, room for four adults plus luggage, and classic good looks. A Lancia Aurelia B.20, in other words.

Abarth

Carlo Abarth should be an inspiration to all you late starters. He built himself maybe the most famous specialty car business in Europe, starting at age forty-one; real life-begins-at-forty stuff. Now Abarth obviously didn't live in a vacuum before then. In the late twenties/early thirties he was a well-known Austrian motorcycle racer. And as these things have a way of happening in the inbred world of racing, he met young Ferry Porsche and through him the legendary Dr. Ferdinand Porsche. When the Nazis blitzkrieged Austria in '38, Abarth crossed over into Yugoslavia, where he sat out the war. When that was over, when all the other refugees were moving around Europe, Abarth made his way to Turin, Italy's equivalent of Detroit City.

Abarth met Piero Dusio and talked himself into a job. This was the time when Dusio was already thinking about a Cisitalia GP car, and Abarth was the one who suggested Dr. Porsche. They had to spring him out of a French jail first, of course, and the GP project bankrupted Cisitalia, but it was Abarth who really got Porsche going, postwar. When Dusio went broke, Abarth started running his Squadra Carlo Abarth. He had three used Cisitalias and a check from Carlo Scagliarini, whose father was a big-time banker and old buddy of Giovanni Agnelli. On April 15, 1949, Abarth and young Scagliarini incorporated to make mufflers and anything else automotive they could think of that might turn a lire.

Abarth mufflers became *the* thing to have, and production zoomed up to half a million units a year by the mid-sixties. Anybody with any sporty car pretensions at all had an Abarth exhaust system, on anything from a smoke-belching Sprite to a new Ferrari. I don't know that anyone ever proved that Abarths *work* any better, but they do *sound* rorty enough, and they're painted in racy-looking black crackle finish, and cost a lot. But mufflers per se are not what you'd call the world's most interesting objects. And right from the beginning, Carlo Abarth gave himself some other more fun things to do besides measuring bits of tubing.

Because of Scagliarini's connections at Fiat, Abarth was able to get parts and advice really cheaply. So in no time at all, Carlo'd become the resident factory racing guru, particularly after the disastrous Siata-Fiat tie-up in the early fifties. Until they bought Abarth & Cie. outright in 1971 and turned it into a separate subsidiary, Fiat never had any money in Abarth the way they did with Ferrari. Abarth didn't need Fiat's money. While Ferrari lost a bundle every year on racing, Abarth made enough off his mufflers to more than finance his cars.

All the Abarth cars were hot rods—sophisticated hot rods, to be sure, but hot rods none-

Brooks Robinson at Meadowdale in 1960, obviously pleased with his 120-mph Fiat-Abarth 1000.

theless. They're the Italian equivalent of John Fitch Corvairs or Shelby's GT-350s . . . modified production cars offering really impressive performance gains for an equally impressive price increase. There were a couple of non-Fiats—a few Porsches, a sleeved-down Alfa Giulietta, and some Simcas when Simca was also associated with Fiat—but mostly, Abarth was a loyal one-marque collaborator. Which was just as well, because the little Fiats were the perfect base on which to build bitsy specials. They were cheap, light, and amazingly tweakable.

Actually, until 1955 Abarth was just kind of beating his head against the wall, trying to make sports cars out of the front-engine Fiat 1100. This was just too out of date to cut it, even in highly modified form. Fiat knew this too, of course, and there was a supplement on the way. What really made Abarth—and Fiat, too, for that matter—was the little rear-engine Fiat 600, designed by Antonio Fessia before he went to Lancia. Abarth started out by doubling the horsepower of the stock cars, adding a few dress-up items, then peddling them out the door at a big markup. But in 1956 he came up with the definitive configuration for Fiat-Abarths, a basic concept that stayed in production for nearly a decade in various forms.

What Abarth did was simple. Since the Fiat 600 had a unit body, it was impossible to do much with it. So he pulled off the front suspension—a simple, independent setup that

used a transverse leaf spring as the lower control arms—and the entire rear suspension/transaxle/engine unit. This weighed almost nothing and featured independent wishbones with coil springs. The 600 engine was bored and stroked to 747cc. Then all these Fiat bits were bolted onto a new tubular chassis, which in turn was sent to Zagato.

Ah, Zagato. He had been specializing in superleggera, luscious bodywork since the late twenties. His best cars were the lithe 1750 Alfa roadsters of the early thirties, but he'd done stripped Ferraris, Maseratis, even the famous Aston Martin DB-4 Zagato coupes later on. But in the mid-fifties, when Abarth came around, Zagato was justly famous for being the one to see if you wanted a few hundred pounds taken off an already lightweight car. Since Abarth had only 47 hp to work with, he had to save every ounce possible.

Zagato, as usual, came through like a champ. He drew up a little bullet-shaped coupe that had a fastback and window treatment very much like the later Ford Mustang coupe and a rounded body reminiscent of the Lotus Elite. There was no grille, just a smooth nose, the headlights being faired in under plastic covers. And there was no add-on decoration *anywhere*. Air got to the engine through a pair of scoops on the trunk, and the roof was pooched out over each passenger's head with a crease down the middle. Zagato had started this roof treatment as a way to cut frontal area and still have some headroom, and it had become a trademark. The new Fiat-Abarth was immediately labeled Double-Bubble because of it.

And could it go. The Double-Bubble 750 would run around 90 mph, even on 47 hp. Hell, it didn't weigh but 1,000 pounds or so, and it had no frontal area to speak of. In the States the Double-Bubble cost a whopping $3,640—*three times* what a lowly Fiat 600 went for. But then, honestly, there wasn't much Fiat left, and soon there was even less. Zagato took out the trademark roof crease, made a single air-scoop on the rear deck, and picked up another 5 mph top end. And Abarth came up with a double-overhead-cam conversion for the tiny Fiat four that gave nearly 70 hp out of 747cc. This was enough to get into triple-figure speeds, for Chrissakes. Of course, the Monza model cost $4,990—more than a Corvette or Jaguar—but then you couldn't race Corvettes in I-production.

Franklin D. Roosevelt, Jr., the East Coast Fiat distributor, financed a team of four Fiat-Abarths in the late fifties/early sixties that absolutely cleaned house in the States. People like Jim Jeffords and Ray Cuomo and Duncan Black had a stranglehold on small-bore SCCA racing and even finished 1-2-3-4 at Sebring and 1-2-3 at Daytona, in their little 1000cc class, of course. Abarths did just as well in Europe, particularly in the hillclimb championships, where they were faster than a lot of the big iron. Between 1949 and 1970, Abarth cars supposedly won something like 7700 races worldwide. In 1966 alone, they won 806 races just in FIA competition. Incredible.

Like everybody else, the Abarths got fatter over the years. There was an 850cc version, and then in 1960 a full 1000, punched out of the revised 600/D. These cars weighed about 1,200 pounds, but they would also go something like 120 mph. Finally, in 1962, Abarth himself revamped the Zagato body to make it even lighter yet. This one was prettier, too, with bigger windows and less overhang. Engine air now came in through conventional louvers in the deck. The cooking version, the Monomille, really would do 100 mph on 1000cc, and it cost only $2,500 at the factory gate. The trick, double-overhead-cam version, the Bialbero, cost an outlandish six grand in Italy in 1962, and even it wasn't the top of the line. For $10,000 you could buy the same

car with a 1300cc Simca engine in the back and the radiator mounted behind a nice little oval grille up front. One of these Simca-Abarths was timed by *Quattroroute* at 150 mph on the Autostrada Torino–Milano, with 0 to 60 in 7.3 seconds. In 1962 this was faster and quicker than anything except a full-house fuel-injected Corvette. And that's not all. You want to hear a real mind boggler? At Le Mans practice in 1962, the 1300cc Simca-Abarths were running *10 seconds a lap faster* than the fastest lightweight Jaguar E-type. No lie.

This kind of performance, despite the price, made these cars immensely popular in Europe. In fact, between 1955 and 1970, when Fiat took over, Abarth sold over 10,000 cars, just about as many as Ferrari sold in the same period. Honest. And pound for pound, Abarth's prices made Il Commendatore's look like Woolworth's. Understand, though, that there has never been a street-legal car that did more with less than the Fiat-Abarth 750/850/1000. No Lotus Elite, no Gordini, no Cisitalia ever came *near* to Abarth levels of performance.

You paid for this performance, I will confess, and not just with steep price tags up front. Driving a Fiat-Abarth is like stuffing rolled-up twenty-dollar bills with nitroglycerin and touching them off by the case. I mean, the Fiat-Abarth is what they were thinking of when they invented the term *nickel rocket*. As collector cars, though, they can't be beat. You wouldn't want to have to drive one every day and also try to keep it in camshafts and big-end bearings. And the

Nickel rocket: 150-mph Simca-Abarth 1300.

aluminum bodywork is pretty flimsy. But the cars *are* relatively inexpensive on an absolute scale; maybe $5,000 for a really superb Double-Bubble or Monza, a little more for a Simca version.

The most famous Abarths are the 750 Double-Bubbles. Only 600 of them were built. Next best are the similar 1000s, and then the later Bialberos. Any of them would be a bona fide blast to own, a watch-pocket Q-ship with all the moves. In this country you're more apt to find one of the early cars, for the simple reason that Frank Roosevelt gave up on his race team around 1962 and the Fiat-Abarth reputation started to die around that time. All told, though, Roosevelt imported 2,800–2,900 Abarth cars of all types, including modified Fiat sedans. Al Consentino at Faza in Florida still has tons of spares and probably knows more about Fiat-Abarths than old Carlo himself. He's *the* man to know.

Bialberos are by far the rarest of all, particularly in the States, for the simple reason that only about seventy were built, all after Roosevelt stopped importing Abarths. Curiously enough, Abarth built one hundred Bialbero bodies, and the remaining thirty leftovers were sold to Radbourne in London in 1967, where another dozen were built with Fiat 124S engines. Radbourne sold *their* remaining spares in 1971, and Lord knows where those other 18 Simca-Abarth bodies have gone now. They're in England somewhere, waiting to be tracked down for parts.

Engines and running gear are no problem, of course, because everything is Fiat 600, with minor tweaks. So really, if you're willing to do a little running around and make a few phone calls to Florida, one of these baby Abarth coupes would be maybe easier to own now than a decade ago, when they were new. And they *are* unique. Because of emissions requirements, I think the smallest cars you'll see in America in the future are going to be VW Rabbit size, 1.5 liters or so. Anything less than that just can't cut it in the modern, sterilized world. And Abarth was getting 70 horsepower out of half that displacement; definitely a dirty business by EPA standards. Which is why Abarth stopped making street cars in 1967. I mean, not only was the handwriting on the wall, the door was already closed. But too late: hundreds of the smoggy little buggers

were already over here, insidious polluters of the landscape and wreckers of the morals of youth. Who knows what evil lurks within 747cc and 70 hp? All wrapped up in Double-Bubbles from Zagato. Gad.

Facel

Jean Daninos was an almost archetypal independent motor car manufacturer, a blustery, hard-driving industrialist who waded into the luxury car field in 1954 and survived a full decade before spending his way out again. But he did something few others have done. Starting from scratch, with no background at all in the car business, Daninos managed to build—and, even more difficult, to sell—a truly grand, high-performance luxury car priced to go against Rolls-Royce and Mercedes but with the *cojones* of a Ferrari or Aston. Even more astonishing, Daninos did this in the mid-fifties—when high-performance luxury cars weren't very much in demand. More amazing still, he did it in France.

After the war, the French car industry never did get it all together again. Ettore Bugatti was dead. Delage and Delahaye and Talbot were as good as dead. The horsepower tax was even more repressive than that in England, with the inevitable result that French roads were clogged with an insane assortment of little shitboxes, and rich folks had to look elsewhere for neat cars to drive.

Jean Daninos was a sheet-metal tycoon, bending and stamping all sorts of things from refrigerator doors to deck furniture. He also did some all-steel bodies for Simca's little Pininfarina coupes and the high-style Ford-France Comète. This branch of the business started in 1949, and by '54 Daninos was ready to get into the car business himself. Now obviously he wasn't going to go head to head with Renault and Peugeot in the mass market. But there was a gaping hole at the upper end of the French car business where Daninos could sell cars to people just like himself. As with most of the world's best cars, Jean Daninos's was designed to be something *he* wanted to drive. A perfect formula for success. It just seems as though you work at it harder when the car you're building is one you expect to live with every day.

Daninos met English club racer Lance Macklin at Le Mans, and Macklin happily agreed to be his chief tester and designer. Macklin never received much credit for his work on Daninos's car, though. But he *has* gone down in racing history. Poor Lance Macklin was the innocent wight who was cut off by Mike Hawthorn's D-Jag at Le Mans in '55, putting his Austin-Healey into the path of Levegh's Mercedes 300SLR and triggering the tragic crash that killed eighty-some spectators. But that was quite a while after he worked for Daninos at Compagnie Facel Metallon, in Pont-à-Mousson.

Macklin drew up a conventional frame made with big tubes, similar to those used by Aston, Ferrari, A. C., and, really, almost any car with serious pretensions to performance in the early fifties. Daninos had an eye on the American market, and he also wanted a big, powerful car to fit with a big, powerful price tag. So like everybody from Reid Railton to Sydney Allard, Daninos had Macklin leave room for a big American V-8. In fact, they picked just about the biggest and best. For the first two years it was the DeSoto version of Chrysler's hemi; from then on, the biggest Chrysler version. This meant 276 cubic inches and 175 hp in 1954 and '55, 330 cubic inches and 255 hp in 1956/'57, 354 cubic inches and 360 hp the next two years, 383 cubic inches and anywhere from 330 to 390 hp until 1963, and a whopping 413 cubes, 425 hp in 1964. Even wilder, as the engines got bigger, the weight went *down*. The first cars weighed over 4,000 pounds; the last ones, only 3,600.

Obviously, the real performance came in the later cars, which is not to say the first cars were slow. You had your choice of either Chrysler's Torqueflite automatic or the big Pont-à-Mousson 4-speed that Daninos later sold to Chrysler itself for early Chrysler 300s. Happily enough, Macklin's chassis was a lot more than a dragster. The front suspension was all independent, of course, with expensive and hefty forged A-arms. The solid rear axle came from Hardy-Spicer in England, and

by 1960 the Facel had four-wheel disc brakes. Together it all sounds drearily pedestrian today, but you have to remember, in the late fifties there was little else on the road that was much more sophisticated.

The Facel chassis, despite (or perhaps because of) its inherent strength and simplicity, not only performed exceptionally well but has lasted well, too. A top speed of 150 mph, quarter-miles of over 90 mph in 16 seconds, and 0 to 100 in less than 20 seconds are definitely not to be sniffed at, even today. And the low center of gravity of the Facel—the big tubular frame rails are 4 inches below the driveshaft level—means, even though it's fairly heavy and nearly as long as the early Camaro/Firebirds, it will go around corners better than any other car of its type. It's no Short Wheelbase Berlinetta, but then it's not a T-bird, either.

By 1954 Facel S. A. had enough experience with car bodies that they could draw up their own and stamp them out. Not surprisingly, the first Facel Vega came out looking very much like an oversized replica of the Ford-France Comète, right down to the slab sides and elegant greenhouse. Made all in steel, it was a lot stronger than most limited-production cars, and the clean styling has turned out to be timeless. The vertical grille evokes a touch of the later Alvises and Talbots, both of which were good things to be resembling in the mid-fifties luxury/sporting market. But in the final analysis, the Facel came out to

Facel HK-500, the only postwar Grand Marque.

be excitingly original, and though various details are reminiscent of other cars—tunneled-in Corvettish taillights, stacked Lincoln/Mercedes headlights, wraparound GM windshield—the whole package is unique. And what's more, successful.

The interior of the Facel is pure personal luxury car, right down to the fake-wood dash, padded tunnel, and leather bucket seats. *Road & Track,* thinking of the interior as much as anything else, called it a French Thunderbird. It's not big inside—it's not big outside, either—but the Facel has to be one of the most comfortable collector cars this side of a Bentley Continental. This all cost, of course. Even in 1954, Facels went for $7,000 in this country. By 1960 they were up to $10,000; in '62 over $12,000 . . . not counting matched and fitted luggage that ran another $600. But for what you got, the price was academic. Daninos managed to sell some 1,024 Chrysler-powered cars in just under a decade, which in the luxury hybrid market is doing quite well, all things considered.

What killed Facel was all those carpies saying, "Why doncha build your own engines, huh?" Daninos did, and wrapped a smaller, $4,000 car around it. But though the Facellia was okay as a car, the little overhead-cam four was an unmitigated disaster. It was immediately dropped. For a while Facel bought Volvo engines, then Austin-Healey sixes, but by then the damage was done. The terrible, unreliable reputation of the Facellia rubbed off on the big car as well, and Facel S. A. went out of the automobile business in 1964.

Max Hoffman was the U.S. importer, and when the marque died he sold all his Facel spares to Packard collector Fred Kanter of Morris Plains, New Jersey. So Kanter has almost all the Facel spares in the country. Happily, he's also a nice guy. Chassis and body parts aren't all *that* expensive through Kanter, and of course Facel mechanical bits are mostly stock Chrysler. The way it stands, a ten-year-old Facel can actually be *easier* to own than lots of more recent cars. At least you know where all the parts are.

Right now, a reasonable Facel II—which is by far the nicest model—will run you $5,000. A really perfect one could go for $9,000. This is cheap enough that you might consider owning his and hers models, or one for every day

of the week or something. I mean, they *can't* depreciate at that level. The only way to go is up. And if 99 percent of the world's car enthusiasts have never heard of them, that's their loss. The Facel II V-8 is among the nicest cars to come out of the fifties. It's a Grand Marque, certainly, and possessed of more class than anything you'll see around for less than twice the price. I mean, people are paying $4,000 for old MGs and Triumphs, and a good Sunbeam Tiger will run you $6,000. But the Facel II is maybe five times as good as all those cars put together. After all, old Jean Daninos was pretty hip, and he was building a car he'd be proud to drive himself. You wouldn't catch Daninos in some worn-out *Deux Cheveau* with rubber-band seats and a centrifugal clutch . . . his transportation had to have a little class.

BMW

If such a thing is possible, BMW is the world's only thoroughly British German car company. Unlike Mercedes-Benz, which has always been a company of overachievers building magnificent classics, BMW has staggered along in a perfectly British way for over sixty years, building airplane engines, motorcycles, and a weird range of cars. The aircraft division traces back to 1916, but BMW as we know it goes back to only 1928. They've always built small, spartan, high-performance sporting cars—Teutonic British sports cars, if you will—and the factory has always raced its own products. Everything from the original BMW Dixie—a British Austin Seven built under license—to the BMW Isetta—an Italian Iso Rivolta bubblecar built under license—was fair game to be raced, no matter how inappropriate as a racing car.

For all intents and purposes, though, there are only two periods of BMW cars worth talking about. During the thirties, a series of six-cylinder cars engineered by Dr. Fritz Fiedler culminated in the classic BMW 328. These incredibly quick roadsters formed the basis for the 1940 Mille Miglia winner, and they literally owned the 2-liter class in the late thirties, too. The 327/328 provided the basis for Bristol's postwar British line and the East German EMW 327/2. And of course the famous Bristol six used in everything from Formula Two cars to Arnolts and A. C.s was nothing more than a hotted-up BMW 328.

The second great period of BMWs, curiously enough, has almost nothing to do with the early cars, except that they were all fathered by the same Dr. Fritz Fiedler. He got Bristol and Frazer Nash straightened out in England between 1945 and 1950, then went back home to Opel. That lasted only a year before he was back as technical director of BMW, where he stayed until his retirement in 1963. The strange thing is that half the sports cars in England used the old BMW six right up till the early sixties. But BMW itself had Fiedler start on a whole new engine concept for 1955.

Fiedler was in overall charge, not running a drafting board any longer. So the new engine was actually drawn by Alfred Boning. Unlike the early engines, the new BMW V-8 was both uninspired and short-lived. A totally conventional overhead-valve V-8, it came in 2.6- and 3.2-liter sizes. In the larger package it made a mild-mannered 140 hp. Fiedler had

this aluminum V-8 stuffed into a 97-inch-wheelbase tubular frame derived ultimately from his prewar 328. It had independent front suspension, torsion bars, and a solid rear axle with transverse Panhard rod. Not the most inspired chassis in the world.

But the BMW 507 is a major classic nonetheless. It was light at 2,600 pounds, so it would go over 130 mph. The big drum brakes were pretty good, so it would stop. The old-fashioned chassis was like a set of railroad tracks, and the 5-speed gearbox was nice and easy to stir. But none of that is worth classic status, not even when you add in a price tag of $10,500 . . . well on the high side of Mercedes's Gullwing. Total production was only 250, but that's beside the point. No, what made—and makes—the BMW 507 a blueblood, double-throw-down classic is the body.

Created by German-American designer Albrecht Goertz, the BMW 507 is easily the most beautiful and timeless German car since the *Sturm und Drang* Porsche-designed SSKs. There is nothing in particular to rave about; Goertz's car simply looks *right*. It is thin in section, yet not at all dachshundlike. It's long and low, but unsquashed. The lightweight, lift-off roof is perfectly shaped and proportioned, yet it dominates nothing. The pointed nose with twin nostrils echoes the classic twin grilles of early BMWs, yet it is perfectly right

Albrecht Goertz's ravishing BMW 507 was a knockout in 1956, even with a $10,500 price tag.

and totally integrated into one of the smoothest, classiest bodies ever. It could be powered by twisted rubber bands and no one would care a whit.

In its day (1956 through '59), the 507 was considered the most beautiful car north of Turin. Hans Stuck, the legendary Auto-Union hill climber, came out of retirement and dabbled with a 507 in '58 and '59. But significantly, when he won his last European hillclimb championship in 1960, it was in BMW's little 700cc coupe. The 507 was an overweight street machine, not a mountain racer. For this reason, BMW 507 drivers tend to be the same sorts as those who own early Aston Martins or Jensens or Bristol 404s—seekers of quality, in other words, not seekers of blinding performance attained by sacrificing all other virtues.

A BMW—any BMW—is usually in above-average shape. As with Porsche owners, the kind of people who buy big BMWs not only usually have good taste but also have enough time and money to keep the cars together. So there's a good chance, in your wanderings through *Autoweek* or *Road & Track,* that you'll spot a perfect-condition 507 every once in a while. Unlike many other modern collector cars, you'll probably have some trouble coming up with major body parts or replacing mechanical bits, so if you do get into a 507, get into a good one. It's not like having a small-block Chevy to worry about.

Your chances are good of finding a nicely kept car, though, with a price that should be around $9,000 these days. Don't go looking for a bargain; you won't find it. And if you do, it'll turn out not to be, in the long run. But if you really *like* the cars and are willing to pay the price, they're pretty enough to take your breath away and give you that tingly feeling behind the old eyes. Oh. Watch out for 507s with small-block Chevys stuffed inside, or full-house Cobra mills. The cars are so pretty and the engines so finicky that a lot of owners have just said the hell with it and spliced in an American V-8. BMW hot rods are nowhere, take it from me.

In 1965 BMW tried again for a real GT car. This one was just the reverse of the old 507. The 2000CS had a grand chassis, but it was, well . . . funny looking. Preposterous, almost, particularly around the front end. And with a little 2-liter four it was embarrassingly

BMW's 3.0CS, a truly desirable combination of perform-

underpowered. But it was a start. Amazingly, by 1969 they worked it around into the definitive version of the best BMW ever built, which, being no dummies, they kept in production until 1975 with only minor changes, all of them improvements. BMW's engineers and directors are famous for having raced and used their own products, right from the early motorcycle/aircraft days, and it's still no different. So logically enough, as the company has matured, the cars have matured, too. The 2800CS/3.0CS coupe is the ultimate, pre-safety bumpers and smog stuff BMW. And despite a price tag of $8,000 when they started and $11,000 when they finished, the little BMWs were consistently compared to Ferraris and Mercedes and Porsches that cost anywhere from 20 to 100 percent more.

Road & Track and *Car and Driver,* either of which would swear black was white if the other one said different, agreed on the CS coupe. "For the person who values finish, detailing, finesse and integrity over pretense, excesses and sure obsolescence . . . no car near the price offers all the BMW has." And like-

ance, comfort, and clean good looks.

never even realized that we weren't going 55 in that BMW, too.

A BMW CS coupe is that kind of car. Inspiring. A machine you can trust, the sort of tight-knit wunderkar you'd think nothing of driving from Maine to Florida on five minutes' notice, knowing all the while that you'll get there, safe and sound. I have never, *never* driven a car that provides such consistent pleasure day in and day out. In a Ferrari you're always worrying about every new little noise you hear. In an Aston you don't go fast at night because maybe all the dim-bulb Lucas lights will go out as you storm into some fast sweeper. And driving a Mercedes is like kissing your sister. But those little BMW coupes are a superb blend of all that's good.

This is another way of saying that, like the best cars, like the GTB/4 Ferrari, for example, CS coupes are perfectly balanced. They don't do any one thing spectacularly, but they will do almost everything better than need be. And it's all done with mirrors, or magic; something. I mean, a casual read through the spec pages won't give you half a clue to why the CS coupe works as well as it does. The chassis was inherited from the old 1800 Ti sedans, with MacPherson struts in front and independent rear. The transmission is a lowly 4-speed. Brakes are disc front and drum rear except on the very last 3.0CS, which finally got four-wheel discs. The single-overhead-cam six was never rated at more than 190 hp no matter which displacement it had. And in any case, 3,000 pounds is a lot for that tiny engine.

But you can prove anything you want with numbers. For all its seeming deficiencies, a BMW 3.0CS coupe will do 16-second quarter-miles at nearly 90 mph, go 130 mph without breathing hard—for hours on end if you can find a place to keep it open that long—stop at nearly .9G, and zap around a skid pad like a Lotus, despite having 55 percent of the weight on the front wheels. On a race track, it probably wouldn't look very good, I will confess. Those CS coupes BMW was racing in IMSA a while ago were as near to a real car as Richard Petty's Dodges are to the sedan your cleaning lady drives.

No, the CS coupe is not for the race track. It's for posting impossibly high averages on the crummy back roads to the country club

wise, "You don't *need* a BMW CS. Unless you need excellence, competence and a car that's near impossible to match anywhere in the automotive world."

Suffice it to say that BMW CS coupes from any year have depreciated not at all. The prices, as the TV pitchmen scream, will never be lower. Now's the time to act. And really, for a real car—not a mantelpiece ego massager, but a real *car*—the CS is just about the best buy you can make in the whole collector car world. They are as finely made as a Rolex, as nimble as a Lotus, as comfortable as a Mercedes, as pretty as a Ferrari. And inspiring? I once drove a BMW 3.0CS test car for two hours down the winding, 1929-era Taconic Parkway through a full-fledged September *hurricane*—50-knot winds, flooded roads, downed power lines and all—never getting below 60 mph and spending most of my time between 80 and 100. Not impressive, you say? Well, the pretty lady who was with me—who is definitely *not* a car enthusiast—was far more used to her father's Mark IV, which never went above a sedate 55. And Nancy and for drawing admiring glances once you get there. The 2000CS was funny looking, but the 2800CS and 3.0CS are beautiful. A delicate greenhouse with huge windows, a sharply pointed bow, and a short, tucked-in stern. Clean, simple, spartan lines, with not an extra geegaw in the place. And plain alloy wheels that are models of understatement, maybe a million times better than those fake spoke wheels Porsche used for much too long.

The BMW is a car of taste, of integrity, and so are most of its owners. So you actually can go buy a used CS coupe and get what you pay for, something you can't guarantee with a Corvette or Shelby. People don't butcher and abuse BMWs, and that's a fact. Or maybe it doesn't matter that they're abused, because the cars are so well made they can shrug it off. In either case, as long as you're prepared for high maintenance costs and a comparatively steep price tag even for a well-used car, there is nothing much around that can compete with the CS. It filled a unique market place when new; it fills a neat collector niche now. And I wouldn't be surprised if the small, tight, roadable coupe isn't the top-line sporting machine of the future. Really, the BMW 3.0CS Gran Turismo coupe is what all those Vega GTs, Mustang II GTs, and Monza GTs are hoping to be when they grow up.

Maserati GTs

Omer Orsi was no dummy. He figured a really neat way to make a lot of money was to provide the beautiful people with high-class, high-price Gran Turismos, derived of course from Maserati's world-famous line of successful racing cars. This plan started perking in his brain in 1946 or so, and he stuck with it through thin and thick, the agony of victory and the thrill of defeat, the defection of the Fratelli Maserati, the near-bankruptcy of the Orsi, till finally, a full decade later, he was able to build his first Maserati street GT.

The obvious idea was to use the Maserati racing name to sell the street cars. Unfortunately for Orsi, it took a good decade to make the postwar Maserati name into something that wasn't a joke. His ultimate coup was going to be to win the Formula One World Championship, the F/I Constructors' Championship *and* the sports car Manufacturers' Championship all in one year. And *then* come out with this great street machine to blow everyone's mind. Orsi was not one to think small.

Fangio delivered the first two championships in 1957, and amazingly enough, except for the famous debacle at Caracas when the entire five-man Maserati team destroyed one another's cars, they would have won the sports-car championship, too. Which was certainly near enough. So Omer Orsi sprang his street machine. What a machine! It was perfectly comparable to the 250GT coupe that Enzo Ferrari had started building in '56. In fact, in many ways the new Maserati was better than the Ferrari. It didn't have a V-12, but it did have a perfectly nice 3485cc version of the 12-plug six from the World Championship 250F Formula One car, which was about as classy as you could get in 1957. It started out with Webers, but by 1962 Maserati had a Lucas fuel-injection unit sorted out and were promising 240 hp.

The rest of Orsi's car was damn near as sophisticated. Instead of trying to make everything himself like Ferrari, he just bought the best bits available. So the 3500 GT had a ZF 5-speed gearbox, four-wheel Girling disc brakes, 16-inch Boranni wire wheels, Pirelli tires, Borg and Beck clutch, Alford & Adler independent front suspension, and Salisbury rigid rear axle. Most of this stuff came off the Aston Martins and Jaguars of the late fifties, which has the nice advantage of giving at least *some* parts swapability.

Maserati built the frame, of course, and the factory bodywork came from decent carrozzeria. Vignale built the roadster—which was nice enough—but Touring's berlinetta was really *good*. It looked a little porkier all around than the equivalent Pininfarina/Boano Ferrari, but at 3,100 pounds, 188 inches overall, on a 102-inch wheelbase, it *was* a little porkier than the 250GT. No matter. The new Maserati coupe was clean and straightforward, without a gimmicky line anywhere.

The grille shape was the traditional Maserati flattened oval with Trident emblem, but the rest of the car was up-to-the-minute with lots of straight surfaces and a rising rear fender line that left room for a decent trunk even. It was at least as pretty as anything you could buy in 1957, and better looking than Boano's similar 250 GT production Ferrari.

The Maserati 3500 GT had fantastic performance, too. Zero to 60 took around 8.5 seconds, the quarter-mile came up in 16, and top speed was a genuine 140 mph. Weight distribution was pretty much 50/50 and the brakes were superb, far superior to Ferrari's old drums. At $12,721 POE the Maserati market was obviously fairly limited in the States, and in Italy there weren't a hundred playboys in the whole country who could afford that kind of price tag. So 3500 GT production kind of lagged. I mean, they built maybe a thousand total before the Touring berlinetta was discontinued in 1965, by which time it was up to 3700cc and $13,000+.

As far as I'm concerned, the 3500 GT is one of the great bargain-basement Italian exoticars. Most people couldn't honestly tell the difference between it and a 250GT Ferrari, yet the most spectacular thing about the Maserati has been depreciation. Ferrari 250GTs are worth over $15,000 for a good one; Maserati 3500 GT prices start under $2,000 and go up to $6,000. Which is incredible. For less than the price of a used Impala, you can get a fully restored, blue-blooded, high-performance GT, with occasional 2 + 2 seats in the back, even, with startlingly sophisticated truly timeless styling, more performance than anyone can ever rightly use—you can break the speed limit in second gear—a prestigious name, and all the little luxury tweaks that the beautiful people paid through the nose for, just a decade and a half ago.

The only flaw is the old parts-and-service runaround. Getting Italian electric windows fixed, for example, can cost more than the goddamn car itself. Other than that, though—and the same thing is true of any Italian exoticar—there's just no reason I can see to buy a Ferrari for twice the price. Except . . . well . . . a Ferrari is a *Ferrari*. A Maserati is a car. If you can get past that mental hurdle, however, the 3500 GT makes Filene's bargain basement look like Bergdorf's.

Maserati 3500 GT Spyder, body by Vignale.

Maserati 3500 GT coupe, body by Touring.

All Maseratis are underpriced right now, every damn one. Now true enough, most of them deserve it. The 3500 GT was followed by some really forgettable cars, like the Mistral and 5000 GT and Quattroporte. Even today's Merak and Khamsin aren't much to write home about. But in the middle there, from 1967 till '72, Maserati built precisely 2,400 examples of *the* most desirable car in the world. The Maserati Ghibli they called it, and it was the most significant Italian car since the landmark Cisitalia coupe two decades earlier. In fact, you can argue a pretty good case that the Cisitalia began the postwar GT phenomenon and the Ghibli summed it up at the end, and that there was really nothing else in between.

Giorgetto Giugiaro's 1967 Maserati Ghibli, the most important design since Pininfarina's Cisitalia.

You think I'm exaggerating. What makes the Ghibli so special? Easy. It's a goddamn purebred work of art is what it is. No question: the Ghibli is a glorious, brilliant masterpiece, no matter how you look at it. Start with the unimportant stuff: the engine. Now I admit that the Ghibli chassis is not up to the rest of the car, but *still*. It's twenty times more sophisticated than anything else around, except for the occasional Ferrari Daytona. I mean, how many 4.9-liter, double-overhead-cam, all-aluminum (block, too), 330-hp V-8s have you seen lately? With *four* twin-throat Webers? Your neighbor's Seville just isn't in the same status league, no matter what he thinks.

And the chassis. The Ghibli front end has conventional independent A-arms like everyone else's. Now of course the rear end *is* nothing more than a rigid axle on leaf springs. What can I say? Even Marisa Berenson has big feet and a trick knee. Thing is, between a Panhard rod and antiroll bar, the Maserati's clunky rear end is about as good as you can get without going to a fully independent setup. And honestly, when you're driving the car, you'd never know the difference. *Car and Driver* tested the third Ghibli in the country and they said, "From inside, the body roll is barely discernible, and the car feels firmly

planted on the road at all times—very reassuring." I rest my case. If you *have* to have a modern rear suspension under you, all I can suggest is a Corvette or a Lotus. Maybe a Mazda Cosmo? Thick-headed peasant.

Anyway. Once you get past the rigid rear axle, the rest of the Ghibli is pure dreamboat. Would you believe four-wheel Girling disc brakes with 543 square inches of swept area? And of course a ZF 5-speed gearbox, huge Pirelli radials on genuine knock-off magnesium-alloy wheels—or knock-off wires, your choice—and a super-strong steel tubing semi-space frame. It looks a lot bigger, but the Ghibli is only 180 inches long, on a 100-inch wheelbase. Total weight, though, is 3,500 pounds, which you have to expect if you want sound-deadening and electric windows and plushy carpets and all the rest of that luxury car stuff.

Once again, it just does not matter to the Maserati V-8 that it's supposed to tow around somewhere over 11 pounds per horsepower, evenly distributed front to rear, with a rear axle ratio good for 45 mph in first, 70 in second, 100 in third, 125 in fourth, and whatever you can get in fifth. And that's with the middlin' all-around performance differential. Put a tall gear in 'er and you can break the speed

Austere, functional, taut—the Ghibli is all of these—a perfect automotive package.

limit in first and run an honest 170 mph without breathing hard. With a 3.54 rear end, the Ghibli ran 0 to 60 in 6.4, 0 to 100 in 16.3, and the quarter-mile in 14.9 at 97 mph for *Car and Driver* in 1968. By comparison, in the same issue, they tested a special 428-cubic-inch Pontiac GTO put together by Royal Pontiac that had a similar 3.55 rear end ratio and about 10 million horsepower. The Goat did the quarter in 13.8 at 104, but with a low-winding Detroit V-8 and 3-speed automatic the best they could get out of it was an asthmatic 117 mph.

Point is, for a car meant to be a balanced, high-speed luxury GT, the Maserati Ghibli wasn't all *that* much slower accelerating than that crazy, stripped-out drag-strip Pontiac, and it had a good 50 mph more at the top end. Granted, in a land of 55-mph speed limits where there's always a smokey ready with his meter-reading pad, should you be daring enough to really wing it away from a stoplight, this kind of acceleration—and this kind of top speed—is totally meaningless, except as a subject for academic comparison. On the other hand, who says things are *supposed* to be this way? I mean, just because the goddamn government is in the hands of a bunch of double-knit peanut farmers, is everyone au-

tomatically supposed to roll over and play dead? Bullshit, I say. How else do you judge a $20,000+ high-performance machine? By the thickness of the foam rubber in the seat cushions?

Suffice it to say, the Maserati Ghibli, with air conditioning, power accessories, and old-fashioned V-8, still has enough *huevos* to see off anything else you're ever likely to meet on the street except a clapped-out super car or Cobra. But compared to most of those acceleration machines, the Ghibli is as snug as Aunt Marian's Vermont living room on a cold winter's evening. Comfortable, well thought out for real people, luxurious, reasonably well put together, and certainly as nice as anything you could buy new today for even three times the price.

I've been saving the best part for last. In addition to the vivid acceleration and unbelievable top speed, the 9.G braking—better than many racing cars—the superbly neutral handling, 17 mpg economy, and perfectly laid out cockpit, the Ghibli has the best exterior styling of any car in two decades. *The best.* You have to understand. Giorgetto Giugiaro is going to be considered the Raphael of automobiles someday. Smart folks think of him that way already. Count off on your fingers and toes the best automotive designs of the last fifteen years. How about the Alfa Romeo GTV and Canguro? The 2000/2600 Sprint? The Fiat Dino coupe, the little Fiat 850 Spyder, the Iso Grifo and Rivolta, the DeTomaso Mangusta, Alfasud, Lotus Esprit, Maserati Bora, Khamsin and Indy, Volkswagen Rabbit and Scirocco? Even the Ducati 860 and Benelli 750 Sei motorcycles. And that's just his good, best-known designs. There are others, for everything from prototype taxicabs to Rowan electric cars. Giorgetto Giugiaro is acknowledged to be the finest automobile stylist of the last two decades, certainly the best since the young Pininfarina, and perhaps, just maybe, he is the very best automobile stylist of this century. Which means the very best *ever*.

Giugiaro's masterpiece is the Maserati Ghibli; nothing else even comes close. Some of his other cars may have been more of an artistic challenge—the Fiat 850 Spyder or VW Scirocco, perhaps, because it's always harder to design a small, mass-market car than a flashy, limited-production GT with an astronomical price tag. Still, when all is said and done, the Ghibli is the best of Giugiaro's oeuvre. No question. Austere, functional, taut . . . the Ghibli is all of these. It's also the most perfect solution yet devised to the problem of beautifully packaging two adults in style and comfort for trips at insanely high speeds.

My art-historian compatriots always begin to laugh when I start going on about the *Automobile as Art.* But think about it. Somebody like Mark DiSuvero bolts together a bunch of old I-beams and logs, precariously balances the whole mess with a couple of chains, and the National Council for the Arts will pay him thirty grand to stick it on the Brooklyn Heights promenade so the neighborhood kids can cover it with graffiti. The thing is, DiSuvero's engineering is straight Tinker-Toy. He takes ten tons of perfectly valuable materials and the only thing it has to do is hold itself up. As a friend of mine said, after thoughtfully examining one of Mark's sculptures, "I liked it better as a telephone pole."

But with a piddling 3,500 pounds worth of aluminum, steel, and rubber, Giugiaro and friends have built a gorgeous chunk of superbly finished sculpture, a three-dimensional entity with easy, natural surface development the equal of any Henry Moore

evolutionary form . . . and the thing will not only carry two people at 170 mph, turn and stop with loads of nearly one gravity, but provide all the services of a small rural house: heat, air conditioning, lights, its own generating plant. *Plus* it will do all these things for years and years and years, if you treat it right. To my mind, the accomplishment of creating an automobile—which is, after all, *the* most significant factor in twentieth-century life—is so far superior to the creation of anything currently being revered by the culture buds in our museums that it doesn't bear talking about.

What makes the Ghibli so special, aside from the fact that it is a marvelous, functional, useful automobile, is that it also functions as a static work of art in three dimensions. The automobile per se is primarily sensation. It provides speed and noise and movement and primary sensory inputs. Obviously, the only time any automobile truly comes alive is when it's in motion. That's what it is built for. On the other hand, it should, in the best of all possible worlds, look good even if it's just sitting there waiting. This is the origin of automobile styling: the making of automobiles to express the essence of motion even at rest.

A limited edition of 2,400, Giugiaro's Maserati Ghibli ca

Nobody does this better than Giorgetto Giugiaro. The Ghibli honestly looks like it's going 100 mph sitting still, which is a cliché, I know, but it really does look like that. And it works on all levels. As a whole, the shape is perfect: tense, mildly angular, aggressive. But all the details work, too. Look at the window shapes and moldings, or the tiny front grille, that shallow, subtle bulge that breaks up the flat plane of the hood without destroying it; the long, thin pencil vents in the front fenders that gracefully echo the powerful, evocative engine compartment; the squared-off but not abrupt fastback; the delicate taillight and bumper treatment. The way even wire wheels are made to seem modern and right through the timeless symmetry of the body itself. There just isn't anything better.

Personally, I think you should be gathering up Ghiblis the way you'd buy Rauschenbergs or Olitskis—as collectible investments guaranteed to appreciate as time goes by. Right now, Ghiblis are at the very bottom of their price cycle. Anything over $15,000 is too much to pay for a good one. And I wouldn't consider anything else. You don't want a tatty work of art, you want the most perfect Maserati Ghibli possible, one that you will then stick in your temperature-stabilized, humidity-con-

trolled gallery where it can be admired by your art collector friends and you can be congratulated on your good taste. I am firmly convinced, if there is any justice left in the world at all, that twenty years from now we'll be trading Maserati Ghiblis the way Marlborough Galleries deals in Impressionists. And people will talk about owning a Giugiaro the way we talk about owning a Picasso. Giorgetto Giugiaro—and his Ghibli—are that good.

Lamborghini

An exotic Italian GT? How does this sound? A double-overhead-cam 4-liter V-12, rated at 430 hp, designed by famed engineer Giotti Bizzarrini, designer of the Iso Grifo, the Bizzarrini, and the 250GT Ferrari. Mounted behind the driver, of course. And not just stuck back there, but cleverly placed *across* the chassis for best weight distribution. A 5-speed transmission. Huge four-wheel disc brakes—an incredible 516 square inches of swept area—covered by wide knock-off magnesium wheels fitted with immense Pirelli VR radials rated for continuous speeds in excess of 165 mph. All-independent suspension, of course, and a lightweight, impressively strong fabricated chassis of the finest steel tubing and sheet steel. The whole chassis designed by Ferrari engineer Gian Paolo Dallara.

Over it all, a lovely, 41-inch-high, low-slung, sensuously erotic berlinetta body designed by that master of the Italian style Giorgetto Giugiaro. And built in aluminum by Nuccio Bertone. It is striking, outlandish . . . and perfectly practical. And without a single add-on aerodynamic device, perfectly stable at 180 mph. This car does the quarter-mile faster than most American super cars, at 108 mph in 13.9 seconds, yet it has a long-legged differential that gives an honest 170 mph in top gear. It weighs less than 3,000 pounds, and will stop with a force better than .9G. It will outhandle any car you can think of, yet the ride is supple and compliant. It even delivers

be collected like fine art.

The 1964 Lamborghini 400 GT by Touring.

14 mpg, for those who care. And the price? A piddling $19,000 in 1970. A mere pittance for the best Italian GT in the world.

As you no doubt realize, I'm *not* describing some forgotten Ferrari, though every word—excepting the compliant ride—could be used to describe a composite of ultimate Ferrari coupes. But no, this is the Lamborghini Miura, the only legitimate challenger to Ferrari for best sports car in the world honors. The Miura was created through the simple expedient of hiring the best engineers and designers in Italy and allowing them totally free rein on an unlimited budget. Happily enough for Ferruccio Lamborghini, the product is worth the expense. Current—that is, circa 1978—Lamborghinis are either illegal to bring into the country or relatively small, mostly emasculated, smog-controlled, be-bumpered people-movers of no great appeal, though the prices are among the highest in the world. But for a while there in the late sixties Lamborghini was *it*—honest and truly better than any Ferrari, no matter which way you cut it.

There's even a semilegendary story behind the founding of Lamborghini, but it's a good tale nonetheless. And Ferruccio Lamborghini swears it's true. The story goes like this. Lamborghini is a major manufacturer, the biggest maker of tractors, air conditioners, and central heating units in Italy. A big industrialist from the north of Italy, tough, smart, and independent; in his own field easily the equal of Il Commendatore. In fact, Ferruccio

is Il Commendatore in his own right, a Knight of Italy, and obviously a very wealthy and powerful person.

Supposedly, he had a 330 GTC Ferrari and the thing was eating differentials like popcorn. So Lamborghini had his designers take the thing apart, figure out what was wrong, and do up some design drawings to fix it. And logically enough in his mind, I suppose, Lamborghini brought his drawings and his car to the factory and showed old Enzo how to fix a Ferrari. According to Lamborghini, Ferrari said, in so many words, that he'd be damned if he'd fix a Ferrari for some lousy tractor maker. So Lamborghini replied in so many words, "Get knotted. I'll build a *better* GT." *"Ehhh, stupido,"* laughed Ferrari. *"Un trattore Gran Turismo."*

This was in 1961. Lamborghini is nothing if not methodical. He spent two years getting his other affairs in order, selecting a new factory, and putting together a design team from all over Italy. And then he sprang. The first Lamborghini was a *very* Ferrari-like front-engine GT. Given the exotic-market segment it was meant for, it was technically ordinary: just a double-overhead-cam V-12, space-frame chassis, all-independent suspension, four-wheel discs, 5-speed. But, unfortunately, one of the weirdest production bodies ever to come out of Touring's shop. Designed by free-lance designer Sargiotto, the shape was fine—sort of an inflated Alfa GTV—but the detailing was horrendous. Quad headlights in little pods, an incised curve down the fender sides, and recessed taillights in a pointed stern were only the most obvious gaffes. The Lamborghini was an *ugly* car, no doubt about it.

Still, *Road & Track* preferred it to the 275 GTB/4, and of course that's precisely what Lamborghini was trying to do . . . out-Ferrari Ferrari. The Lamborghini 350 GT and the larger-displacement 400 GT sold pretty well in the States. And though they were never pretty, they do have a surfeit of visual identity. While all those smooth Pininfarina Ferraris are gliding inconspicuously by, the Lamborghini 350/400 is standing up and shouting "Look at *me!*" Unfortunately for Lamborghini, most of the exotic-car market is slightly more subtle than that. Just *slightly* more subtle, but certainly not as weird as Sargiotto's coupe. Still, there were about 500 of the early

GTs (250 of them were 400 GTs), and prices are in the $15,000 range today.

By 1966, when Lamborghini had Ing. Dallara start work on his new Miura, he'd learned a lot. Lamborghini was now smart enough to head for Bertone's Giugiaro instead of Sargiotto/Touring. So the Miura's styling is maybe a million times more sophisticated than the 350 GT. But it's obvious that Lamborghini had a lot of say in how his cars looked. The Miura is easily the most flamboyant body ever drawn by Giorgetto Giugiaro. It's hard to believe the same man drew this, the Mangusta, and the Maserati Ghibli within months of one another. For one thing, the Miura is about the only mature Giugiaro design that's not in the angular, hard-edged idiom Giugiaro invented and made so much his own. Instead, it's all ersatz Pininfarina—rounded, bulbous, sensuous—covered with fins and louvers and vents, blessed with a smiling, full-width, grilleless mouth like some California special and a naive, unresolved look. Still, it's no worse than most Italian bodies from the mid-sixties. Everything can't be a masterpiece.

The Miura chassis, though, truly is one of the all-time great, strictly street designs. And really, for street use, there's a lot to be said for a car *not* designed for the very peculiar, quite specialized conditions found on a race track. This means the Miura is much more livable, more *comfortable* if it comes to that, than something like a Ferrari 275 GTB/4. And technically of course, even *more* exotic. Really, the Miura is what Ferrari's transverse mid-engine Dino would have been with the 4.3-liter V-12 from the Daytona stuck in the back and the whole car scaled up to match. For 1966 the Miura was just so advanced it's uncanny. It's the acknowledged precursor of the Monteverdi Hai, the Maserati Bora, and Ferrari's own Berlinetta Boxer.

Ronnie Wakefield tested the Miura for *R & T* in 1970 and his comments still stand, I think. "We've never kidded ourselves that the Miura is a practical automobile," he said. "Instead, it should be considered an exercise in automotive art—a design for a particular type of driving that can be practiced only rarely. Its price assures that it will be owned only by people who can afford other cars for other purposes, and taken in this context, it is a masterpiece to be relished by the connoisseur." Indeed. You can make a pretty good case that the best collector cars are those built for collectors—connoisseurs, it means the

The most flamboyant Giugiaro body ever, and totally appropriate to the wild Lamborghini Miura.

same thing—when they were new. And the Miura, certainly, was built for the collector market. Happily enough, today the price of admission is only three-fourths of the $19,000 it took to buy one just five years ago. But it's sure to go up again.

Ferrari [1964-1976]

In 1964 Enzo Ferrari was in a bad way. His sports/racers were in the doldrums and Ford ruled the tracks. Ferrari Formula One cars were nowhere. The engineering department was moribund. Maserati was starting to get its act together with the Mistral that led to the exquisite Ghibli, and Lamborghini already had its funny-looking 400 GT, which *Road & Track* delightedly labeled better than any street Ferrari. Clearly, Ferrari was slipping on all fronts, and he had to do something, *anything,* to turn events around.

The 275 GTB was made for that purpose. It was meant to reestablish Ferrari in no uncertain terms as *the* name in exotic sports cars, at the same time as the fabulous mid-

Pebble smooth, Pininfarina's 1967 275 GTB/4.

engine 275 LM was brought to the track. Of course, the new coupe had to have the Colombo engine. Like every worthwhile Ferrari, the GTB used the short-block V-12. The most successful size until then had been the 3-liter version, but the GTB got a bored-out 3286cc, single-overhead-cam powerhouse with your choice of 260, 280, or 300 hp, depending upon carburetion.

There was a tubular space frame and an all-new suspension with—at last—unequal-length A-arms and coil springs at both front *and* rear. The rear transaxle was a 5-speed, the brakes were four-wheel discs, the wheels were huge Borrani cast-alloy mags. The interior was all-leather; the steel body was styled by Pininfarina and built by Scaglietti. You could go on and on. The GTB isn't a styling milestone like the Cisitalia 1100 or the Maserati Ghibli, it doesn't have earth-shattering performance like a 427 Cobra, it doesn't handle like a Lotus Eleven or cradle you in the luxury of a Rolls-Royce. No single component dominates the others, no one factor stands out to make you pine for a GTB for that and that alone. But when all is said and done, the Ferrari 275 GTB is probably the most balanced street machine ever built, a superb blend of just enough of everything, not too much of anything.

Top speed: around 165 mph with 3.56 gearing. Acceleration: 0 to 60 in 7 seconds, 0 to 100 in 14, the quarter-mile in the mid-14s at over 100 mph. Which is all pretty impressive using just over 3 liters, particularly with a 2,650-pound curb weight. Braking: over .9G consistently, which even today, well over a decade since the last GTB was built, is right at the outer performance limits for street machines. Handling is just as good, with nearly perfect weight distribution (49/51), and even the 15-mpg fuel consumption is still better than many later emissions-controlled V-8s with a lot less performance. Put it all together and you have one of the nicest all-around performance cars you can think of. It's a bit much for everyday use, but not so stupendous as to be unmanageable.

The same is true of the styling. It's not a Raphael that takes your breath away every time you open the garage door, but it is undeniably superior to anything else from its era *except* Giugiaro's Ghibli. In fact, the 275 GTB

The Ferrari 275 GTB/4 has a classic, timeless elegance, the best of Pininfarina's oeuvre.

is kind of the swan song of Pininfarina's bulbous postwar oeuvre, the smooth, aerodynamic, uncluttered style that began with his Cisitalia and will end when Bill Mitchell's Camaro/Firebird finally dies. Giugiaro succeeded Pininfarina as top dog, and he's the one largely responsible for the angular idiom that dominates car styling today, with its intense surface development, hard edges, and linear conception. Pininfarina's classic look seems a bit dated now, precisely because of this change in taste, yet it remains a remarkably pure, timeless style. When the present angularity softens—as it's bound to do in an era of flaccid cars and rubber bumpers—the 275 GTB will be right back in style.

The early cars are great, but after two years Ferrari went to double overhead cams on the V-12, 300 hp in the cooking version, and a new name: 275 GTB/4. The GTB/4 is the ultimate front-engine Ferrari; it's so good you won't believe it. I've spent a fair amount of time in these Ferraris and *never* been disappointed. They are a bit of a handful on the street—the clutch is fierce, there's very little flywheel effect, they overheat sitting in traffic, the steering is heavy at slow speeds, the virtually bumperless body is extremely vulnerable. But low-speed puttering around isn't what these cars are made for, and on an everyday basis most people would be better off driving

some disposable stone. But anyone who's going to buy a GTB/4 isn't going to drive it every day, at least shouldn't expect to, and then it's just one glorious high-speed winding road after another.

The GTB/4 is one of those rare machines that's so good it makes *you* better, too. It will make an average driver feel like Fangio, and Fangio seem like God. You can do *anything* in a GTB/4, and unless you're extremely perceptive, you won't even know you've done something special. The car just hides your mistakes and keeps on pulling for all it's worth. There is nothing, I promise you, that is more concentrated fun to drive than one of these Ferraris in a high-speed, off-camber corner, with the light and sensitive steering feeding back every pebble, the glorious 5-speed shifter notching through the characteristic Ferrari gate, and the instantaneous throttle response letting you dial in your own handling characteristics with a touch of the toe. And that's not to mention the pure, sensuous, palpable shriek of the V-12, redlined at an impressive 8,000, positively howling away, the exhaust blasting you from behind, the clackity-clack of the valve gear pummeling you from in front. It's a visceral, hearty surround-sound they ought to pipe into laggardly offices instead of Muzak. The 275 GTB/4 is one of those rare automotive experiences like

The ultimate Ferrari . . . 300 hp, 2,650 pounds, viceless handling, and superb styling.

eating shell steak with lobster, caviar *and* bay oysters washed down with Cordon Rouge that's just too rich for most men's blood. For those who can stand the protein, though, there's never been anything like it.

On top of everything else, the GTB/4 was one of the bargains of its day. Between 1964 when it appeared and 1968 when Ferrari dropped it in favor of the new 365 GTB Daytona, the GTB/4 went up in price from a paltry $14,500 to $14,900 in America. Peanuts. In 1968 the Aston DBS went for $17,200, Maserati's Ghibli for $18,900. Compared with today's prices for similar new cars, these prices are a joke, but they were considered really *big* less than ten years ago. And the superb GTB/4 cost 20 percent less than the beautiful but comparatively unsophisticated Ghibli or the uninspired, uneven Aston. Even before the GTB/4s were dropped, people could *tell*. And the market never really dipped. They got down to around $8,000 a few years ago, but now a good GTB/4 is worth more than it cost new. The best ones are over $20,000 already, and Lord knows . . . the sky's the limit.

If I were you and wanted to invest in a really guaranteed postwar blue chip but couldn't afford a 300SL or a 427 Cobra, I would sweep together this month's trust-fund interest or trade off some of that Chrysler common that Daddums bought in '49 or whatever and would hie myself down to the local Ferrari owner's club chapter and buy myself the very best GTB/4 that I could find. I'd get an impartial Ferrari mechanic, if such an animal exists, slip him a few bills, and have him curry that rascal with a fine-tooth comb first, of course. And after I'd got it home, I'd massage that monster into just about the best Ferrari anyone had ever seen. And then, and then. And then I'd go find me the twistiest, craziest, dipsy-dooiest road around, and I would fair lay into that little mother and flat straighten it out. Take that GTB/4 and use it like a crowbar, and bend that goddamn road around until it cried "uncle." And then I'd find another road that needed straightening out, and another, and another.

And after *that*, after I'd wrung that GTB/4 out good, I'd *retire* it and keep it perfect as can be. I'd turn it out to stud when my street-racing days were over. Then I'd buy a 365 GTB/4. Ah yes, the fabulous Ferrari Daytona. Guaranteed to go one hunnert sebenty-four miles per hour. That's right, *174*. Documented and guaranteed. *Road & Track* got only 173 out of theirs, but Luigi Chinetti took one to Le Mans—perfectly stock—and had it timed at 179. So it kinda averages out. The Daytona is demonstrably fast. And it handles and

brakes and is wonderful and is the best Ferrari ever built and is great in bed and even makes its own clothes. Okay. At least that's what everyone would like you to think. Don't believe a word of it. The Daytona is truly grand. But somehow, as a package, it just doesn't hold a candle to a good GTB/4. Don't ask me why. Just some little something, that weird body maybe, but at least for me the Daytona just doesn't do it. Would you settle for the second-best Ferrari ever built?

This is irrational, I know. Maybe I should be in analysis or something, but try as I might, I just can't get all *that* excited about the 365 GTB/4 Daytona. Surely, it's good. The heart of any Ferrari is the engine, and the Daytona uses a super-refined 4.4-liter version of the old long-block V-12, complete with double overhead cams. This old blunderbuss is rated at 352 hp at 7,500 rpm. To me this is hardly in the same league with the 300+ hp at 8,000 rpm of the 3.2-liter short block in the GTB/4. I mean, it's still impressive and all, but the specific output—and, more important, that effortless *feel*—just aren't the same. To me, and a lot of other people, there's just no comparison between the Colombo short block and the Lampredi long block, no matter how much they work that big engine over.

Underneath, the Daytona is pretty much identical to the GTB/4: same 94.5-inch wheelbase, same 5-speed transaxle and all-independent suspension, same four-wheel discs and mag wheels, though the Daytona mags have five-pointed star centers patterned after those on Ferrari's big sports/racers. But because of the bigger engine and heavier body, the Daytona weighs almost 300 pounds more than the GTB/4. Still, that extra 50 hp is enough to get the Daytona through the quarter-mile in the low 14s at nearly 110 mph, which is quicker than any street machine ever, except for big Cobras and a few whacked-out super cars.

I guess, really, my objections to the Daytona center on the body and the overall flaccid *feel* of the car. Just as the Pininfarina styling is a lot more gimmicky on the Daytona than on the GTB/4, so the taut, harsh, semiracer feeling of the earlier car has been replaced by something approximating an American personal luxury car. The Daytona, to me, is Ferrari's answer to the Thunderbird, a fancy, overstuffed appearance machine meant to wow 'em down at the car wash. I hate to admit it, but the Daytona *is* more usable. It's more of an everyday sort of car. But that doesn't make it a collector car.

The GTB/4-Daytona situation is analogous to that which surrounds Shelby Mustangs, albeit on a price scale inflated by something like 500 percent. It's like this. The early Shelby GT-350s and Ferrari 275 GTB/4s are really macho, hairy-type street racers, harsh, demanding, and more fun than anything else

Ferrari 365 GTB/4 Daytona, body by Pininfarina.

that's street-legal. The later Ford-built Shelby GT-500s and the Daytonas are bigger, softer, smoother, relatively innocuous machines for people who want the image without the excitement. Predictably, I guess, there're more image seekers than macho seekers in the world. Genuine Shelby GT-350s and GTB/4s are still reasonably priced, in their respective categories, of course, though the later image cars are way overpriced.

Daytonas weren't made U.S.-legal until 1970—they'd been out in Europe for two years before that—and they came in at $19,500. Three years later, when the model was dropped in this country, the tab was a heady $25,200. The thing is that today, just a few years later, that's *still* on the low end of the rate scale. Really good Daytonas, particularly genuine NART cars with documented Le Mans race records (fifth overall in '71, fifth through ninth in '72, sixth, ninth, thirteenth in '73)— have been offered lately for as high as $40,000. Even regular ol' Daytonas are going for $30,000. Which, I suppose, given that the new Boxer flat-12s are going for $60,000 over here, is fair enough. But that makes $20,000–$25,000 for a 275 GTB/4 look like the art bargain of the century. Personally, I'd dip into the trust fund if I were you.

Iso

You have to understand about the Italian car industry. I mean, who else *is* there besides Ferrari? So constantly there's a terrific turnover of new talent in town challenging the top gun. All those spaghetti westerns must have gone to their heads, because half the industrialists in Italy are going broke trying to out-Ferrari Ferrari, and the other half are wishing they had either the guts or the money to try.

One of the most successful—certainly one of the most persistent—Ferrari challengers is Iso. Way back in 1962 now, Il Commendatore Renzo Rivolta—the leading manufacturer of refrigerators in Italy and originator of the crazy Isetta bubblecar that BMW made such a success in the mid-fifties—stepped out onto Main Street in Milan to lay down his challenge to Il Commendatore Ferrari. All things considered, he didn't do such a bad job. The cars were never a match for Ferrari—not even for Lamborghini or Maserati—but Rivolta's Iso did become the top gun in the Italo-American hybrid league, one notch down from Il Big Time.

The reason the Iso doesn't compete with Ferrari is that Rivolta decided to save himself a lot of time and trouble and do an assembled car. It's an old, old concept that worked to a certain extent for everyone from Eddie Rickenbacker and Ned Jordan to Carroll Shelby and Bruce Meyers. Rivolta started by hiring Ferrari engineer Giotti Bizzarrini after the great Maranello massacre of 1962. Bizzarrini had done the Ferrari 250GT, but in 1962 when Commendatore Rivolta came knocking, Bizzarrini was newly out on the sidewalk trying to set up his own free-lance engineering firm. He positively leaped at the chance to do a whole car.

This was the Iso Rivolta, and for a first try it was dynamite. A four-passenger 2 + 2, the Iso Rivolta had four-wheel disc brakes, a DeDion rear, and a solid, 105-inch-wheelbase frame. The fine innards Bizzarrini provided were all covered by a lovely, smooth, all-steel Bertone body *very* similar to the smaller Alfa GTV, and for a very good reason. The Iso Rivolta carries one of the earliest production bodies ever designed by Giorgetto Giugiaro, not much older than a schoolboy in 1962. But you'd never know it from the Iso. Working with his own unique interpretation of Pininfarina's rounded style, Giugiaro gave the Iso some of the best, understated proportions of any car ever. It's not a masterpiece like the Maserati Ghibli, but if the Ghibli is Giugiaro's equivalent of Raphael's *School of Athens,* then the Iso Rivolta is his *Granduca Madonna* . . . the quiet, classical early work that best shows the skills for which he will soon be world-famous.

What kept the Iso as nothing more than just another pretty Italian face was the engine. Rivolta took the easy way out, using the ubiquitous small-block 327 Corvette V-8 and Muncie 4-speed. Now *we* know, breeding and pedigree and overhead cams aside, that the Ed Cole/Harry Barr Chevy V-8 is one of the great, all-time production engines. And it would push the Iso Rivolta up over 140 mph, no sweat, 0 to 60 in 6.2 seconds, 0 to 130 in 29 seconds. Still, when you're trying to compete with Ferrari, the only way to *really* do it is like Lamborghini has—to design and build your own V-12 exotimotor from scratch. On the other hand, if you had to actually *own* one or the other and don't have more money than God, something with an American V-8—whether it's a Cobra, Jensen, or Iso—is *always* going to be a lot less trouble and expense than a pedigreed, thoroughbred Ferrari/Lamborghini/Maserati.

Bizzarrini's same basic Iso Rivolta chassis is still being made as the Iso Lele, with another Giugiaro body done while he was at Ghia. This one looks like an oversized VW Dasher, and nobody's ever suggested it should win any awards. But it *is* significant, I think, that nearly fifteen years after it first appeared, Bizzarrini's Iso chassis can still find a market in the $25,000 range. In Europe only, of course; there hasn't been an Iso brought into the States in years. Perhaps a hundred of the Iso Rivoltas were imported by Inskip, about twice that many Iso Grifos.

Iso Grifo, you say? Indeed. In 1963 Commendatore Rivolta really had his sights on Ferrari. I doubt that Ferrari ever realized it—Clint Eastwood ignoring some gun-crazy kid—but to Rivolta, this was *serious* business. He even picked the Griffon, the mythological enemy of prancing horses, as his emblem. The Iso Grifo is some nice car, right up there with the front-engine Ferraris and Maseratis and Lamborghinis. Except for the engine, of course. Once again, Bizzarrini used the small-block Chevy. But since the Grifo is strictly a two-seater, the wheelbase came down to 98 inches, the overall length to only 175, and the height was kept under four feet, which though not as low as Ford's GT-40 coupe is still pushing the limit for cars you can actually get into and out of on a regular basis.

The Iso Grifo was never meant as a racing car; Rivolta was too smart for that. But still, it's technically about as good as you can get. The transmission in some of the cars was just the plain vanilla Muncie 4-speed, but a lot of them got expensive ZF 5-speeds, the same

The 1962 Iso Rivolta by Bizzarrini/Giugiaro/Chevrolet.

The 1963 Iso Grifo by Bizzarrini/Giugiaro/Chevrolet.

gearbox used by Maserati. Four-wheel Dunlop discs—a giant 12 inches in diameter—with Campagnolo mags were hung on an independent front suspension and DeDion rear. And the standard engine was always the top-of-the-line Corvette V-8, growing in horsepower as the 'Vette did. Around 1967/'68 Rivolta even dropped the aluminum block ZL-1 427 into a handful of Grifos and a few more got the L-88 427 iron block with aluminum heads. This experiment didn't go any further, though, and the production cars were always stuck with the little ol' Chevy small blocks.

With a hydraulic lifter 350-hp 327 running through a 3.31 rear, *Car and Driver* recorded 0 to 60 in 6.5 seconds, the quarter-mile in 15.1 at 94 mph, and a top speed of 160 mph. Although this didn't make 275 GTB/4 owners run for cover, it wasn't bad for a 3,500-pound street fighter with an all-steel body, sunroof, radio, electric windows, and all the rest. It was certainly in the ballpark with a lot of $20,000 cars in 1968, when the Iso Grifo cost a mere $15,000.

Curiously enough, probably the closest car to the Iso Grifo is A. C.'s Cobra-based 428 Coupe, with a Frua body that's been copied from Giugiaro's Iso right down to the twin-nostrils type of nose. Come to think of it, it's Frua who supplied the Monteverdi High Speed body, an obvious copy of Giugiaro's Maserati Ghibli. Which makes Frua a Giugiaro fan and sincere flatterer, if nothing else. Anyway. The other car that comes close to the Iso Grifo in looks and feel, logically enough, is the first-series Corvette Sting Ray coupe. The size, proportions, and power are all about the same, as are the looks and feel.

The Iso, of course, has that little extra something conferred by its $15,000 price tag, something the Sting Ray doesn't have even though it's at least as good a car. Exclusivity, I guess. Collectibility, if you will. I mean, about the only thing wrong with Corvettes as exotic collector cars is they're not very exotic. GM builds something like 50,000 a year. But still they'll rattle, squeak, leak, overheat, and fall apart just as predictably as any Ferrari, for less than half the price. The Iso's no better or worse in that respect, of course, except that like the Corvette the Iso will keep running as it falls apart, thanks to its dull passenger-car engine. The pseudo-racer motor in the Ferrari means that lots of times the car will be falling apart while it's stalled in one place. The assumption, of course, is that the proles who drive mere Corvettes or Chevrolet-powered Isos have to depend on their cars for transportation, whereas it is understood that one doesn't even consider Ferrari ownership without at least one or two other vehicles to use for doing mundane chores and day-to-day transportation.

This leaves the Iso Grifo somewhere in between, in purgatory, as far as lots of collectors are concerned. I'd rather think of it as the perfect combination of the best of both worlds . . . Bizzarrini's Ferrari-taught handling and braking, Giugiaro's exquisite looks, and Chevrolet's dependable power. Certainly it'll never be a blueblood collector car. On the other hand, it's the cheapest decent Italian exotic you can buy outside of a Maserati 3500.

And compared to the Maser, the Grifo is better looking, technically more sophisticated—engine excluded—and capable of *much* higher performance. Not to mention, much rarer and a lot cheaper to maintain.

Really, the Iso Grifo ends up today in the same market position it had more than a decade ago when it first appeared. If all you want is transportation with a little style, buy a 'Vette. If you want an extravagant, expensive, virtually unusable toy, get that Ferrari. But if you want the excitement of being a genuine gunslinger without having to be in the chancy position of top gun, get the Iso. Hell, for $7,000 or something, you can't go wrong. Owning the Ferrari, you're going to use up that much just in Darvon and Valium. And besides, who wants to have every punk gunslinger in the territory gunning for you?

Giotti Bizzarrini finished ninth overall at Le Mans in '6.

Bizzarrini

Yeah, I *know* it sounds like a made-up name. What can I say? But there really *is* a Giotti Bizzarrini, and he really did name his car after himself. Crazy name, crazy car. *Si?* And a crazy story behind it, too. Thing is, Bizzarrini actually had credentials. Real, honest-to-God engineering credentials and a great background in all the right places. He went to the university at Pisa in the early fifties and then became an engineer at Alfa Romeo. He switched from Alfa to Ferrari in 1957 and worked on the 250GT, GTO, and Testa Rossa, which is not a bad group to have in your portfolio, you know? Then, when the famous walkout occurred in 1961 he was one of five Ferrari engineers who left. While the others started ATS, Bizzarrini designed the Lamborghini V-12, then the Iso Rivolta and the Iso Grifo.

That's where this tale starts to get *really* interesting, because the Iso Grifo—with a gorgeous Giorgetto Giugiaro body built by Bertone—was one of the sexiest cars ever built. So what if the Iso used a Corvette V-8 instead of an exotic V-12? Bizzarrini himself drove one into ninth overall and first in class at Le Mans, for Chrissake, back in 1965. I mean, there wasn't anything this boy couldn't do. Eventually, Bizzarrini got fed up with consulting for Iso, who looked like they were going down the drain anyway, and he left.

Thing is, the Iso that Bizzarrini brought to Le Mans was a really good piece, a lightened, wacked-out, full-race version of the basic Iso Grifo. It was his pet project. But after he left, Commendatore Rivolta decided there

...n this Iso Grifo Competition model, which became the Bizzarrini GT.

Bizzarrini GT by Bizzarrini/Giugiaro/Chevrolet.

was more money to be made building boulevard sports cars. So he scratched the race version and concentrated on the heavier, more solid, more luxurious Grifo. There was only one thing to do. Bizzarrini got some backers together and went into the car business himself. He drew up an all-independent suspension, front-engine tubular chassis with a 96-inch wheelbase. Just coincidentally, it was almost identical to his competition version Iso Grifo. So he used the same 327-cubic-inch Corvette V-8 with four Webers and the trusty old Muncie 4-speed. It wasn't very fancy, but it was cheap. And it worked.

Bizzarrini also used four-wheel discs, and great hulking Dunlop tires on pretty mag wheels, and lots of other good chassis bits. And then—*huevos!*—he simply took Giugiaro's magnificent Iso body, cut a few extra slots and slits and holes in it to make it look just a tad different, nostalgically added a twin-nostril nose that was the trademark of his old boss at Ferrari, Ing. Chiti, and called the whole thing the Bizzarrini GT America. Of *course* it was nothing more than the Iso Grifo Le Mans coupe with a few funny styling touches, which was the whole point. Any car that wins its class at Le Mans can't be *all* bad, and everyone had already heard of Iso. No one had heard of Bizzarrini. But everyone would recognize the similarity quick enough.

Somehow, Bizzarrini even talked John Fitch, the purveyor of Corvair Sprints, into being the exclusive American importer. And of course America was where most of the cars went. A fair bunch stayed in Livorno near the factory, and a few more scattered like hawks around the rest of Italy. But the majority of the production came to the States, which isn't as impressive as it sounds. Even at only $10,500—which, though a lot less than a Ferrari was a lot more than a Corvette—Fitch had a hard time scaring up many Bizzarrini buyers. As a car, the Corvette was a *much* better proposition, and as an automotive icon, Ferrari and Lamborghini didn't cost all *that* much more, if that was what you wanted.

By 1969 it was all over. There had been a little Fiat-based 1.5/2.0-liter car, but it was even less popular than the Corvette version. Giotti Bizzarrini disappeared back into the nether world of the Italian automotive industry, having had his fling. A few dozen GT Americas were built at most, and you can be sure that the ones that came in after January 1, 1968, were still labeled '67s. The Bizzarrini was so screamingly bizarre there was no way it could hope to meet the federal safety standards. For starters, it was only 43 inches high, which is pretty hard to do with a front-engine car. Putting side-guard door beams into those little fiberglass panels would have been laughingly difficult. Then there's the matter of front bumpers. Would you believe a decorative chrome strip glued to the fiberglass nose? So much for crash tests.

You get the idea. The Bizzarrini GT was not very far removed from the race track, and though I suppose Bizzarrini *could* have put bumpers on, that would have upset the perfect 50/50 weight distribution he'd worked so hard to achieve. And who knows how much extra would have been added to the lightweight 2,550 pounds of the ready-to-roll car if it had to take side impacts? And eight 45mm Weber carburetor throats, without air cleaners, feeding exquisite fabricated headers? There was no way that setup could have been desmogged. No, it was better to let the Bizzarrini die, the bizarre victim of an equally bizarre set of laws. To do otherwise would have been a violation of aesthetic principles too important to dismiss for such trivialities. Of *course* top speeds of 160 mph make no sense anymore, if in fact they ever did. Of *course* 100 mph quarter-miles are merely of academic interest in a nation with 55-mph speed limits. Of *course.* But that's just the point. Once upon a time, not so long ago, all that wasn't so crazy. Bizzarrini. Crazy name? *Si.* Crazy car? *No.* A thousand times, *No.*

Ferrari Dino

The whole idea of the Dino was—and still is, for that matter—to capitalize on the Ferrari name in the lower-priced Porsche end of the exoticar market. Now the Dino name on V-6/ V-8 Ferrari engines goes back to 1956, when Ferrari's beloved son Alfredo died of leukemia at age twenty-four. Dino Ferrari was to inherit the company and was learning it from the bottom up. This meant studying under Vittorio Jano, easily the most instructive engineer in Italy. Jano and Dino were working together on a 1.5-liter V-6 for Formula Two when young Ferrari died, and his father named that engine—and all subsequent V-6s—Dino.

The first V-6 was a double-overhead-cam racing engine that was scaled up from 1.5 to 2.0, 2.4, and 2.9 liters. In 1957 Jano took half a Colombo V-12 and made a totally different single-overhead-cam V-6 for use in sports/ racers. There have been three different V-8s— including the current 308 aluminum job— called Dino, but really, when you talk about *the* Dino Ferrari, you mean the 246 GT, a strictly street, transverse mid-engine coupe. The V-6 for this Dino was designed in 1965 by Carlo Rocchi, but in typical Ferrari fashion this engine wasn't designed for the car.

Ferrari wanted an engine for the new 1600cc "stock block" Formula Two, which required that at least 500 engines had been built and, presumably, inserted in automobiles. No way was Ferrari *ever* going to find a market for 500 little cars, seeing as how total Ferrari

production in the mid-sixties was only around 400 a year. So Ferrari made a deal, the first step on the way to Fiat's eventual takeover in Maranello. Fiat would build 500 engines to Ferrari specs and insert them in front-engine Fiat roadsters and coupes. Ferrari, meanwhile, would build a real-race version of the same engine for Formula Two and his mid-engine hillclimb sports/racers. And so it came to pass.

Finally, in 1967, Fiat built enough engines. Unfortunately, by then the Lotus/Brabham/Lola hordes were too tough to overcome and the Ferrari Formula Two car went nowhere. The expensive Fiat Dino street machines were a lot closer to Fiat 124s than to Ferraris, so they couldn't give the things away. But Rocchi's engine wasn't bad in itself, however. In it's 1986cc double-overhead-cam form it was rated at 180 hp in street tune, 240 hp for the race cars. In 2418cc form it produced 195 hp at 7,600 rpm in street trim. It was a clean, happy design, one of those all-around *nice* engines that somehow come out to be more than the sum of their parts. The Dino was smooth like a turbine, light like the chunk of aluminum it was, and strong like a bull.

In late '66/early '67 Rocchi mounted one transversely in a tube-frame chassis derived from his little mid-engine mountain championship hillclimb cars. The wheelbase was only 92 inches, the overall length only 165 inches—tiny, in other words. And he came up with a nice 5-speed transaxle that used A-

The first modern GT, Ferrari's 2-liter V-6, mid-engined Dino 246 GT, styled by Pininfarina.

arms and coil springs for an independent rear suspension. At the front was a similar layout. Girling disc brakes all around and big tires on pretty mag wheels, and he was done.

Pininfarina took Rocchi's chassis and clothed it in maybe his best design of the last decade. The car was *so* small and tight that it came across as a really visceral body, a thin skin rippling with hard, well-developed muscles. The pointed nose was similar to that on the bigger GTC 330, with a diminutive slit of an air intake, "sugar scoop" headlights tunneled into the fenders, and louvers in the hood. The greenhouse was light and delicate, with curious buttresses leading back from the top to Kamm-chopped tail. Simple taillights, fat fenders, and rows of louvers in the engine cover/deck lid characterized the rear. But the most unusual feature of Pininfarina's Dino was a curved-glass rear window tunneled into the flying buttresses, which left a vertical slot only a few inches high to see out the back. And where most cars have door handles, the Dino had a long, thin, pointed air scoop carved out of the side. All in all, as lovely a body as you could find, the very epitome of the soft-edge, bulbous period of Pininfarina's mature style. Lovely.

The car is also a goer, and that's the truth. It weighs only 2,400 pounds, and with nearly 200 hp, top speed is claimed to be 145 mph. Acceleration isn't in the same league as the *big* Italian exotics, but then again the big exotics aren't in that league anymore, either. The Dino, it turns out, was remarkably prophetic, the ultimate mid-engine exoticar for a changing world. The performance is still more than adequate for anywhere you'll be able to drive in this hemisphere, yet the car is relatively economical to run, is comparatively inexpensive to buy and maintain, and even makes the EPA smog folks happy.

In America, particularly, Dinos were a grand success. The price was meant to be under $9,000, but by the time they came over here, it was up to $14,500 or $15,000. However, the big Ferrari by that time was the Daytona, and *it* cost upward of $24,000. So if you just wanted *a* Ferrari and didn't care *which* Ferrari, the Dino was a flat-rate bargain that cost no more than a Porsche 911. And honestly, the Porsche is a better car, all things considered. But all things considered again, an

$8,000 Corvette is better than both of them put together, and a Datsun 280-Z is even better than *that*. Ferraris, even Dinos, are not judged by normal standards.

Among Ferraris, among exotic Italian sports cars, even, the Dino is one of the most delightful. Tractable, light, perfect to handle, and compliant to drive. A truly grand Gran Turismo, with all the élan you could possibly expect for $15,000. Even better, there has been virtually zero depreciation. The equivalent new Ferrari, the 308 GT, costs an amazing $25,000, and the big Ferraris are up in $50,000 country. This means that for most people one or the other of the Dinos is as far up the Ferrari ladder as they'll be able to climb, even with the help of their friendly loan arranger. Personally, though I realize the 308 GT is probably a better car mechanically, I don't much like its boxy, sharpened-brick body. It's also considerably heavier, slower, and nowhere near as agile.

What I'm saying, then, is that the 246 GT Dino is maybe the best buy among *all* Ferraris, particularly if you expect to use it on a daily or even weekly basis. The big cars are grand but expensive. The new Dinos are unknown. But the 246 has held its value for the better part of a decade, and it's a particularly happy design to begin with. It's not a car that will win medals for excellence in any one area, but it's one of the nicest packages ever to come out of Italy, and certainly the most enjoyable Ferrari since the 275 GTB/4. Even better, there are a few removable hardtop Targa-style 246 GTSs in this country, and they're the first factory Ferrari convertibles in years and years.

The Dino 246 is so recent that it's more like buying a new car than a classic. It's not what I'd call dependable; no Ferrari is. But certainly it's as pretty as anything on the roads. A real head turner, particularly in Italian blood red with shiny mags or Borrani wire wheels. And it's, well . . . an *amusing* car, in the delicious sense that you can go driving in one and come home smiling and refreshed. It's not a trial to drive as are so many high-performance cars, and it doesn't leave you tied in knots of anxiety as do so many other exotics. Indeed, the Dino 246 is one of the friendliest cars ever built. It's also technically exotic, exquisitely put together, and possessed of the grandest bloodline since Bugatti. Because, even though the name appears nowhere on the car, the Dino 246 GT is one thing, first and foremost: a Ferrari.

Citroën SM

The most complex car ever built for road use is the Citroën SM. Period. End of statement. No arguments. It's the nearest thing yet to NASA technology on four wheels, and the way things are going, it will probably remain the most advanced design of the twentieth century. It is such a significant design that there will always be a market for them. At your price, too. And even better than most collector cars, the SM is, one, relatively inexpensive and, two, magnificently and perfectly usable as a real automobile. Despite its awesome complexity, the Citroën SM is more fun to own than almost anything. And easier. It makes no demands, issues no warnings, makes no statements. It simply and truly *is,* like l'Arc de Triomphe or la Tour Eiffel. In point of fact, in the twenties, Andre Citroën paid a fortune to the city of Paris so that he could spell his name out on the Eiffel Tower one hundred feet high, using a quarter of a million light bulbs. The SM is not that gauche, but it does have the same Citroën panache.

That winsome Gallic flair—not always in the best of taste—has determined Citroën's fortunes since the very beginning in 1919. And since the mid-thirties, Citroëns—like the SM—have always been known for their wildly unorthodox, inexhaustibly effective futuristic designs. In 1934 Citroën introduced the famous Traction Avant—the flat black ones that French police inspectors always drive in Pink Panther movies—with front-wheel drive, unit body/chassis, and torsion bars. It was easily two decades ahead of its time and stayed in production for longer than that with almost no change.

You remember the basking-shark Citroëns of the fifties, those big black whales with

The car of the future, yesterday . . . Citroën SM.

Citroën SM: aerodynamic, complex, and strange.

the pointed noses, narrow sterns, and mysterious adjustable suspensions. They wouldn't get out of their own way—or anybody else's—but they were more comfortable on a bumpy Route Nationale than anything else ever built. Well, the ID-19s and DS-21s were really nothing more than rebodied Traction Avants. And even a decade ago this 1934 design was *still* fantastically ahead of everyone else's. That brings us to the Citroën SM, which is nothing more than the sublime old basking-shark DS-21 stretched out to the ridiculous. But it works, make no mistake. A five-year-old Citroën SM would be a sensation in this year's marketplace, and this year could mean anytime from 1984 to 2001. Like the old Traction Avants, the Citroën SM will *never* be anything so plebeian as obsolete. It probably won't even go out of style, it's so unique already.

What's so advanced? Well, the SM has Citroën's familiar hydropneumatic suspension, with those little rubber globes at each wheel instead of springs. This system can be pressurized at will so you can raise and lower the car whenever you want. It also automatically compensates for heavy loads front or rear to keep the car level and produces squat under braking both front *and* rear, so instead of pitching forward as you stop, you come gliding to a level halt. It sops up all sorts of bumps and holes; it gives great cornering. And all with the most luxuriously soft, fluffy ride imaginable.

The steering is hydraulic, too, and variable ratio, which is no big deal these days. But the power steering *effort* changes with wheel position and speed. At high speeds in a straight line, for example, it's as stiff as a manual steering gear. Sitting at the curb, you can wind it around lock to lock—only two turns—with one finger. And it's self-centering. Let go the wheel and it pops back to dead center. Magic. The suspension is all-independent, of course, and otherwise pretty conventional. Likewise the four-wheel disc brakes and steel wheels.

But the engine is something else. A tiny 2670cc double-overhead-cam V-6, it was made by cutting off part of an old Maserati V-8. That's the M in SM—Maserati. Citroën bought them out in 1968 and sold out again in '75 to Alejandro DeTomaso. But in between, the Maserati engine—the same one as in the little Merak—found its way into Citroën SMs. And though it's not great, it does make 180 hp and match up with a nice 5-speed transaxle, at the front, of course. The tiny Maserati six is less than a foot long and lives *behind* the front axle. So the power goes forward and into the wheels. It's really an ultramodern mid-engine design—it just happens to be *front* mid-engine, not rear mid-engine. And it works: the largish SM, all 3,600 pounds and 192 inches overall, will go 140 mph, do 17-second quarters, and 0 to 60 in under 9 seconds. This isn't startling at first glance, but when you consider the weight-to-displacement ratio, it's simply grand. The SM even gets 16 mpg; not bad considering the ton of hydraulic equipment the little engine has to run.

The body of the SM is pure wind tunnel—like the DS-21—but surpassingly pretty nonetheless. It really is one of those cars that looks right because it is right, and no other four-seater GT is as striking. It's not conventional, for sure, and the original plexiglass-covered sextuple headlights of the European cars disappeared in favor of conventional quads because of U.S. regulations. But even so, it's as pretty a car as you can get from a wind tunnel. And the interior is neat, too, with ribbly seats like Italian show cars, an oval steering wheel, and a cockpitlike dash.

Weird as it is, the whole assemblage *works*. I vividly remember driving the first SM in the country for a magazine road test. It was pouring rain, the photographer wanted to get a moon landscape in a rock quarry in Pennsylvania some three hours away before it got too dark to shoot, and it was all insanely winding road through the lower Catskills and Poconos. I don't claim I had even a small handle on the SM's unique handling and steering. But we averaged over 80 mph for two hours through the mountain roads, and only once or twice did Doug have to cover his eyes with his hands as we went sailing into a corner.

That was my introduction to the SM, and though I've driven them quite a bit since, that marvelous first impression has always remained with me. I felt like a giant that day, in a spectral car that was immune to the indecent vagaries of weather and road that beset mundane motorists. I might as well have been sitting on the Ohio Turnpike as on a junk Pennsylvania two-lane country road covered with treacherous switchbacks, patches, and downright holes. The only way you knew that the road was so miserable was to look; the impeccably mannered SM never let on. When we finally stopped for coffee, I grandly pronounced the Citroën SM one of the finest road cars I had ever driven, and I still see no reason to withdraw that statement.

The Citroën SM cost $11,500 when it first came over here, $13,500 when it left the market. Because of Citroën's troubles with the EPA, it only stayed around for about three years, and because of their limited and ineffective dealer network, not many were sold. Besides which the cars were pretty weird looking to the average American. So Citroën SMs, the most advanced cars ever built, are going for $5,000 and $6,000 today. Which is insane. If I had the money, I'd run right out and buy at least two to drive and another to add to my collection of significant cars of this century. The general public ignored the Citroën SM, but I suspect that engineers in Detroit and Stuttgart and Coventry took them apart piece by piece and marveled. And I do believe that someday in the future *all* cars will be something like the SM . . . small, high-performance engine, totally hydraulic chassis, superbly streamlined body, cavernously comfortable interior. But that's in the future. Right now the only car like that, ironically enough, is no longer even *in* production. If you want the most advanced car ever built, modern as tomorrow, you have to buy it . . . used.

Mercedes-Benz 6.3

In the great years, the Porsche-engineered years of the late twenties, Mercedes was *the* name in motorcars. Great, harsh, brutal things they were, among the classics of all time. And again in the Hitler years, when the street machines had grown fat and arrogant, Rudi Uhlenhaut and Alfred Neubauer, engineer and team manager, made Mercedes the name to be respected on the race courses of the world. From 1952 through '55 the same two teamed up to dominate racing again. And Uhlenhaut and stylist Karl Wilfert created the immortal 300SL. But since then? Mercedes cars, like the company, have grown fat and comfortable once more. The C-111 Wankel experiment of the mid-sixties turned out to be no more than an interesting diversion, a plaything to keep the engineers happy. Otherwise, the old, *vital* Mercedes has been just a memory for the past twenty years.

Tragic. The 300SL Gullwing is the single most important postwar classic, yet no other Mercedes models approach even minor collector status. Some of them are nice cars, sure—the old-fashioned 300S and 300D, the small 250SC coupes, the gargantuan 600 Pullman—but the most sporting cars Mercedes-Benz has made lately are the 280SL and 450SL, the Teutonic Thunderbirds. As expensive personal cars they are wonderful, but as

classics? No. And yet, disguised in all this competent Germanic mediocrity, there is one Mercedes model that flashed across the horizon briefly and then almost immediately disappeared. It was only in production for three years, less than a thousand were built, yet it captured the imagination like no car since the Gullwing.

This was the 300SEL 6.3. A *sedan.* Yes, nominally, a boxy, dumb, dull four-door sedan. But looks can be deceiving; even though it looks for all the world like a cobbled-up Studebaker Lark, the 300SEL 6.3 was a purebred sports car. The 6.3 was called by *Road & Track* "merely the Greatest Sedan in the World," but what they really meant was "one of the greatest *sports cars* in the world that happens to have four doors but don't let that bother you."

The 6.3 was an elaborate engine transplant, a German hot rod. The base car was the 300SEL, which normally came with an inadequate little 2.8-liter six. It had a simple unit body, four-wheel disc brakes, 4-speed automatic, and Mercedes's patented single low-pivot swing axle, the next best thing to a true independent rear suspension. It also had a multitude of luxury car items, from electric door locks to automatic radio antenna. It was big for a modern Mercedes—112-inch wheelbase, 196 inches overall—it was heavy—4,000 pounds—and of course it had all the aerodynamics of a brick wall. But the traditional Mercedes grille was mandatory and it stayed.

Into this nice, dull, conservative package Mercedes slipped a cherry bomb. For their Grosser 600 limousine they'd come up with a monstrous 6329cc, single-overhead-cam 300-hp V-8, with Bosch mechanical fuel injection. It was a simple matter to drop this leviathan into the 300SEL, thus creating the 300SEL 6.3. *Wunderbar!* The car was utterly transformed. In addition to .96G braking and excellent cornering, the lordly 300SEL would now go an honest 130 mph and get into the low 14s at over 90 mph for the quarter-mile. Zero to 60 was a matter of six-point-something-something seconds, which is faster than *any* four-door sedan has a right to go.

The 6.3 was the ultimate Q-ship, a $14,000 putdown for Detroit super cars that was not only superb on bumpy back country roads but as fast around a race track as most spartan

The most desirable Mercedes since the Gullwing: the quiet, unassuming, 130-mph 300SEL 6.3.

sports cars. Mercedes built a handful of semi-factory racers for the European Touring Car Championship and they were simply awesome, kind of like a NASCAR stocker with a stand-up grille and three-pointed star on top. But of course that was patently absurd. The whole point of the 6.3 was luxurious, high-speed grand touring. It was the only logical successor to the Bentley Continental Flying Spur, a car a lady could drive in total comfort but one, too, that a racing driver could drive away from the track and never be bored with.

The 300SEL 6.3 is really what all sedans (and perhaps all sports cars) should be. It was dropped when Mercedes decided that the new 4.5-liter V-8 produced enough power for most people and that the 6.3 was overkill. But nobody's collecting 300SEL 4.5s, and there's a waiting line for 6.3s. Indeed, nearly a decade old, a good 6.3 is worth far more than the fourteen grand it originally cost. The 6.3 obviously has struck a chord somewhere. It's the only Mercedes built since the Gullwing that really has enough power to satisfy American tastes, the only one that's a little larger than life, the only one that's recognized as a genuine classic by those who know. A lot of people are collecting Mercedes-Benz cars lately. It's the thing to do. Antiquated 220s, overpriced 280s, underpowered 230SLs. Maybe they know something the rest of us don't, but as far as I'm concerned they're carefully sifting the wheat from the chaff and hoarding the chaff. *Maybe* the 300S and 300D are collectible, *maybe* the 280SL. But I *know* in my heart of hearts that the 300SEL 6.3 is one of the most important cars

of our decade, and the price reflects (and will continue to reflect) this importance. Try to buy one and see what I mean.

Monteverdi

Ultimate status car: Ferrari 275 GTB/4? Awfully nice, but rather . . . you know, *common.* Same with the Maserati Ghibli—gorgeous, but there're just too many available. Ferrari Daytona? Close, but kind of Buickish, one knows what one means. Mercedes Gullwing? Ah, closer yet. Cobra 427? Very near the ultimate in performance, certainly, but not exactly . . . *class.* What's left? Of *course.* The Movado, the Rolex of automobiles. Monteverdi—Switzerland's watchmaker masterpiece and, really, damn near the very best car in the world. And certainly the rarest exotic piece, a virtual unknown compared to Ferrari and Maserati. Hell, *editors* drive Cobras, and half the rock groupies I know are closet Ferrari freaks. But Monteverdi? Monteverdis are so *in* that even the real gourmets, the connoisseurs of Life among the Fortunate haven't yet gotten wise to the indescribably superb cars of Peter Monteverdi. Their loss, indubitably.

Monteverdis are also very near the ultimate postwar collector cars, for a variety of reasons. Number one, the standard, I mean the plain-Jane model, Pussycat, not only costs in excess of $25,000 but dribbles out at the rate of around four dozen a year. Monteverdi makes fewer of his High Speed model than Rolls-Royce makes of its Camargue, for Chrissake. And the special Monteverdi, the *ne plus ultra*, the $50,000 if-you-have-to-ask-the-price-you-can't-afford-it model, the Hai, comes off the line at a rate of exactly one per month. On a good year. Some years maybe only ten, or less, depending upon supply, demand, and how things are shaping up around the shop.

Now there are lots of limited-production cars. I mean, Bruce Baldwin Mohs didn't build very many Mohs Ostentatienne Opera Sedans, either, but that doesn't make them collector cars. Peter Monteverdi is different. For starters, he has *exquisite* taste. Monteverdi started out building his own M.B.M. racers from 1959 till '62. These ranged from DKW Formula Juniors to a Porsche-engined Formula One car to a little OSCA-powered roadster with Lotus-like Ripple-potato-chip wheels. But as these things go, there wasn't that much demand for racing cars in Switzerland, seeing as how the Swiss had banned *all* racing in reaction to the disastrous 1955 Le Mans.

So Monteverdi switched to selling road cars, which was a lot more lucrative. And in Basel there was no sense being a piker. Garage Monteverdi became the Ferrari/BMW dealer, definitely high class. By 1967 Monteverdi was making so much money he decided to go into the car business again. But like everyone smart from Enzo Ferrari to Colin Chapman, he realized there was no point in building just race cars. Unless you are thrice blessed, the seventh son of a seventh son, there's no way to make money from building racers. But there *is* money to be made in the high-performance luxury GT market, lots of money. When things are good, the super-rich are the ones who spend best, and when things are bad they're the only ones left who *can* spend. If you can carry it off in the proper fashion, the Tiffany/Cartier route is definitely the one to take, particularly in Switzerland, tax haven for the coupon clippers of the world.

So Monteverdi started building cars. Now rich folks, particularly smarty-pants Swiss rich folks, are no dummies. I mean, maybe you can foist off Camargues in Iowa or someplace for $90,000, but when your clientele is also intelligent and tasteful as well as wealthy, your car not only has to be expensive but *good*, too. Monteverdi's cars are better than that. Count them down, starting with the cheapy 375/400 S High Speed. Peter Monteverdi had his bashers weld up a strong ladder frame out of big oval tubes with a 99-inch wheelbase. At the front they fabricated their own independent front suspension around forged A-arms and coil springs, at the rear a nice DeDion tube with twin radius arms and Watts linkage. It's not *the* most sophisticated suspension ever built, but by God it *works*, which is just as good, if not better, sometimes.

Peter Monteverdi's 400 S High Speed, a Chrysler-powered Ghibli copy of great expense.

The brakes are all Girling discs, the wheels are Borranis or knock-off mags, the tires huge Dunlop radials.

Monteverdi sat down with Piero Frua and the two of them came up with a superbly chiseled two-seater coupe body—only 181 inches long—unmistakably based on Giorgetto Giugiaro's masterful Maserati Ghibli. The same subtle angularity is there, the same carefully detailed window shape and trim, the same massive hood, the same simple grille, the same delicate rear treatment and pencil-thin bumpers. Lovely, and though similar, not irritatingly derivative. And it goes without saying, one of the cleanest modern designs of all.

After Monteverdi made the chassis, he shipped them over the mountains to Turin and Frua added these lovely bodies. The interiors were all supergrade leather, air conditioned, with electric windows and heated rear windows and all that sort of thing. When Frua was done, the rolling chassis were shipped back to Basel and Monteverdi put in the engines and transmissions. Understand now, not every Grande Marque has twelve cylinders and double overhead cams. And if that sounds like the beginning of the old Shuffle Off to Buffalo, you're right.

The Monteverdi High Speed (and it really does live up to its name: standing quarter-miles in 13.5 at 106, top speed 156 mph) gets its push from a pushrod Chrysler 440 wedge. *Aargh.* I know. I know. But on the other hand, these stones pump out 50 hp more than Ferrari's fancy 4.4-liter Daytona V-12, double overhead cams and all, and have enough torque to tow Geneva up to Zurich. So what if the redline is 5,500 rpm, you're still going 160 mph, and you can hear the radio, besides. Even better, if it comes to that, all those arguments in favor of Cobras and Corvettes and Cunninghams and Kurtises and Jensens work for the Monteverdi, too. In America, at least, you really can send the second assistant gardener down to the NAPA store in town for a new alternator. It will cost only $38.75 and he can have it on and running this afternoon, not three months and $500 from now.

This has to be an advantage. Really. Out there in Reality Land, where even Beautiful People need starter solenoids *sometimes,* it's nice to know you can make your connection without having to fly Bunkie or Pookie or Re-

Over 500 hp in a 2,750-pound mid-engine chassis, the

Monteverdi Hai . . . body by Frua out of Giugiaro, engine

1970 Monteverdi Hai was a ten-dollar-a-pound bargain.

by Chrysler out of NASCAR.

Re to Maranello for the weekend to pick up the parts you need. Chrysler's big wedge has lots of benefits. Quiet, powerful, cheap, dependable, available. What more could you want besides triple underhead cams and titanium connecting rods? Undoubtedly, the Monteverdi lost status points for this omission when new, but hell, the whole car was so classy it could give away points like that right and left and *still* have it all over the rest of those strokes. A lot of High Speeds even have a 3-speed Torqueflite automatic. Talk about point spreads. But even with the old hydraulic Fluid-Drive there, a decent Monteverdi will still see off the occasional 275 GTB/4 and most Ferrari Daytonas. So what the hell?

Refined as he is, Peter Monteverdi still looks a little like Jerry Quarry, and behind that pugnacious visage lurks a real hard-driving sumbitch. Even Monteverdi realized that the High Speed wasn't a serious contender for the real Star Trek performance crown, so he built his own Starship *Enterprise*. Monteverdi called it the Hai, which means Shark, and the car is as direct as its name. This one was so simple a concept you'll get it right away.

The boys in the back room welded up an all-new frame, with a 100-inch wheelbase. They used the same front and rear suspensions as on the High Speed. And Frua designed the all-steel body again, this time cutting 10 inches off the length, down to 171 inches overall. Pretty tame so far. Then they put in a Z-F 5-speed transaxle. Getting more interesting, right? Because transaxle means . . . mid-engine. Not content with the dull 440 wedge, Monteverdi bought up a batch of NASCAR 426 hemis. And you have to admit, there's probably more racing development time and money in Chrysler's NASCAR motor than in Ferrari's V-12, if it comes to that. Yessir. Right straight from Richard Petty and all them good ol' boys, here was an instant 500 hp in a 2,750-pound car. The Monteverdi Hai is a genuine 180-mph motorcar that does 1 to 100 in an eyeblink over 12 seconds. Until the Ferrari Berlinetta Boxer came along, which has a claimed top speed of 187 mph in high-pollution Italian tune, the Monteverdi Hai was unquestionably the fastest car ever seriously offered for street use.

The thing was low and tiny, with styling very much like the Giugiaro-designed DeTomaso Mangusta/Pantera. In fact, you can think of the Hai as a Pantera carried to the ridiculous: smaller on the outside, bigger on the inside of the engine, and thinner on your wallet after the bills are paid. No matter. The Hai is better than Ferrari's Daytona and at least as good as the Ferrari Boxer. And $10,000 less. Not to mention, although I know it's academic, that parts are *a lot* more available for Chrysler hemis than for Ferrari flat-12s.

There are also a few intriguing possibilities presented by the whole Monteverdi concept. Let's say you buy one. The price for either Monteverdi hasn't depreciated much at all since the High Speed came out in 1967 and the Hai in 1970, but that's a good sign, too. So you plunk down your $30,000 for a really clean collectible car. And you install Bunkie in the passenger seat—she'll really dig these macho stockers—and wind that mother up. And you head dead south for Level Cross, North Carolina. You still with me? You roll it right through town and right into the big tin garage with the little Petty Enterprises sign on the front and the trophy room just inside the door. And you ask for Maurice, Maurice Petty, the engine man. That's pronounced Moh-*russ*. And you get him to dip into his stack of old hemi parts, if you can keep Bunkie away from him long enough, and you get Maurice to build you just the godawfulest Chrysler NASCAR hemi ever put together. And you drop it into that Monteverdi. Now that's what you'd call playing it all ways. Ultimate European luxury GT, ultimate 200-mph *machine*. And ultimate Amurrican hemi motor, complete with that little Petty Enterprises decal on the air cleaner. Status? Hell. You'll have to fight 'em off with a stick.

Mercedes-Benz 300SL

American John Fitch, head thrown back, peaked white helmet pulled low above his hawkish nose, comes slicing into a little nameless Umbrian hill town as fast as his car will go, cutting so close to the stucco house-fronts he leaves a swirling, dusty streak at hip level. Black-clothed farmers' wives retreat into their dark front parlors, hands over ears, but the bespectacled man in the Mercedes passenger seat cannot even be bothered to lift his eyes from the map he is reading. The huge blood red car, vibrating madly, one fender crushed like an egg shell against some forgotten route marker overlooked in the haste of their going, coils itself and springs for the next corner, devouring it as easily as it has swallowed thousands behind and will swallow thousands more to come before the day is done. It disappears with the sudden sadness of a carnival departing, and only the longing eyes of young boys behind the walls and a small tornado of dust no bigger around than a café table mark where it has come.

The official Mercedes-Benz name was 300SL: 300 because of its 3-liter, 3000cc engine, SL for *Super Leicht*. But mostly it was called the Gullwing, for its curious upward-hinging doors. Exactly 1,400 Gullwing Mercedes were built between mid-1954 and mid-1957, but excellence is often inversely dependent upon numbers, and quality is rarely paired with quantity. If there were only 1,000 or 500 or a dozen 300SLs, that handful, that few, that *one car* would *still* be the greatest road car ever built. Why this is so is hard to define exactly. Certainly, the raw numbers barely begin to explain it.

The single-overhead-cam six, 2996cc, stroke unfashionably longer than the bore, was no revelation in 1954. It came from Mercedes's big 300 series limousines and it was a brutish thing . . . heavy, tall, and long. But it was used, simply because it was all they had. Fitted with Bosch mechanical fuel injection, it could be made to deliver 243 hp at 6,100 rpm. More important, it would live at its 6,500-rpm redline for hour after hour. It was not a delicate engine, not at all, but it was strong, unburstable, and perhaps most important, a known quantity to Mercedes-Benz engineers and mechanics alike.

The remainder of the driveline was equally familiar. The 4-speed gearbox, strong in its way as the mighty engine, was fully synchronized, and it, too, was borrowed from the stodgy passenger car line. The front suspension was dully conventional, a standard inde-

John Fitch, Hans Gessel, and their 300SL heading through Parma in the 1955 Mille Miglia.

pendent setup with unequal-length upper and lower control arms and coil springs. At the rear lived the only innovation, a swing-axle independent suspension with trailing arms and coil springs. That it was not a rigid axle or DeDion set it apart from nearly all other cars with which it shared the roads in 1954. That it was not fully independent was a great regret to nearly everyone.

The short, stocky man, full head of gray hair, twisted grin, and white coveralls, is the man who has built this car that Fitch drives so well. Every nut and bolt in it he knows better than a mother knows her child. He has planned for years for this moment, and the lives of others, of John Fitch and his nerveless friend, depend on how well he has done his job. But like a loving mother, he has taken the dare first, months before. This middle-aged man, nearly fifty, looks for all the world like the prosperous Teutonic burgher he is, engineering director of the most respected engineering firm in the world. But set deep in his placid face, if you look, you will see the lightning flash of gunfighter's eyes.

The 300SL coupe first appeared as a racing car in 1952. Rudi Uhlenhaut and his assistants built a team of aluminum-bodied cars for the classic endurance races. From the big six they got 250 hp. Placed in a 1,900-pound aerodynamic car, it was more than enough to blow the doors off everyone else. The engine was strong and durable. The brakes were good, if not great. But the real secret of the 300SL was the tubular space frame, a lightweight, rigid, and totally marvelous assemblage of high-strength steel tubing that gave the chassis a solid backbone, allowing everything to work the way it should. In its day, the handling ability of the 300SL was a near miracle. The racing SLs placed first and second in the Carrera PanAmericana in 1952, the same at Le Mans and Nurburgring, 1–2–3 at Bern, and 2–4 in the Mille Miglia. They were, in a word, overwhelming. Nobody had ever dominated international endurance racing so completely, particularly in their first year, with an untried model. Understandably, once they had proven their point, Mercedes temporarily retired from racing again.

A great machine is not created from nuts and bolts and panels of beaten aluminum. It is made from the hot, dry dust of Italian hill towns, of endless circuits in Nurburg's icy rain, of surpassingly dangerous rounds of Monza's broken pavement. All this and more, neatly penciled into the ever-present black notebooks of assistant engineers, is what Uhlenhaut brought to the 300SL. His twenty years of racing knowledge. One of the great engineering minds of the twentieth century. A winning way that would have his men throw themselves over barbed wire to provide a path for him were he a battlefield commander. What Uhlenhaut brought to Mercedes for the 300SL, their first true sports car in more than a score of years, was his life. Only the things that he had done, the places he had been, prepared Uhlenhaut to create what is universally acknowledged the single most important classic of the past three decades.

At the 1954 New York Auto Show, the incomparable Max Hoffman, at one time or another the American distributor for almost every European marque from Abarth to Zil, lordly guaranteed to buy 1,000 units if Mercedes-Benz would only make a production version of the all-conquering 300SL prototype on display. At war-wracked Mercedes, 1,000 cars were not to be sneezed at in 1954. So Uhlenhaut was told to revamp his fabulous coupe. He gave it fuel injection instead of carburetors, but left the rest alone. Karl Wilfert, director of Mercedes styling, drew up a new, aero-

Rudi Uhlenhaut's unbeatable 300SL of 1952.

Mille Miglia, 1955: The overwhelming 300SLRs are towed

dynamic body incorporating lights and bumpers and all those other things that street machines need. It is not a body of great delicacy, but it is one of the great all-time designs nonetheless: forceful without being brutal, clean but not barren. A splendid mix of powerful motifs, strikingly possessed of character and poise. And utterly timeless.

The production body was steel with aluminum hood and doors. The car weighed nearly 3,000 pounds. And of course, like the racing cars, it had the distinctive Gullwing doors. Uhlenhaut's space frame came straight back as a wide, triangulated bridge girder right where normal doors would be. Wilfert's Gullwings were the brilliant solution to an almost impossible problem. Still, there was no

to scrutineering. Fangio's number 658 was second to Moss's number 722 in the most famous race in history.

room for wind-down windows. The window glass lifted out and stored behind the seats. An awkward, leather-covered shelf separated drivers from the outside and short-skirted passengers from their dignity. Uhlenhaut gleefully accepted this compromise on the body's usefulness as long as he could have his racing space frame. It was a clear matter of priorities. Uhlenhaut was a racer.

His incongruous crash helmet provokes no smiles from the test-day watchers. Moss himself is unusually silent, watching. Jenkinson dances nervously, unconsciously. But the gray-haired man does not see them. He is already accelerating hard through the parabolic at Monza, a lone silver speck in a sea of black. Around he goes, slowly. Around he goes, faster. And faster yet. Faster and faster until he has gone as close to the limit as he can go. If this car will go faster on this track, it will be in the hands of someone like Moss, twenty-five years his junior, young enough to be his son. But Moss, acknowledged the fastest driver ever to enter a sports/racing car, can do no more than match his mentor's time. The old man smiles. He is as fast as Stirling Moss. And he has never, will never, drive a racing car in a competitive event. Rudi Uhlenhaut, director of engineering at Mercedes-Benz, has nothing to prove on a race track. "It would be a waste of a good engineer," he will say. "We need engineers as well as drivers, you know." Said Stirling Moss, "Uhlen-

*haut is the most brilliant driver living today."
What he meant was that this unassuming
man, this engineer, this highly paid company
director, could and did repeatedly best the
times of his team drivers, Juan Manuel Fangio and Stirling Moss, the best racers in history, driving their own racing cars. Had he
chosen, he could have been champion of the
world in a car of his own design. He did not
choose.*

Mercedes's engine, Uhlenhaut's chassis, and
Wilfert's body combined to make the 300SL
one of the highest-performance road cars of
all time, despite the fact that it had only a
mere 3 liters, carried an enormous (and enormously heavy) load of 35 gallons of fuel, and
was fitted throughout as a luxury car ought
to be. It was not extravagant—few Mercedes
have been extravagant—but it epitomized
straightforward good taste as no other car has
done. A Mercedes Gullwing, a clean unrestored car, was tested by *Road & Track* in 1968.
They were conservative with the car, for it
was already thirteen years old. Zero to 60 they
got in 8.2 seconds, 0 to 100 mph in 21, the quarter-mile in an excellent 16 seconds at 89 mph.
And they commented that indeed, impressive
as this was, it wasn't as quick as the new Gullwing they tested in 1955. Still, they achieved
a top speed of 146 mph on a 3.64 differential.
The optional 3.25 would have made that more
like 160 mph, which is what John Fitch's
Mille Miglia coupe would do.

Even more amazing to *R & T*, coasting
from 80 to 40 mph, a reasonable, real-world
test of aerodynamics, the Gullwing set a record of 64.5 seconds, the best aerodynamics the
testers had seen. And this was more than fifteen years after Wilfert's design was first
drawn. For braking and handling they got
only around .7G, which was spectacular in
1954, but mostly because of the old, narrow
tires, mediocre by late-sixties—or late-seven-
ties—standards. With new, wide radial tires
on appropriate rims, a twenty-year-old Gullwing would surely rival today's best sports
cars in both braking and steady-state cornering. And the transient handling, as nimble as
they come, was always a special delight of
the 300SL. Really, two decades after the fact,
there is no newer 3-liter, fully equipped road
machine that can equal the Mercedes's all-

around performance. And on those highly
modified machines that can, engine life expectancy is measured in hours, sometimes in
minutes. The 300SL, by comparison, constructed of the highest-quality materials, was
and is virtually indestructible.

*Mike Hawthorn, champion of the world, was
a strange young man, at twenty-nine already
retired from racing and deeply bereaved. His
one good friend and teammate, his mon ami
mate, Peter Collins, had been killed at Nurburgring the same year. Hawthorn was blank
after that, a burned out, aimless man whose
life had been scarred by strife. His father was
killed violently in a road crash, he himself
was blamed for the tragic 1955 accident that
sent Levegh's Mercedes into the Le Mans
crowd. More than with most people, racing
had sucked the substance out of Mike Hawthorn. Still, he went through the motions. He
ate, he drank, he partied. He drove faster than
he should on the highways. He argued with
friends. Rob Walker, the most beloved figure
in British racing, was one of these. Hawthorn
drove a new Jaguar. Walker had an older Gullwing Mercedes coupe. On the night of January 22, 1959, Hawthorn drove his Jaguar
broadside into an oil truck on the Guildford
bypass. It was pitch dark; it had rained. He
was racing Walker home, determined to show
that a champion's Jaguar was more than a
match for Walker's Mercedes. It wasn't. And
John Michael Hawthorn, whether deliberately or accidentally, ended his life of despair
chasing a phantom Mercedes 300SL. He was
not the only one to lose such a race, merely
the best known.*

The true Mercedes racers were the W196 models, either 2.5-liter GP cars or 3-liter sports/
racers. The sports cars were known as
300SLRs, but they were completely different
from the road-going 300SLs. Still, the stock
300SL was a magnificent competition car,
nearly the equal of the much lighter, more
powerful racing models. In 1955 Stirling Moss
and his passenger Denis Jenkinson won the
Mille Miglia at a record speed. Juan Fangio
was second. Both Moss and Fangio drove incredibly exotic 300SLR racers. John Fitch and
his passenger Hans Gessel were fifth, first in
the production category, in a box stock Gull-

The production 300SL coupe of 1955; tubular space frame, independent suspension, 243 hp, 146 mph.

The production 300SL roadster of 1958, less rigid than the coupe but with a low-pivot swing axle.

wing coupe. Other Gullwings were in seventh and tenth. Mercedes 300SLs ruled production racing worldwide, and Paul O'Shea, Charles Wallace, Tony Settember, and Lance Reventlow all ran them in the United States. O'Shea even won back-to-back SCCA national championships with his Gullwing in '56 and '57. Literally hundreds of minor races were won by the cars.

In 1955 Gullwings were 1–2 in Sweden, first in the Stella Alpina rally and the Dolomite rally, *and* first in the prestigious Liège–Rome–Liège rally, toughest of them all. In 1957 Moss and Garnier were fifth in the Tour de France. A 300SL won its class in the Tulip, was second in Liège–Rome–Liège. Olivier Gendebien, just starting his fabulous endurance racing career, made a shambles of European sports-car racing with his Gullwing, earning a factory Ferrari ride. Back in the era when dual-purpose sports cars were the ideal, the 300SL really *could* be successfully raced in stock condition, with no more preparation than a change to colder spark plugs. Band leader Don Ricardo took one of his street machines to Bonneville and went 160.25 mph. Indeed, there was nothing you couldn't do with a 300SL.

The pretty blond child was seventeen that summer, and she lived in Greenwich. You would have recognized her family name from the papers. Her graduation present, one she had picked out herself, she treated with the casual disinterest she gave to everything else. Her life was lived at the edge of boredom. And the strange car with the tri-pointed star in the grille and the funny doors had bored her almost from the first. All summer she had fried, nauseated, in the closed coupe. Finally she had taken to leaving the gullwing doors open, driving slowly through town in a car that looked like some forgotten prehistoric bird, larger than life. Reduced to tears of frustration on a hot August afternoon, in a moment of pique she had driven into the expansive garage with the doors up, making the most wonderful tearing noise as aluminum and glass showered around her. A sliver of falling glass grazed her forehead, and she appeared in the drawing room dramatically, small drops of blood spattering on the priceless Arak medallion carpet in front of her

mother. "Fuck it," she said. The next day the offending car, wings spitefully broken, was traded in on a white Jaguar roadster with proper doors and an automatic transmission. The 300SL Gullwing was never a car for dilettantes.

When they first appeared in 1954, Mercedes asked only $6,820 for a Gullwing, at which price they were losing money. By 1957 the tab had gone up to $8,905, and still the car was an incredible bargain. But it had its limitations. It was a racing car converted for street use, really, not a docile boulevard sports car. So Uhlenhaut was instructed to come up with a convertible with conventional doors and a folding top for 1957. This looked exactly like the coupe, except that it could be had with a removable hardtop, soft top, or both. And it had real doors. The cutaway frame was not quite as rigid, but nobody complained except Uhlenhaut. And for the first time, the famous Mercedes low-pivot swing axle was tried. So overall, less chassis rigidity for a better rear suspension was just about an even trade-off.

The roadster was $11,099 with one top, $11,573 with both. And in 1961 the roadster was given four-wheel Dunlop disc brakes. A total of 1,858 cars were built between '57 and '62, and Mercedes made money on all of them. The roadsters aren't as much revered by collectors as the early coupes, but that's just one of those irrational collector lapses which means nothing. As a car the roadster is a lot more usable, simply because it has real doors. As a mantelpiece racer the coupe is rarer and more desirable. Best of all from an enthusiast's point of view would be a coupe with the later independent rear suspension and disc brakes. A few of these hybrids were raced in the late fifties, but it's a difficult conversion and one ultimately not worth the time and trouble.

Of the 3,258 300SLs, at least a third are still extant. Many are good originals, most are restored. Some are basket cases. Even a clapped-out roadster is worth $15,000, a good original coupe, an easy $25,000. A concours restored Gullwing is worth nearly $40,000, and prices have been climbing steadily each year. They will never go down again. Of all the blue-chip investment cars there are in the world, of all the four-wheeled machines built

Moss's 1955 Mille Miglia win in a 300SLR racer was good, but Fitch's fifth in a stock 300SL was better.

in the last thirty years, the 300SL is the top. There is no finer collector car. This is what is meant when you hear the word *classic*.

Simon Read quoted Rob Walker in *Automobile Quarterly*. Walker has owned four different Gullwings at various times and still has one. His experience of high-performance cars is as broad as any man's now living; his interest in cars has spanned forty years. For all that time he has indulged himself in whatever car tempted him at the moment, regardless of cost. He is, in other words, a reliable authority. Said Walker, "I think that the 300SL must be the greatest road car that was ever built."

At 6,500 in third gear, the hard metallic sound fills the cockpit, drumming into his skull without the need of listening. An acrid smell of hot metal sifts in from the airvents, and the needle on the big right dial reads 100. The stiff clutch takes a swift boot, the tall, slender lever notches into fourth with a feel of machine, the tach needle drops abruptly down to 40 on the big left-hand dial and starts to climb steadily around again. There is almost no sound from the passing wind, only the flat exhaust noise, the whine of the differential and of the gear-driven camshaft to connect with the passing road. The hard bucket seat rubs on his hip bones, the tightened belt crushes his pelvis. Through soft-soled shoes

he can feel every pebble under braking. The steering goes twitchy and light as the fast sweeper deposits him at the end of a short straight. For miles the road goes on like this, and though the day is cool, beads of sweat form unnoticed on his lean upper lip. There is nothing planned for today other than that he complete a six-hour drive by nightfall and escort a beautiful lady to dinner and to bed. There is no need to hurry, only desire. Each expert flick of his wrists keeps the shining silver car perfectly positioned, each touch of his toe transmits immediately to the road surface. He is flying the car like an airplane, using feet as much as hands. Traveling on the ragged edge of reflexes and good sense, he is enjoying himself immensely. His mind is blank, all his powers of concentration turned to the task at hand. A faint hint of tire squeal and the car's crosswise attitude toward the road are the only hints to how hard he is working. Work? Hah. This is the very essence of life itself. Everything else he will do today pales beside it. Everything else is a duty which he will dutifully perform. But these few hours are his alone, his to share with the magnificent motorcar and the empty, sun-dappled road. They will find perfection together, and pretty ladies in warm beds will have to wait.

PHOTO CREDITS

Photos courtesy of:

A. C. Cars, Ltd., pages 92, 190 (top and bottom), 191

Antique Automobiles, page 28

Michael Antonick, pages 80, 98 (bottom)

Michael Arnolt, pages 45, 47

Automobile Monteverdi, pages 339, 340–41 (top and bottom)

Automobile Quarterly, pages 67 (top), 97 (bottom), 98 (top), 102 (bottom), 196–97, 249, 289 (top)

Bavarian Motoren Werke, pages 313, 314–15

Bristol Aeroplane, pages 149 (top, center, and bottom)

British-Leyland Motors, pages 140, 145, 168, 184, 184–85, 203, 204, 223, 229

Car and Driver, pages 32, 64–65, 66, 84, 85, 108, 113, 117, 126 (top), 129 (top and bottom), 130, 143, 152, 153, 157, 162–66, 167, 172–73, 183, 188–89, 192, 202, 204–5, 212–13, 224, 228–29, 231, 236, 237, 238, 244, 248–49, 250–51, 252–53, 255 (top and bottom), 261, 262 (top), 263, 271, 274–75, 285, 298–99, 308, 318, 319, 320–21, 326–27, 329 (top and bottom), 330–31, 332, 333

Chevrolet Motor Division, pages 51, 54–55 (top and bottom), 78, 79 (top and bottom), 124 (top, center, and bottom)

William Condon, pages 49 (top and bottom)

Ken Costello, page 232

Daimler-Benz, pages 344, 347 (top and bottom)

John Erickson, pages 198 (top), 199 (bottom)

Facel S.A., page 311

John Fitch, pages 30, 33 (top), 34, 141, 171, 240–41, 257, 258–59, 269, 343, 344–45, 349

Ford Motor Company, pages 58, 59, 132–33

Jensen Motors, page 182

Frank Kurtis, pages 18, 19, 21

Richard Langworth, page 220 (bottom)

Lotus Cars, Ltd., pages 220 (top), 226

Karl Ludvigsen, pages 27, 29, 44–45, 82, 106–7, 122–23, 155, 158–59, 187, 208, 210–11, 216, 266–67, 272, 283, 306

William L. Mitchell, pages 76, 77

Morgan Motor Car Company, page 235

Museum of Modern Art, page 245

Pininfarina, page 325

Pontiac Motor Division, pages 126 (bottom), 127

Porsche + Audi, pages 300–1

Carroll Shelby, page 94

Shelby-American Automobile Club, pages 96, 131

Special-Interest Autos, pages 23, 35, 39

Brooks Stevens, pages 40–41, 42–43

Taylor-Constantine, pages ii–iii, 2, 14–15, 20, 22, 24, 26, 33 (bottom), 37, 46, 52–53, 60 (top and bottom), 63 (top and bottom), 67 (bottom), 74–75 (top and bottom), 89, 90–91, 97 (top), 99, 100–1 (top and bottom), 102 (top), 103 (top and bottom), 104, 109, 110, 112–13, 116, 119, 120, 121, 134–35, 136–37, 142, 146–47, 160, 161, 164 (top and bottom), 174–75, 176, 177, 179, 180, 188, 193, 194 (top and bottom), 195, 198 (bottom), 199 (top), 200, 201, 218, 219, 233, 247, 250, 260 (top, center, and bottom), 262 (bottom), 264–65 (top and bottom), 270–71, 277 (top and bottom), 278–79 (top and bottom), 280, 286–87, 289 (bottom), 290 (top and bottom), 291, 292–93, 294 (top and bottom), 295 (top and bottom), 296, 298, 302, 303, 304, 305, 309, 317 (top and bottom), 322, 323, 324, 327, 335 (top and bottom), 338

Road & Track, pages 88, 258

Bob Tronolone, pages 68–69, 70–71, 72–73 (top and bottom)

Bruce Wennerstrom, page 62

Don Yenko, pages 86–87

APPENDICES

Marque Clubs

ABARTH
Abarth Register Newsletter
1298 Birch St.
Uniondale, N.Y. 11553

A. C.
A. C. Owners Club, Ltd.
American Centre
Samuel B. Kane
88 Cushing St.
Hingham, Mass. 02043

ALFA ROMEO
Alfa Romeo Owners Club
Box 331
Northbrook, Ill. 60062
Vintage Alfa Romeo Inter-
national
900 N. College
Fort Collins, Colo. 80521

ALLARD
Allard Register
Hon. Secretary, R. W. May
8 Paget Close
Horsham, W. Sussex
RH13 6HD
England

ARNOLT-BRISTOL
Arnolt-Bristol Owners Club
c/o John Simmons
3900 Langley Rd.
Charlotte, N.C. 28215
Arnolt-Bristol
9382 Gina Dr.
West Chester, Ohio 45069

ASTON MARTIN
Aston Martin Owners Club
c/o Secretariat A.M.O.C.
293 Osborne Rd.
Hornchurch, Essex
England
Aston Martin Owners Club
c/o Joyce Woodgate
324 Echo Valley Ln.
Newton Square, Pa. 19073
Aston Martin Owners Club
U.S.A. West
c/o R. F. Green
7440 Amarillo Rd.
Dublin, Calif. 94566

AUSTIN-HEALEY
Austin-Healey Club Pacific
Center
Box 6267
San Jose, Calif. 94150

AVANTI
Avanti Owners Association
International
Box 322
Uxbridge, Mass. 01569

BENTLEY
Bentley Drivers Club, Ltd.
W. O. Bentley Memorial
Building
16 Chearsley Rd.
Long Crendon, Aylesbury
Bucks HP18 9AW
England

Bentley Drivers Club
Northeast USA Region
34 Snowden Place
Glen Ridge, N.J. 07028
Bentley Owners Club
c/o Klein Kars
Elizabethtown, Pa. 17022

BMW
BMW Automobile Club of
America
Box 401
Hollywood, Calif. 90028
BMW Car Club of America
Two Brewer St.
Cambridge, Mass. 02138
BMW 507 Owners Club
Barry McMillan
Hilltown Pike
Hilltown, Pa. 18927
BMW 700 Register
1733 Falstone Ave.
Hacienda Heights, Calif.
91745
International Association of
BMW Clubs
Box 1312
Garden Grove, Calif. 92642

BRISTOL. *See* ARNOLT-BRIS-
TOL, BMW

CAMARO
The Camaro Club of Amer-
ica
Box 490344
Atlanta, Ga. 30349

CITROËN
Citroën Car Club [also Pan-
hard]
Box 743
Hollywood, Calif. 90028

Citroën Car Club
17 Crossways
Sutton, Surrey
SM2 5LD
England

COBRA. *See* SHELBY

CORVAIR
Corvair Society of America
145 Ivywood
Radnor, Pa. 19087

CORVETTE
Classic Corvette Club 53–55
9417 N. Rich Rd.
Alma, Mich. 48801

National Corvette Restorers
Society
63370 CR 19, Rt. 5
Goshen, Ind. 46526

National Council of Cor-
vette Clubs, Inc.
6672 Balsam Dr.
Reynoldsburg, Ohio 43608

Vintage Corvette Club of
America
Box T
Atascadero, Calif. 93422

CROSLEY
Crosley Automobile Club
200 Ridge Rd. E.
Williamson, N.Y. 14589

Miamisburg Crosley Club
10 Bradstreet Rd., No. 8N
Centerville, Ohio 45459

DELAGE
Les Amis de Delage
4 Blvd. Gabriel Guisthau
44-Nantes, France

DELAHAYE
Club Delahaye
Marco-Polo Galwin C.
06210 Mardelieu, France

DEVIN
The Devin Register
Box 18
Nyack, N.Y. 10960

FACEL
Facel Vega Club
c/o Alan Boring
Box 295
Novi, Mich. 48050

FERRARI
Ferrari Club of America
6250 Woodward Ave.
Detroit, Mich. 48202

Ferrari Owners Club
3460 Wilshire Blvd.
Los Angeles, Calif. 90010

Ferrari Owners Club, Pres-
cott Hill, Gotherington
Cheltenham,
Gloucestershire
England

FIAT
Fiat Club of America, Inc.
Box 192, Union Square
Somerville, Mass. 02143

Fiat Register
Mr. A. Cameron
7 Tudor Gardens
West Wickham, Kent
England

FRAZER NASH
Frazer Nash Section Vin-
tage Sports Car Club
Clink Farm, Frome
Somerset BA11 2EN
England

HEALEY
Historic Sports Car Club
P. Edbrook, Secretary
26 Lower Hey Ln.
Dysarts, Mossley
Lancashire
England

H.R.G.
H.R.G. Association
Hustyn, Packhorse Rd.
Bessels Green, Sevenoaks
Kent, England

JAGUAR
Classic Jaguar Association
Box 61
Costa Mesa, Calif. 92627

Jaguar Clubs of North
America, Inc.
600 Willow Tree Rd.
Leonia, N.J. 07605

Jaguar Drivers Club Ltd.
The Norfolk Hotel
South Kensington
London SW7 3ER
England

Jaguar Owners Club
2707 Granville Ave.
W. Los Angeles, Calif. 90064

LAMBORGHINI
Lamborghini Club of Amer-
ica
c/o G.T. Cars
3054 N. Lake Terrace
Glenview, Ill. 60025

LANCIA
American Lancia Club
110 Bleecker St., Apt. 8E
New York, N.Y. 10012

Lancia Motor Club
"New Grass,"
Down Ampney, Cirencester
Gloucestershire GL7 5QW
England

LOTUS
Club Elite
W. S. Hutton
Box 351
Clarksville, Tenn. 37040

Lotus Ltd.
Box L
College Park, Md. 20704

Lotus West, Inc.
Box 75972
Los Angeles, Calif. 90005

Lotus XI Register
2069 E. Packard Highway
Charlotte, Mich. 48813

MASERATI
Maserati Club
The Paddock, Salisbury Rd.
Abbotts Ann, Andover
Hampshire, England

MERCEDES-BENZ
    Benz Owners Register
    675 Pinewoods Ave.
    Troy, N.Y. 12180

    Gullwing Group, Inc.
    Box 2093
    Sunnyvale, Calif. 94087

    Mercedes-Benz Club of
        America, Inc.
    Box 2183, Dept. A.
    Sunnyvale, Calif. 94087

    Mercedes-Benz Club Ltd.
    Mrs. Gupwell, Secretary
    Thatch Acre, L. Compton
    Warwickshire
    England

    Mercedes Club
    Box 2111
    Sepulveda, Calif. 91343

M.G.
    California M.G. 'T' Reg.
    222 E. Sycamore
    Arcadia, Calif. 91006

    Classic M.G. Club
    1307 Ridgecrest Rd.
    Orlando, Fla. 32806

    MGA Register
    Box 13, Annex Station
    Providence, R.I. 02903

    MGA Twin Cam Register
    Box 191
    Circle Pines, Minn. 55014

    M.G. Car Club Ltd.
    600 Willow Tree Rd.
    Leonia, N.J. 07605

    M.G. Club Ltd.
    273 Green Lane
    Ilford, Essex
    IG3 9TJ England

    New England MG 'T' Reg.
    Box 251
    Abingdon, Conn. 06230

    T.C. Motoring Guild, Inc.
    Box 3452
    Van Nuys, Calif. 91407

MORGAN
    Morgan Car Club of Wash-
        ington, D.C.
    616 Gist Ave.
    Silver Springs, Md. 20910

    Morgan Plus Four Club
    5073 Melbourne Dr.
    Cypress, Calif. 90630

    Morgan Sports Car Club
    23 Seymour Ave.
    Worcester
    England

    Morgan Three-Wheeler
        Club
    USA Group
    1051 16th St.
    Santa Monica, Calif. 90403

    Morgan Three-Wheeler
        Club
    The Secretary, N. H. Lear
    Flat 2, The Grange
    Cannington, Bridgewater
    Somerset England

MUSTANG. See also SHELBY
    Classic Mustang Associa-
        tion International
    Box 10526
    Gladstone, Mo. 64118

    Mustang Owners Club
    115 Fairmont St.
    Malden, Mass. 02148

NASH
    Nash Car Club of America
    c/o James Dworschack
    RR 1, Elvier Rd.
    Clinton, Iowa 52732

NASH-HEALEY
    Nash-Healey Car Club In-
        ternational
    Richard M. Kauffman
    100 Church St.
    Lakeland, Ga. 31635

PANTERA
    Pantera International
    1774 S. Alvira St.
    Los Angeles, Calif. 90035

PORSCHE
    Porsche Club of America,
        Inc.
    Bob Rassa
    5616 Clermont Dr.
    Alexandria, Va. 22310

    Porsche Owners Club
    6229 Outlook Ave.
    Los Angeles, Calif. 90042

    Porsche 4-cam Register
    Box 1120
    Goleta, Calif. 93017

RILEY
    Riley Motor Club
    The Gables, Hinksey Hill
    Oxford
    England

    Riley Motor Club USA
    Box 4162
    Anaheim, Calif. 92803

    Riley Register
    26 Hillcrest Close
    Tamworth, Staffordshire
    B79 8PA, England

SHELBY
    Shelby-American Automo-
        bile Club
    1510 Delaware Ave.
    Wyomissing, Pa. 19610

    Shelby Owners Association
    28 Union Ave.
    Hempstead, N.Y. 11550

SUNBEAM-TALBOT-
    DARRACQ
    Sunbeam-Talbot-Darracq
    5 Woodlodge, Lake Rd.
    Wimbledon, London
    England

SUNBEAM TIGER. See also
    SHELBY
    Sunbeam Tiger Owners
        Association
    5067 Valley Park Ave.
    Fremont, Calif. 94538

    Tigers East
    Box 146
    Jessup, Pa. 18434

THUNDERBIRD
    American Thunderbird As-
        sociation
    Box 7484
    Kansas City, Mo. 64116

    Classic Thunderbird As-
        sociation
    Box 2968
    St. Louis, Mo. 63130

Classic Thunderbird Club
International
Box 2398
Culver City, Calif. 90230

Classic Thunderbird Parts
Club
1115 W. Collins Ave.
Orange, Calif. 92667

Vintage Thunderbird Club
of America
26056 Deerfield
Dearborn Heights, Mich.
48127

TRIUMPH
Triumph Register of Amer-
ica
311 Johnson St. S.W.
Vienna, Va. 22180

Triumph Register of Amer-
ica, Potomac Area
c/o Edna Mans
528 E. Nelson Ave.
Alexandria, Va. 22301

Triumph Roadster Club
Mr. R. Fitsall
11 The Park
Carshlaton, Surrey
England

Triumph Sports Owners As-
sociation
600 Willow Tree Rd.
Leonia, N.J. 07605

Triumph Travelers Sports
Car Club
Box 5881
San Jose, Calif. 95125

Vintage Triumph Register
Box 6934
Grosse Pointe, Mich. 48236

General Clubs

Contemporary Historical Vehi-
cles Association, Inc.
Box 552
Cerritos, Calif. 90701

Midwestern Council of Sports
Car Clubs
1812-R N. Kennicott Ave.
Arlington Heights, Ill. 60004

Milestone Car Society
Box 50850
Indianapolis, Ind. 46250

Sport Custom Registry
1306 Brick St.
Burlington, Iowa 52601

Sports Car Club of America
Box 22476
Denver, Colo. 80222

Sports Car Collectors Society of
America, Inc.
Box 1855
Quantico, Va. 22134

Vintage Sports Car Club
4350 N. Knox Ave.
Chicago, Ill. 60641

Vintage Sports Car Club of
America
170 Wetherill Rd.
Garden City, N.Y. 11530

Publications

Automobile Quarterly
221 Nassau St.
Princeton, N.J. 08540

Car Classics
8943 Fullbright Ave.
Box 547
Chatsworth, Calif. 91311

Cars & Parts
114 E. Franklin Ave.
Box 299
Sesser, Ill. 62884

Hemmings Motor News
Box 380
Bennington, Vt. 05201

The Milestone Car
c/o The Milestone Car Society
Box 50850
Indianapolis, Ind. 46250

Old Cars
Iola, Wisc. 54945

Special-Interest Autos
Box 192
Bennington, Vt. 05201

INDEX